WITHDRAWN

HARVARD LIBRARY

WITHDRAWN

PREACHING IN JUDAISM AND CHRISTIANITY

STUDIA JUDAICA

FORSCHUNGEN ZUR WISSENSCHAFT DES JUDENTUMS

BEGRÜNDET VON
E. L. EHRLICH

HERAUSGEGEBEN VON
G. STEMBERGER

BAND XLI

WALTER DE GRUYTER · BERLIN · NEW YORK

PREACHING IN JUDAISM AND CHRISTIANITY

ENCOUNTERS AND DEVELOPMENTS
FROM BIBLICAL TIMES TO MODERNITY

EDITED BY
ALEXANDER DEEG, WALTER HOMOLKA
AND HEINZ-GÜNTHER SCHÖTTLER

WALTER DE GRUYTER · BERLIN · NEW YORK

∞ Printed on acid-free paper which falls within the guidelines of the ANSI
to ensure permanence and durability.

ISBN 978-3-11-019665-8
ISSN 0585-5306

Library of Congress Cataloging-in-Publication Data

A CIP catalogue record for this book is available from the Library of Congress.

Bibliographic information published by the Deutsche Nationalbibliothek

The Deutsche Nationalbibliothek lists this publication in the Deutsche Nationalbibliografie;
detailed bibliographic data are available in the Internet at http://dnb.d-nb.de.

© Copyright 2008 by Walter de Gruyter GmbH & Co. KG, D-10785 Berlin

All rights reserved, including those of translation into foreign languages. No part of this book may be reproduced or transmitted in any form or by any means, electronic or mechanical, including photocopy, recording or any information storage and retrieval system, without permission in writing from the publisher.

Printed in Germany
Cover Design: Christopher Schneider

Dedicated to

H. E.

Walter Cardinal Kasper

on the occasion
of His 50th Ordination Anniversary

Preface

*Alexander Deeg / Walter Homolka /
Heinz-Günther Schöttler*

We, the editors, are glad to present the papers of the first international conference on "Preaching in Judaism and Christianity", which took place in Bamberg between the 6th and 8th of March 2007. It was jointly organized by the Universities of Bamberg and Erlangen with the Abraham Geiger College at the University of Potsdam. Jews and Christians, rabbis and pastors, students and professors were assembled from Austria, Germany, Great Britain, Hungary, Israel, Italy, Poland, Switzerland, and the United States.

The city of Bamberg with its more than 1,000 years of Jewish and Christian history proved to be a perfect location. Our special thanks go to Heinrich Olmer, chairman of the Jewish congregation in Bamberg, for his hospitality; to the Archbishop of Bamberg, Professor Dr. Ludwig Schick, who provided the conference a warm welcome in his archdiocese; and to the University of Bamberg and its president Professor Dr. Godehard Ruppert for hosting the conference. We are grateful to Walter Cardinal Kasper, the President of the Commission of the Holy See for Religious Relations with the Jews, who sent the executive secretary of the Commission Fr. Dr. Norbert Hofmann SVD as a representative. In his greeting the Archbishop of Bamberg stressed the importance of Jewish-Christian dialogue in order to "'pro-actively' prevent anti-Semitism from ever rising again." The bishop of the Evangelical Lutheran church of Bavaria, Dr. Johannes Friedrich, said that the conference represented "an important new step" in the history of Jewish-Christian relations as it showed ways of cooperation and joint efforts in fields of common interest: the history of Jewish and Christian preaching and current homiletical tasks. Dr. Josef Schuster, President of the *Landesverband der Israelitischen Kultusgemeinden in Bayern*, expressed his delight "that Jews and Christians have been meeting at this International Conference to run a dialogue together and in friendship about the things they have in common, but without concealing the things that separate them." He continued:

"Only if we know each other, will we be able to meet in mutual respect. It is a great pleasure that the Bavarian Universities of Bamberg and Erlangen picked up this dialogue with the Abraham Geiger College Potsdam. Only 50 years ago it would have been impossible that Jews and Christians come together in the manner of a trusting dialogue to debate about basic principles of their religion. Therefore I thank the initiators and supporters, the speakers and participants at this international conference who started this discourse and who hopefully will continue it for a long time."

We, the organizers of the conference and editors of this volume, would finally like to express our thanks to all the participants of the conference and to all the contributors to this volume. We thank the Fritz Thyssen Foundation and the Ministry of the Interior of the Federal Republic of Germany for financing the conference and the publication of this book. We thank Steven Sidore (In-tense Translation, Berlin) for translating some and proof-reading all of the texts in this book, William Hiscott for further proof-reading, Andrea Siebert for the layout-work and production of a print-ready manuscript and Katharina Bach for her help with the indices. We are especially grateful to Prof. Ernst Ludwig Ehrlich and Prof. Günter Stemberger for enabling us to publish this book in the renowned "Studia Judaica" series, and to Dr. Albrecht Döhnert for paving the way for this cooperation with DeGruyter publishing house.

Ernst Ludwig Ehrlich passed away on October 21, 2007, at the age of 86. The editors of this volume mourn the death of a friend and a teacher. Adieu Lutz!

Erlangen/Potsdam/Bamberg, August 2007

Alexander Deeg / Walter Homolka / Heinz-Günther Schöttler

Table of contents

Alexander Deeg/Walter Homolka/Heinz-Günther Schöttler
Preface VII

Alexander Deeg
Two Homiletic Twins. Introduction 1

Walter Cardinal Kasper
Greeting 5

Günter Stemberger
The Derashah in Rabbinic Times 7

Admiel Kosman
On the Spiritual Role of Midrash and Aggada. Response 22

Folker Siegert
The Sermon as an Invention of Hellenistic Judaism 25

Günter Stemberger
Response 45

Annette von Stockhausen
Christian Perception of Jewish Preaching in Early Christianity? .. 49

Richard S. Sarason
Response 71

Marc Saperstein
Medieval Jewish Preaching and Christian Homiletics 73

Richard S. Sarason
Response 89

Klaus Herrmann
Jewish Confirmation Sermons in 19th-Century Germany 91

Yehoyada Amir
Towards Mutual Listening. The Notion of Sermon in
Franz Rosenzweig's Philosophy 113

Alexander Deeg
Response 131

Walter Homolka
Leo Baeck – Preacher and Teacher of Preaching 136

Heinz-Günther Schöttler
Preaching the Hebrew Bible. A Christian Perspective 155

Yehoyada Amir
Jewish and Christian Bible Reading Between Retro-spectivism
and Pro-spectivism. Response 175

Richard S. Sarason
"The Voice is the Voice of Jacob." Contemporary Developments
in US-American Jewish Preaching, Homiletics and Homiletical
Education 182

Martin Nicol
Response 202

Alexander Deeg/Martin Nicol
Jewish Hermeneutics and Christian Preaching.
Scriptural Hermeneutics and its Homiletical Consequences 204

Uta Pohl-Patalong
Through the White Fire to the Black Fire. The Bibliolog as a Path
for Bible Interpretation in Judaism and Christianity 221

Index of Biblical Texts 235
Index of Rabbinic Texts 237
Index of Names 237
Index of Subjects 242

List of Contributors 245

Two Homiletic Twins
Introduction

Alexander Deeg

1. The discovery of the homiletic twin

The story of Jacob and Esau, the twin brothers, was problematic from the very beginning: "The children struggled together within her (Rebecca)" (Gen. 25.22) – so begins their joint way, and it continues in like manner through the sale of Esau's birthright (Gen. 25.29–34), Jacob's obtaining the blessing of the first-born by devious means (Gen. 27.1–40) up to Jacob's flight from his understandably furious brother Esau (Gen. 27.41–28.9). But what is really striking – despite this, the two brothers cannot get away from one another. God himself sends Jacob back into the land of his ancestors, to his relatives, to Esau, the brother whom he cheated (cf. Gen. 31.3). No easy way – and yet the two are reconciled. "To see your face is like seeing the face of God since you have received me with such favour" (Gen. 33.10), Jacob says.

In recent descriptions of the Christian-Jewish dialogue it is sometimes suggested that one should use the not-always-simple interaction of twin brothers as a paradigmatic metaphor for the Christian-Jewish relationship.[1] Just as the stories of the two brothers Jacob and Esau are antagonistic, polemic and yet inseparably intertwined (cf. Rom. 9.10–13), so might one describe the history of the varying relationship between Judaism and Christianity.[2]

Up till now, we have frequently used the model of a "mother-daughter relationship" in Christian-Jewish dialogue, or the model of a Jewish "root" from which Christianity developed. The new pattern of

---

1 Cf. e.g. *Gerard Rouwhorst*, Identität durch Gebet. Gebetstexte als Zeugen eines jahrhundertelangen Ringens um Kontinuität und Differenz zwischen Judentum und Christentum, in: *Albert Gerhards/Andrea Doeker/Peter Ebenbauer* (Eds.), Identität durch Gebet. Zur gemeinschaftsbildenden Funktion institutionalisierten Betens im Judentum und Christentum (Studien zu Judentum und Christentum), Paderborn et. al. 2003, 37–55, here: 39–44.
2 Cf. *Daniel Boyarin*, Dying for God. Martyrdom and the Making of Christianity and Judaism, Stanford (CA) 1999, 1–21; 133–148 (notes).

twin brothers could offer a way to overcome the one-sidedness of the relationship "mother-daughter" or "root-plant" and focus our attention on the *mutual reciprocity* of the relationship. On the other hand, it could also provide the opportunity to look more clearly at the connection of Judaism and Christianity which was not simply given initially as a root but remains *permanent*.

In homiletics, too, a "mother-daughter" paradigm frequently predominates. It was often recognized that Christian preaching somehow had its origin in Jewish preaching.[3] But Christian homiletics has up till now shown very little interest in how Jews over the centuries and in the present interpret the Scriptures in the synagogues, what kind of radical changes and modifications can be observed and what kind of answers Judaism has found and is finding to homiletic and hermeneutic challenges.

Put bluntly: on the Christian side, one usually imagines that one can pursue homiletics without the Jewish twin. Surprisingly this assessment holds true for the majority of recent reflections on homiletics that deliberately orientate themselves to the Christian-Jewish dialogue. These for the most part ask how Christian preaching must change *in content* to avoid anti-Jewish nuances and to achieve a fair representation of Judaism in Christian preaching. They are concerned above all with applying to the Church's preaching that which has been recognized in other branches of theology, particularly in exegesis and dogmatics.[4] Of course this objective was important – and will remain so in future. But it overlooks the potential for learning which might be discovered when there is an earnest appreciation of the Jewish homiletical brother.

By contrast, in his consideration of preaching the Old Testament in his famous "*Predigtlehre*"/Homiletics, which first appeared in 1971,

---

3   Cf. e.g. *Frieder Schulz*, Die jüdischen Wurzeln des christlichen Gottesdienstes, in: *Idem*, Synaxis. Beiträge zur Liturgik (ed. *Gerhard Schwinge*), Göttingen 1997, 15–36, esp. 15; or *Wilfried Engemann*, Einführung in die Homiletik (UTB 2128), Tübingen/ Basel 2002, 88f.

4   I refer simply as an example to *Evelina Volkmann*, Vom 'Judensonntag' zum 'Israelsonntag'. Predigtarbeit im Horizont des christlich-jüdischen Gesprächs, Stuttgart 2002, and *Eadem*, Homiletik und christlich-jüdisches Gespräch, in: PrTh 38/2004, 253–260. Both of these contain references to further literature. So, too, do the two series of meditational sermons, which up to now have arisen in the context of the Christian-Jewish conversations and at best merely glance in passing at Jewish preaching and homiletics; cf. *Arnulf H. Baumann/Ulrich Schwemer* (Eds.), Predigen in Israels Gegenwart. Predigtmeditationen im Horizont des christlich-jüdischen Gesprächs, 3 vol., Gütersloh 1986–1990, and *Wolfgang Kruse/Studium in Israel* (Eds.), Predigtmeditationen im christlich-jüdischen Dialog, Neuhausen 1996–2001; Berlin 2002–2007.

Rudolf Bohren, former Professor of Practical Theology in Wuppertal and Heidelberg, formulated a far reaching perspective. Bohren writes:

> "Only pride and ignorance could prevent the Protestant [and of course, I may also add, the Christian – AD] preacher from learning from the rabbi. […] Even if the preacher should not speak like a rabbi, he still should not preach without the rabbi: The Church cannot discount the Synagogue without losing her Promise."[5]

Even if the preacher should not speak like a rabbi, he still should not preach without the rabbi! This was said more than thirty years ago – but few have really noticed what Bohren said and wrote. One of those who did was Axel Denecke. With regard to preaching Denecke wrote about ten years ago:

> "[…] after all, the Jewish experience of the success and failure of speech about God is twice as old as the Christian. It is really astonishing that up till now – as far as I can see […] – no one has come upon the obvious idea of going as a preacher […] into the Jewish school and learning from Jewish rhetoric for our preaching."[6]

This is why we decided to organize this conference in Bamberg. Because we think that time has come to do homiletics as *twin brothers*. Learning from one another, asking questions together and jointly trying to find answers.

2. "Walking alongside you" as a paradigm of dialogue

Jacob and Esau, the twin brothers, met one another again after years of alienation. After this meeting Esau says: "Let us journey on our way, and I will go with you" (Gen. 33.12). The phrase in Genesis 33.12b can be translated as "I will go opposite to you" or "I will go alongside you" (Buber/Rosenzweig and the NRSV; אלכה לנגדך). A new cooperation of the twin brothers is indicated but in a manner which – if one follows the story in Gen. 33 – by no means denotes that Jacob and Esau now travel in step; Jacob takes the liberty of travelling "leisurely behind" (as we read in v. 14) and lets Esau go first.

If Christian and Jewish homiletics recognize one another as complementary opposite numbers and "go alongside" one another, this will not, should not and cannot mean that common, somehow consensual Jewish-Christian homiletics must be developed. As we Christians have learned in the meantime in ecumenical dialogue, the

---

5   *Rudolf Bohren*, Predigtlehre, Gütersloh ⁶1993, 121.
6   *Axel Denecke*, Als Christ in der Judenschule. Grundsätzliche und praktische Überlegungen zum christlich-jüdischen Gespräch und zur Rede von Gott (Schalom-Bücher 4), Hannover 1996, 84.

stimulus of cooperation does not necessarily lie in agreement but in the jointly reconciled and reciprocally challenging difference.[7] For homiletics this means to go there together and work with one another where this is possible and, for example, to ask questions together about the history of Jewish and Christian homiletics and their interrelation, about the relevance of the sermon today, about the relationship of preaching and liturgy, and about the hermeneutics of sacred texts. But this means at the same time calmly and clearly searching for one's own way. For it is precisely this which will be attractive to the other twin and make it alluring not to look away but to be interested in the other: it is not impossible but is, on the contrary, very likely that one might discover potential for learning and change for one's own way in the other way of the twin brother.

3. Thematic overview

This is exactly what happened in Bamberg in March 2007. Jews and Christians learned together and from each other, discussed the history of Jewish and Christian preaching (with its many open questions!), and faced the challenges for Jewish and Christian preaching today.

Of course, the theme could not be covered completely. And at the end of conference a dozen ideas were collected for further conferences about the "two homiletical traditions". But the conference tried to enter the field and give an overview, also marking questions for further research and clarification. According to its basic aims, the conference was arranged in two main parts: one larger part dealt with the history of Jewish and Christian preaching – and especially with the interrelation, or lacking interrelation, between the homiletic twins. The conference started in hellenistic and rabbinic times and in the times of the Early Church, moved forward to the Middle Ages, and finally reached the 19th and 20th century. The second part focused on current challenges and dealt with homiletical hermeneutics, Christian preaching of the Hebrew/Jewish Bible, developments in Jewish preaching in the USA, and new forms of interpreting the Bible (we chose the so called "*Bibliolog*" as an exemplary learning field).

It is impossible to sum all this up. But it should – we do hope – be possible for the readers of this conference volume to discover the richness and variety of doing research on the "two homiletical traditions" and thus jointly practicing homiletics – as "twin brothers."

---

7   Cf. e.g. *Ilse Bulhof*, Die postmoderne Herausforderung der ökumenischen Bewegung, in: US 50/1995, 15–29.

Greeting
to the conference "Two Homiletical Traditions. Preaching in Judaism and Christianity"

Walter Cardinal Kasper

Jews and Christians share the conviction that the God of Israel made revelations through his efficacious word. Both traditions start with the assumption that this revealed word of God requires interpretation and exegesis for modern listeners to understand it. Homiletic traditions shape both Judaism and Christianity, and it is a worthwhile endeavour for the Jewish-Christian conversation to shine a closer light on this aspect.

This is why I hail the effort by Abraham Geiger College at the University of Potsdam, the Faculty of Catholic Theology at the University of Bamberg, and the Faculty of Protestant Theology at the University of Erlangen to organise a joint Jewish-Christian project centred on the methodical commonalities and differences in the exegesis of God's word. The conference is thereby taking up a fundamental and current topic in the dialogue between Judaism and Christianity.

Since the *Nostra Aetate* Declaration by the Second Vatican Council, Jews and Christians have become more familiar with one another, and thereby come to understand one another better. The declaration involved not just the dispelling of centuries' worth of old misunderstandings and prejudices, but also the discovery of many commonalities in the face of the many fundamental and enduring differences. In 1985, twenty years after *Nostra Aetate*, the Commission for Religious Relations with the Jews published "Notes on the Correct Way to Present Jews and Judaism in the Teaching and Catechesis of the Roman Catholic Church." It instructs:

> "Religious teaching, catechesis and preaching should be a preparation not only for objectivity, justice, tolerance but also for understanding and dialogue. Our two traditions are so related that they cannot ignore each other. Mutual knowledge must be encouraged at every level."

I wish the conference smooth proceedings and fruitful work. May the lectures and discussions contribute to better and deeper understanding for Jews and Christians of their own traditions, as well as the traditions of the other. May the encounter between the two help increase and magnify the transition from dialogue to cooperation in service of the *Repairing of the World – Tiqqun Olam*. This dialogue and better understanding will certainly also serve the Bamberg Conference under the title *"Two Homiletical Traditions. Preaching in Judaism and Christianity."*

The Derashah in Rabbinic Times

Günter Stemberger

When the young Leopold Zunz wrote his magisterial work *Die gottesdienstlichen Vorträge der Juden*,[1] his goal was not only to reconstruct the history of midrash, but to justify with it the renewal of the rabbinic sermon in the Jewish reform movement of his times. Zunz only rarely used the term "sermon", he preferred to speak of *"Vorträge"*, public lectures, speeches in the context of the liturgy; but he seems to use the terms as synonyms.[2] His systematic description of the rabbinic sermon[3] is based on the analysis of the midrashim and therefore comes only after their presentation. Since he was convinced that the transmission of the midrashim for centuries was mainly oral, he saw only one explanation how the midrash could have been preserved and made popular:

> "Nur *ein* Ausweg bleibt uns: die Hagada muss bei verschiedenen Veranlassungen des öffentlichen und des Privatlebens *vorgetragen* worden sein. Da alle öffentlichen Verrichtungen, insonderheit aber was Unterweisung und Gottesdienst betraf, meist in den Synagogen oder in den Lehrhäusern abgemacht wurden, so geschahen die öffentlichen Vorträge höchstwahrscheinlich ebendaselbst" (341, emphasis original).

These sermons were directed to the general public (*"Zuhörer, die aus allen Ständen und beiderlei Geschlechtern bestanden"*, 352). Much of them is preserved in the midrashim:

> "Und in der That bildet der vorzüglichste Inhalt der *ältern Hagada* Theile jener freien Vorträge. Von vielen Fragmenten bezeugen es Inhalt und Tendenz; andere werden ausdrücklich als öffentlicher Vortrag mitgetheilt" (354).

Zunz emphasizes that the public character of the homilies implied that they were delivered in a language the people could understand,

---

1 Leopold Zunz, Die gottesdienstlichen Vorträge der Juden historisch entwickelt, Berlin 1832, Frankfurt/M. ²1892. Hebrew translation: *Ha-Derashot be-Yisrael*, Jerusalem 1954, with updates by Chanoch Albeck.
2 Ibid., XII: "Predigten oder Erbauungs-Vorträge".
3 Ibid., 342–373, chapter 20: "Vortragswesen des Alterthums".

normally in Aramaic; he is convinced that we still have a great store of *aggadah* in its original Aramaic form (*"einen grossen hagadischen Vorrath in seiner ursprünglichen aramäischen Gestalt"*, 370). Texts in Hebrew therefore normally derive from other writings, but there are Hebrew texts consisting of "really delivered sermons, but in the form in which the *darshan* handed it on to friends and students" (*"aus wirklich Vorgetragenem, aber in der Gestalt, wie es der Darschan Freunden und Schülern mitgeteilt hatte"*, 371). Zunz speaks of rhetorical forms typical of the *derashah*, but insists on the great freedom of the preacher regarding form and contents of his homily. He also knows that the sermon in the rabbinic period and its relationship with the biblical readings and the liturgy developed over time, and gives a few examples of earlier and later forms; but his main emphasis is on the multiformity of the homily (thus allowing for a great variety of sermons in the modern period as well).

As the texts quoted above show, Zunz was aware of the fact that not every midrashic text derives from actual sermons; above all, all material in Hebrew was excluded because of his understanding that the rabbinic sermons were intended for the general public including the uneducated people. He also recognized that even homiletic material was at least sometimes reworked for its midrashic context. But in his search for the rabbinic sermon as precedent and model of the homiletical renewal of his own time, Zunz clearly overestimated the extent of rabbinic homilies still preserved.

It was soon recognized, e.g. by Siegmund Maybaum,[4] that hardly any midrashic text can be considered an authentic transcript of a rabbinic sermon delivered as such in a synagogue. One has at the very least to assume that memories of such sermons were joined with other materials and underwent a thorough literary reworking before being inserted into a larger midrashic unit, as Joseph Heinemann has shown in his literary analyses of rabbinic texts supposed to be based on sermons:

> "Though the 'classical' Midrashim undoubtedly drew the bulk of their material from the tens of thousands of sermons which had actually been preached in the synagogues of Palestine during the first four or five centuries C.E., they have hardly ever preserved these sermons in their original form. In many cases, they present mere outlines of actual sermons

---

4   Siegmund Maybaum, Die ältesten Phasen in der Entwickelung der jüdischen Predigt. 19. Bericht der Lehranstalt für die Wissenschaft des Judenthums in Berlin, Berlin 1901.

or of parts of them, while, on the other hand, they take sections from many separate sermons and weld them into new and larger units."[5]

This description of the midrashic material acknowledges its literary shaping, but still insists by far too much on what lies behind it, actual sermons addressed by rabbis to the general public in the synagogues. Richard S. Sarason, among others, has rightly criticised this approach with its insistence on sermons for the public still to be recovered from the preserved midrashim.[6] During the last decades the study of the rabbinic homily has made much progress; all the same, or better as a consequence of it, today we know much less about the rabbinic *derashah* than we used to believe.

1. Historical problems

Zunz saw that there were at least two locations for the public homily, the synagogue and the *Bet ha-Midrash* which sometimes were located in the same building. But he did not sufficiently distinguish between them and the kind of speeches delivered in the respective settings, being interested mainly in the homilies addressed to the general public.

We cannot discuss the rabbinic homily without some knowledge about the institutions where it is supposed to have taken place. At the time of Zunz and even until quite recently, it was supposed that synagogues existed in nearly every town in Palestine and in most Jewish communities in the Diaspora. While for the Diaspora this may be true, in Palestine, more specifically in Judaea, the literary and archaeological evidence before the late third century does not support this assumption. This is not the place to discuss the problem in detail. Some archaeologists are more confident that we have material evidence for at least some synagogues in Judaea which may be dated to the first or second centuries while others doubt the identification in most cases. One may, of course, correctly argue that the early synagogue was a multi-purpose hall and not yet a specifically liturgical building, and thus cannot easily be distinguished from other large and therefore most

---

[5] *Joseph Heinemann*, Art. Preaching. In the Talmudic Period, in: EJ² 16 (2007), 467–470, taken over unchanged from the 1972 edition, 468f. See *Idem*, Sermons in the Talmudic Period, Jerusalem 1970 (Hebrew). The midrashic texts contained in this book are translated in *Idem/Jakob J. Petuchowski*, Literature of the Synagogue, New York 1975.

[6] *Richard S. Sarason*, Toward a New Agendum for the Study of Rabbinic Midrashic Literature, in: *Jakob J. Petuchowski/Ezra Fleischer* (Eds.), Studies in Aggadah, Targum and Jewish Liturgy in Memory of Joseph Heinemann, Jerusalem 1981, 55–73, 62ff. on Heinemann and others.

probably communal buildings. But it is a fact that synagogues, as we know them, became a common and widespread phenomenon in Palestine only from the fourth century onward when the growing visibility of Christianity challenged the Jewish communities also to become more visible in the religious landscape of Palestine, as underlined particularly by Seth Schwartz.[7]

The next question we have to address is the participation of rabbis in the life of the synagogue. Once it was thought that rabbis were the natural leaders of the synagogue and dominated its agenda, regulating the liturgy and the scriptural readings as well as teaching and preaching regularly in the synagogue. Joseph Heinemann states:

> "The importance of the sermon can hardly be overestimated. Not only did it serve as the chief means of instructing all the people – peasants, women, and children – and imparting to all and sundry at least an elementary knowledge of the Torah and its teachings, but it also provided the sages with a means of guiding the people, strengthening their faith, and refuting heretical views" (EJ 16, 467).

But it has become increasingly clear that the rabbis were much less involved in the synagogue than was previously thought. For the tannaitic period we have little evidence: as already said, there are hardly any archaeological remains to be identified as synagogues, and the rabbinic texts have no special interest in them. As Shaye Cohen has shown, among the persons mentioned in synagogue inscriptions we do not find a single person to be identified with a known rabbi of the rabbinic literature.[8] They do not figure among the donors of the synagogue nor are they prominent members of the community. The leaders of the synagogues obviously belonged to the most prominent local families, in a number of cases priests or levites. In most villages, no member of the rabbinic movement was to be found.

Only some of the rabbis started to participate in synagogal life since the third century; the majority always remained aloof from this rather non-rabbinic institution. Only rarely do we find rabbis in the context of the synagogue, especially preaching there. The exact evaluation is still a matter of dispute. Even Lee Levine who is much more positive than I am about the early history of the synagogue and rabbinic participation in its life, formulates rather cautiously:

> "By the third and fourth centuries, the synagogue had assumed a much more central role in rabbinic circles than before. The rabbis' emphasis on the synagogue and regular attendance reflects an identification with this

---

7 *Seth Schwartz*, Imperialism and Jewish society: 200 B.C.E. to 640 C.E., Princeton (NJ) 2002.
8 *Shaye J. D. Cohen*, Epigraphical Rabbis, in: JQR 72/1981, 1–17.

communal institution, and this, in turn, probably indicates that the worship conducted therein met with their approval, and perhaps even followed their dictates. Nevertheless, this point should not be overly exaggerated. The fact that some sages repeatedly emphasized their approval would seem to indicate that there were others who disagreed. As noted above, some sages tended to shy away from the synagogue, preferring instead either the intimacy of their homes or the familiarity of the academy."[9]

It is a question of proportions as to how many synagogues ever saw a member of the rabbinic movement or how many rabbis actually participated in the liturgy of the local synagogues. As has been observed, there is hardly any overlap between places where synagogues have been excavated and towns and villages which are named as places of origin of known rabbis or places where they studied and taught. But this may not be so important for the study of the relationship between midrashic literature and the preaching activity of rabbis. It would make a difference only with regard to the representativity of the texts we have. They would mainly testify to what was going on in rabbinic centers or to the activity of some rabbis more involved in synagogue life (and this is not so different from what we know about Christian preaching traditions of the same period where also we have texts of the theological elite alone and normally do not know what a sermon in a simple village was like).

But how common was it for rabbis to preach? The answer to this question depends on our reading of the rabbinic sources and their relationship with actual sermons. Most authors are convinced that at least some rabbis preached quite regularly to the general public, be it in the synagogue or in the study-house. To give just one prominent example, let me quote again Lee Levine:

> "There seem to have been three major areas of rabbinic involvement in the ancient synagogue. The first is preaching, and several sages are singled out in this regard. Most notable is the third-century amora R. Yohanan, who appears to have preached regularly in the synagogue of Sepphoris [...]. Rabbinic literature preserves numerous examples of rabbinic sermons, but how representative they are of what actually transpired in synagogues is difficult to say. Did rabbis always, sometimes, or only rarely sermonize publicly? The homilies, although not inconsequential in number, do not offer an adequate indication [...] there is little question that a number of sages delivered sermons in synagogues. Rabbinic literature has preserved

---

9   *Lee I. Levine*, The Ancient Synagogue: The First Thousand Years, New Haven (CT) 2000, 459.

a number of interesting references in this regard, as we have noted above."¹⁰

I could go on and give more examples of Levine's understanding of rabbinic texts. He sees the rabbinic sermons in direct continuity from what was common in the first century as he derives from the New Testament (145: "The New Testament evidence makes it crystal clear that the sermon [i.e., the exposition of an idea that appears in the scriptural reading] was a recognized component of the Sabbath service", referring to Jesus in Nazareth and Paul in Antioch in Pisidia: Luke 4.20f.; Acts 13.5). But his reading of the rabbinic evidence (and New Testament texts) is challenged by other scholars as, e.g. most recently, Gary Porton.¹¹

G. Porton is inclined to reduce the activity of rabbis as preachers in a synagogue to an absolute minimum since there are not enough explicit statements to this effect in rabbinic texts: He writes:

> "This paper argues that Rabbinic Midrash is a definable literary phenomenon that finds its primary locus within the Rabbinic schoolhouses of late antiquity. It challenges the claim that much of our current Rabbinic Midrash originated in the Rabbinic sermons of late antiquity. While some rabbis may have delivered sermons in the synagogues of late antiquity or to the 'community' in different public settings, we shall see that there are few specific indications of that fact. When we find rabbis within the context of synagogues, they most often are not delivering sermons. And when rabbis 'preach' to the community, it is often in cities with Rabbinic academies, so it is unclear exactly to whom these 'sermons' were delivered."¹²

Porton opposes the interpretation of Lee Levine¹³ who adduces texts like y. Naz 7.2 as evidence that R. Abbahu preached in the Maradata synagogue of Caesarea:

> "Abbahu teaches, *mty*, but he does not preach. Unlike Levine, I am not willing to argue that a rabbi's teaching in a synagogue necessarily means that he was delivering a sermon there, even if that is one possibility."¹⁴

Most frequently when rabbis are said to have expounded a biblical text, no location is given; normally, the audience seems to have been

---

10 *Ibid.*, 461.465.549.
11 Gary G. Porton, Midrash and the Rabbinic Sermon, in: *Alan J. Avery-Peck/Daniel Harrington/Jacob Neusner* (Eds.), When Judaism & Christianity Began: Essays in Memory of Anthony J. Saldarini (JSJS 85), Leiden 2004, II, 461–482; cf. *Idem*, Midrash, Definitions of, in: *Jacob Neusner/Alan Avery-Peck* (Eds.), Encyclopedia of Midrash, Leiden 2005, 520–534.
12 Porton, When Judaism, 461.
13 *Levine*, The Ancient Synagogue, 461.
14 Porton, When Judaism, 467 n. 20.

students of the rabbi or other rabbis (e.g. Mekhilta Pisha 16: R. Eleazar ben Azariah interprets, *darash*, in Yavneh) but not the normal people of a town or village who simply would not have been knowledgeable enough to understand the intricacies of rabbinic expositions which, by the way, need not have been "sermons". Gary Porton concludes:

> "It remains possible that some of the midrashim originated in Rabbinic sermons and that some of these sermons in fact were delivered to non-rabbis in the synagogues of late antiquity. But it is more likely that most of the midrashim we have come from the Rabbinic schoolhouses of late antiquity and were produced by rabbis for other rabbis or rabbinic students".[15]

I fully agree with Porton that Rabbinic literature offers much less evidence for rabbis preaching in the synagogue to a general public than is usually thought. Most frequently they are presented in an inner-rabbinic setting, even if it is in a synagogue. The verb *darash* normally does not indicate that a rabbi "preached", but that he "expounded, interpreted" a biblical text (e.g. in Mekhilta, Pisha 14); in other cases, the teaching is not even connected with a biblical verse, as in Ruth Rabba 5.12, where R. Simlai taught in public (*darash be-tsibbura*) that a person should have two sets of clothing, one for everyday and one for Sabbath; see also y. Shab 14.4 (14d) where R. Yohanan learns from a non-Jewish practitioner (Domitian's daughter) a prescription against scurvy and the next Sabbath expounds it publicly (*derashah be-tsibbura*). In rabbinic texts, *derashah* is not yet a sermon or an edifying discourse in the synagogue, as it became in the Middle Ages, but "interpretation, exegesis" (e.g. b. BM 86b on Gen. 18.7 *ben baqar rakh we-tov*, "a tender and good calf", understood as three calves – *mi-de-tov le-derashah, rakh nami le-derashah*: "since 'good' serves for interpretation, 'tender' also is for interpretation"). There are cases where a *derashah* looks very much like a homiletic discourse; thus for example in y. Hag 2.1 (87b):

> "R. Meir was sitting and teaching (*darash*) in the schoolhouse (*be-veit midrasha*) of Tiberias. Elisha, his master, passed by, riding on a horse on the Sabbath day. They came and said to him, 'Look, your master is outside'. He stopped his teaching (*pesaq leh min derashah*) and went out to him.
> He said to him: What were you expounding (*darash*) today? He said to him, 'And the Lord blessed the latter days of Job more than his beginning' (Job 42.12).
> Elisha said to him: With what [verse] did you begin to expound it (*u-mah patahta beh*)? He said to him: 'And the Lord gave Job twice as much as he had before' (Job 42:10), for he doubled for him all his wealth [...]".

---

15 *Porton*, Encyclopedia of Midrash, 531.

[Elisha] said to him, 'And what else have you been expounding?' He said to him, 'Better is the end of a thing than its beginning' (Eccles. 7.8). He said to him: How did you begin to expound it (*u-mah patahta beh*)?
He said to him: '[By comparing it] with a man who begot children in his youth and they died, then in his old age he started again. The end of the matter was better than its beginning'" (translation J. Neusner).

The setting of the scene is the schoolhouse on a Sabbath; only his disciples are present when R. Meir gives his lecture. It is based on biblical texts, but not on the reading of the Torah in the synagogue. The first part interprets (*darash*) a verse of Job, and the beginning of the interpretation (*patah*) is from the same chapter, two verses before. The next lesson is based on a verse of Kohelet and might be regarded as a coherent part of the interpretation of Job; but here R. Meir says to have begun (*patah*) his speech with a comparison (not quite a parable). The verses quoted all come from the Hagiographa, not from a Torah reading. They might be considered to introduce a *petihah*, which is normally regarded as a sermon or at least the introductory part of it. But in this case we would expect that it leads up to the first verse of the Torah reading which is not mentioned. The whole passage might offer good material for a sermon, but is not depicted as such. Thus, R. Meir may interrupt his lesson to leave the room and talk to his former master, something not really conceivable in the setting of a formal sermon. The whole scene certainly may not be taken as a report of what actually happened; but even as a story it does not depict the rabbi as a preacher.

We thus have very little direct evidence for rabbis preaching to the public in the Palestinian synagogues. This does not, of course, exclude the possibility that sermons explaining the biblical reading were common and routine in late antique synagogues, as it is frequently claimed to have been the case in pre-70 synagogues. If we assume this possibility, we have to ask ourselves: Who were the preachers? Perhaps simple members of the community, better educated than the rest, who might also have served as *meturgemanim*? We certainly cannot limit the study of the Scriptures to rabbinic circles. But since we have only the writings of the rabbis,[16] our problem is what we can know about the

---

16 Here we should mention the liturgical poetry of the synagogue, the *piyyutim*, of which we have texts at least since the fifth century. Their authors are not to be identified with the rabbis – many apparently came from priestly circles – but their work is clearly in dialogue with the midrashic expositions of their times, thus with regard to ideas not too far away from the rabbis, although the form is completely different. The message of the *piyyutim* might be taken as a kind of homily, but its form in general was too intricate to be fully understood by the simple listener. We would also have to ask how common the recitation of *piyyutim* was in the

way of preaching of people outside the rabbinic world? Would contents of such sermons by lay people and their rhetorical conventions ever enter the writings of the rabbis (or at least the Targum tradition)? Philip Alexander recently suggested[17] that the *petihot* at the beginning of Lamentations Rabbah reflect actual sermons given by people who were not rabbis, referring especially to the unrabbinic theology of *Petihah* 24, close to the ideology of the Avele Zion. Interesting though it is, I find it difficult to verify this hypothesis, and in general prefer to consider "non-rabbinic" reasoning in rabbinic texts as reflecting later developments. This would be worthy of a systematic study. For the time being, we just have to try to approach the question of the rabbinic *derashah* (now more cautiously defined as elements of preaching to be discovered in rabbinic literature) from another angle.

2. Formal analysis of the derashah

In spite of so many open questions as to the historical situation, we are all used to speaking of "homiletical" midrashim and to see in them rhetorical conventions characteristic of sermons. Some of the literary forms or components of such "homilies" have been thoroughly analysed, most of all the *petihah* and the *hatimah*.

As to the *petihah*, so called because of its standard introduction R. X *patah*, i.e. 'opened (the sermon)' or 'preached', it clearly follows a rhetorical pattern in dealing with selected verses of Scripture and thus might originally have had its *Sitz im Leben* in oral performance. The simplest form of the *petihah* starts with a biblical verse most commonly taken from the *Ketuvim*, i.e. a group of biblical texts not used for public reading, and leads up to the first verse of the Torah reading or the *Haftarah*. This lopsided structure of the *petihah* has been explained by its function as a short introductory sermon before the Scriptural reading (but see the objection by Arnold Goldberg[18] that this understanding of the *petihah* does not fit the known structure of the liturgy which does not allow a place for such a prooemium before the reading; at least the *berakhah* would be interposed between the introduction and the reading). Others think that it normally did not serve as an independent

---

synagogues of the Talmudic period. Perhaps they were recited only in the intellectual centers, not in the common village synagogues.

17 *Philip Alexander*, in a lecture given on February 26, 2007, in the Institute of Jewish Studies, University of Vienna.

18 *Arnold Goldberg*, Rabbinische Texte als Gegenstand der Auslegung. Gesammelte Studien II, ed. by *Margarethe Schlüter/Peter Schäfer* (TSAJ 73), Tübingen 1999, 328f.

unit, but has to be understood as a component of a larger rhetorical unit, the composite rabbinic sermon. Structurally it can serve both purposes. But there is not only the classical simple *petiḥah*; there are circular *petiḥot* and more complex composite structures. Many aspects of the *petiḥot* preserved in rabbinic literature (as, e.g., the quotation of one or several rabbis in them) suggest that, although originally based on a rhetorical pattern, in the midrashim as we have them, they primarily serve literary purposes. Richard Sarason writes:

> "[...] while the petihta-form undoubtedly originated in the oral exposition of Scripture, the composite petihtot which we find in the early midrashic compilations surely are literary creations of the editor(s), constructed in the processes of redaction. These editors made use of the petihta-form, on the model of oral discourses, as a convenient and, to them, logical formal device for ordering the disparate materials at hand and forming larger units for the literary encapsulation and transmission of these inherited materials".[19]

The *ḥatimah*, the concluding part of most 'homiletical' units, leads up to a verse from the prophetic reading. It clearly never served an independent function, but always was the eschatological kerygma at the end of a longer text dealing with selected aspects of a biblical pericope. Formally it is less strict than the *petiḥah*; thus it is frequently difficult to recognize its beginning, but working back from the end one can see where the text begins to prepare this ending with its message of consolation and comfort, contrasting the troubles of this world with the blessings of the world to come. Regarding the body proper of the homiletical unit, structural criteria to a large extent are still unexplored (if there ever were such defined criteria beyond the topic of the biblical reading).[20]

Arnold Goldberg has devoted much of his research to the formal description of distinct units of midrashic literature, the midrashic sentence, the *petiḥah*, the *semikhah*, the *ḥarizah* and the *ḥatimah* etc.[21] On the basis of these studies by Goldberg, Doris Lenhard has worked out a large-scale form-analytical description of the rabbinic homily.[22] In the

---

19 *Sarason*, Toward a New Agendum, 67 n. 29.
20 *Felix Böhl*, Aufbau und literarische Formen des aggadischen Teils im Jelamdenu-Midrasch, Wiesbaden 1977, addresses this question only in part, switching continuously between the Yelamdenu-homily and the document called Yelamdenu. Cf. the criticism of *Doris Lenhard*, Die Rabbinische Homilie. Ein formanalytischer Index (FJS 10), Frankfurt/M. 1998, 6 n. 21.
21 These essays have been collected in *Goldberg*, Rabbinische Texte.
22 *Doris Lenhard*, Die Rabbinische Homilie; cf. *Eadem*, Document or Individual Homily? A Critical Evaluation of Neusner's Methodology in the Light of the Results of Form-Analysis, in: JSQ 4/1997, 339–356.

introduction, she quotes from a text written by Goldberg which was intended as preface to her volume:

> "Rabbinische Homilien sind Texte von einer bestimmten Form, die regelmäßig bei der Herstellung realisiert wird. Sie sprechen über Schriftverse oder kurze Perikopen der Schrift in den Formen des Yelamdenu, der Petiḥa, der Semikha, der Inyanauslegung und der Ḥatima. An den Texten läßt sich eine bestimmte Verwendung nicht erkennen (noch ist es uns möglich, einen Zusammenhang zwischen Zweck und Form zu finden).
> Die Vorfindlichkeit solcher formbestimmter Texte in größerer Anzahl, und zwar in Sammlungen, die nicht von den Homilien, sondern eher vom Wunsch der angemessenen Thesaurierung (Abfolge der Schrift, der Feiertage, etc.) bestimmt sind, ließen es sinnvoll erscheinen, die jeweils einzelnen Texteinheiten 'Homilie zu ...' nach formalen Kriterien darzustellen [...]. Die Summe dieser formalen Beschreibung ist dann auch die Summe aller (uns zugänglichen) Texteinheiten, die wir 'rabbinische Homilien' nennen und die in den Sammlungen WaR, DevR, Tan, TanB, PesK und PesR vorliegen."[23]

This introduction makes it fully clear that Goldberg and, following him, Lenhard, do not pretend to describe actual rabbinic homilies. It speaks of *texts* with recurrent literary forms. What purpose these texts served, we cannot know nor can we recognize a connection between purpose and form. The collections of these texts (the "homiletical midrashim") are determined not by the homilies, but rather by the wish to provide an adequate thesaurus of homilies according to the sequence of Scripture or the festival days. The texts and their formal characteristics are all we have. Historical questions are completely beyond the scope of this analysis; they simply cannot be answered on the basis of the texts. This strict approach to midrash as pure literature beyond which we may never go, will not satisfy most of us who still have historical questions on our mind; but it is at least the necessary first step before historical questions may be approached.

Having analysed all the 411 homiletic units in Leviticus Rabbah, both versions of the Tanḥuma and both Pesiqtot, Lenhard categorizes the compositional units of the macro-form of the rabbinic homily. These smaller 'functional forms' – so called because they stand in a functional relationship to each other, connecting the different parts of the homily – normally appear in the following sequence: *Yelamdenu* (a halakhic section, called after its introduction *Yelamdenu rabbenu*, "let our master teach us"), *petiḥah*, *semikhah* (a section which links the following inyan to the biblical verse preceding it), *inyan* (the central

---

23 *Lenhard*, Die Rabbinische Homilie, 1f.

part of the homily) and *hatimah*. *Yelamdenu* and *semikhah* are optional whereas *petihah*, *inyan* and *hatimah* are the essential elements of the homily. For each of the sub-units of the macro-form Lenhard catalogues a whole series of sub-forms, deviations from the expected standard form or mixed forms: She counts 30 subforms for the *yelamdenu*, 40 for the *petihah*, 26 for the *semikhah*, 17 for the *inyan* and 15 for the *hatimah*. Thus there is no standard literary form of the rabbinic homily to be expected, the ideal type or prototype never occurs in the preserved texts.

The mere fact that there are so many subforms of the single parts of the rabbinic homily as analysed by Arnold Goldberg and Doris Lenhard, and that even the sequence of its constituent parts is not absolutely stable, clearly shows the difficulties inherent in any formal description of the homily, but also its necessity, if we ever want to move beyond an impressionistic approach to it. This has been pointed out in a lengthy review-essay by Alexander Samely who emphasises

> "[...] that rabbinic homiletic texts can differ from each other to such a degree that even the distinction between homiletic and non-homiletic texts is insecure [...] it cannot be doubted that in the case of rabbinic homiletic texts a considerable proportion of the literary variety now found is due to accidental historical factors, not compositional decisions or conventions. An account of the rabbinic 'form' homily has to be able to draw a line between the sense and the nonsense; and no definition of the genre could save the textual evidence as it stands in all cases and sources."[24]

3. How useful is the distinction between exegetical and homiletical midrashim?

In the index worked out by D. Lenhard, it becomes immediately clear that especially the central part of the homily defies clear formal definiton. The *inyan*, as this part is called in the Goldberg-school, consists of interpretations of a series of lemmata of the text on which the homily is based. The fact that the first lemma frequently coincides with attested beginnings of weekly Torah lessons, is normally considered as a criterion that we really are dealing with some kind of sermon on them. In most cases these units could quite as well be found in a classical 'exegetical' midrash. The same is true of mixed forms of the *petihah*. On the other hand, the *petihah* as the most essential "homiletical" form occurs very frequently in Genesis Rabbah, an

---

24 *Alexander Samely*, An Account of the Rabbinic Homily: Lenhard's Form-Analytical Index, in: JJS 53/2002, 371–379, 374.

'exegetical' midrash, and other works regarded to belong to this category (Maybaum used Genesis Rabbah as the basis of his study of the rabbinic homily!).

Lamentations Rabbah begins with a whole block of *petiḥot* (normally 36 according to the numerical value of the first word of the biblical book, *ekhah*; but the manuscripts vary), but the work as such is not considered as a homiletical midrash, and we have no early evidence for preaching on the book of Lamentations on the ninth of Av.

Leviticus Rabbah, generally considered a particularly fine example of a collection of homilies, has recently been subjected to a thorough and most stimulating new analysis by Burton Visotzky. He rightly emphasises that the midrash

> "[...] does organize some chapters around what may have been verses in a triennial lectionary; but at most only one-half to two-thirds of the chapters may be accounted for by this assumption. It is more accurate to speak of LR as a collection of texts organized loosely around clusters of traditions on selected verses of Leviticus [...] a type of quasi-encyclopedia of traditions somehow related to Leviticus."[25]

Visotzky sees the midrash structured according to contemporary Greek literary models and not at all as a 'homiletical' midrash. This does not exclude the possibility that some parts in it may derive from a homiletic context or have been useful for such a context afterwards. The rather unquestioned use of Leviticus Rabbah as one of the sources for Lenhard's Index seems to follow purely formal criteria since she states that our knowledge about reading cycles or festival cycles cannot serve

> "[...] als Ausgangspunkt für eine Definition [...], will man nicht weite Teile der Homilienmidrashim – wie etwa WaR und Teile der PesR, für die kein Sitz in der Liturgie plausibel gemacht werden kann, von vornherein ausklammern."[26]

Doris Lenhard seems to assume that the midrashim she has analysed are the full corpus of such texts;[27] but there is not only the somewhat problematic categorization of Leviticus Rabbah,[28] but also the omission

---

25 Burton L. Visotzky, Golden Bells and Pomegranates. Studies in Midrash Leviticus Rabbah (TSAJ 94), Tübingen 2003, 178.
26 Lenhard, Die Rabbinische Homilie, 8.
27 She explicitly says of her Index: "The availability of this comprehensive evidence, namely *all* homilies [her emphasis] makes it possible for the first time to contrast a form-analytical definition of the texts with their definition by way of works" (as proposed by J. Neusner: Lenhard, 'Document', 340).
28 Lenhard, Die Rabbinische Homilie, 540, presents a list of non-homiletic materials (Nicht-Homilien). Most passages listed here come from the two versions of *Tanḥuma*, but only three from Leviticus Rabbah.

of so much material, formally fully comparable to texts analyzed by her, in midrashim usually not qualified as 'homiletical midrashim'.

The traditional division of midrashic works partly breaks down; the common criterion that 'homiletical' midrashim follow the order of lectionaries for the Sabbath (*Tanhuma*) and for feasts (*Pesiqta*) to a large extent still works, but how useful is it?

4. Can we recover the derashah of the rabbinic period and its theological message?

What has been said up to now may be considered to be rather negative, a collection of problems and doubts. I think that in spite of all the historical and literary problems regarding the practice of preaching in the rabbinic period, we still may search the midrashim for homiletical materials and their basic theological message. The rhetorical (or, more cautiously, literary) devices found in the midrashim may still serve for a better understanding of how the biblical texts read in the synagogues could be used for the instruction and spiritual edification of the community, be they listeners to sermons, students in a rabbinical school or readers of such texts.

This paper does not claim that there was no regular preaching in the synagogues of the rabbinic period; it only insists on the fact that from the texts we have, we cannot derive certain knowledge as to the practice of the sermon, who were the preachers or what the "normal" sermon looked like. If we were prepared to include not only formal sermons, but every kind of edifying use of biblical texts for every group of people assembled in the synagogue, we would have more evidence, but even then many questions would remain unanswered. We may no longer pretend to know the historical details regarding preaching in the rabbinic period, but we may still derive our lessons from a study of the literary constructs to be found in the midrashim and see in them at least the most fundamental aspects of the biblical theology behind them.

The recognition that most midrashic 'homilies' (I continue to use the word as a short-cut) are built not on the Torah reading alone, but also on the prophetic reading, the *haftarah* (something Jacob Mann sought to establish in his monumental *The Bible as Read and Preached in the Synagogue*[29]), underlines the essential unity of the Hebrew Bible, a

---

29 Jacob Mann, The Bible as Read and Preached in the Old Synagogue: A Study in the Cycles of the Readings from Torah and Prophets, as well as from Psalms, and in the Structure of the Midrashic Homilies, vol. I, New York 1971 (reprint of 1940, with a

thought also served by the structure of the *petiḥah* which normally starts with a verse from the Hagiographa. Texts that explicitly state that a teaching may be derived from all three parts of the Scriptures are not too frequent, but the thought behind such texts is very common. The Torah is the most privileged text in the public reading, but the other parts of the Bible also get their hearing. The other theological aspect common to most homiletical units of the midrash, is the message of the *ḥatimah*, a message of hope and optimism in spite of the calamities of the present times. God is the Lord of history and will put everything right.

Messages such as these inform rabbinic thought; the rhetorical forms found in the midrashim, mainly the *petiḥah* and the *ḥatimah*, can be used to convey these messages to the community. Thus we have in these texts some formal aspects as to how a sermon could be constructed, and central elements of the contents to be transmitted in such a sermon. In the context of this symposium, this seems to me more important than the elusive answers to how it really was in rabbinic times and what the exact background of these texts is. For centuries the midrashic texts have been an inspirational source for homilies and similar purposes which escape clear definitions. This alone finally counts.

---

prolegomenon by *Ben Zion Wacholder*); vol. II, by *Jacob Mann/Isaiah Sonne*, New York 1966.

On the Spiritual Role of Midrash and Aggada Response

Admiel Kosman

The question that lies at the center of the discussion by Prof. Stemberger is indeed the historical one: to which extent – if at all – we can show evidently that the written *Derashah* (sermon) that we find in the Midrashic corpus took place in reality in the ancient synagogues in the first hundred years of the creation of Midrash.

Those doubts and considerations have their own place – and Prof. Stemberger has explained them in his erudite lecture.

However, I would try in my response to draw attention to another aspect that maybe can shed light on the subject we are trying now to investigate.

The fact is that if we pay attention to the *content* of the Midrashim we will see immediately that there are – roughly speaking – two types of Midrashim: those which reflect the higher spiritual level of the Aggadists' literary tradition, and those which are the outcome of the folklore type (which might be considered as some drafts of materials that were told in front of lay people).

It would be quite right, I think, to say that in general the first type of materials was the creation of the "Beit Midrash" circles, and the second type is closer to the "synagogue environment".[1]

Even if one insists in saying that all the written materials of the Midrashim that we have in front of us were not preached at all in any event in front of any audience in Eretz Israel at that time – that very fact alone, that a group of learned people, mostly spread over the towns of the Galil in the first hundred years after the destruction of the Temple, was so eager to create such a huge and highly sophisticated corpus (even if we assume that all is mere a literary work) – that fact alone counts in order to draw the conclusion that those ideas were so powerful to become in the end the sole ideology that survived and was later accepted indeed to be the new religious canon for the entire

---

1   As a summarized discussion for this long dispute see: *Marc Hirshman*, On Midrash as Creation: its Creators and its forms, Madaei HaYahadut 32/1992, 83–90 [Hebrew].

Jewish communities all over the world in the long way of the exile – from the ancient world up to the modern time.

That alone counts for us. The question whether those materials were "vocally" really preached in this way or the other in the synagogue is just a secondary question; as all the researchers accept the fact that in the end of the day those materials shaped the new form of Judaism in exile.

In this respect one can say that practically only the higher type of those Midrashic materials later became significant as subject to infinite discussions and interpretations that have influenced the later modes of the rabbinic Jewish culture.

What indeed can we say briefly, in this short response, about the content of those Midrashim?

I think that the most accurate description was given by Prof. Yonah Fraenkel[2] – who explains that the function of this type of Midrash (the "higher" one) is rather daring: to convey in a literary "cover" the message of a high "peak" that one can "climb" in his inner religious life, challenging the individuals (*"Hassidim"*) to be devoted by those means to God.

In the Jewish double-system of *Halakhah* and *Aggada* this message is quite significant, as it emphasizes that the fulfilling of the "recipe" (*"Rezept"*) of the *Halakhah* is the just the *beginning* of another religious path: the "Aggadic" one.[3]

This elite Midrashic message is therefore intended in its core not to the laymen – but rather to the sensitive ear of the individuals whom you can trust that they would be wise enough to uncover the "clothes" of the literary design, and follow the inner Jewish spiritual path.

One can easily understand that this "cover-uncover" midrashic method was especially important for the rabbis after the rise of the new religion, Christianity – which indeed claims constantly that Jews have to leave aside the system of the *Halakhah* (flesh) and join the new spiritual path (spirit). Therefore the "politic" of the Midrash is always rather cunning: on one hand to be careful enough not to be understood as a "Christian" message which degrades the importance of the *Halakhah* – but on the other hand to gently convey the "secret" message that never should not be declared publicly: if one invest his energy only in

---

2 Cf. *Yonah Fraenkel*, The Ways of the Aggada and the Midrash, Givatayim 1991, 484–487 [Hebrew].

3 See in this respect my discussion in both articles: The Female Breast and the Male Mouth Opened in Prayer in a Talmudic Vignette (BT Bava Batra 9a–b), in: JSQ 11/2004, 293–312; The Extended 'Hand' and the Pilgrim 'Foot': On Individual, Authentic Sacrifice and 'Seeing God's Face' in an Ancient Story from Palestine and in Late Hasidic Story, in: Kabbalah 10/2004, 227–248 [Hebrew].

keeping the "recipe" of the *halakhah* – one will never be able to "cross" into the holy realm; one is even sometimes doomed to be considered – as Nachmanides formulated it later in the middle ages – as purely "mean person" – although one fulfills all the demands of the commandment-system (*"Naval bi-Reshut haTora"* = a mean person who lives in the framework of the Torah).[4]

In this respect one can understand why the term Torah was always considered to be strongly connected with secret. What the rabbis saw as the unspoken intimate secret that exists always between the loving groom and its beloved bride.[5]

---

4 Cf. Nachmanides in his commentary to Lev. 19.1 and to Deut. 6.18, and see the discussion of *Chayim Henoch*, Nachmanides: Philosopher and Mystic, Jerusalem 1982, 123–131 [Hebrew].

5 On Torah as "Kalla" (bride) see: *Chanoch Albeck* (Ed.), Midrash Bereshit Rabbati, Toldot 27, Jerusalem 1940, 111, and see b. Ber 57a: "'Moses commanded us a law [Torah], an inheritance of the congregation of Jacob' (Deut. 33.4) – Read not morashah [inheritance], but me'orasah [betrothed]".

The Sermon as an Invention of Hellenistic Judaism[1]

Folker Siegert

1. On origins and ancient terms

1.1 The origins

Jewish homiletics took its origin as the adaptation of Greek hermeneutic and rhetoric to the needs of publicly teaching the Jewish Bible. This need was felt in Greek-speaking Diaspora synagogues, and it was so for two reasons:

– There was no other cult available than praying together and, if more should be done, reading and meditating on the Holy Scriptures.
– A linguistic gap had opened between *eretz Yisrael* and the Western diaspora in that the latter's cult was done in the vernacular.

So not only the Septuagint translation (2nd–1st century BCE) became necessary, but also its cultic use in replacement of what the texts were about. This applies in particular to the five books of the Torah, called "Pentateuch" (because, in Greek, they were physically five scrolls), but we shall also see the beginnings of some use of the "Prophets" and "Writings" (Hagiographa).

1.2 Proposal of terminology

There is no specific term for "sermon" or *d^erashah* in the classical languages. The Greek *homilia* and the Latin *sermo*, both originally meaning 'conversation', may be used to refer to a religious speech, as

---

[1] This paper is a revised reprint of the article "Homily and panegyrical sermon" in: Stanley E. Porter (Ed.), Handbook of Classical Rhetoric in the Hellenistic Period 330 B.C.–A.D. 400, Leiden 1997, 421–443. For fuller notes see there.

Augustine attests in the 4th century CE.² Thus we are dealing with a phenomenon which made its way gradually into ancient culture from its fringes. Teachers of rhetoric, as they were normally pagans, did not take note of it; so it does not appear in their terminology.

For our modern purposes, "sermon" may be defined as 'public explanation of a sacred doctrine or a sacred text', with its *Sitz im Leben* being worship. It is a remarkable fact of the history of religions that of all religious cults known in Antiquity, only Jewish worship as it took place outside the Temple in the synagogues – and Christian worship which imitated it – demanded a speaker's rhetorical activity.

Ancient religious celebrations normally kept worship separate from teaching. Religious cult, including the worship done in the Jerusalem Temple, consisted of processions, performing symbolic acts, singing, praying, burning incense, slaughtering animals for sacrifice (in paganism also: observing prodigies), and so on. There was no occasion for teaching.

In order to adapt ancient rhetorical terminology to the known phenomena of public religious teaching, the following distinctions may be made:

	Speeches on religious matters	Speeches explaining a sacred doctrine/text in a liturgical setting (*sermon*)
Professional level (mass communication, literature)	**(A)** religious panegyric	**(C)** panegyrical sermon
Colloquial level (private or classroom communication)	**(B)** religious diatribe	**(D)** homily
Used by	most ancient religions	Judaism and Christianity only

Examples for (A): Dio Chrysostom, *Orat.* 36 (on Zeus); Aelius Aristides (frequently praising Asclepius); *4. Maccabees*;
Examples for (B): Epictetus, *Dissertations*; LXX: the *Letter of Jeremiah*; NT: the Epistle of James;
Examples for (C): Ps.-Philo, *On Jonah*; *On Samson*; Melito, *On the Passah*;

---

2 In his preface to the exposition of the 118th (Hebrew: 119th) Psalm; see *Albert Blaise*, Dictionnaire latin-français des auteurs chrétiens, Turnhout 1954, s.v. *sermo*.

Examples for (D): Origen's *Homilies* on OT- and NT-texts; John Chrysostom, *On Genesis, On the Psalms*; pope Gregory I, *Homilies on the Gospels*.

In what follows I will speak only about cases (C) and (D).

2. The problem of orality

2.1 Eventualities

The requirement of orality that is assumed with the liturgical setting of cases (C) and (D) poses some problems, since there were smooth transitions between oral and literary communication. Even if we take for granted that orators practically never read from a manuscript, there remain at least three possibilities of how oral delivery may be linked to a written text (to be transmitted later on):

(a) the text may have been written in advance in order to be memorized and delivered,
(b) it may have been taken down in shorthand at the time of delivery,
(c) it may have been written down afterwards, from memory.

As all these eventualities are irrelevant for invention, disposition and elocution, ancient manuals rarely distinguish oral from written communication.

The problem with our sources, however, is not to determine *when* an oral text was written down, but to establish *whether* it ever was an oral text. According to our definition, a given text can only be labelled as 'sermon' if it may have (or even must have) served as part of a religious ceremony, with the function of explaining some of the doctrines underlying that ceremony.

This requirement is not easily met in any of the New Testament writings, including their supposed oral components. Luke 4.16–21 mentions Jesus preaching in the synagogue at Capharnaum; but of his sermon the Evangelist gives only a summary in one single phrase (v. 21). The Epistle to the Romans may have originated from several oral diatribes of its author: 1.18–4.25; 5–8; 9–11; but they have been transformed into a fairly homogeneous epistolary unit. Many *pericopae* of the New Testament may have served as liturgical lessons, as did all of the epistles (cf. 1Thess. 5.27; Col. 4.16); but then they were not sermons. *Hebrews* may be an exception: this rhetorically-styled text with its balanced constructions and its frequent rhythms meets the requirements of orality; it is more of a sermon than of a lesson. In a kind of appendix it is called a *logos paraklēseōs* (13.22; cf. Acts 13.15).

This may be regarded as the oldest attested term for a synagogue sermon.

2.2 The vertical distinction

To come back to our diagram: The vertical distinction scheme allows us to single out a trait that distinguishes Judaism and Christianity from their Hellenistic background. (C) is a specialization of (A) as (D) is a specialization of (B). Both rely on the intellectual bias of the Jewish-Christian tradition.

One could be tempted to add as a further requirement for the right-hand column its being based on a sacred text. This would provide us with an even clearer distinction between Hellenistic religion and its Jewish-Christian counterpart. But there are also non-exegetical sermons; and whether a Biblical text has been read beforehand cannot always be determined. In the book of *Acts*, e.g., where Paul is reported to have spoken in synagogue services no less than ten times,[3] he never acts as commentator of a Scriptural pericope. He speaks, rather, at the end, where either greetings from community to community are appropriate or, at the most, a *haftarah*. Paul, however, makes use of these occasions to extend his role to something quite different, which might have been one motive for throwing him out.

As regards Christianity in its earliest period, we should make a distinction between "missionary proclamation" as Paul would give and "artistic sermon" as it developed later on, with certain written precursors in New Testament epistles, notably *Hebrews*. After the creation of Christian sacred rooms in the (2nd and) 3rd century, artistic sermon came to replace the more primitive forms of proclamation. The only thing reminiscent of the simplicity of Christian origins was the *homily*, being more or less in between; cf. chap. 9.

Now my main thesis is as follows: Religious speeches, esp. if based on a sacred text, are a Hellenistic Jewish innovation taken over by – and only attested by – the Christians. Greek paganism, as far as it may be compared here, had developed an art of interpreting religious texts, especially Homer on the one hand, with the art of public speaking called 'rhetoric' on the other; but in the pagan world they were rarely combined. On occasion, a sophist like the 2nd-century orator Dio Chrysostom might base a moral teaching on a passage of Homer (*Or.* 57, on *Il.* 1.260–274). But these are rare cases, none of which is linked to an ongoing cult.

---

3   Acts 9.20; 13.5, 15–41; 14.1–3; 16.13f; 17.10–12, 17; 18.4, 19; 19.8.

In Hellenism there were myths, there were *hieroi logoi* (occasionally read but never published), and there was religious philosophy and oratory; but there was nothing like a sacred doctrine. It is sufficient, therefore, to define "sermon" (*d^erashah*) as an exposition either of a sacred text or of a sacred doctrine, delivered in a liturgical setting.

This linking up with ancient terminology presents us with a historical paradox. The Jews and their religion were a marginal phenomenon in the Graeco-Roman world. They probably had no access to the places and institutions of public communication, at least not for the transmission of their religious message. They had to create their own auditoria in erecting synagogues. For Christians, the means of publicly proclaiming their message called the Gospel were likewise restricted, and even more so after their expulsion from the synagogues.

2.3 The horizontal distinction

As to the horizontal distinction in the above scheme, it follows a properly rhetorical point of view, being a distinction of stylistic levels. The plain style is excluded from the upper level (A, C) just as the grand style is not called for in the lower (B, D). The domain of rhetoric proper, of course, is the upper level. Here the activities of well-trained persons, orators and their pupils are to be placed. It is a recent innovation that "rhetorical" analyses[4] are also done on texts of the lower level.

Using the ancient distinction of styles, we may more clearly discern the degree of commitment to Hellenistic culture, and we may also assess the possible size of the audience. As to the commitment to Hellenistic culture, this may vary even within paganism. The Cynics, whose behaviour and teaching have considerable affinities to that of Jesus, despised ornate speech and a formal social setting. As regards the size of the audience, it should be kept in mind that public communication – in a period long before the invention of the microphone, the transmission of images, etc. – required high artistic skills, just as television does today. The colloquial style was not fit for speaking in a theatre or for mastering the acoustic problems of a market place. This explains the extensive use of the expressive means and the

---

4   E.g., there is a wealth of literature on the "rhetoric" of Paul, even though he rightly claims not to have been trained in rhetoric.

musical treat of "Asianic" rhetoric[5] that we find in the only surviving specimens of synagogue preaching.

Thus Greek *encomium* – also labelled as *panegyric* or *logos* in a specific sense – found its counterpart within Hellenistic Judaism and within the Christian Church, yielding what should be called a *panegyrical sermon*. One of its oldest surviving specimens terms itself an *encomium*.[6] The fact that both texts are part of a liturgy, being the explanation of a sacred text read beforehand, is evident from the texts, but not specified in these terms. This is why I propose to use the compound term "panegyrical sermon".

3. Further remarks on terminology

3.1 Kerygma and logos

Our endeavour to define what can be called a "sermon" in Graeco-Roman antiquity would be incomplete without a discussion of some terms which were current during the period itself.

In translating the New Testament, where speakers are seen at work there, *kēryssein* has often been rendered as "to preach"; but this cannot be taken in our specific sense. *Kēryssein* means "to proclaim": a sovereign's words are repeated aloud. This excludes by definition the rhetorical effort of embellishment, amplification etc., let alone interpretation. Ancient sources associate a *kēryx* (herald) with a trumpet, which is significant: in Antiquity trumpets were not instruments of music, but a means of (magically) distorting and amplifying the human voice. Ancient trumpeters did not "interpret" music any more than heralds interpreted a message. Jonah did not preach to the Ninivites, but just proclaimed one sentence (Jon. 3.4b; verb: *ekēryxen*); he delivered a *kērygma* (Q/Luke 11.32). The Jewish speaker of the harangue *On Jonah*, to be sure, does quite a different thing. He pronounces what everybody would call a *logos* (in the sense of "speech").

In New Testament writings the word *logos* is rarely or never used with reference to a formal speech. The so-called "Sermon" on the Mount consists of sayings, but it is not a speech; see Mat. 7.28: "When

---

5 Cf. *Eduard Norden*, Die antike Kunstprosa vom VI. Jahrhundert vor Christus bis in die Zeit der Renaissance, 2 vol., Darmstadt ⁷1974, vol. 1, 126–155, 266ff., 367ff. a.fr.

6 *Ps.-Philo*, On Samson 10 (retranslated); cf. *logos, ibid.*, 4, and the verbs used in *Ps.-Philo*, On Jonah, proem.

Jesus had finished these words [*logous*] ..." Peter's Pentecost address are *rhēmata* (Acts 2.14). Later on, in the Church Fathers' writings, *logos* = *oratio* is a more or less clear alternative to *homilia* = *sermo*, a term to which we may now turn.

3.2 "Homily"

Whereas a religious speech on the stylistic level of a panegyric was labelled as (one kind of) *logos*, its modest counterpart on the level of a diatribe[7] came to be termed *homilia* – our *homily*. The idea conveyed by that term is that of a 'conversation' of a religious leader with a group of persons which he knows personally: thus Xenophon, *Mem.* 1.2.6 (of a Sophist's teaching), the Jewish *Epistle of Aristaeus* 171 (with reference to the High Priest giving instructions to a group of visitors), and other writers; cf. the verb *homilein* in Acts 20.11 (of Paul) and *homilian poieisthai* in Josephus, *Life* 222. Later on it was the Christians who used it to refer to an address dealing with religious matters: thus Ignatius of Antioch, *Polyc.* 5.1 (*homilian poieisthai*), Theophilus of Antioch, Origen, John Chrysostom, and many others.

The refusal to use fine rhetoric on the part of those who would perhaps have been able to use it – the Cynics in particular – testifies to their aloofness from a society which they criticised. The low style of the early Christian message has been interpreted that way; and there is no doubt that early Christians, such as Luke and the author of the *Epistle to the Hebrews*, are more "conformed" and acculturated to Hellenism as is, e.g., the apostle Paul. In this sense Paul's scorn of rhetoric (1Cor. 1.17, 20; 2.4f., 13 etc.) could be termed "cynical". With respect to the paltriness and intellectual mediocrity of many utterances of second century Christianity, however, it may be asked to what degree rhetorical restraint was based on voluntary discretion. Wasn't the Christian mission from its very inception dependent upon the use of the available means of communication? In line with Mat. 28.18–20 is the fact that the bishops soon became rhetoricians – or, to put it more exactly, that Christian rhetoricians became bishops.

In this respect Gnosticism was quicker than Catholic Christianity. Clement of Alexandria, *Str.* 6.6.52.3, quotes a *peri philōn homilia* by the Gnostic Valentinus. The few quotations he gives from this text may be embarrassing for our definition purposes, as they are of a highly

---

7   This term was used for an extended or intensified conversation. It includes a range of rhetorical devices on a lower level. The apostle Paul is one of its best-known exponents.

rhetorical character using prose rhythms. Moreover, the text is qualified not as a speech, but as a writing (*kata lexin graphei*), and its title suggests that it was not concerned with interpreting a Biblical text. There is little to support our definition given above. For an explanation, the fact may be recalled that *homilia* was not a well-defined term: in the very rhetorical fragment attached to the *Epistle to Diognetus* (chs. 11–12) it is the Word himself (*Logos* without article) 'who communicates (*homilei*) by what means he wants and when he wants' (11,7). It is rather the Latin usage which restricted *homilia* to 'popular' ways of speaking, as may be seen from Blaises's dictionary. For the purposes of our present inquiry the narrower definition will be retained.

4. Antecedents of the art of preaching in the Hebrew and Greek Scriptures

4.1 Hebrew Bible and "intertestamental" literature

It has been stated above that sermons are an innovation due to Greek-speaking Judaism. Now in the Bible, be it Hebrew or be it Christian, we find references to persons speaking on a sacred text, beginning with Ezra the scribe in Neh. 9.[8] But we do not know whether these performances were speeches in the rhetorical sense of the term, nor whether the Biblical narrator considers them to be so. The first question, at least, may safely be denied, as the cultural and social requirements for a Semitic parallel to Greek oratory were not given. One of the proofs of the superiority of Hellenism, after all, was public *logos*, including its social and architectural requirements. There is a marked distance between Jesus sitting in a boat and "teaching" the people with parables and *logia* ("sayings"), and an orator pronouncing a well-organized and ornate speech.

The refinement of mass communication, which so deeply characterises the epoch of Graeco-Roman Hellenism, was part of an *urban* civilization. Judaic civilization, however, was mainly rural. Jerusalem, its religious centre, was known for its Temple, the sacrifices, and the treasure, but not for its exploits in the domains of oratory or literature. The theatre erected by Herod I does not seem to have been important, being alien to Jewish religion and lifestyle, and little is

---

8   Luther's translation of Gen. 4.26 (speaking of Seth and Enosh) may be quoted here, be it as a curiosity: "Zu derselbigen Zeit fing man an zu predigen in des HERRN Namen." Here the Reformation is somehow projected back into ante-diluvian times. For public preaching not on texts the Moses of Deuteronomy may be recalled.

known of the library in which Nicolaus of Damascus, Herod's pagan court historian, wrote his (now lost) 144 books of universal history.

No Jewish citizen of Jerusalem is known to have been an orator. Josephus, to be sure, styles himself as such, and it may be safely held that the Judaean kings were able to pronounce, in Aramaic, an address to the people. One may compare Peter's speech in Acts 2.14–36 (cf. sect. III, above) and Paul's Aramaic address to the crowds of Jerusalem in Acts 22.1–21. These were local events that do not prove that there was an Aramaic art of oratory comparable to what was called *Hellēnismos*. The Greek writings which Josephus composed with the assistance of a secretary are one thing, and his Aramaic performance in front of the walls of burning Jerusalem is another. In all of Hebrew and Aramaic literature there is nothing that resembles a Greek *logos*.

4.2 New Testament

Let us now consider three prominent Jews of the 1st century CE: Jesus of Nazareth, Paul of Tarsus, and – less known, but no less significant – Apollos of Alexandria.

Jesus eschewed the cities of his homeland. Even though he had contacts with paganism, he did not take up the challenge of Hellenism, except negatively. Two of the group of the Twelve bear Greek names (Philip and Andrew), and according to John 12.20–22 they were bilingual. Besides this, there is not much to note. Sepphoris, which was a centre in Galilee, is not mentioned in the New Testament; Caesarea Philippi and Caesarea-on-the-Sea are passed over in Jesus' itinerary. In Tiberias, where there was one of the largest synagogues of his time, he did not speak; and his disputes in the Jerusalem Temple are not an example of oratory. The *exousia* ("authority") of his teaching has nothing to do with rhetorical *deinotēs* or "impressiveness".

The same holds true for the apostle Paul, even though he was perfectly bilingual, speaking "Hebrew" (Aramaic) as well as Greek. He was an able teacher and debater, but not an orator. In his native town Tarsus there was a famous school of rhetoric, but he does not seem to have attended it. There are no traces of professional rhetoric in his letters, as he rightly claims himself (1Cor. 2.1–5), not without some pride. In the provinces of Asia Minor, Paul was occasionally admired as an incarnation of Hermes (Acts 14.12), and passages like Rom. 9–11 or 2Cor. 6 may be impressive through their dialectical skill or their emotionality.[9] In Corinth the Christians admitted that "his letters are

---

9 Cf. *Stanley Kent Stowers*, The Diatribe and Paul's Letter to the Romans (SBL Diss. Ser. 57), Chico (CA) 1981.

impressive and moving"; but they added that "his actual presence is feeble and his speaking beneath contempt" (2Cor. 10.10, trans. Phillips). Paul's failure on the Areopagus (Acts 17.32; cf. 17.18) illustrates the same point: Paul's oral delivery was deficient, be it by some corporeal shortcoming, or be it by lack of professional skill.

This seems not to be the case for Paul's companion Apollos, a Jew from Alexandria whom Luke qualifies as *anēr logios* ("a man versed in speech", Acts 18.24). Unfortunately we have little information of his person.[10] But we do have sufficient information on Jewish culture in Alexandria.

In the entire New Testament the only writers trained to cope with the requirements of mass communication are: the author of *Hebrews*, who might well have been a professional orator, of Jewish origin as it seems; second, the author of the *Epistle of James*, again a Jewish Christian; and third, Luke as a literary man.[11] But in order to spot the origin of Christian homiletics we have to turn our attention to the centres of diaspora Judaism. Let us now speak of the synagogue in general and of Alexandria in particular.

5. The 'Intelligent Worship' of the Synagogue and its Christian imitation

5.1 The impact of ancient cult critique

When Paul summoned the Roman Christians to render by their lives a *logikē latreia* (Rom. 12.1), he alluded to an ideal of worship which had been developed in theory by Pythagorean and Stoic Philosophers, but put into liturgical practice by Judaism alone. The Pythagoreans were against bloodshed, in profane life as well as in the cult. Blood does not establish good relations with the divine, their criticism held; but prayer of a pure heart and a righteous, pure life will do so. They used the oxymoron *anhaimaktos bōmos* ("unbloody altar") to denote this ideal. In calling a similar thing a *logikē latreia* Paul evokes also the Stoic *logos*,

---

10 Acts 18.24, 28 speaks rather of the contents of his teaching, and 19.1–4 of certain shortcomings on that level. Apollos was well-trained in oratory, but unaware of the Holy Spirit's working.

11 Cf. *Folker Siegert*, Mass communication and prose rhythm in Luke/Acts, in: *Stanley E. Porter/Thomas H. Olbricht* (Eds.), Rhetoric and the New Testament, JSNT.S 90, Sheffield 1993, 42–58.

which was believed to be the intermediary (in both directions) between the divine and the mortals. *Logos* was revelation and prayer as well.

5.2 Turning cult critique positively: the synagogue

When the synagogue worship had evolved – its origins lie perhaps as early as in the Babylonian exile, where no sacrificial atonement was available – Alexandrian Jewish apologists did not fail to recognize its modernity by philosophical standards. Philo (b. ca. 15/10 BCE) praises the Jewish Legislator for having instituted the Sabbath as a day of learning for everybody:[12]

> "He required them to assemble in the same place on these seventh days, and sitting together in a respectful and orderly manner hear the laws read so that none should be ignorant of them. And indeed they do always assemble and sit together, most of them in silence except when it is the practice to add something to signify approval of what is read. But some priest who is present or one of the elders reads the holy laws to them and expounds them point by point till about the late afternoon, when they depart having gained both expert knowledge of the holy laws and considerable advance in piety."

Such was the *Sitz im Leben* of the Jewish art of preaching. There were synagogues throughout the Jewish Diaspora;[13] there also were synagogues in the mainland including Jerusalem (as the famous Theodotus inscription shows). The largest of all synagogues was in Alexandria; a copy of it (as scholars presume) served as town hall in Tiberias.

The innovation of the synagogue service can best be evaluated in ancient terms: Of all Graeco-Roman religions, Judaism alone managed to develop a non-sacrificial monotheistic cult. Most philosophers professed a theoretical monotheism; but there were no means of establishing a cult that corresponded to their lofty ideas. Jewish "philosophy", however, put it into practice not only on the level of everyday behaviour, but also in worship.

Synagogue worship consisted of singing psalms and hymns, praying, reading the Torah – and explaining the Torah lesson (the

---

12 Fragment from *Philo*, Hypothetica, quoted in *Eusebius*, Praeparatio evangelica 8.7.12-12 (trans. *F. H. Colson* in the LCL Philo, IX, 1941, 431–433). There are many similar passages in Philo. On synagogues in general, see e.g. *Lee I. Levine*, The Ancient Synagogue: The First Thousand Years, New Haven (CT), esp. 139–179.

13 See, e.g., *Hanswulf Bloedhorn/(Frowald) Gil Hüttenmeister*, The Synagogue, in: *William Horbury/William David Davies/John Sturdy* (Eds.), The Cambridge History of Judaism III, Cambridge 1999, 267–297.

parashah of Rabbinic terminology) or the lesson associated with it (the *haftarah*). Philo, as it appears from his own writings, spent his life teaching Torah. We cannot be sure but we can reasonably suppose that he engaged personally in the job of preaching.[14] At any rate he would not have been the only person capable of doing so.

In early Christian times Christian worship had only one model: the Jewish synagogue service. The Eucharist was added, so that the sermon was no longer at the end of the celebration. Other elements (taken, e.g., from mystery cults) modified it without denying its intellectual (*logikos*) character.

6. Alexandria: a centre of Jewish eloquence

Alexandria, founded in 331 BCE by Alexander himself, soon became one of the largest cities of Antiquity. It housed the richest library of the Hellenistic-Roman period, and it was the home of numerous world-renowned scholars and literary men such as Euclid, Herophilus, and Ptolemaeus on the one hand (in mathematics and sciences) and Aristarchus, Callimachus, and Theocritus on the other (in the humanities). The indigenous Egyptians, as well as the Jews who soon came to settle there, had few to no citizens' rights, but – as for the Jews – a certain amount of self-administration. Alexandria was the seat of the Ptolemaic kings, none of whom understood the language of his Pharaonic predecessors. In Roman times, when Egypt had become the emperor's personal property, Alexandria was distinguished from the province of Egypt as *Alexandria ad Ægyptum*.

This city may well have been the cradle of the art of preaching, at least so far as rhetorically refined preaching is concerned. One of her five quarters, numbered Delta (4), was assigned to the Jews; but Jews were also living all over the city. They only spoke Greek (hence the Septuagint translation) and wanted to count with the Greek, and not the Egyptian, inhabitants of the city. Their Greek culture is far in advance of all we know of Roman, Antiochian, and other Jewish populations. Aristobulus, the anonymous author of the *Letter of Aristaeus* (or Aristeas), and Philo the Jewish philosopher became their most famous exponents. As to Philo, in a kind of double identity he

---

14 This may be surmised from his writings. Some are rather technical (the "Questions"), but many are in the style of a very high-level diatribe, notably his so-called Exposition of the Law (vols. 4–5 in the LCL series). As to oral performance (or "delivery"), he must have been capable of it as he was chosen to speak before the emperor Gaius Caligula (see his "Legatio ad Gaium").

claimed to be a citizen of a Greek city, which was his *patrís*, and to belong to a people whose *mētropolis* was Jerusalem.

In Alexandria stood the largest synagogue known to Antiquity. This building was called a *diplostoon* because of its five naves which were divided by two double rows of columns. The Tosephta[15] wants us to believe that there was an assistant standing on its *bimah* charged to give a signal with a cloth after a prayer so that the assembly would say amen. This building may have been the very place where the earliest panegyrical sermons known to us were first held.

7. Specimens of Hellenistic Jewish eloquence: The sermons *On Jonah* and *On Samson*

7.1 Two forgotten texts

Much speculation on the origins of the art of preaching is hampered by the ignorance of the only existing specimens, the Jewish panegyrical sermons *On Jonah* and *On Samson*. Published in 1826 from manuscripts of the only surviving Armenian translation, they were soon forgotten, perhaps due to philological difficulties, but also due to their very rhetorical character which did not appeal to the historians of religion until recently. There is now a German translation;[16] a French one has appeared in the *Sources chrétiennes* (nr. 435), an English one is in the hands of Professor Louis Feldman.

7.2 The liturgical setting

As a date, Philo's day seems most likely for both sermons. Their content, however, clearly disproves Philonic authorship: there is no allegorizing, no 'modern' cosmology and science drawn upon, no speculation on divine names, etc. The *Sitz im Leben* for *On Jonah*

---

15 t. Suk 4.6 etc.; cf. *Bloedhorn/Hüttenmeister*, Synagogue, 287 n. 51.
16 Cf. *Folker Siegert*, Drei hellenistisch-jüdische Predigten: Ps.-Philon, „Über Jona", „Über Simson" und „Über die Gottesbezeichnung ‚wohltätig verzehrendes Feuer'", vol. 1: Übersetzung aus dem Armenischen und sprachliche Erläuterungen (WUNT 20), Tübingen 1980. The third text dealt with in this publication is not a sermon, but has turned out to be a fragment from one of the lost books of Philo's "De somniis". Cf. also *Idem*, Drei hellenistisch-jüdische Predigten: Ps.-Philon, "Über Jona", "Über Jona" (Fragment) und "Über Simson", vol. 2: Kommentar nebst Beobachtungen zur hellenistischen Vorgeschichte der Bibelhermeneutik (WUNT 61), Tübingen 1992.

probably is the afternoon of *Yom Kippur* (if we may rely on the Rabbinic liturgical calendar – sect. 5, above); there is one reference to a previous reading of the biblical text to the community (*On Jonah* 67). *On Samson*, which is on Judg. 13.2–14.19, would fit with the Sabbath on which, as we know from later sources, the law of the Nazirites (Num. 4.21–7.89) was read.[17]

7.3 The intellectual and rhetorical style

Among the most striking features of these "period pieces" of Asianic eloquence may be named the absence of any exclusivism or esoterism and a marked sense of humour. These are fanciful, imaginative masterpieces of narrative preaching – rather long by modern standards (about 30 printed pages each), but never tiresome. Their author is an expert of the grand style, even more than the author of 3Macc. (with which there are notable parallels of language and imagery) and more than Philo. Its *copia verborum* is evident, and the use of various flourishes and even prose rhythms can be proved even though the transmitted text is only a translation. (Happily, it is a mechanical one, a kind of linguistic mimicry.) Quotations from Scripture (i.e., Septuagint) are rare, due perhaps to the low stylistic level of the Septuagint version.

We said that, unlike Philo, this preacher does not use allegorical hermeneutics. He is all the more successful in the rhetorical amplification of his text. His difference from Rabbinical midrash lies *inter alia* in the very skilled psychological observation and motivation of the characters' – and even God's – behaviour. Every detail in Scripture is made plausible, except in *On Samson* those which the orator tacitly omits (e.g., many of Samson's curious exploits among the Philistines).

The sermons are rich in ethos and pathos passages. *On Jonah* relies more on the former, and *De Sampsone* on the latter: curiously, *On Jonah* advocates openness towards heathens, Jonah's warning of the Ninivites being a sign of God's general philanthropy, whereas in *On Samson* the *allophyloi* (this is the Philistines' name in the LXX) deserve no compassion whatsoever.

---

17 In Philo's "Questions on Genesis" and "On Exodus" there are clear traces of the existence of the annual cycle of Torah lessons such as the Rabbis have transmitted it to our day. Whether there already was a list of selected lessons from the (Former and Latter) Prophets cannot be proved, but there is some evidence in favour of a positive answer, e.g. 2Macc. 15.9; 4Macc. 18.15.

One of the sermons, *On Samson*, bears in its transmitted title the notice that it has been improvised: the Armenian term corresponds to *autoschedios* or *autoschediatos* (*logos*). This is quite plausible if we take account of the highly developed art of rhetorical improvisation in all of classical Antiquity. There are some inconsistencies in *On Samson* itself and a certain lack of structure which may be typical of improvising.

As is the rule in most of ancient religious discourse, no reference is made to the hearers' historical situation. In Antiquity a good sermon was not an attempt to speak 'concretely' in the modern sense of the term; it rather was a music of words that led astray as much as possible from everyday concerns.

7.4 Message and theological content

The pseudo-Philonic Sermons propagate their message by means of Greek notions and values. In *On Jonah* it is God's philanthropy and the ineluctable constraint of his vocation; in *On Samson* it is the virtue of temperance (!) and of righteousness that the hero illustrates by his life. However, the speaker admits that of the six spiritual gifts of Isa. 11.2 his hero only received wisdom and strength (chap. 24).

But to come back to the more reflected sermon *On Jonah*, in its last part we find a styled dialogue between Jonah, who would have delighted in seeing Nineveh perish, and God, the great Philanthropist. There the preacher discusses the question, more than once raised at *Yom Kippur* through the ages, whether it is worthy of God to change in response to human repentance (§ 160–196). There are three answers, the coherence of which is left to the hearers' consideration. The first answer claims God's right or power of everything, including changing himself (§ 185–198). Changing a human society's morals, the third answer holds, is kind of a miracle and an exploit superior to the successful siege of a city (§ 196). In between comes the surprising, but etymologically founded argument that God had announced to "overthrow" the city, what, in fact, he did concerning its morals (§ 190–194).[18] So, with respect to his eternal intention, he did not change.

Jonah, who has not been a philanthropist so far, does not follow this reasoning. He objects (§ 195),

"But the city was not destroyed, neither its houses nor its walls!"

God answers (§ 195f.):

---

18 The Greek *catastrophe*, the orator holds, may be an "overthrow".

"But the heart and life of the inhabitants (were returned): the former through piety; the latter (which) must have been expecting destruction, your message restored it. I do not need to turn over rocks and buildings! To knock down walls would be a change quite easy to provoke: the walls fall under enemy attack and under war machines. But to turn evil intentions into good – such an upheaval is the performance of a divine hand."

There is no apocalyptic material in these sermons, but a strong emphasis on natural theology and on Providence, which ranks the preacher among the upper class. There is no jurisprudence either, as in most of Philo's exegeses and in Rabbinic literature. Instead, the imagery of the Greek Heracles legends penetrates the account of Jonah's adventure in the sea monster and the other account of Samson's prowess. The conceptual framework is largely Stoic: it consists of God's providence and philanthropy, the notion of a cosmic polis, the notion of *sōtēria* meaning "preservation" (rather than "rescue"), and other elements in the domain of ethics. In *On Samson* 9–11 there is a curious reflection on the angel's way of communicating with Samson's timid father Manoah. Using a rhetorical notion, the preacher extols the *epieikeia* (mildness, fairness, condescension) of the heavenly messenger.

7.5 A note on impact

Outside Armenian literature (which is much less anti-Jewish than Greek, Latin and Syriac ecclesiastical literature) there are no traces of an impact of these two masterpieces of synagogal eloquence. But against the background of Philo's and others' descriptions of synagogue worship (cf. sect. 5, above) they are quite what can be expected. One may wonder where the preacher got his excellent training, since we do not know of any ancient Jewish school of rhetoric. We may wonder even more where he got his practice, because nearly all opportunities of speaking in public would involve compromises with polytheism.

8. Panegyrical sermon in the Church

We noted already (sect. 4) that there was little opportunity for Christian missionaries' public oratory in Apostolic or post-Apostolic times. It had no *Sitz im Leben*. Peter proclaiming the Gospel in Solomon's Colonnades (Acts 3.11–4.4; 5.12) was impeded, and Paul's efforts to do the same on the Areopagus – a rare occasion – met with failure. Synagogues were notoriously reluctant. The School of Tyrannus (Acts

19.9f.) in Ephesus gave Paul some relief. From his letters we may imagine the way he explained the new doctrine in such a setting; it was the typical situation of diatribe, but not the one of public oratory. Christian mission was not so much a public event as a naive reading of the *Acts of the Apostles* would have us believe.

There is no means of knowing what Apollos' teaching in the synagogue of Ephesus (Acts 18.24f.) – certainly not a modest building – was like, except if we suppose the same Asianic taste as we saw in Philo and in Pseudo-Philo. The first documents of formal Christian oratory appear from 160/70 onwards and confirm this supposition. These are the following:

The speech *On the Passah* by bishop Melito of Sardis is a panegyric of about 30 printed pages in rhythmical prose, nearly a poem, rich in rhymes and other effects. Stylistically it is a curious specimen of "Asianic" oratory: there are no periods in the classical sense; instead, there are hammering repetitions of short structures (*cola*). This speech was destined for the celebration of the (quartodeciman) Easter night. It is clearly for oral delivery; so one might wonder where late 2nd-century Asian Christians got a hall large enough to celebrate their rite with a formal encomium. Its content recalls and amplifies the Exodus event by a host of allegorical and typological associations. Its very emotional style leads up to treating the execution of Jesus as a "murder" (§ 96). This is the oldest attestation of the worst of all anti-Jewish slanders.[19] – Other panegyrics by Melito have been preserved in fragmentary manner.

Ps.-Hippolytus, *On the Epiphany* is a casual sermon for a baptism, based on the pericope of the baptism of Jesus (Mat. 3.13–17). Prose rhythms and other embellishments are regularly used. The hermeneutic of this piece is similar to that of Melito.

In the Latin church the oldest existing panegyric may be an *Adversus Iudaeos* attributed to Cyprian of Carthage. This is a counterpart of Melito's Passah speech, maybe its conscious imitation. Its contents and tendency are very similar, and its style is also similar to that of Melito, though less accomplished. The piece is rather short and probably incomplete. It may be dated about 200 CE.

---

19   As to its content, it lies far outside any reasonable theology or Christology. Would Melito have preferred Jesus to die of old age without having achieved a "Messianic" turn? Melito's words, of course, are purely emotional, but they admit of a historical reading (as do the Johannine writings, belonging to the same milieu): In the 2nd century the Jews of Asia Minor were culturally (and politically) assimilated and well off, even in Hadrian's day, which the Christians were not. Thus they reproached to them to be a "synagogue of Satan" (Rev. 2.9), this "Satan" being identical to Hadrian and his successors.

Let us come back to Greek examples. At the end of the *Epistle to Diognetus*, chs. 11–12, the *peroratio* of an anonymous speech has been attached whose speaker qualifies himself as a disciple of Apostles and his activity as *homilein* (ch. 11 at the beginning). His style is marked by "Asianic" short *cola*, rhymes, and prose rhythms. The verb *homilein* obviously does not refer to a 'homily' in the sense defined here (sect. III), but to oral delivery. Ch. 11.5 gives a clue as to the original liturgical setting in the feast of Epiphany.

From the writings of Clement of Alexandria (dated before 215 CE) we may mention his speech on "How a rich man may be saved" (*Quis dives salvetur*), a panegyric covering about 30 printed pages.[20] Its proem resembles in content and terminology the one of *On Jonah*. In the following exposition of Mark 10.17–31, however, there is much quoting, mostly from the New Testament, and the stylistic ambition ceases to some extent. The diction comes near to that of the New Testament epistles or to that of an exegetical homily (cf. sect. 9).

Later on, the Church Fathers' volumes abound with panegyrics to celebrate Christian feasts or Saints. John Chrysostom, Severian of Gabala, the Cappadocian Fathers, Basilius of Seleucia and many others were trained orators – not to speak of their Latin counterparts, especially Augustine. It is a significant fact that in the 4th century CE, the Antiochian rhetor Libanius, a notorious gentile, had the pagan Eunapius as pupil, as well as the son of the Jewish patriarch[21] and Christians like John Chrysostom and Gregory Nazianzen. Later on, Jewish culture divorced from Hellenism, whereas Christian culture, being associated with political power, did not, except in abandoning temples and theatres, which the Jews had done long since.

9. Jewish and Christian homily

9.1 "Homily" as conversation

In sect. 3 we defined "homily" as an address to an audience with which the speaker is familiar. Its antecedents are dialogues on an intellectual level. In ps.-Plutarch Minos, king of Crete, is said to have "talked" with

---

20 This seems to have been a standard length. One reason for the length of synagogue and church festivals and cults surely was the endeavour to keep people aloof from work or from trifling and unholy distractions. Or, to put it positively, this was the Jewish and Christian world's cinema.

21 *Epist.* 1098,1; see the text, translation and comments in *Menachem Stern*, Greek and Latin Authors on Jews and Judaism, 3 vol., Jerusalem 1976/1980/1984, vol. 2, no. 502, 595f.

Zeus (*homilein*) in order to obtain the wisdom required for his legislation; the text goes on: "their conversation was learning jurisprudence" (*hē d' homilia nomōn mathēsis ēn*). In one of Plutarch's genuine treatises Minos is called a "disciple conversant (*homilētēs kai mathētēs*) with the Great God" – as it were, a Greek Moses.

The *Letter of Aristaeus*, a 2nd-century BCE Jewish pseudepigraphon already cited, gives a literary example of such a "conversation" in § 128–171. A group of visitors to Jerusalem receive some teaching by the High Priest. These paragraphs are marked by considerable hermeneutical efforts to get a symbolic meaning for awkward food and purity laws. There is no stylistic ambition; the text meets perfectly with the definition of "diatribe".[22] In fact, it is a speech conveying religious doctrine in a sacred place (but not during service) – according to our diagram, case B. We may easily imagine similar efforts in ancient synagogue services where there was a need to make the Torah lessons understandable and acceptable to a public composed of Jews and heathens (the "God-fearers" of Josephus and the book of Acts).

For the Christian Church, the scene of Luke 24.14–49 with the risen Christ speaking to some of his disciples and being recognised later on became a model of homiletics. The oldest surviving texts, however, which might be called a homily are reminiscent of the hortatory (paraenetic) conclusions of the Pauline letters. Justin Martyr (*Apol.* 65–67) and Tertullian (*Apol.* 39) mention exhortations (*dia logou nouthesia*; Lat. *exhortationes*) as a part of the Christian worship.

A much quoted example is the so-called *Second Epistle of Clement* (2nd century CE), chs. 1–18. It is a moral exhortation, in Greek, abounding with biblical quotations (OT and NT), but devoid of rhetoric. It is structured by associations; there is no main text discernible.[23]

9.2 Exegetical homily

A sub-species of homily has been called "exegetical homily", or just "homily" in the narrowest sense of the term. Once again we have to speak of a Jewish innovation.[24] Philo was proud of the diligence with

---

22 See note 7, above.
23 Chs. 19–20 of that epistle have led to confusion, being a mere appendix. 19.1 refers *back* to the previous text as an exhortation (or intercession) to be delivered by *reading*. Such was the secondary use of this sermon, as it has often happened to sermons.
24 Cf. *Folker Siegert*, Art. Hellenistic Jewish Midrash I: Beginnings, in: *Jacob Neusner/Alan J. Avery-Peck* (Eds.), Encyclopedia of Midrash. Biblical Interpretation in

which a synagogue teacher would "expound point by point" the holy laws: *kath' hekaston exēgeitai*.[25] Christian exegesis in all its facets is nothing but Jewish exegesis modified by the new hermeneutical viewpoints that derived from the unique role attributed to Jesus as Christ.

Now along with ps.-Philo's *On Jonah*, another Jewish fragment bearing the same title has been transmitted which may be cited here. It is remarkable for quoting Jon. 1.8, 1.11 and 1.12 in the space of half a page. If all of this speech followed the Biblical text as closely, it may count as an early – or even the earliest – example of an exegetical homily.

Other "homilies" by Christian scholars and bishops, especially Origen and John Chrysostom, are nothing but a running commentary taken down in shorthand from oral delivery. Being a kind of diatribe, they do not affect the grand style, except perhaps in the proem. Catechesis and liturgical sermon become undistinguishable. At occasions, such as Saints' days and Christian feasts, however, the bishops were required to use all the resources of the grand style in order to "edify" and entertain their public.

As to the art of improvisation, already mentioned with reference to synagogue preaching (7.3), there are clear traces of it in Christian sources, too. We may conveniently conclude this account in citing the scene transmitted in Origen's homily on the witch at Endor (1Sam. 28.3–25). Four *pericopae* have been read, and Origen asks the bishop which pericope to choose for an exposition. The bishop gives a sign, and Origen begins with the Endor pericope. This is a difficult text indeed; yet it should be said that it was much discussed at that period. Origen had solutions of the exegetical problems in his mind; he proposes them by improvising much in the style of Clement of Alexandria (who was one of his predecessors). Much of Origen's and others' homilies (*homiliai, tractatus*) may be due to similar situations.

One would like to know whether Origen's Jewish dialogue partner, Osha'yah Rabba, the aggadist whose name has stuck to the *rabba* commentaries, ever achieved the same, and if so, in which language.

Formative Judaism, 2 vol., vol. 1, Leiden/Boston (MA) 2005, 199–220; *Idem*, Art. Hellenistic Jewish Midrash II: Adopting the Allegorical Method, ibid., 220–232; *Idem*, Art. Hellenistic Jewish Midrash III: Developed Non-Allegorical Forms. Josephus, ibid., 232–250.

25 In the fragment of his "Hypothetica", quoted above (n. 12).

Response

Günter Stemberger

The Diaspora existence of many Jews in antiquity, far away from their religious centre at the Temple of Jerusalem, forced them to create new forms of religious life and to find ways of worship without sacrificial cult. Synagogues were instituted as centres of the Jewish communities in the Diaspora in order to preserve their religious identity. Common prayer and instruction in the biblical tradition were essential parts of Jewish religious life in the Diaspora. Synagogues and the religious services conducted in them had no counterpart in other religions of antiquity; they also were introduced only much later into the Jewish homeland. Galilee seems to have been the first part of Palestine to erect synagogues if we accept the testimony of the gospels. This region was so far away from Jerusalem that most people could never make the pilgrimage to the Temple. In many respects, Galilee therefore shared the characteristics of the Diaspora, whereas closer to Jerusalem synagogues were accepted only very late (the Theodotos-synagogue in Jerusalem most probably served mainly diaspora-Jews, above all pilgrims to the Temple who had to be instructed which rules to observe when going there). It is only in the synagogues that the study of the biblical texts and traditions and instruction in them became a central element of Jewish liturgy.

It is thus most probable that many elements of the synagogue service were first developed in the Diaspora before being taken over by Palestinian synagogues. The homily as part of such services may also have its origin in the Diaspora and owe its formal aspects to Hellenistic rhetoric. Philo and Pseudo-Philo may thus be considered as valuable sources for early Jewish homilies.

Thus far I can accept most of Folker Siegert's presentation. Much depends, of course, on Siegert's definition of a homily. Defining sermons as "speeches explaining a sacred doctrine/text in a liturgical setting" seems to be neutral enough. But how formal must such a speech be to qualify and what exactly do we understand by a "liturgical setting"? Siegert excludes most texts of the New Testament because they would not qualify as speeches according to Hellenistic standards.

But is this the only permissible standard? I can hardly imagine that there was no kind of public oratory in an Aramaic or Hebrew language environment although one has to concede that most rhetorical forms we encounter in Jewish texts of the Second Temple period or in rabbinic writings have their parallels in Hellenism and probably derive from it.

As to rabbinic literature, we have great problems in identifying remains of actual sermons in the synagogue not only because practically all texts seem to have been reworked for their literary context, but also because most texts which by contents and some formal aspects would qualify occur in settings more typical of a *bet ha-midrash*, the instruction of students by a rabbi. The liturgical setting is hardly ever explicit; the distinction between instruction and sermon is not as clear-cut as might be expected. From the texts presented by Prof. Siegert, I have the impression that for Hellenistic Jewish texts the situation is not so different. He quotes Philo praising the Jewish Legislator for having instituted the Sabbath as a day of learning for everybody (Hypothetica 7.13) and then concludes: "Such was the *Sitz im Leben* of the Jewish art of preaching". What is described in this text is the common study of the biblical laws with a priest or one of the elders expounding them. Philo describes a study session, but does not include any element that might be viewed as typical of a formal speech. What is described here is not really different from the nightly study sessions referred to in the texts of Qumran. I do not know any clear-cut differences between an "exegetical homily" and more edifying study sessions.

The main examples of Hellenistic-Jewish sermons presented by Folker Siegert are the two texts *De Jona* and *De Sampsone* wrongly attributed to Philo but deriving from an unknown author of the first century. These texts conform to the requirements of a "panegyrical sermon" as Siegert describes them. But does this guarantee that the texts as such were orally performed in a liturgical setting? We have them only in an Armenian translation, mentally retranslated into Greek by Prof. Siegert when he did his German translation. Even if we had the original Greek text, it would be difficult to prove their origin in oral performance, even allowing for their preparation in writing beforehand or their being written down after an oral presentation.

The statement that Philo "spent his life teaching Torah" is certainly correct; but can we therefore conclude, as Siegert continues: "we can reasonably suppose that he engaged personally in the job of preaching"? As long as this is formulated as a reasonable hypothesis, I can certainly accept it; but taking the strict criteria we are used to in the study of rabbinic texts, I would have to say that there is no real evidence for this statement although it is very reasonable. Teaching Torah (perhaps even mainly in writing) and preaching is not the same.

Folker Siegert is not the only scholar claiming that in Philo we find "clear traces of the existence of the annual cycle of Torah lessons such as the rabbis have transmitted it to our day", but again there is no hard evidence. It is clear that certain texts were read in correspondence with the cycle of yearly feasts; but this is no proof of a fixed and stable reading cycle, not for the Torah and even less so for the Prophets which play such a minor role in the writings of Philo. Scholars like Ezra Fleischer claim that also the yearly cycle of Torah reading had its origin in Palestine (and not in Babylonia, as frequently claimed) and was abandoned in favour of the "triennial" cycle when the reading from the Torah was no longer the only or at least the main element of the synagogue service; with the addition of other elements as the sermon, the service would have become too long; therefore the sections to be read in the synagogue were broken up into smaller units. Details of the development of the Torah reading in the rabbinic period are not yet clear; we do not have any evidence at all that in this regard the rabbis took over traditions from the Diaspora. Their insistence on reading the Hebrew text alone and to distinguish it clearly from the Targum to be recited afterwards by another person rather speaks against it.

As to the pseudo-Philonic "sermons" on Jonah and Samson, it has to be emphasized that neither text ever was a liturgical reading in rabbinic Judaism; the story of Jonah never received an extended comment before the ninth century (Pirqe de-R. Eliezer 10). The recently published anthology of ancient *piyyutim* for Yom Kippur contains no single quotation from or allusion to Jonah.[1] The book of Jonah became the reading for Yom Kippur only in the Middle Ages. This is not to say that this text which by its contents is very appropriate for Yom Kippur could not have been used long before in this context, but we do not have any evidence for it. I would therefore hesitate to place the pseudo-Philonic *De Jona* in a liturgical setting for this day.

Siegert's suggestion that Alexandria "may well have been the cradle of the art of preaching, at least so far as rhetorically refined preaching is concerned" is a good possibility. But it remains astonishing that we have to turn to two texts preserved only in Armenian to find the only really convincing examples of such texts. Thus the statement that "against the background of Philo's and Josephus's descriptions of synagogue worship [...] they are quite what can be expected" remains in the sphere of hypothesis. Philo certainly is

---

1 *Michael D. Swartz/Joseph Yahalom (Eds. & translators)*, Avodah: an anthology of ancient poetry for Yom Kippur, University Park (PA) 2005.

the better witness. As to Josephus, he actually never describes a synagogue service, and I should guess that as a priest he was hardly interested in it and in Judaea would hardly have had the chance to participate in such a service. In his long years in Rome he certainly would have had the opportunity if he had cared to do so, but he remains silent about it.

Prof. Siegert's paper is well founded and highly illuminating, but a number of assumptions made in it remain open to doubt. It is one thing to reconstruct the antecedents of later liturgical developments; hypotheses are unavoidable in such reconstructions and are justified. Different is the task of the critical historian, by definition sceptical and prone to a certain minimalism. What she/he accepts as proven is certainly much less than what actually existed. It remains difficult to responsibly mediate between the two positions; this is a task which will never be finished.

Christian Perception of Jewish Preaching in Early Christianity?

Annette von Stockhausen

1. Introduction

When I began my research on the topic, I was quite optimistic that there would be evidence of a "Christian perception of Jewish preaching". I thought that the attraction that Judaism had from the very beginnings for Christians – former Jews and former pagans alike – was at least partly due to the preaching in the synagogues. And I thought that therefore there should be some reflection of this fact in the masses of treatises, letters, sermons, exegetical works, etc. that were written by ancient Christian writers and that have come down to our days.

This – as it turned out – over-estimation of the role of the preaching in the synagogues was surely also caused by my own Protestant heritage, and by the importance of the sermon in this tradition.

After having looked through presumably relevant ancient Christian texts in Latin, Greek, and Syriac, originating from Spain in the west[1] to Persia in the east[2], and from the New Testament to the Byzantine era,[3] I'd now rather like to put a question mark after the title of my paper

---

1 I. e. the "Epistula Severi" on the conversion of the Jewish community on the island of Menorca, cf. *E. D. Hunt*, St. Stephen in Minorca: An Episode in Jewish-Christian Relations in the Early 5th Century A.D., in: JThS 33/1982, 106–123, and *Scott Bradbury* (Ed.), Severus of Minorca: Letter on the Conversion of the Jews (OECT), Oxford 1996.

2 I. e. Aphrahat's Demonstrations, cf. *Jacob Neusner*, Aphrahat and Judaism. The Christian-Jewish Argument in Fourth-Century Iran (StPB 19), Leiden 1971.

3 Cf. the texts mentioned and treated by *Averil Cameron*, Byzantines and the Jews: Some Recent Work on Early Byzantium, in: BMGS 20/1996, 249–274, *Andreas Külzer*, Disputationes graecae contra Iudaeos. Untersuchungen zur byzantinischen antijüdischen Dialogliteratur und ihrem Judenbild (ByA 18), Stuttgart/Leipzig 1999, *Andrew Sharf*, Byzantine Jewry from Justinian to the Fourth Crusade, London 1971, *Andrew Sharf*, Jews and Other Minorities in Byzantium, Jerusalem 1995, *Gilbert Dagron*, Judaïser, TMCB 11/1991, 359–380, and *Gilbert Dagron/Vincent Déroche*, Juifs et Chrétiens dans l'Orient du VIIème siècle, TMCB 11/1991, 17–273.

and ask: Is there a "Christian Perception of Jewish Preaching in Early Christianity" at all?

And as I will show, the answer is almost entirely a negative one.[4]

But before I present the few texts that seem to be relevant and before I consider their meaning, it is necessary to settle two terminological and methodological issues:

(1) What kind of speech do we mean at all, if we use the term "preaching"? And what is the *Sitz im Leben* of this "preaching"?

(2) What kind of sources are at our disposal, and what can we therefore hope to learn from them?

1.1 "Preaching"

Because there are already extensive studies, it is not necessary to discuss this matter here in depth.[5] In my following considerations I'd like, therefore, to understand "preaching" and sermons in the special sense of texts originally orally spoken during a religious service which comment in one form or another on Scripture:[6] The *Sitz im Leben* of preaching is the service/prayer in the synagogue or in the church, and there is also a necessary connection between preaching and the reading of the Holy Writ during this service/prayer.

I'd like, therefore, to distinguish this kind of speech from lectures in the context of "school" on the one hand and from panegyrics

---

4   The, as far as I see, first evidence for Christian perception of Jewish preaching (at least in the Latin speaking world) is the 9th century bishop Agobard of Lyon, who complains in his treatise "De insolentia Judaeorum" (written in 826/27 to the Emperor Louis the Pious) about the thriving Jews in general and especially that some Christians find the preaching of the Jews better than that of their own priests (*L. Van Acker* [Ed.], Agobardi Lugdunensis Opera Omnia, Opusculum XI [CChr.CM 52], Turnhout 1981, 191–195, here: 194,125f.): "... ad hoc peruenitur, ut dicant imperiti christiani melius eis praedicare Iudeos quam presbiteros nostros." "... it reaches the point that inexperienced Christians say that the Jews preach to them better than our priests."

5   See the discussion of the evidence by *Alexandre Olivar*, La Predicación cristiana antigua (BHer.FT 189), Barcelona 1991, 641–669.

6   Cf. the definitions made by *Klaus Berger*, Hellenistische Gattungen im Neuen Testament, in: ANRW II 25.2/1984, 1031–1432, here: 1363–1371, *Maurice Sachot*, Art. Homilie, in: RAC 16 (1994), 148–175, here: 148.170–172, *Folker Siegert*, Drei hellenistisch-jüdische Predigten. Ps.-Philon, "Über Jona", "Über Jona" (Fragment) und "Über Simson", vol. 2: Kommentar nebst Beobachtungen zur hellenistischen Vorgeschichte der Bibelhermeneutik (WUNT 61), Tübingen 1992, 3–12, and *Folker Siegert*, Homily and Panegyrical Sermon, in: *Stanley E. Porter* (Ed.), Handbook of Classical Rhetoric in the Hellenistic Period (330 B.C.–A.D. 400), Leiden 1997, 421–443.

(πανηγυρικοί) – even in the broader context of the service[7] – on the other hand.

Although school or teaching and service or ritual/prayer are connected to each other (especially in Judaism),[8] we have to distinguish between the two: teaching and preaching are two different kinds of speaking to a religious community that have both their own *Sitz im Leben* and place.

Before the 3rd century this distinction seems not to have been made, as there is no "terminus technicus" at all used in our sources, but only more general words like "speech" (λόγος) or even "teaching" (διδασκαλία). Only later on we find more special terms like ὁμιλία, *tractatus* and *sermo* in connection with texts that are sermons in this strict sense.[9]

1.2 What kind of sources do we have?

A further problem, and the most vital one for our undertaking, is the question of which sources we can consult on our matter: what relevant sources do we have? And what kind of sources do we have?

Excursus: Christian Preaching

But before we look at possible Christian sources for Jewish preaching it seems to me reasonable to take a look at the sources for *Christian* preaching,[10] because in view of that evidence the problem we are confronted with becomes all the more obvious.

---

7   Like homilies on the lives of martyrs or saints or orations on occasion of the consecration of a church. I would also count the pseudo-philonic "sermons" "De Jona" and "De Sampsone" among this genre and not look at them as sermons in the strict sense; but see *Siegert*, Drei hellenistisch-jüdische Predigten, vol. 2 (as in note 6), 7–9.

8   Cf. *Hanswulf Bloedhorn/Gil Hüttenmeister*, The synagogue, in: *William Horbury/ William David Davies/John Sturdy* (Eds.), The Cambridge History of Judaism, vol. 3: The Early Roman Period, Cambridge 1999, 267–297, here: 292–294, who point at the difference between praying (in the synagogue) and teaching (in the *"Lehrhaus"*), but who also state that synagogues were time and again used as places for teaching.

9   Cf. *Olivar*, Predicación cristiana (as in note 5), 487–514.

10 On Christian preaching generally cf. *David G. Hunter* (Ed.), Preaching in the Patristic Age. Studies in Honor of Walter J. Burghard, S.J., New York 1989, *Sachot*, Homilie (as in note 6), 155–175, and especially the comprehensive approach by *Olivar*, Predicación cristiana (as in note 5), but see also *Jean Bernardi*, La prédication des pères Cappadociens. Le prédicateur et son auditoire (Publications de la Faculté des

Contrary to the findings regarding the Jewish evidence, there is an abundant amount of Christian sermons, filling many volumes of Jean-Paul Migne's *Patrologia latina* and *Patrologia graeca*. Therefore we do know very well what Christian preaching – at least starting from the 2nd half of the 2nd century onwards[11] – actually looked like: we know when, where and how often they preached;[12] we can read the very words of these sermons;[13] we know which exegetical and hermeneutical methods

---

Lettres et Sciences Humaines de l'Université de Montpellier 30), Paris 1968. The *opinio communis* on the origins of Christian preaching is that it is dependent of Jewish preaching (*derashah*), cf. for example *Hans Martin Müller*, Art. Homiletik, in: TRE 15 (1986), 526–565, here: 528; I have reservations about this, but cannot deal with this subject here.

11 Justin Martyr, 1 apol. 67 (on this text *Gerard A. M. Rouwhorst*, The Reading of Scripture in Early Christian Liturgy, in: *Leonard Victor Rutgers* [Ed.], What Athens has to do with Jerusalem. Essays on Classical, Jewish, and Early Christian Art and Archaeology in Honor of Gideon Foerster [Interdisciplinary studies in ancient culture and religion 1], Leuven 2002, 305–331, here: 323.326) is commonly reckoned the first clear evidence of Christian preaching after the reading of the Scriptures in the service on Sundays besides the New Testament evidence: Εἶτα παυσαμένου τοῦ ἀναγινώσκοντος ὁ προεστὼς διὰ λόγου τὴν νουθεσίαν καὶ πρόκλησιν τῆς τῶν καλῶν τούτων μιμήσεως ποιεῖται. (*Miroslav Marcovich* [Ed.], Iustini Martyris Apologiae pro Christianis [PTS 38], Berlin/New York 1994, 129,9–11) "Then, when the reader has ceased, the president verbally instructs, and exhorts to the imitation of these good things." (*Alexander Roberts/James Donaldson/A. Cleveland Coxe*, The Apostolic Fathers, Justin Martyr, Irenaeus [The Ante-Nicene Fathers 1], ND Grand Rapids [MI] 1989, 186) But it is not evident that this exhorting speech is connected with and about the apostolic or prophetic text read before (τὰ ᾽Απομνημονεύματα τῶν ἀποστόλων ἢ τὰ συγγράματα τῶν προφητῶν [*Marcovich*, Iustini Martyris Apologiae pro Christianis, 129,8]).

But there are also extant texts like Melito's Passah-homily (an exegetical sermon on Ex. 12 cf. Mel., pass. 1 and 11 [*Othmar Perler* (Ed.), Méliton de Sardes, Sur la Pâque et fragments (SCh 123), Paris 1966, 60,3 and 66,72f.]) or the fragments of Valentinus Gnosticus transmitted by Clement of Alexandria (Val. Gn., fragm. 4 and 6 [Clem., str. IV 89,1–3 and VI 52,3–53,1]; cf. the commentary by *Christoph Markschies*, Valentinus Gnosticus? Untersuchungen zur valentinianischen Gnosis mit einem Kommentar zu den Fragmenten Valentins [WUNT 65], Tübingen 1992, 118–152.186–204, especially 122–124). There are also 2 Clement (but see *Wilhelm Pratscher*, Der zweite Clemensbrief [KAV 3], Göttingen 2007, 25–27) and Clement of Alexandria's "Quis dives salvetur" to be mentioned, but I doubt whether they are speeches given during a service.

12 Cf. the short account by *Hans Georg Thümmel*, Materialien zum liturgischen Ort der Predigt in der Alten Kirche, in: *Ekkehard Mühlenberg/Johannes van Oort* (Eds.), Predigt in der Alten Kirche, Kampen 1994, 115–122.

13 There is a discussion about the relation between the actual delivered sermon and its literary form, i. e. between orality and literacy, which I can set aside here as irrelevant for the purpose of my study.

the preachers used, which style, we even know how they reacted to disturbances by their audience.[14]

We have furthermore traces of a theoretical analysis of the "art of preaching": Augustine instructs the diacon Deogratias in Carthage on how to compose a catechesis in his *"De cathechizandis rudibus"*;[15] and the fourth book of his *"De doctrina christiana"*[16] could well be called a preacher's handbook. Augustine also tells us in his *"Confessiones"* how he perceived the preaching of Ambrosius.[17] He comments sometimes in his sermons on what he does when he preaches and how his audience reacts, as do Origen, John Chrysostom, and others.[18]

In stark contrast to these results obviously no ancient Christian author ever intended to write a treatise on Jewish worship in general or on Jewish preaching specifically. There is no extant *tractatus de praedicatione Iudaeorum* – and it is quite unlikely that we will ever discover a treatise like that.

Early Christian authors had no interest in this topic. And that is because they apparently saw no need to deal with it. I will return to this point later after having examined the evidence, when I will ask for the reasons for this lack of evidence.

---

14 On preacher and audience cf. *Ramsay MacMullen*, The preacher's audience (AD 350–400), in: JThS 40/1989, 503–511; *Marc Hirshman*, The Preacher and his Public in Third-Century Palestine, in: JJS 42/1991, 108–114; *Christoph Markschies*, "… für die Gemeinde im Grossen und Ganzen nicht geeignet …"? Erwägungen zu Absicht und Wirkung der Predigten des Origenes, in: ZThK 94/1997, 39–68; *Philipp Rousseau*, "The Preacher's Audience": A More Optimistic View, in: T. W. Hillard et al. (Eds.), Ancient History in a Modern University, vol. 2: Early Christianity, Late Antiquity and Beyond, Grand Rapids (MI)/Cambridge 1998, 391–400; *Mary B. Cunningham/Pauline Allen* (Eds.), Preacher and Audience. Studies in Early Christian and Byzantine Homiletics (A New History of the Sermon 1), Leiden/Boston (MA)/Köln 1998; *Wendy Mayer*, John Chrysostom: Extraordinary Preacher, Ordinary Audience, in: *Cunningham/Allen*, Preacher and Audience, 105–137; *Robert C. Hill*, Reading the Old Testament in Antioch (Bible in Ancient Christianity 5), Leiden/Boston (MA) 2005, 184–186.

15 Edition: *I. B. Bauer*, De cathechizandis rudibus, in: Aurelii Augustini Opera XIII,2 (CChr.SL 46), Turnhout 1969, 115–178.

16 Edition: *Joseph Martin*, De doctrina christiana libri IV, in: Aurelii Augustini Opera IV,1 (CChr.SL 32), Turnhout 1962, here: 116–167; cf. *M. Avilés Bartina*, Predicación de san Agustín. La teoría de la retórica agustiniana y la práctica de sus sermones, in: Augustinus 28/1983, 391–417.

17 Aug., conf. V 13.23 (*Lucas Verheijen* [Ed.], Sancti Augustini Confessionum Libri XIII [CChr.SL 27], Turnhout ²1990, 70); VI 4,6 (*Verheijen*, Confessiones, 77).

18 Cf. *Olivar*, Predicación cristiana (as in note 5), 774–878, and the literature mentioned in fn. 14.

This gap is all the more important as early Christian writers otherwise did have great interest in topics related to Jews and Judaism and quite a lot of texts covering this field are in our hands.[19]

Many if not most of them are part of the early Christian literature *adversus Judaeos*. There are treatises and sermons,[20] parts of anti-heretical works and lives of saints, but also documents of synods and Church laws or texts in dialogue form.[21]

But if we look through all these writings we observe two things:

(1) They deal principally with *theological* themes, in the first place with the question of Jesus being the Messiah and later on with issues regarding the Trinity.

(2) They deal with Jewish religious practices for the most part only in regard to the keeping of the Sabbath and the festivals, to the observation of *kashrut*, and to circumcision. Prayer does not play an important part;[22] only a minor theme in this regard is the *birkat ha-minim* as part of the prayers.[23]

And more than a few of these texts are directed not to Jews at all and do also not reflect a Christian-Jewish discussion, but are part of the development of a Christian self-consciousness and are but one step towards formulating a Christian "orthodoxy".

Furthermore, and as has also already often been remarked, the controversy with Judaism was to a large extent a literary one, so that even if Jewish theological positions are mentioned, we often cannot decide whether these theological positions are not merely a literary frame for a dogmatic discussion based on exegesis of the biblical texts, especially based on the prophets' critique of the people for not keeping the precepts God had given to them.

To sum up: we have to keep in mind that we solely depend on sources that do not intend to give an answer to our question.

---

19 Cf. the texts treated by *Heinz Schreckenberg*, Die christlichen Adversus-Judaeos-Texte und ihr literarisches und historisches Umfeld (1.–11. Jh.) (EHS.T 172), Frankfurt/M. et al. ⁴1999 and the comprehensive "classic" studies by *James William Parkes*, The Conflict of the Church and the Synagogue. A Study in the Origins of Antisemitism, London 1934, and *Marcel Simon*, Verus Israel. Étude sur les relations entre chrétiens et Juifs dans l'Empire romain (135–425) (BEFAR 166), Paris 1948.

20 Cf. *Bernard Blumenkranz*, Die Judenpredigt Augustins. Ein Beitrag zur Geschichte der jüdisch-christlichen Beziehungen in den ersten Jahrhunderten, Basel 1946.

21 Cf. the literature treated in the works mentioned in note 19.

22 On Christian evidence of synagogue *prayer* in general cf. *William Horbury*, Jews and Christians in contact and controversy, Edinburgh 1998, 236–240.

23 On the problems in connection with the *birkat ha-minim* cf. now *Steven T. Katz*, The Rabbinic Response to Christianity, in: *Idem* (Ed.), The Cambridge History of Judaism, vol. 4: The Late Roman-Rabbinic Period, Cambridge 2006, 259–298, here: 280–294.

Sometimes we have to read them even against the intention of their author – and sometimes there is nothing to read at all.

2. What do we know about Jewish preaching in antiquity – apart from any supposed Christian evidence?

Talking about Jewish preaching in antiquity seems to me like entering a minefield, as it is much disputed – and not at all as clear as it always seemed to be – what we definitely can say about it in historical perspective.[24] I therefore shall only touch on the problems connected to our knowledge of Jewish preaching, but will give no answers. The following questions are crucial:

(1) What were "synagogues" like?[25] Was there a religious "service" at all? Or was the synagogue more a room for common study and discussion – on religious topics as well as on political ones?[26] And were there differences between *Eretz Israel* and the Diaspora, between Hebrew/Aramaic-speaking and Greek-speaking Judaism?[27] What was the service in the synagogue like?[28] Did it comprise prayer, reading of

---

24 Cf. the articles by *G. Stemberger* and *F. Siegert* in this volume and the literature mentioned in the following notes. *Horbury*, Jews and Christians in contact and controversy (as in note 22), 226, has rightly pointed to the general scarcity of evidence.

25 Cf. on the late evidence for synagogues *Shaye J. D. Cohen*, Pagan and Christian Evidence on the Ancient Synagogue, in: *Lee I. Levine* (Ed.), The Synagogue in Late Antiquity, Philadelphia 1987, 159–181; a more optimistic view with emphasis on the New Testament evidence can be found in *Horbury*, Jews and Christians in contact and controversy (as in note 22), 228–232. Also on the scholarship on synagogue service *Rouwhorst*, Reading of Scripture (as in note 11), 315–318.

26 Cf. *Bloedhorn/Hüttenmeister*, Synagogue (as in note 8), 268, *Heather A. McKay*, Sabbath and Synagogue. The Question of Sabbath Worship in Ancient Judaism (Religions in the Graeco-Roman World 122), Leiden et al. 1994, and *Seth Schwartz*, Imperialism and Jewish Society. 200 B.C.E. to 640 C.E (Jews, Christians, and Muslims from the ancient to the modern world), Princeton (NJ) 2001, 221–225, on the first century evidence.

27 Cf. *Levine*, Synagogue in Late Antiquity (as in note 25); *Cohen*, Pagan and Christian Evidence (as in note 25), 159–181; *Avigdor Shinan*, Sermons, Targums, and the Reading from Scriptures in the Ancient Synagogue, in: *Levine* (Ed.), Synagogue in Late Antiquity (as in note 25), 97–110; *Schwartz*, Imperialism and Jewish Society (as in note 26), 215–239.

28 Cf. the articles in the collections by *Levine* (Ed.), Synagogue in Late Antiquity (as in note 25), *Steven Fine* (Ed.), Sacred Realm. The Emergence of the Synagogue in the Ancient World, New York/Oxford 1996, *Steven Fine* (Ed.), Jews, Christians and Polytheists in the ancient synagogue: cultural interaction during the Greco-Roman period (Baltimore studies in the history of Judaism), London/New York 1999, and by *Howard C. Kee/Lynn H. Cohick* (Eds.), Evolution of the Synagogue. Problems and

the Torah and the Prophets, the *Targum* or translation and a sermon about these readings?[29] Did it comprise only one or two of these elements, but not all four? What is the relation of the *Targum* to the sermon? Was prayer or reading first? What is the role of the *"piyyut"*?[30]

(2) Further questions relate to the sermon in particular: What was the sermon in Greek-speaking Judaism like?[31] Are the *petihtot* we find in the *midrashim* really parts or reflections of actually held sermons?[32]

Progress, Harrisburg (PA) 1999, and the accounts of *Stefan C. Reif*, Judaism and Hebrew Prayer. New Perspectives on Jewish Liturgical History, Cambridge 1993, especially 53–87, and *Bloedhorn/Hüttenmeister*, Synagogue (as in note 8), especially 267–270 and 291f.; a summarizing account on the second temple period synagogues and on the later development of the synagogue is made by *Peter Wick*, Die urchristlichen Gottesdienste. Entstehung und Entwicklung im Rahmen der frühjüdischen Tempel-, Synagogen- und Hausfrömmigkeit (BZWANT 150), Stuttgart/Berlin/Köln 2002, 88–116.383–385. See also the discussion on how the synagogue is called and whether we can conclude from its naming as συναγωγή or προσευχή on its function *Bloedhorn/Hüttenmeister*, Synagogue (as in note 8), 270–272, and *Schwartz*, Imperialism and Jewish Society (as in note 26), 216f.

29 This seems to be the *opinio communis* since *Leopold Zunz*, Die gottesdienstlichen Vorträge der Juden historisch entwickelt. Ein Beitrag zur Alterthumskunde und biblischen Kritik, zur Literatur- und Religionsgeschichte, Berlin 1832, cf. *Ismar Elbogen*, Der jüdische Gottesdienst in seiner geschichtlichen Entwicklung. Dritte, verbesserte Auflage, Frankfurt/M. 1931, 194–198; *Hermann L. Strack/Paul Billerbeck*, Kommentar zum Neuen Testament aus Talmud und Midrasch. Vierter Band: Exkurse zu einzelnen Stellen des Neuen Testaments. Erster Teil, München ²1956, 153–188, especially 171–188; *Paul Billerbeck*, Ein Synagogengottesdienst in Jesu Tagen, in: ZNW 55/1964, 143–161, here: 157–161; *Wolfgang Schrage*, Art. συναγωγή etc., in: ThWNT 7 (1964), 798–850; *Emil Schürer/Geza Vermes/Fergus Millar/Matthew Black* (Eds.), The History of the Jewish People in the Age of Jesus Christ (175 B.C.–A.D. 135). A New English Version, vol. 2, Edinburgh 1979, 447–454, esp. 453; *Joseph A. Fitzmyer*, The Gospel According to Luke (I–IX) (AncB), Garden City (NY) ²1983, 531; *Sachot*, Homilie (as in note 6), 149f. *Reif*, Judaism and Hebrew Prayer (as in note 28), 63f., at least puts it only as an assumption that there was a sermon in the synagogue.

30 Cf. *Schwartz*, Imperialism and Jewish Society (as in note 26), 263–274.

31 Cf. *Hartwig Thyen*, Der Stil der jüdisch-hellenistischen Homilie, Göttingen 1955, and *Siegert*, Homily and Panegyrical Sermon (as in note 6), 421–443; *Folker Siegert*, Drei hellenistisch-jüdische Predigten. Ps.-Philon, "Über Jona", "Über Simson" und "Über die Gottesbezeichnung 'wohltätig verzehrendes Feuer'", vol. 1: Übersetzung aus dem Armenischen und sprachliche Erläuterungen (WUNT 20), Tübingen 1980; *Siegert*, Drei hellenistisch-jüdische Predigten, vol. 2 (as in note 6).

32 There is a broad consent that they are, cf. *Joseph Heinemann*, Art. Preaching. In the Talmudic Period, in: EJ 13 (1971), 994–998; *Shinan*, Sermons (as in note 27), 97–110; *William-Richard Stegner*, The ancient Jewish synagogue homily, in: *David Edward Aune* (Ed.), Greco-Roman literature and the New Testament. Selected Forms and Genres (SBibSt 21), Atlanta (GA) 1988, 51–69; but see the article by Günter Stemberger in this volume.

Or are they rather a literary phenomenon? And what is the role of the rabbis in the synagogues? Did they preach in the synagogues?[33]

The problem that evolves from these questions and their disputed answers for the subject of our study is that we have no clear picture in which we can embed the no less obscure and complex evidence by Christian authors.

3. Supposed evidence of Christian knowledge of Jewish preaching

Generally speaking the evidence for Jewish preaching in the first centuries CE is very sparse, both in Jewish and in Christian writings. And being so sparse, there is always the danger of finding evidence where there actually is none.

Therefore I will now deal with texts that have been referred to as evidence for Christian perception of Jewish preaching in the synagogues.

3.1 The alleged evidence of knowledge about Jewish preaching in Jerome's work

Our main source here is Jerome, monk and man of letters who lived and worked almost half of his life in Bethlehem at the turn of the 4th to the 5th century. He is *the* father of the church who is – besides Origen and to a degree also Eusebius – most dealt with when it comes to the question of borrowing Jewish exegetical knowledge by Christian authors.[34]

---

33   Cf. *Sachot*, Homilie (as in note 6), 150–155, and *Shaye J. D. Cohen*, Were Pharisees and Rabbis the Leaders of Communal Prayer and Torah Study in Antiquity? The Evidence of the New Testament, Josephus, and the Early Church Fathers, in: *Kee/Cohick*, Evolution of the Synagogue (as in note 28), 89–105.

34   Cf. for example *Benjamin Kedar-Kopfstein*, Jewish Traditions in the Writings of Jerome, in: *Derek R. G. Beattie/Martin J. McNamara* (Eds.), The Aramaic Bible. Targums in their Historical Context (JSOT.S 166), Sheffield 1994, 420–430; *Günter Stemberger*, Exegetical Contacts between Christians and Jews in the Roman Empire, in: *Magne Sæbø* (Ed.), Hebrew Bible/Old Testament. The History of Its Interpretation, vol. 1: From the Beginnings to the Middle Ages (Until 1300). Part 1: Antiquity, Göttingen 1996, 569–586, here: 576–586, especially 581–583 on Jerome; *Christoph Markschies*, Hieronymus und die "Hebraica Veritas". Ein Beitrag zur Archäologie des protestantischen Schriftverständnisses?, in: *Martin Hengel/Anna Maria Schwemer* (Eds.), Die Septuaginta zwischen Judentum und Christentum (WUNT 72), Tübingen 1994, 131–181; *Schreckenberg*, Christliche Adversus-Judaeos-Texte (as in note 19), 333–339;

Samuel Krauss refers in his still much cited article "The Jews in the Works of the Church Fathers"[35] to some alleged remarks on Jewish preaching that Jerome[36] makes on various occasions in his commentaries to the Old Testament, namely in his Commentaries on Isaiah (written between 408 and 410) and on Ezekiel (written between 410 and 414).[37]

I can be brief here because Günter Stemberger has – in his contribution to the Festschrift for Heinz Schreckenberg[38] – already shown that Samuel Krauss took the texts out of their original context and has rather made them fit what he wanted to read rather than interpreted them in their proper meaning and context.

(1) Samuel Krauss cites a text from Jerome's commentary on Ezekiel and translates it as follows: "They say one to another: Come, let us listen to this or that Rabbi who expounds the divine law, with such marvellous eloquence; then they applaud and make a noise, and gesticulate with their hands."[39] The Latin text is: *tales sunt usque hodie multi in ecclesiis, qui aiunt: "uenite audiamus illum et illum", mira eloquentia praedicationis suae uerba uoluentem, plausus que commouent et uociferantur et iactant manus.*[40]

First of all Krauss does not translate *"in ecclesiis"* at all, which is crucial; secondly, there is no word "rabbi" in the Latin text.

If we look at the context of this section, it becomes clear that it is a commentary on Ezekiel 33.30–32:

Wolfram Kinzig, Jewish and "Judaising" Eschatologies in Jerome, in: *Richard Kalmin* (Ed.), Jewish Culture and Society under the Christian Roman Empire (Interdisciplinary studies in ancient culture and religion 3), Leuven 2003, 409–429.

35 *Samuel Krauss*, The Jews in the Works of the Church Fathers I–III, in: JQR 5/1892, 122–157; *Idem*, The Jews in the Works of the Church Fathers IV–V, in: JQR 6/1893, 82–99; *Idem*, The Jews in the Works of the Church Fathers VI, in: JQR 6/1894, 225–261.

36 On Jerome's attitude to Judaism generally and the caution to be applied regarding his knowledge of Jewish traditions cf. *Günter Stemberger*, Hieronymus und die Juden seiner Zeit, in: *Dietrich-Alex Koch/Hermann Lichtenberger* (Eds.), Begegnungen zwischen Christentum und Judentum in Antike und Mittelalter. Festschrift für Heinz Schreckenberg (SIJD 1), Göttingen 1993, 347–364; *Markschies*, Hieronymus (as in note 34), 131–181; *Hillel I. Newmann*, Jerome's Judaizers, in: Journal of Early Christian Studies 9/2001, 421–452.

37 *Krauss*, Jews in the Works of the Church Fathers VI (as in note 35), 228.234–236. The argument of Krauss is for example repeated by *Hirshman*, Preacher and his Public (as in note 14), 111–113, cf. also *Horbury*, Jews and Christians in contact and controversy (as in note 22), 242.

38 *Stemberger*, Hieronymus (as in note 36), 361f.

39 *Krauss*, Jews in the Works of the Church Fathers VI (as in note 35), 234.

40 *Franciscus Glorie* (Ed.), S. Hieronymi Presbyteri opera. Pars I. Opera exegetica 4. Commentariorum in Hiezechielem Libri XIV (CChr.SL 75), Turnhout 1964, 479.

Jerome comments on the verses Ez. 33.30–32 with an actualising comparison: Like the target group for the prophet in former times people nowadays go to the theatre to have a good time as they go to the church and hear a sermon to enjoy themselves; they do this for pleasure only, and never intend to act according to what they have heard.

There is no anti-Judaic undertone in this text; it is a critique which Jerome directs against his fellow-Christians. And there are many other texts, mostly in sermons, which confirm that "theatromania" was not uncommon with Christians in the time of the ancient Church.[41]

We therefore cannot conclude from this text, as Krauss has done, that there were famous preachers in the synagogues that attracted the Jews to come and hear them and that the people that heard their sermons showed their enthusiasm by applauding and cheering.

(2) In the commentary on Ezekiel, in book 11 on Ez. 34, Jerome states: *qui cum populo persuaserint uera esse quae fingunt, et in theatralem modum plausus concitauerint, et clamores immemores fiunt imperitiae suae, et, adducto supercilio libratis que sermonibus atque trutinatis, magistrorum sibi assumunt auctoritatem.*[42] Krauss translates this once more in a way that fits his intended interpretation: "The Preachers make the people believe that the fictions which they invent are true; and after they have in theatrical fashion called forth applause [...] they arrogantly step forward, speak proudly and usurp the authority of rulers." He eventually explains this text with the following statement: "Jerome was an attentive observer; the Jewish preacher's theatrical manner is also mentioned by his contemporary, St John Chrysostom."[43]

But Jerome is not at all talking about Jewish preachers – as again Günter Stemberger has already observed[44] – but about heretics and teachers in the church who teach not the right doctrine, as he states in the preceding sentence: *quod et omnes quidem haeretici faciunt, ut carpant eloquia scripturarum, et quantum in se est maculent; sed ecclesiastici uiri qui dogmatum non custodiunt ueritatem, sed de suo corde confingunt magistram que habent praesumptionem suam, simili errore retinentur.*[45]

More instructive for our question may be another text which Samuel Krauss cites.[46] It is from book XVI of Jerome's commentaries on Isaiah, the explanation of Isa. 58.2: "Yet they seek me daily, and delight

---

41   Cf. for example John Chrysostom, Jud. IV 7.
42   *Glorie*, Commentariorum in Hiezechielem Libri XIV (as in note 40), 488.
43   *Krauss*, Jews in the Works of the Church Fathers VI (as in note 35), 234f.
44   *Stemberger*, Hieronymus (as in note 36), 362.
45   *Glorie*, Commentariorum in Hiezechielem Libri XIV (as in note 40), 487f.
46   *Krauss*, Jews in the Works of the Church Fathers VI (as in note 35), 235f.

to know my ways: as a nation that did righteousness, and didn't forsake the ordinance of their God, they ask of me righteous judgments." Jerome comments on this verse with the following words: *hoc proprie iudaeis conuenit, qui per singulos dies currunt ad synagogas, et in dei lege meditantur, scire cupientes quid abraham, isaac et iacob, quid ceteri sanctorum fecerint, et libros prophetarum ac moysi memoriter reuoluentes, decantant diuina mandata, quibus rectissime illud aptabitur: quaerent me mali, et non inuenient. sic enim scriptum est: omnis qui quaerit inuenit.*[47]

In contrast to the last text we have here clearly a polemical, anti-Judaic undertone: in this text Jerome does really speak about Jews – and criticizes their way of religious life.

We learn from this commentary that Jerome at least seems to have knowledge of the following Jewish practices: Jews meet on certain days in the synagogue (*per singulos dies currunt ad synagogas*) and study the "Law of the Lord" (*in dei lege meditantur*). They want to know the deeds of the patriarchs and the other "saints" (*scire cupientes quid abraham, isaac et iacob, quid ceteri sanctorum fecerint*); they repeat from memory the books of the prophets and of Moses (*libros prophetarum ac moysi memoriter reuoluentes*) and they say over and over again the divine precepts (*decantant diuina mandata*).

Granted that Jerome's description – despite the pejorative tone – is reflecting Jewish customs of his time, we can discern only one part of Jewish religious practice as it was performed in the synagogue: the study of the Torah and of the prophets by heart. There is no mention of either prayers or reading of Torah and Haftarah, or of a sermon. As Jerome states that the Jews meet *"per singulos dies"*, it seems reasonable to assume that he is not talking about the prayer on Sabbath but that he has something more like common learning in mind.

Therefore this text proves to be of no relevance for our question either.

3.2 The New Testament evidence

The evidence we find in the New Testament is different from that.[48] But the New Testament itself is a very different kind of source in comparison to Jerome or the work of any other Christian writer. First

---

47 Marcus Adriaen (Ed.), S. Hieronymi presbyteri opera. Pars I. Opera exegetica 2A. Commentariorum in Esaiam libri XII–XVIII. In Esaia parvula adbreviatio (CChr.SL 73A), Turnhout 1963, 660.

48 The New Testament evidence plays a crucial part in almost all the studies on the early history of the synagogue and is often used in a quite uncritical way. Cf. the literature mentioned in fn. 28.

and foremost because it is clearly to be placed before the "parting of the ways" of Judaism and the emerging Christianity.

It is therefore also a methodological question whether we can make use of the New Testament to obtain evidence of *Jewish* preaching at all. We have to ask whether the preaching Jesus and Paul in New Testament texts are an image of a Jewish preacher or rather the prototypes of the Christian?

There are quite a few passages in the New Testament that show us Jesus or one of the apostles preaching or – as I would rather put it – teaching in the synagogue.[49] But besides the quite stereotyped (and often very short) accounts in Matthew, Mark and John we find broader and more elaborate evidence in Luke and Acts.[50] And I think we must pay special attention to this fact, because we have to judge whether the "sermons" Luke cites are transcripts of "real" sermons Jesus or Paul gave or whether they are rather part of his historiographical approach to the life of Jesus and the early history of the church in accordance with the rules of ancient Greek and Roman historiography.[51]

What can we learn then from Luke's portrayal?

The first text is *Luke 4.16–21*:[52] Luke tells us something about prayer on the Sabbath in the synagogue.[53] There is a reading from the scriptures, i. e. from the prophet Isaiah,[54] and Jesus *stands* while he is performing this ritual reading (v. 16); he opens the book and reads from it (v. 17) and he shuts it again after having read, and returns it to the servant who gave it to him (v. 20) – and then at last he *sits down* and teaches the people in the synagogue.

---

49   Cf. (besides the texts mentioned in the following: Luke 4.16–21 and Acts 13.14–44) Mat. 4.23 (διδάσκων ... καὶ κηρύσσων); 9.35 (διδάσκων ... καὶ κηρύσσων); 13.54 (ἐδίδασκεν); Mark 1.21 (ἐδίδασκεν); 6.2 (διδάσκειν); Luke 6,6 (διδάσκειν); 13,10 (διδάσκων); John 6.59 (διδάσκων); 18.20 (ἐδίδαξα); Acts 9.20 (ἐκήρυσσεν); 16.13 (ἐλαλοῦμεν); 17.2f. (διελέξατο); 19.8 (ἐπαρρησιάζετο).
50   On Luke's attitude toward the synagogue cf. also *Wick*, Die urchristlichen Gottesdienste (as in note 28), 273–281.
51   On the historical value of the writings of Luke cf. *Fitzmyer*, Gospel According to Luke (as in note 29), 14–18.
52   Cf. the commentary on this text by *Fitzmyer*, Gospel According to Luke (as in note 29), 526–540.
53   Only Luke stresses that Jesus was frequenting the synagogue (*Fitzmyer*, Gospel According to Luke [as in note 29], 530) as later on the apostles and the early Christians frequently went to the temple (Acts 2.46; 3.1; 4.1; 5.12, 42; 21.26).
54   One should not infer from that that there was a *haftarah* already common in the synagogue of Jesus' time. The fact that Jesus is reading the verses of Isa. 61.1f. has more to do with what Luke as an author wants Jesus to show to us: Jesus reading a part of the Torah would not have helped Luke in his intention of showing the "proof from prophecy" that Jesus is the Messiah.

We see that for Luke there is something like an exegetical sermon after the reading of the scriptures and that this sermon is performed sitting while the ritual reading is performed standing up. The scenario Luke presents us is more like the scenario of a teacher talking to his not-too-many pupils, at any rate it is not the scenario of an oration given before a huge crowd.

Can we regard this as a sermon? All the more as Jesus, according to Luke, only says one sentence? I have doubts.

In the second text, *Acts 13.14–44*, Luke presents us a different picture:[55] Here the reading of the scriptures and exegesis are connected, too. Paul and Barnabas sit in the synagogue in Pisidian Antioch (v. 14) – apparently they also sit during the reading of Law and Prophets (v. 15). After the readings the archisynagogues[56] ask them to give a comforting speech, a λόγος παρακλήσεως (v. 15). Paul stands up and delivers an elaborate oration in the classical Greek manner (vv. 16–41).

After having left the synagogue Paul and Barnabas are asked to speak again on the following Sabbath (v. 42) and many of the Jews and the Godfearers follow them and urge them to stay (v. 43). On the following Sabbath in contrast to the beginning of the scene, not only the Jews, but almost the entire city come to hear the word of God (v. 44). The missionary plan of Paul and Barnabas to bring the word of God to Jews and pagans alike is accomplished.

Now, in contrary to the scene in Luke 4.16–21, Paul and Barnabas and probably the whole community are sitting while hearing the reading, and Paul is standing while he delivers his speech. Here we have the scenario of an ordinary public speech in the Hellenistic world, and also the style of the speech Paul is delivering points to that genre.[57] So this text fits more to our notion of a sermon. But is it necessarily also a reflection of historical reality? I rather think that this "sermon" is caused by the genre Luke chose for his *Acts of the Apostles*: he writes a historical work,[58] and one of the fundamental characteristics of ancient Hellenistic historiography is the composition of great speeches delivered by the protagonists at crucial points of the account. With this

---

55 Cf. the commentaries on this text by *Joseph A. Fitzmyer*, The Acts of the Apostles (AncB), New York et al. 1998, 505–524, and *Charles K. Barrett*, A Critical and Exegetical Commentary on the Acts of the Apostles, vol. 1: Preliminary Introduction and Commentary on Acts I–XIV (ICC 5), Edinburgh 1998, 620–661.

56 Cf. *Bloedhorn/Hüttenmeister*, Synagogue (as in note 8), 294f., on the office of archisynagogos.

57 *Barrett*, Acts of the Apostles I (as in note 55), 625; on the speeches in Acts cf. *Fitzmyer*, Acts of the Apostles (as in note 55), 103–108.

58 Cf. *Berger*, Hellenistische Gattungen (as in note 6), 1275–1277.

speech (as well as with the other speeches in Acts) Luke complies with this rule of the genre.

Excursus: Jews as listeners to Christian sermons

While we have no evidence that there were Christians going to the synagogue in order to listen to a sermon, there is one text that gives evidence that Jews went to the church to listen to a Christian sermon – but only to lead Christians afterwards, at the end of the liturgy, astray, as the author concludes in polemical tone.[59]

This text can be found in one of the homilies of Proclus, the 5th century Archbishop of Constantinople, in Homily 2 "On the incarnation and On the Lampstand of Zechariah", § 9:[60]

> "But I see that you are crowded together by force, and that it would be better at this point to finish my discourse. But if you are forcefully crowded together, remember that the kingdom of God belongs to those who take it by force. Permit me then to add but this: there may by chance to be a Jew in our midst, like the fox of Judah lurking in the vineyard of Christ. After the congregation is dismissed, he might stand outside and mock our words, saying such things as these: 'Why do you Christians invent such novelties and boast of things which cannot be proved? When did God ever appear on earth? Never, except in the time of Moses.'"

---

59 Cf. the commentary on this text by *Jan H. Barkhuizen*, Proclus of Constantinople: A Popular Preacher in Fifth-Century Constantinople, in: *Cunningham/Allen*, Preacher and audience (as in note 14), 179–200, here: 193–195.

60 Ἀλλ᾽ ὁρῶ ὑμᾶς στενοχωρουμένους καὶ βέλτιον ἐνθάδε κατευνάσαι τὸν λόγον. εἰ δὲ βιασταί ἐστε, τῶν «βιαζομένων δέ ἐστιν ἡ βασιλεία.» προσθήσω τοῖς εἰρημένοις· εἰκὸς τῶν Ἰουδαίων τινὰ παρεῖναι ἐνταῦθα, καὶ ἐν τῷ ἀμπελῶνι τοῦ Χριστοῦ λανθάνειν τὴν ἀλώπεκα τῆς Ἰουδαίας, καὶ μετὰ τὸ ἀπολυθῆναι τὴν ἐκκλησίαν στήκειν ἔξω καὶ σκώπτειν τοὺς λόγους καὶ λέγειν τοιαῦτα· «διὰ τί, Χριστιανοί, καινοτομεῖτε ταῦτα, καὶ κομπάζετε ἐπὶ πράγμασιν ἀναποδείκτοις· Θεὸς ἐπὶ γῆς ὤφθη πότε· οὐδέποτε ἄλλοτε εἰ μὴ μόνον ἐπὶ Μωϋσέως.» Text and translation *Nicholas Constas*, Proclus of Constantinople and the Cult of the Virgin in Late Antiquity (SVigChr 66), Leiden/Boston (MA) 2003, 170–172. A further, similar text can be found in Homily 33 "On the apostle Thomas", § 8 (*François Joseph Leroy*, L' homilétique de Proclus de Constantinople. Tradition manuscrite, inédits, études connexes [StT 247], Città del Vaticano 1967, 242): Κἂν τις τῶν Ἰουδαίων εἴπη πρός μέ· «Ἀμήχανα καὶ ξένα κηρύττεις καὶ παντελῶς ἄπιστα πράγματα· πῶς γὰρ ἠδύνατο διὰ κεκλεισμένων θυρῶν σῶμα παρελθεῖν»· ἐρῶ πρὸς αὐτόν· «Πῶς ἠδυνήθη καταγαγεῖν ὁ ἄγγελος τὸν Ἀμβακοὺμ εἰς τὸν λάκκον τῶν λεόντων καὶ πάλιν ἀναγαγεῖν καὶ τὰς ἐπικειμένας σφραγῖδας ἐρρωμένας καταλιπεῖν· Ὁ δοῦλος ὅπερ ἠθέλησεν ἤνυσεν καὶ ὁ Δεσπότης οὐκ ἴσχυσεν ὅπερ ηὐδόκησεν· Ὥσπερ οὖν ἐκεῖνο γεγένηται βουληθέντος Θεοῦ, οὕτω καὶ τοῦτο πέπρακται τοῦ ἐνανθρωπήσαντος Θεοῦ Λόγου θελήσαντος».

But here also we cannot discern clearly whether it is a *real* Jew Proclus is dealing with, and it seems more probable that it is not. But it certainly reflects the competition of Jews and Christians.[61]

4. Reasons for the lack of evidence

The answer to the question whether there is a Christian perception of Jewish preaching in Early Christianity is therefore a negative one.

But why is that? In a further step I will try to explain why early Christians tell us essentially nothing about Jewish preaching, especially while they do tell us a lot about Jews and Jewish life in general (of course – as we have already seen – highly mixed with polemics).

4.1 What attracted Christians to Judaism?

But what then attracted Christians to Judaism? From the second century onwards we hear again and again warnings that Christians should not "Judaize",[62] that they should not live like Jews,[63] that they should not adhere to Jewish customs, and above all that they should not go to the synagogues.[64]

---

61 On this topic see also Ambrose, ep. 74, especially § 10 and 20 (*Michaela Zelzer*, Sancti Ambrosii Opera. Pars decima: Epistularum liber decimus. Epistulae extra collectionem. Gesta Concilii Aquileiensis [CSEL 82/3], Wien 1982, 54–73) on the affair of the burnt-down synagogue of Callinicum and above all John Chrysostom's Orations against the Jews.

62 Cf. for example the title of Clement of Alexandria's lost Κανὼν ἐκκλησιαστικὸς ἢ πρὸς τοὺς Ἰουδαΐζοντας (Eus., h.e. VI 13,3).

63 Ign., Magn. 10,3: Ἄτοπόν ἐστιν, Ἰησοῦν Χριστὸν λαλεῖν καὶ ἰουδαΐζειν. Ὁ γὰρ Χριστιανισμὸς οὐκ εἰς Ἰουδαϊσμὸν ἐπίστευσεν, ἀλλ' Ἰουδαϊσμὸς εἰς Χριστιανισμόν, εἰς ὃν πᾶσα γλῶσσα πιστεύσασα εἰς θεὸν συνήχθη. "It is silly to speak of Jesus Christ and to judaize. Christianity did not belief in Judaism, but Judaism in Christianity, to which every soul that believes in God is brought."; Philad. 6,1: Ἐὰν δέ τις Ἰουδαϊσμὸν ἑρμηνεύῃ ὑμῖν, μὴ ἀκούετε αὐτοῦ. Ἄμεινον γάρ ἐστιν παρὰ ἀνδρὸς περιτομὴν ἔχοντος Χριστιανισμὸν ἀκούειν, ἢ παρὰ ἀκροβύστου Ἰουδαϊσμόν. "If someone is explaining to you Judaism, don't pay attention! It is better for a circumcised man to hear about Christianity than for a man not circumcised to hear about Judaism."

64 See for example Martyrium Pionii 13 (*Herbert Musurillo*, The Acts of the Christian Martyrs [OECT], Oxford 1972, 152,18–20/153), written about 300 AD: Ἀκούω δὲ ὅτι καί τινας ὑμῶν Ἰουδαῖοι καλοῦσιν εἰς συναγωγάς. διὸ προσέχετε μή ποτε ὑμῶν καὶ μεῖζον καὶ ἑκούσιον ἁμάρτημα ἥψηται, ... "I understand also that the Jews have been inviting some of you to their synagogues. Beware lest you fall into a greater, more deliberate sin ...".

But what did Christians do there? What made the synagogue for Christians as attractive[65] as the theatre, against which the fathers of the church polemicise again and again as it was obviously seen by them as a similar threat?

Canones

The best evidence for questions like that are found in the law of the Church, the *canones*, promulgated by synods from the 4th century onwards, and in Church orders.[66]

The relevant – and, I think, well known – canons for the question on Judaising Christians are to be found in the canons of the Synod of Elvira in Spain,[67] in the canons of the Synod of Laodicea,[68] in the so called Apostolic Canons,[69] and in the Church order of the so called Apostolic Constitutions,[70] all dating to late 4th century AD. Most of these canons are repeated again and again in later collections as well in the "orthodox", Chalcedonian and in the non-Chalcedonian "mono-" and "dyo-physite" churches.

If we look at what the canons prohibit, we can gather what Christians obviously did in connection with Judaism – and what they obviously did not, too:[71]

– Christians went into the synagogues.[72]

---

65 Cf. *Steven Fine*, Non-Jews in the synagogues of late-antique Palestine: Rabbinic and archeological evidence, in: *Idem*, Jews, Christians and Polytheists in the ancient synagogue (as in note 28), 224–242, here: esp. 231–236 on the rabbinic and archaeological evidence.
66 Cf. *Bernhard Blumenkranz*, Die jüdisch-christliche Missionskonkurrenz (3. bis 6. Jahrhundert), in: Klio 39/1961, 227–233, here: 230f.; see also *Charlotte Elisheva Fonrobert*, Jewish Christians, Judaizers, and Christian Anti-Judaism, in: *Virginia Burrus* (Ed.), A People's History of Christianity, vol. 2: Late Ancient Christianity, Minneapolis 2005, 234–254, here: 243–250, on the Didascalia Apostolorum which cannot be further discussed here.
67 Cf. *Pio de Luis*, Art. Elvira, Council of, in: EECh 1/1992, 270, and *Eckhard Reichert*, Art. Elvira, Synode von, in: RGG⁴ 2 (1999), 1242f.
68 *Carlo Nardi*, Art. Laodicea, Councils of, in: EECh 1 (1992), 472f.
69 Cf. *Bruno Steimer*, Art. Apostolische Canones, LACL (1998), 46.
70 Cf. *Marcel Metzger*, Art. Konstitutionen, (Pseud-)Apostolische, TRE 19 (1990), 540–544, and *Bruno Steimer*, Art. Apostolische Konstitutionen, LACL (1998), 46f.
71 See, for example, in this regard also Augustin's ep. 196 (CSEL 57, 216–230) to the catholic bishop Asellicus, the answer to his question on the relevance of Jewish customs in the church. Regarding Augustin's attitude to Judaism generally cf. *Blumenkranz*, Judenpredigt Augustins (as in note 20).

- They prayed in the synagogue.[73]
- They brought with them oil into the synagogue and lit with it lamps.[74]
- They observed the Jewish ritual.[75]
- They asked Jews to bless their fruit.[76]
- They collected gifts from the Jews[77] and especially unleavened bread.[78]

---

72 Const. App. II pinax 61 (*Marcel Metzger* [Ed.], Les Constitutions apostoliques. Tome I. Livres I et II [SCh 320], Paris 1985, 142): ... καὶ ὅτι οὐ χρὴ συντρέχειν τὸν πιστὸν εἰς Ἰουδαίων συναγωγὰς ἢ αἱρετικῶν εὐκτήριον ἢ Ἑλλήνων θεάματα; cf. Chrys., Jud. II (Μονὴ Λείμωνος 27, f. 129ra = *Wendy Pradels/Rudolf Brändle/Martin Heimgartner*, Das bisher vermisste Textstück in Johannes Chrysostomus, Adversus Judaeos, Oration 2, in: ZAC 5/2001, 23–49, here: 46): Τί γὰρ ταύτης τῆς ὕβρεως χεῖρον· ἐλευθέρα γυνὴ καὶ πιστὴ τῆς οἰκίας πρόεισιν, εἰπέ μοι, καὶ εἰς συναγωγὴν ἄπεισιν;
73 Can. App. 65 (*Marcel Metzger* [Ed.], Les Constitutions apostoliques. Tome III. Livre VII et VIII [SCh 336], Paris 1987, 298): Εἴ τις κληρικὸς ἢ λαϊκὸς εἰσέλθοι εἰς συναγωγὴν Ἰουδαίων ἢ αἱρετικῶν προσεύξασθαι, καθαιρείσθω καὶ ἀφοριζέσθω.
74 Can. App. 71 (*Metzger*, Constitutions apostoliques III [as in note 73], 300): Εἴ τις Χριστιανὸς ἔλαιον ἀπενέγκοι εἰς ἱερὸν ἐθνῶν ἢ εἰς συναγωγὴν Ἰουδαίων ἢ λύχνους, ἀφοριζέσθω.
75 Const. App. V pinax 12 (*Marcel Metzger* [Ed.], Les Constitutions apostoliques. Tome II. Livres III–IV [SCh 329], Paris 1986, 200): Ὅτι μὴ προσήκει ᾠδὴν ἐθνικὴν ᾄδειν οὔτε ἐπομνύεσθαι εἴδωλον οὔτε οἰωνοῖς ἢ κληδόσιν ἢ μαντείαις ἢ παλμοῖς ἢ παρατηρήσεσιν ἰουδαϊκαῖς προσανέχειν· ἀσεβὲς γὰρ τοῦτο καὶ τῆς τοῦ Θεοῦ γνώσεως ἐχθρόν; VI pinax 27 (*Metzger*, Constitutions apostoliques II [as in note 75], 292): Περὶ παρατηρημάτων ἰουδαϊκῶν καὶ ἑλληνικῶν, γονορροίας, ὀνειρώξεως, πλησιασμοῦ, ἀφέδρου, μίξεως νομίμου, τοκετοῦ, ἀποβολῆς, μώμου σώματος, κηδίας νεκροῦ ἢ ὀστέων, μνήματος ἢ διαφορᾶς βρωμάτων; VI 26 (*Metzger*, Constitutions apostoliques II [as in note 75], 378): Εἰ δέ τινες παρατηρούμενοι φυλάσσουσιν ἔθιμα ἰουδαϊκά, γονορροίας, ὀνειρώξεις, πλησιασμοὺς τοὺς κατὰ νόμον, λεγέτωσαν ἡμῖν, εἰ ἐν αἷς ὥραις ἢ ἡμέραις ἕν τι τούτων ὑπομείνωσιν παρατηροῦνται προσεύξασθαι ἢ εὐχαριστίας μεταλαβεῖν ἢ βιβλίου θίγειν, καὶ ἐὰν συνθῶνται, δῆλον ὡς τοῦ ἁγίου Πνεύματος κενοὶ τυγχάνουσιν τοῦ ἀεὶ παραμένοντος τοῖς πιστοῖς; on the efficacy of the Jewish rites cf. *Robert Louis Wilken*, John Chrysostom and the Jews. Rhetoric and Reality in the Late 4th Century, Berkeley (CA) 1983, 88–94.
76 Elvira Can. 49 (*Friedrich Lauchert*, Die Kanones der wichtigsten altkirchlichen Concilien nebst den apostolischen Kanones [SQS 12], ND Frankfurt/M. 1961, 21,12–17): "De frugibus fidelium ne a Iudaeis benedicantur. Admoneri placuit possessores, ut non patiantur fructus suos, quos a Deo percipiunt cum gratiarum actione, a Iudaeis benedici, ne nostram irritam et informam faciant benedictionem: si quis post interdictum facere usurpaverit, penitus ab ecclesia abiciatur."
77 Laodicea Can. 37 (*Lauchert*, Kanones [as in note 76], 76,17–19): Ὅτι οὐ δεῖ παρὰ τῶν Ἰουδαίων ἢ αἱρετικῶν τὰ πεμπόμενα ἑορταστικὰ λαμβάνειν, οὐδὲ συνεορτάζειν αὐτοῖς; Can. App. 70 (*Metzger*, Constitutions apostoliques III [as in note 73], 300): Εἴ τις ἐπίσκοπος ἢ ἄλλος κληρικὸς νηστεύει μετὰ Ἰουδαίων ἢ ἑορτάζει μετ᾽ αὐτῶν ἢ δέχεται αὐτῶν τὰ τῆς ἑορτῆς ξένια, οἷον ἄζυμα ἤ τι τοιοῦτον, καθαιρείσθω· εἰ δὲ λαϊκός, ἀφοριζέσθω.

- They went to Jewish physicians.[79]
- They went to the Jewish *Miqve*.[80]
- They dined with Jews.[81]
- They celebrated together with the Jews,[82] especially Passover.[83]
- They married Jewish women.[84]
- They rested together with the Jews on the Sabbath.[85]
- They fasted together with the Jews.[86]

It is to be noted that there is no mention of Christians listening to a sermon in the synagogue; this obviously posed no problem.

---

[78] Laodicea Can. 38 (*Lauchert*, Kanones [as in note 76], 76,20f.): Ὅτι οὐ δεῖ παρὰ τῶν Ἰουδαίων ἄζυμα λαμβάνειν ἢ κοινωνεῖν ταῖς ἀσεβείαις αὐτῶν; Can. App. 70 (cf. the preceding footnote); Quinisextum Can. 11 (*Georges Neungatt/Silvano Agrestini*, Concilium Trullanum 691–692, in: *Guiseppe Alberigo* et al. [Eds.], Conciliorum Oecumenicorum Generaliumque Decreta. Editio Critica. I. The Oecumenical Councils. From Nicea I to Niceas II (325–787) [CChr.COGD 1], Turnhout 2006, 203–293, here: 237,746–755): Μηδεὶς τῶν ἐν ἱερατικῷ τάγματι ἢ λαϊκὸς τὰ παρὰ τῶν Ἰουδαίων ἄζυμα ἐσθιέτω ἢ τούτοις προσοικειούσθω καὶ ἰατρείας παρ᾽ αὐτῶν λαμβανέτω ἢ ἐν βαλανείῳ παντελῶς τούτοις συλλουέσθω· εἰ δέ τις τοῦτο πρᾶξαι ἐπιχειροίη, εἰ μὲν κληρικὸς εἴη, καθαιρείσθω, εἰ δὲ λαϊκός, ἀφοριζέσθω.
[79] Quinisextum Can. 11 (cf. the preceding footnote).
[80] Quinisextum Can. 11 (cf. fn. 78).
[81] Elvira Can. 50 (*Lauchert*, Kanones [as in note 76], 21,18–21): "De Christianis qui cum Iudaeis vescuntur. Si vero quis clericus vel fidelis cum Iudaeis cibum sumpserit, placuit eum a communione abstineri, ut debeat emendari."
[82] Const. App. V pinax 17 (*Metzger*, Constitutions apostoliques II [as in note 75], 200): Ὅπως ὀφείλει γίνεσθαι τὸ πάσχα καὶ πότε, καὶ ὅτι οὐ δεῖ μετὰ Ἰουδαίων ἑορτάζειν.
[83] Can. App. 7 (*Metzger*, Constitutions apostoliques III [as in note 73], 276): Εἴ τις ἐπίσκοπος ἢ πρεσβύτερος ἢ διάκονος τὴν ἁγίαν τοῦ πάσχα ἡμέραν πρὸ τῆς ἐαρινῆς ἰσημερίας μετὰ Ἰουδαίων ἐπιτελέσῃ, καθαιρείσθω.
[84] Elvira Can. 78 (*Lauchert*, Kanones [as in note 76], 25,29–26,2): "De fidelibus coniugatis si cum Iudaea vel gentili moechati fuerint. Si quis fidelis habens uxorem cum Iudaea vel gentili fuerit moechatus, a communione arceatur: quod si alius eum detexerit, post quinquennium acta legitima poenitentia poterit dominicae sociari communione."
[85] Laodicea Can. 29 (*Lauchert*, Kanones [as in note 76], 75,17–21): Ὅτι οὐ δεῖ χριστιανοὺς ἰουδαΐζειν καὶ ἐν σαββάτῳ σχολάζειν, ἀλλ᾽ ἐργάζεσθαι αὐτοὺς ἐν αὐτῇ τῇ ἡμέρᾳ, τὴν κυριακὴν προτιμῶντας, εἴ γε δύναιτο, σχολάζειν ὡς χριστιανοί· εἰ δὲ εὑρεθεῖεν ἰουδαϊσταί, ἔστωσαν ἀνάθεμα παρὰ τῷ Χριστῷ; cf. Chrys., hom. 3 in Tit. 2 (PG 62,679).
[86] Can. App. 64 (*Metzger*, Constitutions apostoliques III [as in note 73], 298): Εἴ τις κληρικὸς εὑρεθῇ τὴν κυριακὴν ἡμέραν ἢ τὸ σάββατον νηστεύων πλὴν τοῦ ἑνὸς σαββάτου, καθαιρείσθω· ἐὰν δὲ λαϊκός, ἀφοριζέσθω; Can. App. 70 (cf. fn. 77); cf. Chrys., Jud. III 1 (PG 48,857); hom. 3 in Tit. 2 (PG 62,679).

John Chrysostom

To this impression can be added the evidence to be found in the notorious "Orations against the Jews" (or better "against Judaising Christians") by John Chrysostom,[87] which can be dated to the autumn of 386 (Jud. I), to January (Jud. III) and to the autumn of 387 (Jud. IV, II, V–VIII).[88]

For example Chrysostom tells us that Christians went to the synagogue to swear an oath, because they thought that oaths sworn in the synagogue were more effective.[89] Or. in Jud. I 5 and on various other occasions he remarks that Christians go to the synagogue to see and hear the trumpets.[90]

As we can see already in this small example, Chrysostom not only mentions Christian Judaising customs, but also gives us an explanation why they were so attracted to Jewish rituals and customs. It seems that to a great extent the attractiveness of Judaism was caused by the fact that the Jews kept festivals and customs that were described in the "Bible", but which were never or not any longer kept by the Church – even though they were commanded in the Scriptures that were, after the exclusion of the Marcionites, regarded by Christians as "holy".

---

[87] The literature on Chrysostom's Homilies on the Jews is abundant, cf. among others *Marcel Simon*, La pólemique antijuive de s. Jean Chrysostome et le mouvement judaïsant d'Antioche, in: AIPh 4/1936, 403–421; *Adolf Martin Ritter*, Erwägungen zum Antisemitismus in der Alten Kirche. Johannes Chrysostomus, "Acht Reden gegen die Juden", in: Bernd Moeller/Gerhard Ruhbach (Eds.), Bleibendes im Wandel der Kirchengeschichte, Tübingen 1973, 71–91; *E. A. Grissom*, Chrysostom and the Jews. Studies in Jewish-Christian relations in fourth-cent. Antioch, Ph.D. Southwest Baptist Theological Seminary Louisville (KY) 1978; *Anne-Marie Malingrey*, La controverse antijudaïque dans l'oeuvre de Jean Chrysostome d'après les discours Adversus-Judaeos, in: *Valentin Nikiprowetzky* (Ed.), De l'antijudaïsme antique à l'antisémitisme contemporain, Lille 1979, 87–104; *Wilken*, John Chrysostom and the Jews (as in note 75); *Rudolf Brändle*, Christen und Juden in Antiochien in den Jahren 386/87. Ein Beitrag zur Geschichte altkirchlicher Judenfeindschaft, in: Jud. 43/1987, 142–160; *Adolf Martin Ritter*, Chrysostomus und die Juden – neu überlegt, in: KuI 2/1990, 109–122; *Rudolf Brändle/Verena Jegher-Bucher*, Art. Johannes Chrysostomus I, in: RAC 18 (1998), 426–503; *Mayer*, Preacher and Audience (as in note 14), 105–137; *Fonrobert*, Jewish Christians (as in note 66), 236–243.

[88] *Wendy Pradels/Rudolf Brändle/Martin Heimgartner*, The Sequence and Dating of the Series of John Chrysostom's Eighth Discourses Adversus Iudaeos, in: ZAC 6/2002, 90–116, table with dates and sequence of the orations in *Pradels/Brändle/Heimgartner*, Sequence and Dating (as in note 88), 106.

[89] Chrys., Jud. I 3 (PG 48,847).

[90] Σάλπιγγας θεωροῦντα: He obviously refers to Rosh Hashana. Chrys., Jud. I 5 and 8 (PG 48,850 and 855f.); cf. II [Μονὴ Λείμωνος 27, f. 127vb–128va = *Pradels/Brändle/Heimgartner*, Textstück (as in note 72), 44–46] and IV 7 (PG 48,881).

Christian writers did their very best to cope with the not-keeping of the Old Testament law by applying several hermeneutical techniques and doctrines, but at least the rank and file Christian obviously did not always conform to these teachings.[91]

Further points of attraction[92] according to Chrysostom's account have been: Jews were regarded as wise men (Jud. III 3) and the Jewish teachers as more believable than the Christian ones (Jud. III 6). Jewish magic was believed as quite effective (Jud. I 6; VIII 5–7).[93]

I will take now two sections of the first oration against the Jews which focus on the matter of "holy books".[94] As Chrysostom tells us, Judaisers think of the synagogue as a σεμνὸς τόπος, because the books of the Law and the Prophets are kept in the synagogue.[95] This is especially repulsive for Chrysostom because the Jews do not make the right use of these books – otherwise they would already have become Christians. Again, preaching is not mentioned. Chrysostom fears that the image of Christianity will be a negative one, if Christians go to the synagogue; especially weak Christians will be challenged whether Christianity is the right way at all (§ 5). For Chrysostom there is only right or wrong: if the Jewish customs and synagogues are holy, then the church must be wrong. The only exception to this rule is the Bible, because the Bible leads to salvation (§ 6).

The Christians had a problem: They relate to the Bible as a holy book – as do the Jews. But unlike them, they have it only in a translation and there were repeated controversies on the right wording of the text. Christians therefore always had a sense of inferiority vis-à-vis the Jews.

This sense of inferiority is still obvious in a document as late as the second half of the 6th century, in the famous "novella 146" by

---

91 Cf. also the argument in *Fonrobert*, Jewish Christians (as in note 66), 234–254.
92 Cf. on the attraction of Judaism in general *Wilken*, John Chrysostom and the Jews (as in note 75), 66–94.
93 Cf. *Wilken*, John Chrysostom and the Jews (as in note 75), 83–88, and *Giancarlo Lacerenza*, Jewish Magicians and Christian Clients in Late Antiquity: The Testimony of Amulets and Inscriptions, in: *Leonard V. Rutgers* (Ed.), What Athens has to do with Jerusalem. Essays on Classical, Jewish, and Early Christian Art and Archeology in Honor of Gideon Foerster (Interdisciplinary Studies in Ancient Culture and Religion 1), Leuven 2002, 393–419.
94 Jud. I 5f. (PG 48,850–852). An English translation is to be found in *Paul W. Harkins*, Saint John Chrysostom. Discourses against Judaizing Christians (FaCh 68), Washington (DC) 1979, 18–24.
95 Cf. *Wilken*, John Chrysostom and the Jews (as in note 75), 79–83, and *Horbury*, Jews and Christians in contact and controversy (as in note 22), 234f.

Justinian.⁹⁶ I subscribe to the view Leonard Rutgers pointed out some years ago:⁹⁷ Justinian acts here not on the initiative of Jewish opponents regarding the use of Greek in the synagogues (as is stated in the preface). His law is rather an instrument of suppression: Jews should only use the Greek (or Latin) translation – or the Septuagint or Aquilas' translation – and refrain henceforth from their δευτέρωσις, their own oral traditions. Thereby they will loose the advantage of having the "original" text, and will hopefully find their way to the true religion.

This is the most elaborate law we have on the Jewish religion, but again Jewish preaching is not seen as part of the Jewish threat to Christianity.

4.2 The lack of evidence – one final reason

I think I have sufficiently shown that there is no Christian perception of Jewish preaching in the first centuries CE. I have also reasoned what could have been the cause for this lack of perception.

Maybe there is one more reason for why there is no Christian perception of Jewish preaching: maybe the reason is that there was no such *preaching* in the synagogues in the late antique Roman Empire at all⁹⁸ or that it at least was not as significant for Jewish worship as it was for the Christian. But that is a supposition I cannot prove.

---

96 The text (with a commentary) is to be found in *Amnon Linder*, The Jews in Roman Imperial Legislation, Detroit (MI)/Jerusalem 1987, 402–411, but see also *Guiseppe Veltri*, Die Novelle 146 περὶ Ἑβραίων. Das Verbot des Targumvortrags in Justinians Politik, in: *Martin Hengel/Anna Maria Schwemer* (Eds.), Die Septuaginta zwischen Judentum und Christentum (WUNT 72), Tübingen 1994, 116–130. On laws regarding Jews in general cf. *Linder*, Jews in Roman Imperial Legislation (as in note 96), and *Robert Louis Wilken*, The Jews and Christian apologetics after Theodosius I Cunctos populos, in: HThR 73/1980, 451–471. On laws against Christian participating in synagogue service cf. also CTh XVI 8,1.

97 *Leonard V. Rutgers*, Justinian's Novella 146 Between Jews and Christians, in: *Kalmin*, Jewish Culture and Society (as in note 34), 385–407.

98 That does not imply that there was no *teaching*; but the "Sitz im Leben" of the teaching is different of that of preaching, cf. above I.1.

Response

Richard S. Sarason

Interactions between competing, yet proximate, religious communities such as those of Jews and Christians in late antiquity, the Byzantine world, and medieval Europe are subtle and often surprising. The "official" pronouncements of these communities and their leaders never tell the whole story. While it is a mistake to look for interaction and conscious response to the Other in every corner, it is equally a mistake to view these communities' religious and cultural traditions as developing in blissful ignorance of, and total unconcern with, each other.[1] The difficult hermeneutical issue for the modern scholar is how to walk this thin line without veering too much to one side or the other – often without being able to know when the thin line has been crossed.

The main concern of Christian preaching is, of course, with Christians, just as the main concern of Jewish preaching is with Jews. Awareness of the Other usually figures in when one feels challenged to respond to the Other, either by way of substance or by way of style, form, and aesthetic. Something on "the other side" is either perceived as potentially attractive or potentially dangerous (and the "dangerous," of course, often is labeled as such precisely because it is attractive!). Thus, as Dr. von Stockhausen points out, John Chrysostom and the authors of a number of fourth-century canons find to their dismay that members of their Christian flock are attracted to synagogues by the presence there of the scrolls of sacred scriptures in the original

---

1   Thus, for example, many scholars have remarked on parallel developments in synagogue and church art and architecture in the land of Israel during the Byzantine period and reasonably assumed that there is some relationship between the two. See *Lee I. Levine*, The Ancient Synagogue. The First Thousand Years, pb. ed. New Haven (CT) ²2005, 210–380, and *Steven Fine*, Art and Judaism in the Greco-Roman World. Toward a New Jewish Archaeology, Cambridge 2005, 187ff. Similarly, the flowering of liturgical hymn-writing in the Byzantine synagogue and church as well as among the Samaritans (Yannai and his contemporaries and followers on the Jewish side, Ephrem the Syrian and Romanos the Melode – thought to be a Jewish convert to Christianity – on the Christian side, Marqah on the Samaritan side) is certainly not to be viewed as coincidental. See *Levine*, op. cit., 583–588, and the literature cited there.

language, which are deemed to be powerful and efficacious mediators of divine blessings, and by the practice there of rites that are mandated in those scriptures but which Christians do not observe!

Given the attested areas of Christian interest in Jewish religious practice in synagogues during the late Roman and Byzantine periods, Dr. von Stockhausen is initially surprised that there is no evidence for Christian awareness of Jewish sermons. But she correctly notes that "Jewish sermons" is itself a problematic concept during this period, as Prof. Günter Stemberger has spelled out in detail in his paper. Even allowing for the presence of *derashot* of some kind, a *derashah* is not the same thing as a "sermon" or a "homily," as these terms (and rhetorical forms) were understood in Latin and Greek. Also worth recalling is that the midrashic literature that bears a putative relationship to *derashot* is localized to the Galilee region of the land of Israel and does not testify at all to the situation in the Mediterranean, Greek-speaking Jewish Diaspora. The linguistic issue (Aramaic/Hebrew vs. Greek or Latin) additionally is relevant to the question of an outsider's awareness of what is transpiring during synagogue services in a particular locale.

Perhaps, indeed, the question needs to be rephrased: rather than Christian awareness of Jewish "sermons," we should be inquiring about Christian interest in, and awareness of, Jewish scriptural interpretation more generally (where, of course, a keen interest was evinced particularly with regard to those scriptural passages that were deemed by the Church to foretell aspects of the Christ-event and the Christian story of salvation). It is also likely that what took place in (some?) synagogues in late antiquity and the Byzantine period bore more of a resemblance to scriptural interpretation and exposition than to what Dr. Alexander Deeg has labeled "metascriptural" homiletics. Even the so-called "homiletical" midrashic literature is far more "intertextual" (that is to say, using Scripture to interpret Scripture) than "meta-textual" in its predominant rhetorical and exegetical forms. So the lack of evidence that Dr. von Stockhausen points out might additionally result from a kind of "category error" in framing the question.

Medieval Jewish Preaching and Christian Homiletics

Marc Saperstein

Since completing my two books that treat medieval material (*Jewish Preaching 1200–1800*, and *"Your Voice Like a Ram's Horn": Themes and Texts in Traditional Jewish Preaching*), I have been working on post-medieval material. My last published book was based on the 550 autograph sermon texts written by Saul Levi Morteira, the leading rabbi of the Portuguese Community of Amsterdam from 1619 until his death in 1660. My current book is *Jewish Preaching in Times of War, 1800–2001* – even further from the medieval period. When I began to gather material to fulfil my assignment, I discovered that much of what I wanted to say I had already published in one of the first two books or subsequent articles. Therefore, I have decided to provide a general introduction to the topic, including a brief overview of Christian influences on medieval Jewish preaching and especially the philosophical influences that seem to have come from Christian scholasticism. Then, I will focus on a specific topic, in order to illustrate and exemplify this dynamic: the problem of *repentance* in late medieval Jewish preaching.

I will not be addressing here the subject of references to Christians or Christian doctrine in the Jewish sermons, as I have treated these topics elsewhere.[1] Rather, I will attempt to my assignment regarding "the impact of Christian homiletics", especially with regard to philosophical material.

1. Structure: The thematic sermon

A powerful example of the impact of medieval Christian preaching on the Jewish sermon is reflected in the structure of the sermon, a topic I have discussed in my general introduction to *Jewish Preaching 1200–*

---

1 See, for example, *Marc Saperstein*, Jewish Preaching 1200–1800, New Haven (CT) 1989, 177–179, on Jewish responsibility for the Crucifixion, and *Idem*, "Your Voice Like a Ram's Horn". Themes and Texts in Traditional Jewish Preaching, Cincinnati (OH) 1996, chapters 5 and 6, 45–74.

1800.² When we begin to find texts of Jewish sermons written by specific authors – and this does not precede the thirteenth century, although the evidence for Jewish preaching in the preceding centuries is substantial – we find that a very specific form predominates. The preacher begins with a verse from the Hagiographa, most frequently from Proverbs. He gives several different interpretations to the verse. The final interpretation relates it to a verse in the Torah lesson read that week in the synagogue. This generally occurs somewhere around the middle of the sermon. The remainder is devoted to issues related to the *parashah*, often in the form of a homily that discusses several consecutive verses each in turn.

Anyone familiar with the rabbinic literature will immediately recognize this form as characteristic of many passages in the Midrashim on the Torah. It is known as the "proem" or "*petihta*". There, as in our sermons, a tension is created through the selection of a verse that is often apparently far removed from the subject matter of the *parashah*; the preacher's art is revealed in demonstrating an unsuspected unity in these disparate passages from the Hebrew Scripture. There is a scholarly consensus that this *petihta* was derived from the oral sermon. But the *petihta* ends with the verse from the lesson; nothing follows it in the units preserved in the midrashic literature. Scholars have debated whether each *petihta* introduced a full sermon, the bodies of which have been lost, or whether the petihtas, which may take only a minute or two to read, were the full sermons, read before the Torah reading as an introduction to that. The medieval material reveals full sermons with the continuation focused on verses from the Pentateuchal lesson following the citation of the first Torah verse. They suggest an ongoing tradition of preaching from the rabbinic period to the High Middle Ages.

This form continues into the fifteenth century. But by the end of that century, as a result of a process that cannot yet be fully documented, many sermons by Spanish preachers reveal a strikingly different form. The sermon regularly begins with a verse not from the Hagiographa but from the lesson itself. Second, this verse has acquired a technical term, widely used to characterize it, and continuing in this function for many centuries: the *nosé*. This is clearly the Hebrew equivalent of the Latin *thema*, the technical term for the opening biblical verse of the Scholastic thematic sermon.³ Indeed occasionally the word "thema", written in Hebrew letters, is actually used in the Jewish texts.

---

2   See especially pp. 63–75.
3   On the development of this form, cf. *Nicole Bériou*, Les sermons latins après 1200, in: *Beverley Mayne Kienzle* (Ed.), The Sermon, Turnhout 2000, 394–398.

The choice of the *nosé* is determined not by the need to connect it with another biblical verse, but rather by the subject the preacher wants to address. The influence of the Christian thematic sermon seems beyond any question, although the more than two-century lag-time from its use in Christian preaching to its appearance in Jewish texts is somewhat surprising.

Despite this incorporation of a major structural element from contemporary Christian preaching, this classical Sephardic sermon form retains a distinctively Jewish component. Following the *nosé*, the preacher reads a second text, this one from the rabbinic literature, almost always of a non-legal nature, called the *ma'amar* or dictum, which frequently has no obvious connection with the *nosé*. This may be ignored for most of the sermon, but at some strategic point, the preacher will introduce it and connect it with the subject of the sermon, revealing an unsuspected connection. The preacher's challenge now seems no longer to be to demonstrate the unity in different parts of the Bible, but rather the unity of the Bible with the subsequent rabbinic literature.

2. Christian philosophical influences

Other forms of late medieval Jewish preaching seem clearly to be influenced by philosophical modes of argumentation and discourse that most plausibly entered Jewish homiletics by way of Christian models. In order to make this case, we need to review the evidence that Jews were aware of what Christian preachers were doing. In the early middle ages, a Christian writer, Agobard, archbishop of Lyons, reported with shock that simple Christians say the Jews preach better than do their own elders.[4] By the late middle ages, the pattern was reversed: Spanish Jews were said to listen to Christian sermons and come away impressed by the high calibre of the discourse, complaining that Jewish preachers fall short by comparison. Isaac Arama, one of the most gifted homileticians from the generation of the Expulsion, wrote in the introduction to his classic homiletical work about the "profound and articulate speakers" among the Christian neighbours of the Jews. It is a passage worth citing at length:

"In every city, their scholars master all branches of knowledge, their priests and princes stand at the fore in philosophy, integrating it with their theological doctrine. They have written many books, on the basis of which

---

4   Agobard of Lyons, De insolentia iudaeorum, cited in *Jeremy Cohen*, Living Letters of the Law: Ideas of the Jew in Medieval Christianity, Berkeley (CA) 1999, 127.

biblical texts are expounded before large congregations. Each day their preachers give important insights into their religion and faith, thereby sustaining it.

For some time now, calls have gone out far and wide, summoning the people to hear their learned discourses. They have fulfilled their promise. Among those who came were Jews. They heard the preachers and found them impressive; their appetites were whetted for similar fare. This is what they say: 'The Christian scholars and sages raise questions and seek answers in their academies and churches, thereby adding to the glory of the Torah and the prophets, as do the sages of every people. [...] The Gentiles search enthusiastically for religious and ethical content, using all appropriate hermeneutical techniques. But our Torah commentators do not employ this method that everyone admires. Their purpose is only to explain the grammatical forms of words and the simple meaning of the stories and commandments. They have not attempted to fill our need or to exalt the image of our Torah to our own people by regaling them with gems from its narratives and laws.'"[5]

This passage provides striking evidence of cultural competition in the best sense: Jewish awareness of the achievements of philosophically trained Christian theologians in the Spanish universities with a ripple effect felt in the pulpits. According to Arama, Jews have heard Spanish preachers, come away impressed with their sophisticated approach to biblical texts, and demanded a higher level of discourse in their own synagogues. This is obviously a very different dynamic from the common conception of medieval Jews stuffing their ears when forced to attend conversionary sermons. Arama – who himself held at most an extremely moderate philosophical worldview – presents himself as responding to this pressure.

What were these hermeneutical techniques being used in the sermons and applied to theological problems? Hayim Ibn Musa, a mid-fifteenth-century Spanish polemicist, wrote in a letter to his son with considerable dissatisfaction of a "new type of preacher" overly influenced by philosophy: "most of their sermons consists of syllogistic arguments and quotations from the philosophers. They mention by name Aristotle, Alexander, Themistius, Plato, Averroes, and Ptolemy, while Abaye and Rava are concealed in their mouths."[6] By the end of

---

5 *Isaac Arama*, Aqedat Yitshaq, Warsaw 1883, 8a, translation in *Saperstein*, Jewish Preaching 1200–1800, New Haven (CT) 1989, 392f.

6 *Hayyim ibn Musa*, "Letter to His Son," translated in *Saperstein*, Jewish Preaching, 392f. Cf. also the complaint by Joseph ibn Shem Tov, himself much more positively inclined toward philosophical literature, complaining about contemporary preachers who "think they excel at syllogistic proofs, but for the most part they preach about things that neither they nor their listeners understand" (cited in *Saperstein*, "Your Voice Like a Ram's Horn", 78).

the fifteenth century, we have clear evidence of the use of syllogisms as a basic mode of argumentation in Jewish sermons – a technique that clearly did not originate in Jewish traditions. Here, for example, is the beginning of a sermon by the noted Talmudist Isaac Aboab:

> "*You who cleave to the Lord your God live* (Deut. 4:4). This thesis is based upon true premises, which we shall state. The first is, 'Whoever cleaves to God lives'. The second is 'You cleave to God'. The necessary conclusion is, therefore, 'You live'. This is a syllogism of the first form ... Now the major premise I have taken can be established from (empirical) reality, for we see that the closer anything approaches God, the greater the portion of life it attains. [...]"[7]

Although the preacher was one of the greatest Talmudists of the generation of the Expulsion, his analysis of a biblical verse as the product of an Aristotelian syllogism is obviously far removed from the traditional rabbinic *derash*.

A second example is from a sermon by Joel ibn Shu'eib. Shortly after the beginning, he states,

> "We shall explain that intellectual pleasure is more distinguished [than sensual pleasure] by three arguments. The first: The more choice pleasure is that derived from the more choice faculty. But that is the intellect. If so, etc. (QED). The major premise is established because pleasure is dependent upon the activity of the appropriate faculty, as is written in the Eighth Chapter of [Aristotle's] *Ethics*. The minor premise is established because the intellect is superior to all other faculties, for its activity is the apprehension of metaphysical matters, essences abstracted from matter. [...] Therefore, the proper pleasure is the one specific to this faculty."[8]

In both of these examples, the conclusion itself is totally unremarkable; indeed, it is quite commonplace. But the syllogistic form of the argument indicates that this was a mode of thinking that many found convincing, and that could readily be followed in an oral discourse. The premises themselves could be established through an appeal to a philosophical text, or by biblical verses and rabbinic statements. But this is clearly a new manner of preaching; it seems to be a response to the demand, recorded by Isaac Arama, for new tools to approach the Bible, because of the preaching of Christian scholars.[9]

Even more surprising than the syllogisms is the appearance of the "Disputed Question" in fifteenth-century sermons, for this was a mode

---

7   *Isaac Aboab*, Nehar Pishon, Zolkiew 1806, 23a.
8   *Joel ibn Shu'eib*, Olat Shabbat, Venice 1577, 105a–b.
9   One scholar has spoken of "the passion for the syllogism which dominates" the sermons of the thirteenth-century Franciscan preacher Servasanto da Faenzo: *Carlo Delcorno*, Medieval Preaching in Italy (1200–1500), in *Kienzle* (Ed.), The Sermon, 480f.

of argumentation derived not from Aristotelian logic but from medieval Christian scholasticism.[10] One form of this argument can be seen in Hasdai Crescas's sermon, probably for the Sabbath preceding Passover, in which he raises the question "Whether or not the miracle creates faith in the human soul without the concurrence of the will?"[11] Crescas gives four arguments on one side – that the will must always be involved in the attainment of faith – three of which are in the form of a *reductio ad absurdum*. Then he gives four arguments on the other side – that the will is not involved in the process by which a miracle produces faith. This turns out to be the position Crescas accepts, and he goes on to refute the four original arguments that appeared to oppose it.[12] When Crescas incorporated this problem into his philosophical work, *Or ha-Shem*, he eliminated the formal aspect of the Disputed Question by including only the arguments on the side he favored. Apparently he considered the Disputed Question more appropriate for a sermon than for a philosophical work.

A second example comes from the circle of disciples of Crescas, which I translated from a St. Petersburg manuscript in *Your Voice Like a Ram's Horn*. Several pages of this text are devoted to the question, "Is the act performed by means of a vow and acceptance [of it as obligatory] more praiseworthy [...] [than] the very same act done without a vow and acceptance [of its obligatory nature]." Five arguments are brought for the superiority of an act performed freely without the constraint of the vow, then four for the superiority of the act in fulfilment of a vow, then five universally accepted premises, arranged in syllogisms, to prove the superiority of the act fulfilling a vow, and finally the refutation of the first five arguments purporting to sustain the antithesis.[13] We are certainly far closer to the disputations of the medieval universities than to the argumentation of the Tosafists.

Finally, from the end of the century. The manuscript called *Dover Mesharim*, an extremely rich text in the Oxford Christ Church Library

---

10 On philosophy in medieval Christian sermons see *Louis Bataillon*, L'emploi du langage philosophique dans les sermons du treizième siècle, in: *Jan P. Beckmann* (Ed.), Miscellanea mediaevalia, vol. 12/2: Sprache und Erkenntnis im Mittelalter, Berlin 1981. The Hebrew word *derush*, commonly used today to refer to all homiletical literature, was in the Middle Ages a technical term, equivalent to the Latin quaestio.

11 On the formulation of this question compare *Thomas Aquinas*, Summa theologica II-II Question 6, Article 1.

12 See on this work (and other similar texts) *Aviezer Ravitzky*, Derashat ha-Pesaḥ le-R. Hasdai Crescas u-meḥqarim be-Mishnato ha-Pilosofit, Jerusalem 1991.

13 Hebrew text: *Saperstein*, "Your Voice Like a Ram's Horn", 231–238; translation: 200–207.

that has never been properly studied, contains several disputed questions. One is "Whether one who professes a religion is able to investigate whether or not his religion is divine, and if he investigates it and he is not satisfied, whether he is able to change it for another"[14] (54b) – a question argued not infrequently in the fifteenth century, with obvious relevance to the problem of the conversos. The second is whether or not God forgives the penitent; I shall return to this in the next part of my presentation. At this point it is significant to note that before presenting the question itself, the preacher gives an introductory justification of the permissibility of preaching in this mode "in the presence of the Torah, for whoever does so is required in some way to give support for the proposition antithetical to the truth, and this may sometimes cause problems for the masses." What he means, of course, is that some among the listeners may remember the argument for the heretical position that is ultimately rejected and forget the argument for the accepted position. His defence draws on precedents in the Bible, the rabbinic literature, and the work of the philosophers (Maimonides and Gersonides). We have here an artful integration of this alien form with the theme verse and the rabbinic dictum.[15]

3. The problematics of repentance in late medieval sephardic preaching

As the Sabbath of Repentance is one of the preaching occasions mandated by ancient custom, it is not surprising that the theme of repentance is a significant homiletical motif in many collections of Jewish sermons. It is particularly pronounced in sermons from the generation of the Expulsion from Spain. I would like to highlight a problem in this material, warning in advance that I have no definitive solution to it.

There seems to be no question of the importance of the doctrine of repentance, which both Abravanel and Arama describe as "the peg upon which redemption is hung, the cure for all ills and the repair of all

---

14 Israel, "Dover Meisharim", Oxford Christ Church MS 197 (Neubauer 2447), fol. 54b.
15 For the translation of this introductory passage, see *Saperstein*, Jewish Preaching, 395f. Because of the defense of propositions ultimately rejected, the scholastic disputed question was also not at first encouraged in Christian preaching, although it eventually became more fashionable, especially in sermons addressed to the clergy, as "little by little, scholastic thought was introduced more and more massively into sermons": *Bériou*, Les sermons latins après 1200, in: *Kienzle* (Ed.), The Sermon, 403f.

curses."[16] Nevertheless, one is struck by the extent to which it appears to have become deeply problematic. This is not the case for earlier medieval sermons. Here, for example, is the rationalist preacher Jacob Anatoli in a sermon on the lesson *Nitsavim*, comparing the Christian and Jewish modes of repentance:

> "It [repentance] is considerably easier for a Jew than it is for the peoples who imitate the Torah in their laws [that is, the Christians]. Do you not see that they require the penitent to undergo many afflictions, such as travelling beyond the sea or to other distant places. Not so the Torah of Moses, which commands only the confession of the mouth and of the heart (cf. Deut. 30:14)."[17]

The rhetorical thrust of this passage is to undercut the Pauline claim that the Law is an impossible burden leaving no realistic opportunity for justification, and to call upon his listeners not to fail in what is after all an easier task than that imposed upon their neighbours. The efficacy of such repentance does not seem to be in question.

By the middle of the fifteenth century, the issue has changed. Since repentance is understood to be one of the commandments of the Torah, it is certainly understandable for Jewish thinkers to ask whether it falls in Saadia's category of the rational or the traditional commandments. Or whether God's acceptance of repentance is an act of justice or of totally unmerited divine grace. My sense is that the insistence by almost all Jewish thinkers that the efficacy of repentance is *not* rational, *not* justice, leaves them and their listeners in something of a quandary.

Thus, in the second of a recently-published series of sermons on repentance, the courtier-philosopher Joseph ibn Shem Tov insists that the atonement for sins sought from God "is not according to law and justice, but rather total grace from God" (לא כדין וכצדק אבל היה בחסד גמור (מהש"י).[18] He sets out the arguments for this position in various ways, including the claim that according to the standards of justice, for sins against God there "must be punishment for eternity, without any atonement; that is the law without doubt" (192). Rational argument concludes that divine pardon due to repentance cannot be justified by the law and pure speculation, but only by divine grace and mercy (ומזה

---

16 *Isaac Abravanel*, Peirush al ha-Torah, 3 vol., Jerusalem 1964, Deuteronomy 283c. Cf. *Arama*, Aqedat Yitzhaq, end of Sha'ar 100, Deuteronomy, 86c.

17 *Jacob Anatoli*, Malmad ha-Talmidim, Lyck 1866, 174b, in: *Saperstein*, "Your Voice ...", 61. For the theme of repentance in late medieval Christian preaching see *Manuel Ambrosio Sánchez Sánchez*, Vernacular Preaching in Spanish, Portuguese and Catalan, in: *Kienzle* (Ed.), The Sermon, 767–777, 772f., 855, and *Carlo Delcorno*, Medieval Preaching in Italy (1200–1500), in ibid., 451f., 472.

18 *Shaul Regev*, Derashot al ha-Teshuvah le-Rabbi Yosef ibn Shem Tov, in: Asufot 5/1991, 191.

יתבאר בהקש השכלי שהמחילה בעבור התשובה הוא דבר לא תחייבהו הדין והעיון הגמור זולתי החסד והרחמים האלוהיים) (193). A considerable part of the sermon is devoted to presenting the argument against the rationality of repentance.[19]

A generation later, Joseph's son, Shem Tov ibn Shem Tov – like his father (and unlike his grandfather) a believer in the value of philosophy – wrote a book containing eight sermons on repentance. For him, the problem arises in a different way, through well-known rabbinic aggadot, such as the statements that as a result of repentance, willful sins are transformed into merits (b. Yom 86b), and "In the place where the penitent stand, the totally righteous cannot stand" (b. Ber 34b) – statements that he characterizes as "absolutely strange" (בתכלית הזרות). Here is how he continues: "How can it be said that perversion and evil become virtues and merits? This is something difficult to say, all the more so to believe. And how can it be said that the stature of a man who has sinned is higher than one who never sinned throughout his life and who serves God truthfully and faithfully? Human reason cannot tolerate the idea that a woman who has sinned (סרחה) and betrayed, then returns in repentance can sit with the righteous women and be of a higher level than they in holiness and purity? This is not right; it cannot be!"[20] This does not sound like someone who is indulging in an intellectual exercise by making a case that he knows can be easily refuted. To me this sounds like an anguished man wrestling with a real problem.

After reviewing various attempts to answer this quandary by providing a plausible, rational exegesis of these statements,[21] he eventually gives up, throwing the matter back on tradition and faith: "What the sages said, they received from the prophets and the holy spirit. It is their *tradition* that the penitent are on a higher level than the righteous and than the ministering angels. But human intellect is unable to know this mystery ..." The one thing he insists on is that the

---

19 Ibid., 192, 193. This is taken up again in a later sermon: it is only "God's gracious compassion" that provides a way for human beings to return to their "pristine stature" following sin (207). On grace, see also sources in *Saperstein*, "Your Voice ...", 319 n. 104: Nissim, Crescas, Isaac Karo. Joseph ibn Shem Tov's definition of repentance appears to show the influence not of traditional rabbinic literature but of Scholastic discourse: "an act performed by a sinner to return to God to the end that God might pardon him of his sins and replace punishment with merit." Following this definition, he proceeds to explain each element in the definition (196).
20 *Shem Tov ibn Shem Tov*, Derashot, Salonika 1525, 162b.
21 For example, "Some say this is said homiletically, in order to motivate people to repent, but the truth is that level of the righteous is higher [...]" (ibid., 163a). But this approach – that the sages stated things they knew to be false in order to motivate Jews to act properly – is rejected.

righteous who have no need for repentance will not be disenfranchised by the glorified status of the penitent: "There is no doubt that God will reward the righteous according to the fruit of their deeds."[22]

Isaac Arama discusses the aggadic dictum about "the place where the penitent stand" in a manner rather similar to Shem Tov, actually going further in specifying the conflict with philosophical tradition: "Now indeed this view conflicts with what is found in the writings of the Philosopher [Aristotle], in chapters 1 and 12 of the 7th book of the *Ethics* [...] and in chapter 11 of the first book [...] Maimonides, in the 6th chapter of his introduction to Avot mentioned this view [of Aristotle] and supported it with the following verse. [...] He then challenged [Aristotle] with the rabbinic statements. [...] Then he reconciled the two positions. [...]" But Maimonides' reconciliation is not satisfying to Arama, who ends – as does Shem Tov – unable to make peace between the two traditions: דברי תורה לחוד ודברי פילוסופים לחוד.[23] Unlike Shem Tov, Arama uses this conflict to expose the inadequacy of reason and philosophical analysis for him. Yet for many, this discussion would have left the rabbinic statement about repentance as a puzzle and a problem.

Similar problems can be seen in the work of other preachers and commentators from the generation of the Expulsion. Isaac Karo, uncle of the celebrated Joseph, recapitulates the position we have heard from Joseph ibn Shem Tov: "The efficacy of repentance is total grace. Why should it avail a murderer that he makes repentance? The soul of the dead person will not return to its body by means of this repentance! If one profanes the Sabbath, it will not return re-sanctified as a result of repentance! It is certainly nothing but total grace."[24] Isaac Aboab, another of the leading Talmudists of the generation, raises the same issue in strikingly similar terms in one of his sermons. By law, repentance should be of no avail. "For what is the use of repentance made with the mouth for one who has denied God through his deeds? Furthermore, who can annul the reality of things that have already occurred? Who can set right what they have perverted? [...] The sages taught [...] that according to reason and strict justice, the sinner should not be able to achieve atonement through a verbal utterance."

---

22   Ibid., 163b. This confession on the part of someone obviously committed to philosophy of an utter inability to comprehend or make sense of a rabbinic statement which appears to be repugnant to reason, nevertheless reaffirming its validity as an authentic tradition, echoes skeptical formulations of Abraham ibn Ezra.

23   *Arama*, Aqedat Yitshaq, Sha'ar 100, Deuteronomy, 84a.

24   *Isaac Karo*, Toledot Yitzhak, Riva di Trento 1558, Re'eh, 103b.

Finally, we have an extraordinary discussion of repentance from a preacher known only by the title of his manuscript sermon collection, "Dover Mesharim." The discussion is in the form of a *"disputed question"*, one of the most characteristic modes of scholastic argumentation which increasingly finds its way into 15th-century Spanish Jewish discourse. In this form, two *antithetical positions* on a theological question are supported with arguments from reason and authority, before a resolution is reached. Now our preacher realizes that this is a controversial preaching technique, and he begins his sermon by justifying its use in the pulpit. Then he turns to the issue at hand: "Whether God forgives the penitent." Taking his cue from the theme verse of the *parashat Nitsavim*, "The Lord will not be willing to forgive him" (לא יאבה יי סלוח לו), the preacher goes on to bring an argument from "experience": we see in the example of Saul, that "even though he admitted his transgression and said 'I have sinned' several times, his repentance was not accepted."

More provocative is the argument from *reason*:

"Assume that God decrees at the time of the commission of the sin that the evil person shall die, or be given whatever punishment is appropriate. Then if it is true that afterward He decrees that the one who is supposed to die because of his sin will be accepted, and He removes from upon him what has already been decreed, the result is that God changes from wanting something to not wanting it. But whoever thinks this has thought something monstrously heretical, attributing a significant defect to God's stature."

The preacher continues his case for the irrationality of repentance with a straightforward philosophical argument: change entails movement, movement can occur only in time, if God changes, He must be subject to time, but that is false, as God created time. In conclusion, "the assumption that God accepts the penitent entails the conclusion that God changes, and this is total heresy. Therefore, we must necessarily conclude that God does not pardon and does not accept the penitent." Of course the preacher does not leave it at this; he proceeds to argue the other side, and then to resolve the conflict. But why does he make such a strong argument against the efficacy of repentance to begin with?

Virtually alone, Abraham Saba insists the opposite: that the efficacy of repentance is totally rational. It seems as if he is arguing explicitly against the position we have seen: "What you say – that once a person has sinned and transgressed there is no remedy for it – that is a lie. […] That was the position in which Adam erred […]; he had doubt about repentance, thinking that having sinned against God, there was no remedy […] but Cain did repentance" (and Adam learned of its efficacy from Cain). And in another comment, "Therefore this passage [from

Nitsavim] comes to remove this error from the hearts of people who think that repentance cannot benefit one who has sinned against God. […] 'It is not distant' from reason, for reason requires that if one admits his sins, feels sorrow for them, and never repeats them, God will accept his repentance."[25] His very insistence on this matter indicates his recognition of a troubling problem.

Similarly, the author of "Dover Mesharim" produces his own argument from reason for the rationality of repentance (as well as arguments from the Scriptural lesson and biblical and Talmudic models that illustrate its efficacy). God brings souls into this world for their own benefit, no one is free from sin, were it not for the efficacy of repentance all souls would be doomed to destruction, so that God would have created them for this end. But, echoing the conclusion of his first part, "Whoever thinks this way has attributed to God an abomination, a significant defect to God's stature." In this argument – which parallels classical Christian theological arguments for the necessity of the Incarnation and Passion – not only the possibility but the necessity of efficacious repentance is rationally demonstrated. The preacher then proceeds, in accordance with the requirements of his form, to rebut the original argument from reason. Change due to new knowledge applies to human beings who do not know the future, but God knows who will repent and who will not repent, and His knowledge therefore does not change when repentance occurs. "Yet despite this knowledge [of the future], the power of contingency [the possible] remains, as we have already explained in our previous sermon that while all is foreseen by God, free choice is given".[26] It appears, then, that this preacher ends by sustaining the minority position that the efficacy of repentance does not violate the standards of reason. But the long road he has taken to arrive at this conclusion suggests a measure of ambivalence.

What are we to make of this problematizing of repentance in the sermons and commentaries from the generation of the expulsion? What does it mean, as a cultural statement, to insist that the efficacy of repentance is irrational, in conflict with reason and justice? I have no conclusive answer, but I will suggest some possibilities. One caveat is to note that the valence of such statements may vary, as we have seen in the similar passages of Arama and Shem Tov which nevertheless point,

---

25 Abraham Saba, Tseror ha-Mor: Perush al ha-Torah, Venice 1567, reprint edition Tel Aviv 1975, Deuteronomy 27b, 27c; also 28a; cf. *Abraham Gross*, Iberian Jewry from Twilight to Dawn, Leiden 1995, 121 n. 96, 159.

26 Israel, "Dover Meisharim", fols. 175r–182v, partially translated in *Saperstein*, Jewish Preaching, 395–398.

I believe, in different directions. Each passage must be studied carefully, in context, with attention paid to the nuances of formulation and tone before definitive conclusions can be drawn.

It is possible – though I personally do not believe it to be so – that the material I have cited might serve as evidence for what Yizhak Baer and others, based on some contemporary sources, viewed as the corrosive effects of philosophical study on the foundations of Jewish belief. In this view, as philosophical analysis penetrates here into pulpit discourse that insists on using it as a touchstone, it thereby undermines the simple faith in one of Judaism's core values.[27]

Another possibility is that these passages reveal the power not of philosophy but of the Christian theology of grace. Some of these passages do, indeed, recall the classical Christian teachings denigrating the centrality of works as a means to salvation, insisting that sins against God cannot be atoned by finite human efforts, and promising to the sinner God's favour as an expression of totally unmerited love. Thus one influential fifteenth-century Christian preacher wrote that even with 1000 mortal sins, if the person only thinks contrition and mercy, God will pardon him and he will not go to hell. God's *greatest* wonder is *incarnation*, but the second – the preacher maintains – greater even than creation of the world, is the *conversion of the sinner*.[28] If Christian theology could promise its sinners divine favour *beyond* what reason and justice could validate or explain, should Jewish teaching promise less?

A third context in which to evaluate this material is that of the *conversos*. Most discussions of repentance in this period have focused on this theme, analyzing the positions of Abravanel, Arama, and others on the relevance of repentance for those living as Christians.[29] Does the

---

27 I am not convinced that such an interpretation is valid. The scholars I have cited were not at all of the same ilk as the radical preachers condemned in the Rashba's herem of 1305 (on which see *Saperstein*, Jewish Preaching, 380–383). Isaac Aboab and Isaac Karo were distinguished Talmudists whose absolute commitment to Judaism is beyond any question. Shem Tov ibn Shem Tov, while a strong defender of Maimonidean philosophy, was not as far as we know attacked for heretical philosophical doctrine in his sermons. The work of such preachers shows rather that rabbinic leaders of the generation incorporated philosophy and rational categories into their sermons and commentaries without viewing it as a threat. For a fuller argument about the Jewish "Averroists" see *Marc Saperstein*, The Social and Cultural Context: Thirteenth to Fifteenth Centuries, in: *Daniel H. Frank/Oliver Leaman* (Eds.), History of Jewish Philosophy, London/New York 1997, 310–313.

28 See the German Franciscan Johannes von Werden, Dormi Secure: Models of Holiness, 308.

29 *Benzion Netanyahu*, The Marranos of Spain, New York 1966, chap. 4 on "Homiletical and Exegetic Literature." Abravanel introduces this category explicitly into his

problem lurk in the background even of our material? Is the emphasis on the irrationality of repentance a way of appealing to the *conversos* – perhaps through their familiarity with the Christian doctrine – by saying that even though it makes no apparent sense, God will accept your return? Or a way of addressing the Jews who may have been thinking, "It's not *fair* that we have continued to sacrifice to live as Jews, while *they* can be on the same level, indeed even a *higher* level, simply by a deathbed repentance."

Finally, we should realize that repentance was not the only aspect of Judaism that was being problematized in this period. Virtually *everything* about the Bible and the aggadic literature was. Abravanel and Arama are well known for their exegetical technique of raising a series of "doubts" or intellectual problems with every passage they discuss and then resolving them. What is not as well known, as I have shown in a different study, is that this technique was *omnipresent* in that generation, appearing in all of the writers and preachers I have cited, and many more, in contexts that have nothing to do with repentance.[30] Apparently it was considered intellectually and aesthetically *de rigeur* to problematize the tradition in this way, so long as one could provide resolutions – despite the danger that the listeners or readers might remember the doubts and forget the resolutions. In this sense as well, the discussions of repentance would be part of a larger cultural trend.

Whatever may serve best to illuminate this puzzlement over repentance, I do not want to suggest that the discourse was limited to the *theory* of repentance and overlooked, completely, its practical manifestations. I continue, therefore, with another brief passage from the philosopher Shem Tov ibn Shem Tov, which invokes repentance not as intellectual problem but as moral challenge. It is a sermon for Yom Kippur, and the preacher makes use of the Haftarah from Jonah. After discussing some conceptual and exegetical matters, he makes the application to his listeners: "And now you, O congregation of Israel,

---

discussions of repentance, speaking, for example, of "the victims of duress who have left the category of religion. Regarding these it is said, 'You shall take it to heart' (Deut. 30:1), for their repentance will be in the heart, not in the mouth, for they will not be able to proclaim their repentance and their faith publicly" (*Abravanel*, Perush al ha-Torah, Deuteronomy 283a).

30 *Marc Saperstein*, The Method of Doubts: Problematizing the Bible in Late Medieval Jewish Exegesis, in: *Jane Dammen McAuliffe/Barry D. Walfish/Joseph W. Goering* (Eds.), With Reverence for the Word: Medieval Scriptural Exegesis in Judaism, Christianity, and Islam, New York 2003, 133–156. Recall what Arama said in the introduction to his homiletical work: "The Christian scholars and sages raise questions and seek answers in their academies and churches, thereby adding to the glory of the Torah and the Prophets," referring to the scholastic method of raising dubitationes, which became the Hebrew technical term *sefeqot*.

hear in how many ways the repentance of the nations is different from the repentance of Israel!" As expected in the tradition of the *tokhehah*, the Jews come off second best.[31] Unlike the Ninevites, the Jews failed to repent despite many prophets, they insisted that their prophets bring signs of authenticity and that their prophets explicitly invoke God's name.

The punch comes in the final contrast, no longer in the Biblical past but in the present: "Fourth, Israel repents only by fasting, and weeping, and affliction, but not by deeds. [...] No Jew has ever repented by returning that which he has stolen. But the nations, before anything else, made repentance and returned what they had stolen [*not* in Jonah]. No, *even on this sacred fast*, every Jew seeks out a place where he will be honored. In this way, our atonement needs atonement, and this Day of Atonement needs something that will atone for the sins and the transgressions that are performed on it!"[32] No matter how problematic the theory of repentance may have become, it could still serve to inspire a primary function of the preacher – in the words of Isaiah: והגד לעמי פשעם – "to tell my people its sin" (Isa. 58.1).

I conclude with one of my favourite passages, not from an actual sermon but from an ethical work written in the wake of the anti-Jewish riots of 1391, in which the author identifies those aspects of Jewish behaviour provoking the divine wrath manifest in the riots. One might imagine that a Jewish writer who lived through these events would express a bitterly negative view of Christian society. But here is what Solomon Alami wrote:

> "Look what happens when a congregation gathers to hear words of Torah from a rabbinical scholar. Slumber weighs upon the eyes of the officers; others converse about trivial affairs. The preacher is dumbfounded by the talking of men and the chattering of women standing behind the synagogue. If he should reproach them because of their behaviour, they continue to sin, behaving corruptly, abominably.
> This is the opposite of the Christians. When their men and women gather to hear a preacher, they stand together in absolute silence, marvelling at his rebuke. Not one of them dozes as he pours out his words upon them. They await him as they do the rain, eager for the waters of his counsel. We have not learned properly from those around us."[33]

This, of course, uses the same rhetorical trope we have seen in the concluding citation from Shem Tov ibn Shem Tov: shaming one's own

---

31 See on this rhetorical mode *Marc Saperstein*, Jews and Christians: Some Positive Images, in: *Idem*, "Your Voice ...", 45–54.
32 Shem Tov ibn Shem Tov, Derashot, 179a.
33 *Solomon Alami*, Iggeret Musar, 27, in: *Saperstein*, Jewish Preaching, 383f.

community by identifying areas in which they fall short of their neighbors, pointing to the Other in a manner that transcends conflict and resentment and recognizes aspects of behaviour that are worthy of emulation. Needless to say, Christian moralists and preachers complained about the behaviour of their own congregations while the sermon was being delivered,[34] and they sometimes identified aspects of Jewish behaviour that Christians should take to heart.[35] At moments like these, we see something different from the conflict model that predominates in so much of our discourse about the past, and sense something that might be identified as a model, if not of mutual admiration, then perhaps of creative competition.

---

34   See the examples given in *Delcorno*, Medieval Preaching in Italy, 468f.
35   For examples see *Saperstein*, Jews and Christians.

Response

Richard S. Sarason

Prof. Saperstein has noted the aesthetic and formal impact of the Christian scholastic thematic sermon on Spanish Jewish preachers beginning in the late fifteenth century. He also wonders why it took approximately two centuries for this influence to be felt. Clearly something in the larger cultural interaction between Spanish Jews and Christians during this period is impacting in this sphere (and likely in other spheres as well). The question is whether our extant data permit a sufficiently thick cultural description to properly contextualize and account for this fact. Also noteworthy in Prof. Saperstein's account is the observation that, notwithstanding the formal influence from Christian sermons, Spanish preaching during this period also retains a characteristically Jewish formal element: the homiletical integration of biblical with rabbinic texts, already present in late Byzantine Jewish homiletical literature (the Tanhuma-Yelamdenu genre). The point here is that the Christian formal influence has been *integrated* into a Jewish rhetorical context.

Prof. Saperstein's fascinating presentation of the treatment of repentance in Jewish sermons of the mid-fifteenth century admirably offers a number of possible contexts through which to evaluate this phenomenon. Since I am not a medievalist, I cannot responsibly weigh in here, except to note that the three hermeneutical lenses that seem most reasonable to him appear so to me as well, and that I deem as exemplary the manner in which he approaches the issue.

Another fruitful observation of Prof. Saperstein's is that, at various points during the Middle Ages, *both* Jews and Christians complained that their own preachers fell short by comparison with those "on the other side of the street." But he also directs our attention to the *rhetorical* context of these comparisons: the Jewish instance, at least, takes place in a penitential context, where the *darshan*'s goal was to shame his congregation into repentance by pointing out that even the despised Christians in this instance behave better than the Jews who otherwise view themselves as superior!

The ultimate point is that cultural interaction extends in both directions, even though in any particular time and place it may be more one-sided. Prof. Saperstein rightly notes that "this is obviously a very different dynamic from the common conception of medieval Jews stuffing their ears when forced to attend conversionary sermons." The actual dynamic was clearly more nuanced and complicated, as he has sought to demonstrate here – and likely spurred more vibrant homiletical activity in both communities.[1]

---

1   A parenthetical observation out of my own field of expertise, classical rabbinic literature: Prof. Saperstein points out that the earliest form of individually authored Jewish sermons, which do not precede the thirteenth century, clearly is patterned on that of classical homiletical *midrashim*. Whether this represents "an ongoing [living, oral] tradition of preaching from the rabbinic period to the High Middle Ages," as he suggests, or the conscious appropriation at some point (either in the thirteenth century or earlier) of an inherited *literary* tradition, known primarily through texts, cannot be determined. On the *petiḥta*-form (*not* a "proem"), see my articles, Toward a New Agendum for the Study of Rabbinic Midrashic Literature, in: *Jakob J. Petuchowski/Ezra Fleischer* (Eds.), Studies in Aggadah, Targum and Jewish Liturgy in Memory of Joseph Heinemann, Jerusalem 1981, English section, 55–73, and The Petihtot in Leviticus Rabba. "Oral Homilies" or Redactional Constructions?, in: JJS 33/1982, 557–568, and the literature cited there. The fact that the intertextual technique characteristic of the *petiḥta* is also to be found in contemporary liturgical hymns, such as those of Yannai and Shimon bar Megas, that clearly were composed for and performed in the synagogue, suggests a synagogal context for *petiḥtot* in some form.

Jewish Confirmation Sermons in 19th-Century Germany

Klaus Herrmann

1. The beginnings of Jewish confirmation ceremonies

I would like to begin my paper with an excerpt by Leopold Zunz (1794–1886), the famous founder of the scientific study of Judaism, *Wissenschaft des Judentums*, and the first Jewish "confirmand",[1] who described his time as a schoolboy in Wolfenbüttel from 1803 to 1807 as follows:

> "On Sunday noon, the 5th of June in the year 1803 I arrived with my uncle in the [school] courtyard [...]. The study of the Talmud now began straightaway from the very next day on [...]. There were no school rules, no protocol, to a certain extent no pedagogy. Friday afternoons we sorted beans and peas; in our games and rough-and-tumble we were left on our own [...]. I think Inspector Ehrenberg turned up at the end of 1806 or in January 1807 [...]. In one day we literally moved over from a medieval age into a modern one, at the same time stepping out of Jewish helotism into bourgeois freedom. Just think vividly of all that I had been deprived of until then: parents, love, instruction, and educational materials [...]. The first confirmation that Inspector Ehrenberg performed was my own, Sabbath 22 August 1807."[2]

Zunz's vivid description of an old-style traditional Jewish *shul* at the beginning of the 19th century, marked by ignorance of modern teaching methods and the needs of a young boy while putting much stock on gardening and working in the teacher's household, ends with the

---

1 According to some sources confirmation ceremonies were already being performed in the Freischule in Dessau as early as 1803; but reliable testimony has yet to be uncovered; cf. Mordechai Eliav, Jüdische Erziehung in Deutschland im Zeitalter der Aufklärung und der Emanzipation, Erstausgabe Jerusalem 1960, für die deutschsprachige Ausgabe vom Autor überarbeitet und ergänzt, aus dem Hebräischen von Maike Strobel, Münster et al. 2001 (Chap. 10: „Die Konfirmation", 330–347), here: 340 n. 48.
2 Quoted according to Jahrbuch für jüdische Geschichte und Literatur, Berlin 1937, 131–172: „Zum Andenken an Leopold Zunz gestorben 17. März 1886"; quotation: 131f. and 138 (first published by Zunz in 1843).

confirmation ceremony which neatly symbolizes Zunz's own abrupt entrance into a new age, the Age of Enlightenment. For his training in modern secular subjects with modern pedagogical goals Zunz was indebted to his teacher Samuel Meyer Ehrenberg until the latter's death in 1853. Zunz's experiences are reflected in the many Jewish confirmation sermons that became so fashionable in Judaism, first in the so-called *Freischulen* and later on in the synagogues themselves. In these sermons the traditional Bar Mitzvah is especially criticised as a ceremony which forced young boys to read a portion of the Torah lacking any relevance to their own life experiences and incomprehensible in its Hebrew wording. By listening to these sermons, the young boys were supposed to feel grateful for no longer living in the Middle Ages and thus for being able to participate in the new age of Enlightenment and to reap its fruit. I would like to start with a quotation from a sermon by Israel Jacobson, the founder of the Reform temple in Seesen and the initiator of the modern Jewish Reform service. I will come back to the temple in Seesen later on. In 1812 on the occasion of a conformation service in Seesen he pointed out:

> „Denn so lautet der Zuruf des heiligen Propheten Jesaja: ‚Und betet Ihr noch so viel, so höre ich nicht, denn eure Hände (eure Werke) sind nicht schuldlos!'.[3] Verachtungswert muß euch besonders jeder seyn, der zu gottesdienstlichen Verrichtungen, zwar in Gemeinschaft mit seinen Brüdern im Tempel erscheint, jedoch seine und die allgemeine Andacht durch Plaudereien oder wohl gar durch Zank und Streit unterbricht. O meine Kinder, lasset euch nie hinreißen, dieser in unserer Synagogen leider oft anzutreffenden Sitte, nachzuahmen."[4]

Jacobson's plea to the children is a good example of a confirmation sermon in the early phase of the Reform movement. According to its message the old synagogue service had to be replaced by a new one embodying both true devotion and edification. In the introduction to the sermon he delivered on the occasion of a confirmation ritual in the "Synagogue of Battenfeld" (located in Hesse [Hessen]) in 1817, Elias Birkenstein praised the newly introduced profession of faith (*Glaubensbekenntnis*) while lamenting its lack in the old synagogue service. Instead the boys in the old service had had to bleat like sheep in Hebrew, often without understanding a word of what they were reciting:

---

3   Isa. 1.15.
4   Rede des Präsidenten (Israel) Jacobson bei der von ihm Sabbaths den 8. Nissan 5572 in der hiesigen Synagoge verrichteten Konfirmation. Nebst Religions-Bekenntnis der Konfirmanden, Kassel 1812, 10.

„Es war mir schon längst sehr anstößig, der Gebrauch wurde schon längst von jeglichem hell denkenden Israeliten getadelt, daß unsere Kinder statt der Confirmation kein Bekenntniß von irgend einer Glaubens- und Pflichtenlehre ablegen, sondern nur den Sabbath-Text und zwar in der hebräischen Sprache so daher blöken [this means that they bleated like sheep in Hebrew], ohne oft nur ein einziges Wort von dem zu verstehen, welches sie bey dieser Gelegenheit mit der grössesten Genauigkeit vortragen müssen."[5]

A similar impression was conveyed to the young boys and girls (I'll come back to the girls later on) in the Reform congregation in Hamburg when Eduard Kley (*Israelitischer Tempel zu Hamburg*, 1819) reflected on his own Bar Mitzvah:

„Aber wie dunkel, wie freudlos liegt jener Tag hinter uns, ein leeres Schattenbild; ohne Geist, ohne Leben und ohne Wärme schwebt die Feyer vor unserer Seele, wie sie uns zu Theil geworden; und was wir in schwacher Erinnerung noch von ihr erblicken, erfüllt uns mit traurigen Gefühlen."[6]

By the way: Kley uses in his sermon the term "*Verächter des göttlichen Wortes*" (despiser of the divine word) – a clear reference to the great Protestant theologian Friedrich Schleiermacher whose deep influence on some Reform rabbis was demonstrated by Alexander Altmann in his article "*Zur Frühgeschichte der jüdischen Predigt in Deutschland*".[7] It is known that Schleiermacher visited the Jewish Reform Temple in Berlin before it was closed down by the Prussian king in 1823.

As mentioned before, the Jewish confirmation ceremony had its origins in the so-called Jewish *Freischule*, which over time replaced the traditional Jewish *shul* by implementing modern teaching concepts espoused by the surrounding German-Christian society. Soon the Jewish confirmation became an integral part of the modernised Jewish synagogue service itself and in the course of time was also adopted in some traditional or even orthodox synagogues.

---

5   *Elias Birkenstein*, Rede bey der Confirmation eines jungen Israeliten, welcher in der Synagoge zu Battenfeld den 8ten November 1817 sein Glaubensbekenntnis öffentlich abgelegt hat, Frankfurt/Leipzig s. a., 3.
6   *Eduard Kley*, Predigten in dem neuen Israelitischen Tempel zu Hamburg, Hamburg 1819, 128–149: „Neunte Predigt. Zur Confirmation der Knaben", here: 129.
7   Zur Frühgeschichte der jüdischen Predigt in Deutschland. Leopold Zunz als Prediger, YLBI 6/1961, 3–59.

2. The confirmation ceremony within the Synagogue service

If there is anything like a birth date for this modern Jewish Reform service, then it is the 17th of July 1810, for this day witnessed the ceremonial dedication of the first Reform "temple" in the small town of Seesen in the Harz Mountains region of Central Germany. Dubbed "Jacobson's Temple" after its founder, Israel Jacobson (1768–1828), it was to assume a model character for the whole subsequent movement. What may strike us at first is the proximity of the 17th to the 14th of July, the day commemorated for the storming of the Bastille. And indeed the dedication ceremony of the Seesen temple bore the imprint of the ideals of the Enlightenment and the political changes that had occurred in the wake of the French Revolution. We are well informed about the day's course of events: a detailed report is found in the periodical *Sulamith*, one of the most important publications of the *Haskalah*, the Jewish Enlightenment.[8] In this report special attention is paid to the pealing of bells, the organ music, the singing of chorales – this report of the dedication ceremony immediately indicates how much the program of Jacobson's Temple was conceived with a (self-)conscious sidelong glance at the culture of its Christian surroundings, with respect not only to the interior decor, but also to the external appearance of the temple, which was destroyed in the Nazi period.

Even though the reform in Seesen was catalysed by the events of the French Revolution, nevertheless the influence of the Protestant cultural surroundings is unmistakably evident in the shaping of the worship service.[9] Here the Reformation served in this respect as a model for having marked a break with tradition and convention; rationalism and universalism in the Protestantism of the Enlightenment Era could be adapted without any problem. And as we will soon see, the Protestant confirmation ceremony of that time neatly fitted this

---

8   Quoted from *Sulamith*. Eine Zeitschrift zur Beförderung der Kultur und Humanität unter den Israeliten [A Periodical for the Promotion of Culture and Humanity among the Israelites], *David Fränkel*, Consistorial Councilor and School Principal, 3rd year, vol. 1, Kassel 1810, 298ff., here: 298–301. For more details of the whole ceremony see the standard work on the Reform movement by *Michael A. Meyer*, Response to Modernity. A History of the Reform Movement in Judaism, New York 1988, 56ff., and *Klaus Herrmann*, Von *Die Deutsche Synagoge* (1817) bis zum *Einheitsgebetbuch* (1929). Liberale Jüdische Gebetbücher in Deutschland vor der Shoa, in: Walter Homolka (Ed.), Liturgie als Theologie. Das Gebet als Zentrum im jüdischen Denken, Berlin 2005, 63–98.

9   On preaching in the Jewish Reform movement see *Alexander Deeg*, Predigt und Derascha. Homiletische Textlektüre im Dialog mit dem Judentum, Göttingen 2006, 121–161.

modernised Jewish service, addressed as it was, according to Jacobson, especially to young people.

From the very beginning, the Jewish confirmation contained the same features as the Protestant version did; Zunz described this ceremony as follows:

> "A hymn, prayer and speech by the teacher, the examination, the teacher's address and exhortation to the boy, the confirmand's profession of faith and prayer, the giving of the blessing, a prayer, the final hymn."[10]

For the religious training of the young generation dozens of catechisms and *Religionslehrbücher* (religious educational textbooks) were published in the 19th century, most of which were meant for the preparatory classes which started at least several months before the confirmation ritual. Like the Protestant confirmation, the examination of the candidate was a central feature of the ceremony. And as in the Protestant ceremony, the main part of this examination consisted of a series of questions and responses. The confirmation itself became the bearer of the ideals of the Jewish Reform movement. Thus already in the first years after the introduction of this ritual we find sermons devoted to the whole spectrum of enlightenment-worldview themes such as pleas for humanism, tolerance, brotherly love [*Nächstenliebe*]. Young boys were encouraged to envision a better future that would be free of the old hatred against Jews. This hope was taken up in the sermons again and again over the next decades. I want to give you only one example from a confirmation service which took place in Berlin in 1871, the year when – at least on paper – equal rights were guaranteed to all Jews in the newly founded German *Kaiserreich* (the German Empire).

> „Übertraget Eure Liebe auf alle Menschen und wenn sie Euerer bedürfen, so fraget nicht erst, in welcher Kirche sie zu ihrem Gotte beten. Das sind die Christen nicht mehr, die uns wie Feinde hassen und verfolgen, wie dies einst in den schwarzen und bangen Jahrhunderten längst vergangener Zeiten ihre Väter an unseren Vätern gethan. Diese Christen unserer Tage sind unsere Brüder und Freunde [the last sentence is emphasized in the original text]!"[11]

We should bear in mind that this sermon and its hope for an enlightened partnership between Jews and Christians was delivered only a few years before the vitriolic anti-Semitic attacks by the Berlin history professor Heinrich von Treitschke (1834–1896) – in the so-called

---

10 Zunz, Antworten auf Kultusfragen, in: Gesammelte Schriften, vol. 2, 214.
11 J. Landsberger, *'ad qarnot ha-mizbeah*. An die Hörner des Altars. Confirmationsrede gehalten am 28. Mai 1871 in der neuen Synagoge der Kaiserstraße zu Berlin, Berlin 1871, 13f.

Berliner *Antisemitismusstreit* – and Adolf Stöcker (1835–1909), a staunch anti-Semite and believer in *"Verjudung,"* the idea that German culture was being corrupted by the newly emancipated Jews.

The fact that the Jewish confirmation was modelled on the Protestant ritual does not mean that the Jewish confirmation entirely dispensed with the Hebrew language. In Seesen the benediction formula (*"Einsegnungsworte"*) was spoken in Hebrew.[12] Some bilingual sermons show a Jewish society in transition in the early phase. Thus the confirmation sermon itself became something of a battlefield over the question of the extent to which the Hebrew language should be used in the modernised Jewish service. This question was one of the most important issues of the so-called Rabbinical Assemblies that took place in the 1840s in Brunswick (Braunschweig), Frankfurt-on-Main and Breslau (today: Wrocław in Poland). The overall impression is that Hebrew became less and less important in the confirmation ritual, but sometimes the opposite trend can be found as well. Thus Hebrew was added to the German translations of biblical passages in textbooks designed to prepare Jewish children for the confirmation ritual in order to give them an idea of the original Hebrew texts.

From the very outset the Jewish confirmation ritual was attacked by the Orthodox camp, even though some Orthodox rabbis introduced the ceremony in the synagogue life of their own communities as well. The best known ones are Rabbi Sabel Egers (1769–1842), who performed the first confirmation ritual in Brunswick in 1831, and Rabbi Samson Wolf Rosenfeld (1783–1862) in Bamberg in 1833: fully committed to the Jewish law but also willing to modernise the Jewish school system and service, he introduced the confirmation for boys at the age of 13 and for girls at the age of 12; however, as we will see later on, it was precisely the confirmation for girls which was criticised by the Orthodox camp.[13] Of course, the main argument against the Jewish confirmation was its Protestant origin, an origin even more obvious when we remind ourselves of the songs chosen for the ritual. In the early phase of the Reform movement Protestant hymns embellished the service. When the temple in Seesen was inaugurated, composers like Louis Lewandowski or Salomon Sulzer who so deeply influenced synagogal music in the second half of the 19th century either had yet to be born or, as in the case of Sulzer, were still small children. Thus expressly Protestant hymns were quite common in Reform synagogues and in the Kingdom

---

12 Cf. Rede des Präsidenten (Israel) Jacobson bei der von ihm Sabbaths den 8. Nissan 5572 in der hiesigen Synagoge verrichteten Konfirmation. Nebst Religions-Bekenntnis der Konfirmanden, Kassel 1812, 38f.

13 Cf. A. Eckstein, Die israelitische Kultusgemeinde Bamberg, 75.

of Wuerttemberg Rabbi Joseph von Maier – his official title was *Oberkirchenrath* [High Consistorial Councillor] – tried to base the Jewish songbook on the *Evangelisches Würtembergisches Gesangbuch*, first published in 1791. Naturally, all texts with the slightest reference to Jesus or other Christian themes were omitted or replaced by a new wording often based on the psalms.

I would like to give you an example from a confirmation ceremony which took place in 1843 in Heddernheim, located close to Frankfurt-on-Main (now a suburb of Frankfurt). The credo of the Christian tradition was of course replaced in the Jewish confirmation ceremony by the 13 *Iqqarim* of Maimonides. A poetical form of the 13 *Iqqarim* (principles of faith) is included in the Siddur known as *Yigdal*. In 1843 the sound of the confirmation ritual was a bit different. Thus the Hebrew wording of the *Yigdal* was enhanced by the melody of a now very familiar Christmas carol: "*O du fröhliche, o du selige, gnadenbringende Weihnachtszeit.*"[14] By the way, its composer, Johannes Daniel Falk (1768–1826) originally wrote it as a so-called *"Dreifeiertagslied"* [The Three Holidays Song] dedicated to Christmas, Easter and Pentecost. (Its melody is actually of Sicilian origin.) Therefore I would be inclined to argue – the proof has yet to be provided, however – that this was a favourite song in the Christian confirmation service in and around Heddernheim at that time.

In order to understand the emergence of the Jewish confirmation in the 19th century it is necessary to recall the changes that the Protestant rite had undergone in the 18th and 19th centuries. To put it in a few words, it can be said that the Protestant confirmation of the Age of Enlightenment did not have much to do with the cause originally championed by Protestant Reformation figures, first and foremost the Strassbourg Reformer Bucer (who incidentally happened to be outspokenly hostile to Jews): for those early Reformers the confirmation was supposed to secure for Christian youngsters, girls and boys, the God-given grace they had received through baptism and to incorporate them into the communion-supper community with the obligation to submit themselves to the ecclesiastical order of the community. The acting subject is hence the community itself.

---

14 The whole ceremony of this Jewish confirmation service was published in: *I. Löwenstein*, Jom ha-Bikkurim. Eine vollständige israelitische Confirmationshandlung am Schebuoth-Feste, Frankfurt/M. 1843 (appendix). Cf. also *Wolfgang Se'ev Zink*, Synagogenordnungen in Hessen 1815–1848. Formen, Probleme und Ergebnisse des Wandels synagogaler G'ttesdienstgestaltung und ihrer Institutionen im frühen 19. Jahrhundert. Originale Archivdokumente hessischer Staaten und preußisch-rheinländischer Enklaven mit Einbeziehung des Königreiches Württemberg, Aachen 1998, 659ff.

In 17th-century Pietism, however, the girls and boys to be confirmed step onto the centre-stage of the event with their personal profession of faith. It was precisely this declaration of faith that proved to be a particularly controversial issue in the debate about the Jewish confirmation. This can best be illustrated by comparing the synagogal rules [*Synagogenordnung*] of the Kingdom of Wuerttemberg with those of Mecklenburg-Schwerin. The synagogal rules drawn up by the aforementioned *Oberkirchenrath* Joseph von Maier in 1838 also included of course a paragraph on the Jewish confirmation in which Maier actually affirmed all of the determinative elements of the Protestant confirmation only to stress, however, that the profession of faith did not belong in the synagogue.

Samuel Holdheim adopted these synagogal rules for Mecklenburg-Schwerin in 1843. Even if he himself had wished for much more radical reforms for the restructuring tasks he envisioned, nevertheless, according to his own testimony he accepted this synagogal rule-book in the hope of achievng a more unified course in the Jewish Reform movement (and, indeed, Maier's synagogal rules were positively received in the Rabbinical Assemblies, too). But Holdheim's readiness to compromise had its limits: the Jewish confirmation. Here Holdheim attached the greatest importance to positioning the confirmand's declaration of faith in the centre of the ceremony precisely according to the pietistic understanding of the Protestant confirmation.

3. The Protestant background of the Jewish confirmation ceremony

Let's go back now to the Protestant confirmation of the 18th and 19th centuries. The Age of Enlightenment brought with it a rationalist understanding of the confirmation, according to which pupils were supposed to be instructed about how to lead a virtuous life. The confirmands (whether boys or girls) explained in front of the community that they had gained a clear understanding of how to make the right decisions in all of life's situations and solemnly vowed to orient their lives according to the divine commandments.

At this point it is important to stress that Christian Enlightenment theologians accorded Judaism and its faithfulness to the commandments a positive appraisal in their sermons. Transferred to the Protestant confirmation, this means that the ritual became a *"Tugendweihe"* or ceremony of consecration to virtue and was expressly designated as such. Thus the boy or girl to be confirmed had to go up to the altar and say: "I raise my hand and swear that I will be faithful to virtue for the honor of Jesus Christ and be religious." [„*Ich erhebe die Hand und schwöre, ich will bei Jesu Christi Ehre der Tugend treu und gläubig sein.*"] I suspect that I may now disappoint my readers, for a good section of the 19th-century Jewish confirmation sermon is nothing other than such a Jewish *"Tugendweihe"* or consecration to virtue, i.e. [in other words] the sermons assume a quite moralising tone to our ears. I would like to limit the examples to the following ones:

In 1820 Gotthold Salomon, who was one of the preachers at the Reform temple in Hamburg, summarised the Jewish religion as follows:

> „Gott, Tugend, Religion, Menschengröße und Menschenwürde, Tod und Unsterblichkeit – dieses Siebengestirn müsst ihr immer vor Augen haben, und ihr werdet das Leben verstehen, werdet seinen wahren Werth fassen und ihn an euch bewähren."[15]

In most of the sermons at that time the influence of the Enlightenment is obvious. Some of the sermons remind us more of an introduction to Kant's *"Praktische Vernunft"* (Practical Reason) rather than of an introduction to the Jewish faith. Or to put it in other words: the Jewish religion is equated with the ideal of the Age of Enlightenment. A good example for this tendency we can find among the most radical reformers in the 19th century like Samuel Holdheim. I quote from a confirmation sermon which he delivered to the Reform congregation in Berlin in 1852:

> „Religion ist ohne Tugend nicht denkbar […]. Wir vermögen nicht auf dem Boden des Judenthums, Religion und Tugend von einander zu trennen und zu scheiden […]. Tugend ist die schönste Frucht unseres Lebens, Religion aber ist diese Frucht und der Duft ihrer Blüthe zugleich.[16]

In other sermons we can clearly recognise Goethe's *"Edel sei der Mensch, hilfreich und gut"*: "Noble is man, helpful and good," which became the manifesto for German Classicism.

Some of the most popular songs which were used for the Jewish confirmation ritual contain the same message. I quote from the second stanza of the song *"Gepriesen sei die Stunde, dem Höchsten jetzt geweiht"* [Praised be the hour dedicated to the Highest Being] (the melody stems from the Protestant songbook:)

---

15 *Gotthold Salomon*, Predigten in dem neuen israelitischen Tempel zu Hamburg ("Siebente Predigt: Zur Confirmation der Mädchen," 122–155), Hamburg 1820, here: 149.

16 *Samuel Holdheim*, Neue Sammlung jüdischer Predigte: worunter über alle Feste des Jahres gehalten im Gotteshause der jüdischen Reform-Gemeinde zu Berlin, Berlin 1852, 58f.

„Der Tugend soll ich leben
Den kleinsten Fehler flieh'n
Der Gottheit fromm ergeben
Soll ihr mein Innres glüh'n
Doch werd' ich sie erfüllen,
Die ernste, hohe Pflicht?
O Gott! Du kennst den Willen!
Gieb Du mir Kraft und Licht!"[17]

This reorientation of the confimation rite in 18th-century German Protestantism brought further changes in its wake: because the judgment competency of the confirmands was given such prominence the confirmation celebration mutated ever more from a church ritual into a civil affair. The confirmands were now viewed more as members of adult middle-class society than as members of the religious fellowship. The confirmation became an initiation rite marking the attainment of the age of majority and Jews, who were still struggling for equal rights in German society, just wanted to participate in this process.

Therefore it may not surprise you to hear that I owe a part of my historical outline of the Protestant confirmation to a Jewish scholar, the one who in 1835 presented an early basic scholarly reflection of the confirmation rite, after he himself had already established the Jewish confirmation as a fixed feature of community life – Salomon Herxheimer.[18] With respect to Herxheimer it should be pointed out that the Protestant confirmation of that period was not that of the Reformation, but the one that had newly evolved "with great deviations", as he himself emphasised, during the Age of Enlightenment. In fact, the church rite in the Protestant Church became a generally practiced event there only after the confirmation had already become a standard custom in many Jewish communities. The increasingly popular confirmation service in contemporary Protestantism, which had originally been designed in the Reformation period to replace the sacrament of confirmation as practiced by the

---

17 Quoted according: Allgemeines Israelitisches Gesangbuch, eingeführt in dem Neuen Israelitischen Tempel zu Hamburg, Hamburg 1833, 510 (song no. 413); the melody derives from „Ich bin ein Gast auf Erden", a very famous Protestant song by Paul Gerhardt.
18 See his article: Über die synagogale Zulässigkeit und Einrichtung der Confirmation, Wissenschaftliche Zeitschrift für jüdische Theologie, vol. 1, 1835, 68–96. The Jewish confirmation was only seldom mentioned by Protestant theologians; a short chapter on the Jewish confirmation was included in: *H. W. Bödeker*, Ueber Confirmation und Confirmanden-Unterricht. Ein historisch-practischer Versuch, Göttingen 1823, 355–359.

Catholic Church, misled Herxheimer finally to observe: "It is still not valid as a sacrament in the Protestant Church even today" ["*Als Sacrament gilt sie in der protestantischen Kirche heute noch nicht*"].[19] For Reform Jewish scholars and rabbis at that time their high esteem of the Protestant confirmation rite had apparently already assumed a semi-sacramental character!

In view of the history of the Protestant confirmation it is more than understandable that Jewish confirmation sermons tried to defend the new institution against those critics who bewailed the adoption of a non-Jewish custom. Of course, Reform rabbis indeed had to admit that the confirmation was not rooted in Jewish tradition, even mentioning this fact in their own sermons. But as apologists always try to do – for lack of more sophisticated arguments – they pointed out that many of the "traditional" Jewish customs accepted as undisputed and widely believed to go back to biblical times actually had their origins in Christian traditions of the Middle Ages.

4. Some protests among the Orthodox camp and among the parents

But not everyone was pleased by the new ritual and frequently the strongest opponents of the Jewish confirmation were the parents of the children themselves. In addition Orthodox journals tried to mobilise the parents and decried the ritual. I quote from the Orthodox journal *Jeschurun*:

> „Also ist die sogenannte Relgionsweihe ein Akt, welchen die Willkür moderner jüdischer Pfaffen den christlichen Religionsgebrauch entnommen haben und dem Judenthum gewaltsam aufoktroyiren wollen. Es wäre Zeit, dieses Unjüdische aus der jüdischen Gemeinschaft zu verdrängen. Und dieses können am besten die Eltern. Gebt eure Kinder nicht her zu solchem Nonsens! Handelt ihr und helft euch selbst, euch will ich ermahnen; zu den jüdischen Pfaffen zu reden, wäre vergebliche Mühe."[20]

Again and again Reform-oriented rabbis complain about having to contend with much reluctance to accept the Jewish confirmation. Twentieth-century Jewish scholars have pointed out that Jewish communities were forced by the governments of the Protestant German states to introduce the confirmation against their own will. In 1821 a

---

19 Ibid., 70.
20 Quoted from the article: *Isaac Hirsch*, Konfirmation und Judenthum, Jeshurun 18/1885, 241–243, here: 243.

ducal decree was enacted for the first time specifying that all Jewish children were obliged to participate in the confirmation ceremony.[21] To me this view seems to be too one-sided, especially since the archives reveal another picture: whereas the communities opposed the confirmation ritual and boys continued to attend the traditional Bar Mitzvah, the Reform rabbis clearly wanted the state to take steps to introduce the newer ritual. This wish of some reform-oriented rabbis ended up becoming the very theme of the confirmation sermon itself (in most cases the preface of the respective collections of sermons was seen as the right place for these complaints). One example I would like to quote comes from a sermon delivered by Gotthold Salomon in 1841:

> „Von so vielen Kindern, die den Unterricht in dem väterlichen Glauben genossen, waren nach einem Stillstand von drei Jahren, wie ihr seht, nicht mehr als sechs Seelen dem Herrn geweiht am heutigen Tag. Darüber könne, dürfte man klagen, dass die Menschen zum Guten und Besseren *gezwungen* sein wollen [the term *„gezwungen"* is emphasized in the original text]. – Denn würde die Staatsbehörde die Konfirmation der israelitischen Jugend anordnen, wie es in vielen Ländern bereits geschehen ist: dann würde sich Niemand auszuschließen wagen."[22]

On the other hand we have teachers and rabbis who though strongly opposed to the confirmation ritual nevertheless felt forced to introduce it, like Salomon Plessner in Berlin. In his collection of "Confirmationsreden für die israelitische Jugend", published in 1839, we find the blurb: "*Zugleich ein passendes Geschenk am Einsegnungstage*" – "at the same time a suitable gift for confirmation day." However, the preface makes the book seem quite the opposite, unsuited for this occasion at least: here Plessner made no attempt to conceal his feeling that he mostly hated to deliver confirmation sermons, precisely because the confirmation had no roots in Jewish tradition.

> „Habe ich jemals mit Ueberwindung Vorträge gehalten, mit noch größerer aber, nach vorangegangenem vieljährigen Aufforderungen, mich zu ihrer Herausgabe entschlossen, so waren es die vorliegenden Konfirmationsreden. […] So sehr mir nun auch die ganze Sache der Konfirmation als etwas Unjüdisches erschien, und noch erscheint, und ich ohne Bedenken, wenn sie in Israel heute aufgehoben, dafür aber der Jugend ein gründlicher hebräischer Sprach- und Religionsunterricht ertheilt werden soll, der erste sein würde, der mit Freude dies unterschrieb; könnte ich doch nicht umhin, die bestehende Sitte einstweilen zu nehmen wie sie ist, und es zu

---

21 See *Sulamith*, vol. VI/I, 399. The first attempt was undertaken by the Westfälischen Konsistorium; see Eliav (above note 1), 340 n. 53.
22 *Gotthold Salomon*, Die Einsegnung der Jugend als eine Confirmations-Feier im neuen Israelitischen Tempel in Hamburg am 2. Mai 1841, Hamburg 1841, 15.

versuchen, eine möglichst natürliche israelitische Handhabung derselben auf die Bahn zu bringen."[23]

Plessner's confirmation sermons are far removed from the pedagogical standards of his own time. Shortly after the publication of these sermons he left Berlin and went to Posen.

5. A ceremony for boys and girls

Comparing the Jewish confirmation sermon with its Protestant model, we can single out one major difference. The language of the Protestant sermon is a unisex one with words like "Jugend", "Kinder" and "Söhne und Töchter", because in the Protestant tradition the confirmation was always addressed equally to boys and girls. In the Jewish tradition, of course, the traditional Bar Mitzvah was, as its name indicates, only meant for boys. Thus the gender aspect became very prominent in the debate on the Jewish confirmation, as it was directly linked to the general debate about women in the Judaism of that time and taken up again and again in the confirmation sermons themselves. During the Enlightenment period the traditional role of women in Judaism underwent rapid changes, first and foremost in the field of education. At the outset these changes were first seen in connection with the so-called Berliner Salons of the early 19th century, represented by Rahel (Levin-) Varnhagen, Henriette Herz and others. In the religious area we find at first more practical rather than theoretical changes. In education equal standards for boys and girls were being demanded.

And it was in Berlin that in 1817 the first confirmation of Jewish girls took place in a synagogue, in the so-called Beerschen Temple, the Reform temple of Isaac Beer (Giaccomo Meyerbeer's father), which had been established only two years earlier, in 1815 by Israel Jacobson. We have a vividly enthusiastic report of this ceremony, which I would like to quote now:

> „Dr. Kley [one of the preachers at the temple] confirmed two daughters of Jewish parents (Demoiselle Bernsdorf and Demoiselle Bevern) in the splendid Beerschen Temple here [in Berlin] in an extremely ceremonial manner. A gathering of 400 people, as many as the temple could accommodate, dissolved – so to speak – into tears. All of those present were uplifted by the excellent sermon of this good speaker and by this solemn confirmation. The lighted lamps, the two girls, the first in Israel who have [ever] been confirmed, having passed their examination with the

---

23   *Salomon Plessner*, Confirmationsreden für die israelitische Jugend, Berlin 1839, Vff.

greatest praise; in short, everything made this one of the most festive and most beautiful celebrations."[24]

In the following years more and more boys and girls were confirmed, at times even together, in the synagogue, which of course provoked protests among conservative community members. It then became more and more common for boys and girls to study together in mixed classes with school books dedicated to both Israelite boys and girls ("Israelitische Knaben und Mädchen").

In the light of these reforms it is understandable that passages which contradicted the new worldview were then removed from the prayerbooks. It was again in Berlin that the first prayerbook was published in 1817, the same year in which the first confirmation of girls took place. The prayerbook was published by Eduard Kley, the very same man who performed the confirmation ceremony, and Carl Siegfried Günsburg. In this prayerbook – entitled "The German Synagogue" (*Die deutsche Synagoge*) – the passage where men praise and thank God that they have not been created as women (*she-lo asani ishah*) was removed.

In 1837 the first text on women by a Reform rabbi that can be termed truly emancipatory appeared in the "Wissenschaftliche Zeitschrift für jüdische Theologie" ["Scientific Journal of Jewish Theology"]. Authored by Abraham Geiger (1810–1874), the article was entitled: "Concerning the Position of the Female Sex in Judaism of Our Time" ["*Zur Stellung des weiblichen Geschlechts in dem Judenthume unserer Zeit*"]. Its opening words make very clear Geiger's basic emancipatory attitude:

> "The position of the female sex, according to existing Judaism, has so much that is unnatural and unfavorable for our times [*zeitwidriges*], [and] has moreover so many ills in its wake that an immediate and sufficient alteration of several existing customs, the reason and meaning of which have already been repudiated by our time, is urgently needed."

Geiger's view is shared by many authors of Jewish confirmation sermons addressed specifically to girls. In these sermons the confirmation ceremony itself is sometimes seen as a declaration of the religious maturity of women.

The first quotation comes from a sermon delivered by the educator, scholar, mathematician and Reform advocate Michael Creizenach (1789–1842) in 1828 at a confirmation ceremony for boys and girls in the *Frankfurter Israelitische Realschule*:

---

24 Anonymous, Aus einem Briefe aus Berlin, in: *Sulamith*, vol. 5, 1817/1820, No. 1, 279.

„Es soll hiermit gar nicht gesagt werden, dass der jetzige Religionsunterricht nicht sehr bedeutender Verbesserungen fähig ist; dass aber derjenige, welche noch Viele unter uns erhalten haben, entschieden schlecht war, und eine gänzliche Unbekanntschaft mit dem Geiste unsrer heiligen Lehre voraussetzte, verräth sich schon dadurch allein, dass für die religiöse Bildung der Töchter ganz und gar nichts geschah; als wenn das Weib nicht auch einen Gott zu verehren und Pflichten zu erfüllen hätte. Unsere Nachkommen werden es kaum glauben, wenn sie erzählt bekommen, dass es eine Zeit gab, wo man es nicht für nöthig hielt, das heranwachsende Mädchen durch einen geregelten Unterricht mit den Grundlehren der Religion bekannt zu machen, wo das verheiratete Weib allein zum Gottesdienst angehalten und zugelassen wurde, wo weibliche Dienstboten oft lebenslänglich davon ausgeschlossen waren, und sie werden darin allein eine befriedigende Erklärung der traurigen Erscheinung finden, dass ein Volk, dem Gott so weise und vernünftige Gesetze gegeben hat, unglücklicher als alle übrigen werden konnte."[25]

Herxheimer's sermon published in his collection *Gelegenheitspredigten* (occasional sermons) in 1838 points in a similar direction:

„Ja, Tausende eurer Brüder, und noch mehr eurer Schwestern, lebten verwaist, kennen nicht die Mutter Religion, nicht den Vater über sich, nicht die Unsterblichkeit vor sich ... O fühlet dieses Glück meine Lieben! Fühlet, Jungfrauen, wie an euch wahr geworden die tröstliche Verheißung Gottes: ich will dich wieder erbauen, auf daß du erbauet bleibst, Jungfrau Israels (Jirm 31.3)."[26]

The quotation from Jer. 31.3 has, of course, a messianic connotation. Here the messianic time has been transferred from the traditional messianic hope to contemporary Germany, where Israel is facing a new future. Incidentally, most of the confirmation sermons at this early stage lack quotations from the Talmudic tradition or even condemn the rabbinical world.

These sermons reflect to some extent the very radical demands for the equal status of women in Judaism which were summarized in David Einhorn's "Report of the Committee on the Religious Status of Women in Judaism" at the third Rabbinical Conference in Breslau in 1846.

Most of the confirmation sermons delivered to girls state more or less explicitly – but sometimes very pointedly and aggressively – that it was precisely the Talmudic tradition that was proving to be an obstacle

---

25 *Michael Creizenach*, Confirmations-Feier für mehrere Schüler und Schülerinnen der Frankfurter israelitischen Realschule, gehalten im Lokale dieser Anstalt den 12. Januar 1828, Frankfurt/M. 1828, 9.
26 *Salomon Herxheimer*, Sabbath-, Fest- und Gelegenheitspredigten, Bernburg 1839, 342f.

to the emancipation of women in the religious sphere. But we find an outstanding exception as well: a sermon delivered in 1847 by Rabbi Adolph Jellinek in Leipzig, where Reform services were held during the famous annual fair. To Jellinek religious maturity did not mean abandoning the Talmud – on the contrary women should study the Talmudic tradition like men and not only the Talmud. By the way, his sermon marked the first use in Jewish history of the term "Bat Mitzvah" namely in the German phrase: *"Pflichtbare Tochter der Synagoge"* – "dutiful daughter of the synagogue" – a fact which seems to me to have been completely neglected by scholars so far. I quote from the sermon:

> „Bedeutungsvoll ist diese Stunde, weil es gerade eine Israelitin ist, die vor Gott heute erscheint. Ihr wisset, m.Br., in welchem Grade die Vergangenheit die religiöse Erziehung des weiblichen Geschlechts vernachlässigte; wie sie von dem falschen Grundsatze ausging, das zartere Geschlecht bedürfe einer geringeren Sorgfalt und weniger Eifer und Pflege in der Heranbildung für das köstliche Gut Israels, für die Religion, obwohl, wie unsere Weisen bemerken, Gott selbst sich an die Frauen wandte: ‚So sprich zum Hause Jakob' (Ex 19.3) erklärt der Midrasch אלו הנשים ‚das sind die Frauen'. Allein unsere bewegte Zeit hat uns enttäuscht. Sie hat uns nachdrücklich belehrt, dass die religiöse Erziehung des Hauses, der Familie fast ganz und gar in den Händen des weiblichen Geschlechtes liege und dass, so wir den Bund, den Gott mit unseren Vätern am Horeb geschlossen, für kommende Zeiten aufrecht erhalten wollen, wir die Knospe des weiblichen Herzens schon frühzeitig den Sonnenstrahlen der Religion öffnen und den Israelitinnen eine gleiche Sorgfalt in der religiösen Erziehung widmen müssen, wie den Israeliten. Denn auch sie sind Kinder des einig-einzigen Vaters, der in seiner Gnade Alle mit gleicher Liebe umfasset, auch sie stehen in demselben Verhältnis zu Gott wie die Israeliten. Welches ist aber überhaupt das wahre Verhältniß des Israeliten zu seinem Gotte?"[27]

The following speech by Jellinek is based on the Shema Yisrael, the basic profession of faith in Judaism, which also plays a central role in the Jewish confirmation ritual. As part of the inquiry-response cycle the female *"Konfirmandin"* (confirmee) had to answer the question about the main sources of the Jewish religion (*"israelitische Religion"*). The correct answer was to point out the existence of two sources: the written and the oral Torah. This answer is explained by Jellinek in the following way:

> „Richtig hast Du die Quellen unserer Religion angegeben. Allein die erste, sie ist fast ein Weltquelle geworden, aus der in Synagogen, Kirchen und

---

27 *Adolph Jellinek*, Die erste Confirmations-Feier in der Leipzig-Berliner Synagoge am zweiten Tage des Wochenfestes 5607 (22. Mai 1847), Leipzig 1847, 7f.

Moscheen geschöpft wird; die zweite Quelle ist eine ausschließlich israelitische. Ahme nicht jene Modethorheit nach, welche den Talmud verdammt, ohne ihn auch nur zu kennen. Du hattest oft Gelegenheit, die sinnreichen Sprüche, Gleichnisse, Erzählungen, Parabeln und Allegorien desselben kennen zu lernen; Du weißt, dass die geistigen Schätze von mehr denn fünf Jahrhunderten in demselben aufbewahrt sind; dass zahlreiche Gelehrte die Spuren ihrer Geistesthätigkeit in demselben hinterlassen haben und dass wir den richtigen Sinn und die wahre Deutung der Schrift oft nur durch ihn erlangen können. Auch die dritte Quelle ist nicht minder wichtig. Du kennst Saadja Gaon, den Stern des Morgenlandes, Moses Maimun, den Adler des Mittelalters, Moses Mendelssohn, der den Israeliten das Licht der Bildung angezündet; Du kennst jenes dichterische Dreigestirn Salomo Ibn Gabirol, Jehuda ha-Lewi und Moses Ibn Esra, die unser heutiges Fest in Hymnen und Lobgesängen gefeiert haben; Du weißt, wie viel glänzende Namen unsere Geschichte aufzählt. Labe Dich an allen diesen Quellen."[28]

Jellinek's sermon is most meaningful in several aspects. First his hymn of praise on the Jewish tradition: the Talmud, the philosophical tradition and the Jewish poetry of the Middle Ages. Within the Reform tradition we find here a clear refusal of those sermons which used the Biblical tradition to knock out the Talmudic one. Jellinek's sermon marks a clear paradigm shift in the Reform movement itself and coincides with decisive, even radical changes in the Reform movement that affected virtually all aspects of community and liturgical life, even extending to the building of synagogues in the distinctively Moorish or Oriental architectural style, then so fashionable.[29] During these years the basic structures of a liberal worship service started to crystallize, a worship which had shown itself to be quite open to the influences of the Protestant majority culture in its beginnings and indeed had quite consciously begun to distance itself from it as a model in the following decades. This development was also reflected in synagogal music. As we noted in connection with the inaugural ceremony of the Seesener Temple, the influence of Protestant culture at the outset of the Jewish Reform movement was especially strong in musical matters. The paradigmatic shift of direction then taking place was adumbrated by the composer Louis Lewandowski (1821–1894), who left an enduring musical imprint on the modern Jewish service, in the preface to his songbook "Kol Rinah u-T'ffilah. Ein- und zweistimmige Gesänge für

---

28 Ibid., 19f.
29 Not until the increasingly virulent anti-Semitism of the Second German Empire [after 1870] did the Moorish style disappear, because of the fear of giving a fillip to the infamous idea that with such an architecture Jews as an Oriental people would never really be able to be acculturated in Germany.

den israelitischen Gottesdienst" [Songs for Solo and Two Voices for the Israelite Service], dated 1871, at a time when he was music director of the Moorish-styled New Synagogue in Berlin:

> "The great Christian masters in the area of church music, Bach and Handel, did not try to invent new hymn melodies for the congregations. These Gentlemen [the reformers of the synagogue music], however, with an unprecedented shamelessness and recklessness and lacking any talent or musical knowledge, delighted congregations with their most trivial tunes, and now those who lead the prayers and the communities, who, through their honest efforts are taking the trouble to free the Israelite service from all ordinariness, already need to apply all their energies to removing these melodies from the house of God for all time."[30]

It goes without saying that we ought to interpret these words not as a qualified judgment on the music, but as a strongly polemic statement against the uncritical adoption of Protestant aesthetics in the divine service in the early phase of the Reform movement, aesthetics that Lewandowski countered by employing the traditional recitative synagogal singing in his own works.

6. The decline of the ceremony

In the second half of the 19th century we find a decline of the confirmation ceremony. In 1867, at the so-called Jewish synod in Leipzig, it became clear that the confirmation would never replace the traditional Bar Mitzvah in the synagogues – with the exception of the radical Reform congregations. For that reason we find far fewer published confirmation sermons in the second half of the 19th century than in the decades before. Moreover, at this time the first comprehensive Jewish homiletical work, published by Siegmund Maybaum, devoted one chapter to the contents of an ideal confirmation sermon. Maybaum himself complained that the parents were much too reluctant to welcome the confirmation ceremony in Judaism.[31] To be honest, however, Maybaum's own confirmation sermons as well as those of many of his rabbi-colleagues contained simple moral pleas that would hardly have appealed to children. Yet we do find some exceptions too, e.g., when the preacher discusses in his sermon modern concepts like the idea of Nietzsche's *"Übermensch"* [Superman] and the

---

30 Louis *Lewandowski*, Kol Rinah u-T'ffilah. Ein- und zweistimmige Gesänge für den israelitischen Gottesdienst, Berlin 1871, Preface.
31 See his Jüdische Homiletik. Nebst einer Auswahl von Texten und Themen, Berlin 1890.

dangers inherent in such ideologies.³² On the other hand, it is understandable that a rabbi would not have wanted to burden the children on a day which was supposed to evoke a pleasant memory. And even in the radical Reform communities the confirmation ceremony lost its acceptance-standing among young people.

I started with a quotation by Zunz declaring the confirmation to be the beginning of a new age in Judaism. I would like to close this paper with a quotation by Victor Klemperer (1881–1960) whose father, Wilhelm, was one of the three preachers at the Berlin Reform Assembly. His memories ("Curriculum Vitae, Erinnerungen 1881–1918") clearly reflect this change in the attitude toward the confirmation among the youth in a German society which was becoming more and more secularised. His confirmation took place in 1885:

> "When I was confirmed, I accused Father of hypocrisy and of, so to speak, dishonourably earning his living. In this point Father chose with me a middle-of-the-road solution; together with a group of boys and girls I was confirmed according to the German convention of the Reform community, but already at Easter 1895, and thus much closer to the traditional Orthodox [Bar Mitzvah] age of 13 than to the usual age in the Reform community. Up to then the attitude of my relatives to religion had seemed to me to be something natural which I didn't have to think about. [...] I had never been haunted by religious anxieties. I said my evening prayer just as one cleans one's teeth [...]. Confessions I viewed like clothes that one wore customarily according to the locality and the time; Judaism was an old and un-German traditional mode of dress ["*Tracht*"], Protestantism a North German fashion, Catholicism a fashion common in South Germany and Austria [...]. Yet I really ought to have shown a certain understanding. How did I deal with my evening prayer? I still continued to say it, however no longer with casual inattentiveness, but with the shameful awareness: 'You aren't giving it any thought' and could not stop doing it nonetheless. It wasn't until the confirmation ritual itself, when we were reminded to lead a virtuous life in the Lord, that I swore to myself, to leave it from now on, in order, as I told myself, 'not to play the hypocrite any more' ['*nicht mehr mitzuheucheln*']."³³

---

32 See *Julius Jelski*, Aus großer Zeit. Predigten gehalten im Gotteshause der Jüdischen Reform-Gemeinde in Berlin, Berlin 1915, 123ff.
33 *Victor Klemperer*, Curriculum Vitae, Erinnerungen 1881–1918, vol. 1, Berlin 1996, 111ff.

7. The Jewish confirmation before the Shoa

During the time of murderous persecution and social ostracism from German society, for German Jewish children the confirmation ritual again became more meaningful than it had been in previous decades. A very fine example for this tendency is a sermon delivered by Rabbi Dr. Karl Rosenthal at the Berlin Reform congregation on the occasion of the *"Einsegnung der Konfirmanden"* on 12 April 1936, at which 30 boys and girls were confirmed.[34] Rosenthal, born in 1889, had studied at the universities of Berlin and Cologne before starting his career as a rabbi in Dortmund, whence he went to Berlin in 1924 to work as a rabbi for the Reform congregation there. Many of his writings criticised the Nazi ideology, and he was arrested several times. On *Kristallnacht* Rosenthal was arrested and sent to the Sachsenhausen concentration camp. Released three months later, he migrated to England. In 1946 Rosenthal was appointed Rabbi of a Reform congregation in Fredericksburg, Virginia. He later worked in Springfield, Illinois, and Wilmington, North Carolina, where he died in 1952. The main theme of his 1936 sermon is the idea of freedom, which he expands by relying on the fact that the confirmation was taking place on Passover: Israel was freed from the house of slavery in Egypt. Then he continues:

> „Aber, so fragen wir schließlich, wenn wir diese Bindung an Gott, wenn wir diese Bindung durch die Kraft der Religion bejahen und in ihr unsere wahre göttliche Freiheit sehen, brauchen wir dann gerade *Judentum*? Ist es nicht genug, wenn wir *allgemein* die Religion bejahen, *müssen wir unser Judentum haben*? Müßt ihr, liebe Freunde, liebe Schüler und Schülerinnen, Juden sein, um diese Freiheit im Göttlichen bewähren zu können? – Liebe Kinder, Religion kann und darf nicht farblos sein, Religion muß Charakter haben, wenn sie uns etwas bedeuten soll. Unsere jüdische Religion aber,

---

34 In earlier years the confirmation sermons had been published in the *Mitteilungen der Jüdischen Reformgemeinde zu Berlin*. During the Nazi period the publication of this kind of sermon in a journal was obviously no longer possible. The sermon by Rosenthal (published as a leaflet under the title: "Predigt zur Einsegnung der Konfirmanden am 12. April 1936 im Gotteshause der Jüdischen Reformgemeinde zu Berlin") clearly indicates his undisguised frankness about Nazi oppressive politics, which would hardly have been tolerated by the German authorities. The last issue of the *Mitteilungen der Jüdischen Reformgemeinde* was published 15 October 1938. On the end of the Jewish Reform congregation in Berlin see *Peter Galliner/Simone Ladwig-Winters* (Eds.), Freiheit und Bindung. Zur Geschichte der jüdischen Reformgemeinde zu Berlin von den Anfängen bis zu ihrem Ende 1939, Berlin 2004, 175ff. I would like to thank Aubrey Pomerance, Chief Archivist of the Jewish Museum Berlin, who gathered together materials on confirmation from the museum's archive and from the branch of the Leo Baeck Institute Archive located there and granted me permission to quote from Rosenthal's confirmation sermon.

sie hat ihre Farbe aus ihrer *Geschichte*, sie hat ihre Farbe aus unserer *Ethik*, sie hat ihre Farbe aus unserem jüdischen *Optimismus*. *Aus* unserer Geschichte, da schöpfen wir *Kraft*, aus unserer Ethik, da schöpfen wir unseren *Stolz*, aus unserem Optimismus gewinnen wir *Geduld*, die uns ausharren läßt in diesem Kampf um unser Leben. Wir brauchen dieses Judentum, weil in seiner Geschichte, in seiner Ethik, in seinem Optimismus diejenigen Kräfte offenbar werden, die uns wahrhaft zur inneren Freiheit, zur Freiheit unseres jüdischen Menschen führen. – Ja, liebe Schüler, *Ihr braucht Judentum*, mehr als jemals eine Generation Judentum gebraucht hat. Ihr lebt in einer Welt, die für uns Juden düster ist, in einer Welt, in der wir viel Unfreundlichkeit, viel Härte erfahren, viel Leid, viel Weh, viel Kummer und Not, in einer Zeit, in der Ihr den bitteren Haß der Welt da draußen um Euch Tag um Tag erfahren müßt. Ihr lebt in einer Welt, die dunkel ist, weil Eure Menschlichkeit, weil Euer menschliches Drängen nach echter Freiheit in dieser Welt der Düsternis keine Erfüllung findet. Darum braucht Ihr Euer Judentum.

In der Passahgeschichte, von der wir ausgingen, wird uns berichtet, daß die vorletzte unter den 10 Plagen, durch die Pharao vom Ewigen gezwungen wurde, Israel freizulassen, eine dreitägige *Finsternis* war, die über ganz Ägypten kam. Und Ihr kennt alle, liebe Jugend, jenes Bild des großen jüdischen Künstlers, das sich in dem Vorraum unseres Gemeindehauses befindet, und das da zeigt, wie Mose auf Gottes Befehl die Finsternis über Aegypten bringt. Solche Finsternis ist nun um Euch, solche Finsternis ist nun um uns. Aber unsere Thora berichtet uns: während ganz Aegypten erfüllt war von der Finsternis seines Unglaubens, war bei den Kindern Israels *Licht*! Dieses Licht, liebe Jugend, das auch im Dunkeln leuchtet heute und in kommenden Tagen, *das ist unser Judentum*. Dieses Judentum ist nicht eine allgemeine Religion, nicht eine Allerwelts-Religion; sondern unser Judentum mit *seiner* Geschichte, mit *seiner* Ethik, mit *seinem* Optimismus soll Licht und Heiligkeit tragen in Eure Herzen und Eure Seelen. Aus diesem Judentum soll Euch in den Tagen der Finsternis *Stolz des Herzens* wachsen, Stolz, der nicht gebeugt werden kann, wie finster und hart auch die Welt um Euch da draußen ist. Dieser Stolz Eures Judeseins soll Euch Heiligkeit geben in Eurem Leben, menschliche Freiheit. Ja, wie hart dieses Leben Euch packt, wie tief man uns auch unser Judentum und seine Lehre immer wieder herabwürdigt in dieser Zeit, das *Wissen um dieses Judentum* soll Euch einen Stolz geben, einen herrlichen Stolz, der durch nichts, durch nichts in der Welt überwunden werden kann! Diesen Stolz, den schöpft Ihr allein aus Eurem Wissen um unser Judentum, um unsere Ethik, um unsere Zehn Gebote, die das Sittengesetz der ganzen Menschheit geworden sind. Diesen Stolz schöpft Ihr aus der heiligen Ueberzeugung, daß Israel durch seine Religion der *Bannerträger der Moral* für alle Völker geworden ist ... Ja, liebe Konfirmanden, Israel steht seit dreitausend Jahren *allein*, allein in der Wüste des Vorurteils, des Hasses und des Aberglaubens. Israel steht allein in der Wüste – aber *mit ihm ist Gott*! Zu Ihm sollt Ihr Euch bekennen. *Glaubt* an Sein ewiges Wirken! Lebt in der Hoffnung auf *Sein Reich*! Mag die Welt

Euch knechten – im Glauben an Ihn seid ihr frei Israel steht allein, aber Gott ist mit ihm. Durch Ihn und mit Ihm werdet Ihr frei, durch Ihn, in Ihm sei Euer Leben glücklich! Amen."[35]

In this sermon Rosenthal compares the darkness in Egypt with the darkness in Nazi-Germany. To remember the dark period of slavery in Egypt means, however, to be optimistic and hopeful for the future: Israel was freed from Egypt. We all know that for many of the Jewish children confirmed in Berlin in 1936 this optimism and hope was destroyed in the extermination camps.

At the end of this article I would like to mention the testimonials of the last witnesses of the Jewish confirmation in Germany, a ceremony which was completely annihilated in the destruction of the Jewish communities. At the Free University in Berlin we now have access to the 52,000 video-tapes of Shoah survivors which were collected in the late 1990s on the initiative of Steven Spielberg after he had produced his film "Schindler's List." In several of the interviews the confirmation rite is described as one of the last important and vivid memories in an otherwise dark time.[36]

---

35 Predigt zur Einsegnung der Konfirmanden am 12. April 1936 im Gotteshause der Jüdischen Reformgemeinde zu Berlin, 10–14; emphasis as in the original text.

36 At the conference in Bamberg, *Two Homiletical Traditions: Preaching in Judaism and Christianity*, several videos were shown which could not be included in this conference volume. A transcription of the videos concerning the confirmation service together with an analysis of these oral-history witnesses will be published in a separate booklet.

Towards Mutual Listening
The Notion of Sermon in Franz Rosenzweig's Philosophy

Yehoyada Amir

1. Introduction – The sermon in modern Jewish life

Since the first steps of liberal Judaism in Germany, taken during the first decades of 19th century, the sermon has become a major component of Jewish *Gottesdienst*.[1] It is characteristic that when the Hamburg Temple hired professionals, they were hired as "preachers" (*Prediger*) rather than rabbis.[2] Conducting sermons every Sabbath and for Festival services became one of the prominent components of rabbinical function in liberal congregations[3] and sooner or later in all modern congregations in Central Europe, including the Orthodox ones.[4] The sermon gave the rabbi room to exercise direct influence on his congregants, to lead them in the complicated path of modern religiosity, and to leave a personal mark on his congregation.[5] While prayers were conducted in a mixture of Hebrew and German, the sermon was given in German and was much more accessible to the audience. While prayer was based to a large extent on antique traditional formulations, even when re-formed and reinterpreted, the sermon enabled the rabbi to interweave Jewish sources and German literature and to demonstrate how natural the combination of modern European culture and Jewish identity could be. While prayer and chanting from the Torah was ritually bounded and repetitive, the sermon could be new every Sabbath.

---

1   *Alexander Altmann*, Zur Frühgeschichte der jüdischen Predigt in Deutschland. Leopold Zunz als Prediger, in: YLBI 6/1961, 3–59.
2   *Michael A. Meyer*, Response to Modernity. A History of the Reform Movement in Judaism, Detroit (MI) 1995, 55.
3   Ibid., 129.
4   Cf. for example: *Solomon Breuer*, Chochmo u'Mussar. An original Approach to Sidra interpretation, Jerusalem 1996.
5   Cf. *Gerda Budde*, Predigen aus Berufung, in: Truma 6/1997, 151–177.

There is no doubt that this development is anchored in the direct and explicit influence that the Christian *Gottesdienst* had on liberal Judaism. Like music and other aesthetic elements, the Christian – more so Protestant than Catholic – sermon served as the basis for the renewal of the Jewish sermon in this environment. Since Jewish knowledge deteriorated among non-professional Jews, rabbis had to use the occasion of the sermon in order to teach, formulate basic religious notions, and establish a sense of spiritual authority. Leopold Zunz's book, "Die Gottesdienstlichen Vorträge der Juden – Historisch entwickelt" [The Sermons of the Jews – Historical Development] (1832) aimed apologetically to prove that this new development was really a revival of antique Jewish notions, and hence not merely an adoption of Christian liturgical component but rather a new face in a long history of Jewish worship. Regardless of its scholarly contribution and even of its political *Sitz im Leben*, through the need to prove – to Jews as well as to the governmental authorities – that sermons and preaching were an authentic and legitimate component of Jewish religious life from the Rabbinic era onwards, the book proves how vital and energetic this new component was for those Jews and how desperately they needed to integrate it into their notion of Jewish tradition.

This scholarly effort is only one literary expression of the new status that the sermon gained in modern Jewish life in Central Europe and in a parallel way in the United States of America. As another expression one can view the growing number of collections of sermons published by rabbis of all streams. Nevertheless, this new development hardly found an expression in the reflective field of Jewish philosophy. Some philosophers do tend to give their thoughts more or less a form of midrash or a sermon.[6] But almost none of them view the sermon, taking place at the synagogue in the middle of the service, as a phenomenon which one needs to philosophically analyse and evaluate within the context of Jewish worship. The only philosopher who does so and offers a philosophical-theological understanding of the sermon's

---

6   See for example: *Joseph Dov Soloveitchik*, The Lonely Man of Faith, in: Tradition 7/1965, 2, 5–67; *Emmanuel Lévinas*, Beyond the Verse – Talmudic readings and lectures, tr. by Gary D. Mole, Bloomington (IN) 1994; *Idem*, New Talmudic Readings, tr. by Richard A. Cohen, Pittsburgh (PA) 1999. Emil Fackenheim promoted the notion that Jewish thought can cure itself after the Holocaust only through developing itself as philosophic midrash. See: *Emil L. Fackenheim*, To Mend the World. Foundations of Post-Holocaust Jewish Thought, New York 1982, 256ff.

role in Jewish religious life is Franz Rosenzweig in his "Stern der Erlösung."[7]

The main object of this article is to discuss this analysis by Rosenzweig, and its systematic role and place within Jewish life in particular and religious life in general. In order to do so we have to delve briefly into the questions of the relationship between revelation and religious life in Rosenzweig's philosophy and of the role that Judaism and Christianity play in constituting the supreme level of human life and language.

2. Revelation and redemption in Rosenzweig's philosophy

Revelation is at the architectonic and substantial heart of the "Star of Redemption". It constitutes the point-of-view (*Standpunkt*) from which all discussion in this complicated and multifaceted work takes place. Revelation is perceived by Rosenzweig as an encounter between the individual, who ceases to be a closed self, and God, who expresses with his command "you shall love God" His own love to the human individual. Through this shaking transformative experience (*Erlebnis*) the individual opens her- or himself to the other, be it a human being or may it be God himself. When Rosenzweig speaks of revelation he does not refer to the great events described in the Hebrew Bible or in the New Testament, but rather to the "here and now" experience that occurs to the individual in her or his intimate sphere.[8]

It is revelation that creates human language. Man speaks because God spoke to him. The Divine call "אַיֶּכָּה", "where are you", seeking a reply from the first human beings, is answered a few generations later with Abraham's "הִנֵּנִי" "here I am".[9] Language is "entirely in a relation of 'identity' with Revelation", says Rosenzweig.[10] The Star's second part examines the three revelatory relationships: creation, revelation, and

---

7 Franz *Rosenzweig*, Der Stern der Erlösung, Haag 1976; English: The Star of Redemption (tr. by Barbara E. Galli), Madison (WI) 2005 (later cited as 'Stern' and 'Star').

8 Cf. *Yehoyada Amir*, Die Offenbarung Gottes und des Menschen aus den Quellen des Judentums. Eine Studie zu Rosenzweigs Stern der Erlösung, in: *Martin Brasser* (Ed.), Rosenzweig als Leser. Kontextuelle Kommentare zum „Stern der Erlösung," Tübingen 2004, 429–451.

9 Gen. 3.9; 22.1. Rosenzweig develops in the Star a comprehensive *midrash*, describing the rise of dialogue between God and man. He composes it from Gen. 1, 3 and 22.

10 Stern, 164; Star, 160. Cf. *Joseph Turner*, Emuna ve-Humanism. Iyunim ba-Philosophiya ha-Datit shel Franz Rosenzweig, Tel Aviv 2001, 47–72.

redemption. In each of these discussions Rosenzweig deals also with the lingual level that corresponds to this "event." Creation corresponds to the factual lingual level, namely the objects and the past tense. The story of Genesis is a perfect example to Rosenzweig's mind of this layer. It speaks about the facts of the past, about done-deal deeds and about objects: heaven, earth, stars, sun, man, etc.[11]

The lingual level that corresponds to revelation is that of the dialogue, the spontaneous cry, the command. At the heart of revelation is God's commandment "You shall love the Lord your God,"[12] calling each and every individual to submit her- or himself to God's love and to respond with love. This new, staggering experience evokes a complicated reaction on the side of the human partner, whose peak is the spontaneous prayer. "This is the last that is reached in revelation, an overflowing of the soul's supreme and perfect trust: prayer. It is not at all a question here of knowing whether the prayer will be satisfied. The prayer itself is the answer. The soul prays with the words of the psalm 'Let not my payer, nor your love withdraw from me'."[13] The ability and inevitability of prayer does not yet constitute a liturgical prayer, a community or pre-designed texts. It is only about the individual who gives voice to his or her trust, who cries out, expressing the new faculty awarded to him or her by revelation. In terms of the biblical text Rosenzweig refers to the intimate dialogue of the lover and the beloved in the Song of Songs, constituting their presence as a perfect example for the lingual layer of revelation.[14]

In regards to creation, language was only a means of expression, a way to communicate its factuality. With revelation, we met much stronger connectivity between the lingual aspect and the theological event itself. God called upon the soul and commanded with words; the soul corresponded with prayer, a spontaneous one, but nevertheless one that can be articulated in words. Redemption's connectivity to language is even stronger. Rosenzweig understands redemption as the human task to redeem the word, backed by God's command "You shall love your neighbour."[15] Contrary to revelation, it is not the isolated individual who carries on this duty but rather the community, the

---

11 *Joseph Turner*, Franz Rosenzweig's Interpretation of the Creation Narrative, in: Journal of Jewish Thought and Philosophy 4/1994, 23–37.
12 Deut. 6.5. Rosenzweig refers to this text as an essential element of Jewish liturgy (*keri'at shema*) much more than in its original Biblical context.
13 Stern, 205; Star, 198. Rosenzweig cites from Ps. 66.20.
14 *Inken Rühle*, Das Hohelied – ein weltliches Liebeslied als Kernbuch der Offenbarung? Zur Bedeutung der Auslegungsgeschichte von Schir haSchirim im Stern der Erlösung, in: Rosenzweig als Leser (see above nr. 8), 453–479.
15 Lev. 19.18.

togetherness of individuals who gain power from their cooperation before God. The main tool of this *Gemeinschaft*, Rosenzweig believes, is prayer, a different one than that which marked revelation. It is the prayer of the many, of the choir composed by the redeemed-redeeming ones who praise God.

The essential difference between these two layers of prayer and language lies in two dimensions. First, it is clear that a singing choir cannot be spontaneous like the individual who cries, expressing her or his emotions and spiritual energy. The choir needs pre-composed music and pre-designed text. When performing, it enters the universe of this complex of text and music; it does not create it. Even an improvising choir or musical band must be anchored in a specific school of music, in a pre-determined framework that can serve as the basis of its newly designed music. The lingual layer that Rosenzweig attributes to redemption is hence poetry, the pre-designed texture of words, attempting in many cases to artistically transmit again and again what the spontaneous cry could only express on the spot.

In terms of the prayer, it means that the redeemed-redeeming *Gemeinschaft* must be rooted in a liturgical tradition that will determine if not the exact liturgical texts it will speak and sing, at least the framework of its prayer. It is no surprise then, that the biblical text Rosenzweig chooses as the perfect example of redemption's language is a Psalm (115).[16]

The other dimension that marks the difference between the prayer of revelation and that of redemption is even more essential. Revelation's prayer gave voice to that what already happened. God had already commanded the individual human to love Him; the individual human being was already shocked and by the new horizon opened to her or him with this commandment. The prayer of revelation did not create the experience or even the human reaction to the Divine call. It only brought it to its peak and completion by awarding it voice and words. With redemption the situation is entirely different. There is no new "experience" upon which to base this prayer. In a matter of fact, redemption is based on that very experience of revelation. We are commanded to love our neighbors by the one who expressed His love to us through His commandment to love Him. This time prayer does not seek to give expression to an already-occurred experience. In contrast to revelation's prayer the prayer itself is not "the answer". This time, prayer wishes to achieve a goal, to create a new reality, to award

---

16 Norbert M. *Samuelson*, Tracing Rosenzweig's literary sources. Psalm 115, in: Rosenzweig als Leser (above nr. 8), 481–497.

human life with a higher layer of significance and language, and to encounter it with eternity.[17]

3. Sociological, aesthetical, and lingual role of Judaism and Christianity

Rosenzweig's notion of religion is a complicated question which cannot be dealt with here in its full scope.[18] Rosenzweig is quite ambivalent in regards to religion. He makes clear that his work is in no way a philosophy of religion but rather "a system of philosophy."[19] In its first two parts neither the notion of religion nor Judaism or Christianity are explicitly mentioned. The first, "philosophic", deals with ancient Greek idolatry and far eastern religious philosophies. The second, "theological", develops its discussions from the point of view of that which Rosenzweig calls "faith", overcoming and contradicting Idolatry. It is easy to see that the notion of faith represents a common context of Judaism and Christianity. This notion of common context of Judaism and Christianity is expressed through the selection of classic sources Rosenzweig cites or refers to in this part[20] and by his polemic treatment of Islam.[21] Nevertheless, Judaism and Christianity are not mentioned in

---

17 Cf. *Moshe Schwartz*, The idea of Prayer in Franz Rosenzweig's "Star of Redemption", in: *Gabriel Cohn Gabriel/Harold Fish* (Eds.), Prayer in Judaism. Continuity and Change, Northvale (NJ) 1996, 163–175; *Daniel Hoffmann*, Die Stimmung der jüdischen Liturgie in Franz Rosenzweigs Stern der Erlösung, in: *Wolfdietrich Schmied-Kowarzik* (Ed.), Franz Rosenzweigs "neues Denken", München 2006, 938–945; *Joost Jansen*, Gebet und Liturgie im Stern der Erlösung, in: ibid., 946–955; *Yehoyada Amir*, Da'at Ma'amina. Iyunim be-Mishnato shel Franz Rosenzweig, Tel Aviv 2004, 197–213.

18 Cf. *Luc Anckaert's* and *Yehoyada Amir's* papers in: *Luc Anckaert/Martin Brasser/Norbert Samuelson* (Eds.), The Legacy of Franz Rosenzweig. Collected Essays, Leuven 2004, and *Leora Batnizky*, The New Thinking. Philosophy or Religion, in: Franz Rosenzweigs "neues Denken" (above nr. 17), 79–89.

19 *Franz Rosenzweig*, Zweistromland. Kleinere Schriften, Dordrecht 1984, 140; English: Philosophical and Theological Writings (tr. by Paul W. Franks and Michael L. Morgan), Indianapolis (IN) 2000, 69.

20 Hebrew Biblical sources: Gen. 1, Song of Songs, Ps. 115, Decalogue, the paradise narrative and Abraham's life etc.; Jewish sources: Kri'at Shema, Yom Kippur, Yehuda ha-Levi, etc.; Christian sources: Church Fathers, Augustine, Schleiermacher, etc.

21 Rosenzweig deals polemically with Islam in seven chapters of this part, in which he systematically attempts to prove that all basic components characterizing "faith" and anchored in its rootedness in the notion of revelation appear in Islam in a reversed way. He wishes to show that Islam is not really rooted in revelation and hence does not belong to the context of "faith," constituted by Christianity and Judaism. Rosenzweig claims that these passages are the only element of the Star that

name, nor are their actual life and traditions discussed in this part. He does not discuss here the institutionalized traditions but rather the theological bases that lie beneath these traditions and are being expressed through them.

This state of affairs changes radically during the Star's last, third part. The role of religion in general and Judaism and Christianity in particular which seemed to be quite unclear and undetermined in the first two parts is explicitly the theme of this part. The discussion in this part is based on an analysis of prayer, to which Rosenzweig devotes its introduction. We have met the difference between revelation's prayer and that of redemption. While the first merely gives voice to an experience, the last aims to change reality. As such it has to be a social deed, a work of a common, coordinated "choir". In the introduction to the third part Rosenzweig returns to the social nature of liturgical prayer and systematically analyses its superiority over that of the isolated individual.

Redemption is a deed of love, aimed at the neighbor, namely the person who happens to be next to you. Prayer aims to lighten one's eyes and direct that deed. In this potency to lighten our eyes lies prayer's power, but also the risk it bares in its very nature. The blind act of love has no determined direction. It is a pure expression of the commandment to love thy neighbor, anchored in God's love and in His commandment to love Him. A conscious and directed effort to redeem the word might be much more effective; it can also mislead the beloved-redeeming soul.

Individual intuition cannot guarantee us against being misled and from slowing and damaging the growth of God's kingdom by our very misdirected act of love. It is too subjective, too individual. Only faith-community may award prayer with the right universalistic, over-subjective direction and enable it to entreat the Divine Kingdom. Only such a togetherness that accedes each of its individuals and encounters them with the absolute, can provide human life with the presence of eternity. Rosenzweig believes that this role can be fulfilled by Jewish and Christian traditions, not because they are institutionalised religions, but rather because they create two faith communities which

---

could be called "philosophy of religion" (Zweistromland, 154; Philosophical and Theological Writings, 110). Cf. *Yossef Schwartz*, Die entfremdete Nähe. Rosenzweigs Blick auf den Islam, in: *Franz Rosenzweig*, „Innerlich bleibt die Welt Eine". Ausgewählte Schriften zum Islam, Berlin 2003, 111–147; *Matthias B. Lehmann*, Franz Rosenzweigs Kritik des Islam im Stern der Erlösung, in: JSQ 1/1993/1994, 4, 340–361; *Gesine Palmer*, Der verkannte Islam, in: Franz Rosenzweig "neues Denken" (above nr. 17), 1109–1118.

can provide the individual believer with a higher sphere of being, that which he calls "Hyper-Cosmos" (*Überwelt*).²²

The role of Judaism and Christianity is to create through its togetherness and tradition a holistic atmosphere, a designed time and space that will provide human life with the faculty of touching and anticipating eternity, namely with being in dialogue with that which is beyond life, beyond time, and beyond language. Rosenzweig interprets both the weekly cycle (based on the contents of Sabbath or Sunday) and the calendar cycle (flowing through the main holidays of each religion) as essential building-blocks of the encounter with eternity. They create an ongoing, repetitive visualisation of the presence of creation-revelation-redemption; thus they hint, each tradition in its unique manner, towards eternity itself.

Rosenzweig describes his discussion of Judaism and Christianity, taking place mostly during the first two "books" of the Star's third part, as "sociological". He explains that by choosing such method he deliberately adopted a point of view alien to that which constitutes each religion's self-consciousness. Judaism tends to understand itself as a realization of the Law (*Torah*); Christianity – of faith.²³ By distancing himself from those points of view Rosenzweig aimed not only to create a common ground for the discussions of both traditions, but also to provide a functional description, one that allows the reader to understand not only what the two traditions do but also how they function for their believers and how they design the faith-communities ("Glaubensgemeinden") that carry them.

For our discussion it is essential to add to Rosenzweig's own attribution of his discussion as "sociological" two others: the discussion he develops is also both aesthetical and lingual. The aesthetic dimension is very visible. Already in the Star's first two parts Rosenzweig develops a comprehensive discussion of the aesthetic, relating to plastic arts in the first part and to literature and poetry in the second part. In the third part he discusses, in regards to both traditions, the aesthetic elements of the design of the Hyper-Cosmos. At the peak of this discussion is Rosenzweig's statement that while physical-mathematical space is only an abstraction, it is architecture in general and that of the Church in particular, that really creates space, a pre-

---

22 See: *Christoph Askani*, Die Gestaltung der Zeit durch die Liturgie im Judentum und Christentum, in: Franz Rosenzweigs "neues Denken" (above nr. 17), 956–981; *Caspar Bernhard*, Theo-logie als Geschehen des Gebets. Eine Anleitung Franz Rosenzweigs Stern der Erlösung zu lesen, in: The Legacy of Franz Rosenzweig (above nr. 18), 219–227.
23 Zweistromland, 156; Philosophical and Theological Writings, 132. Cf. *Amir*, Da'at Ma'amina (above nr. 17), 214–252.

designed, pre-designated, and human space. "And on the other hand there is among buildings only the one kind that is simply space, that is to say not split into spaces that serve purposes. [...] Nowhere does man linger in order simply to linger mutually with others in one room. Such space is for him quite simply only in the house of God, the only one of all with the same firm orientation everywhere and necessarily with one room".[24] In a parallel way Rosenzweig speaks of the aesthetics of Jewish ritual, reaching its peak in those gestures that he interprets in terms of dancing.[25]

The lingual quality of the third part's discussion is a bit less apparent but in no way of lesser essentiality. Like the aesthetic one, it is based on the lingual-grammatical discussions in the first two parts. In contrary to the aesthetic one, it does not only bring the previous discussions to their peak, but rather offers a new category that enlightens those of the first parts of the work in a new light. In the first part Rosenzweig dealt with what he saw as pre-languages as the underground basis for the language-to-be, namely the communicative quality of plastic art and the structural texture of mathematics. Real language is, as we saw, the topic of part two, in which revelation is at the center. Language's climax seems to be poetry and the mutual singing of the choir. Part three introduces a higher lingual level, that of the supreme, over-lingual mutual silence. "Because in eternity the word ceases to exist in the silence of harmonious gathering – for we are united only in silence; the word unites, but those who are united grow silent – therefore the mirror that collects the sunbeams of eternity in the tiny cycle of the year, the liturgy, must introduce man into this silence".[26] Liturgy, with its texts and musical elements, architecture and non-verbal gestures, aims towards something which lies beyond all of these. Silence is neither part of Jewish tradition nor of the Christian one; it manifests neither Jewish anticipation of eternity, namely "eternal life", nor Christian anticipation, namely "eternal way". It manifests eternity itself and therefore lies beyond Judaism and Christianity, beyond life and liturgy. But it is the liturgical apparatus of both traditions which not only hints towards silence but also assists the believers in climbing through the levels of lingual expression towards silence. The main educational tool of which it makes use is mutual listening.

---

24   Stern, 396; Star, 377.
25   Stern, 414; Star, 395.
26   Stern, 342; Star, 327. Cf. *Almut Sh. Bruckstein*, Zur Phänomenologie der Jüdischen Liturgie in Rosenzwegs *Stern der Erlösung*. Ein Versuch über das Schweigen mit Husserl, in: Rosenzweig als Leser (above nr. 8), 357–368.

4. Jewish sermon as mutual listening

Rosenzweig's discussions of Judaism and Christianity draw quite a few parallels between the two traditions. Sabbath is parallel to Sunday; Passover, the Jewish festival of creation, is parallel to Christmas, which plays the same role in the Christian year; Shavu'ot, the Jewish holiday of revelation, is parallel to the Christian festival of revelation, namely Easter. Nevertheless, there are some elements that are perceived as unique to Judaism and find no parallels in Christian tradition. Yom Kippur, the day of direct encounter with eternity, cannot have a parallel day within Christianity, since this religion does not confront the believer directly with eternity; it only places her or him "in the middle" of the way between the two moments, in which eternity penetrates time, the first coming of Christ as the beginning of time, and his future, second coming, namely the end of history. In the same way, there was no Jewish parallel to the "real space" that the Church represents, since the Jewish faith-community is not created by the gathering in the house of God, but rather in the very fact of birth into the Jewish people.

Despite these examples, in which one can easily explain why the general parallelism between Judaism and Christianity ceases, it is hard to understand why the sermon, *derashah*, is dealt with and analyzed by Rosenzweig only in the Jewish context. A Christian parallel to the Jewish sermon can be vaguely found only in the notion of sacrament. Rosenzweig is well aware of the fact that the sermon not only takes place in Christianity, but that it was the Protestant sermon that played a decisive role in the formation of the modern notion of the Jewish sermon. Nevertheless, he overlooks it. We will return to this later. As for our discussion, we will have to temporarily limit our horizon, in line with Rosenzweig, to the Jewish context.

The discussion of Jewish tradition and the way it designs the Jewish *Überwelt* is composed of two parts. In the first part Rosenzweig deals with the nature of Judaism as a faith community based on a people and its unique encounter with eternity. The second part describes and analyzes the two cycles that together create the Jewish tempo: that of the week and that of the year. The bridging passage that combines the two into one whole is the discussion of the sermon as a mutual listening and anticipation of supreme silence.[27]

Liturgy's main role is, as we have already seen, to "introduce man into this silence. In the liturgy, too, of course the mutual silence can

---

27   Stern, 342–344; Star, 327–329. Cf. *Norbert M. Samuelson*, A User's Guide to Franz Rosenzweig's Star of Redemption, Richmond Surrey, 257f.

only be that which is last, and all that precedes is only the preparatory school for this which comes last. In such an education, the word still rules. The word itself must guide man so that he may learn to grow mutually silent. The beginning of this education is that he may learn to listen." The words used in liturgy do not serve in the same manner that words usually serve in human life. Normally it is their content that counts, maybe also the load of associations they create, the emotions they arouse, and the kind of atmosphere created by the way they are being delivered. In other cases the words might be accompanied by music or motions that might have an essential part in delivering the message. All of these dimensions take place in regards to the liturgical language. But Rosenzweig believes that the essential role of liturgy lies much beyond them, namely in building the road towards silence, in total overcoming language altogether, in acceding to that very tradition in which liturgy is anchored. In that sense liturgy has an educational role. It should teach us how to reach silence. The first step in this educational process is to learn how to develop a mutual listening. As a first step it must take place within the world of language and words. We cannot reach silence yet; we should at least be silent and listen to the words that are being spoken to us. The words and the way they are delivered should not create the will to react and respond. They should create a kind of active silent listening that will unite the gathering community. What kind of words can reach such a goal? How can the sermon create such a situation?

Rosenzweig analyses the sermon as a kind of communication in order to define the kind of listening it creates. In order to do so, he compares the sermon both to the dialogical conversation and to a speech held in front of a public. In the first instance, Rosenzweig argues, listening is only apparent, not real. It is true that when a conversation takes place, there are normally periods in which one conversation partner listens to that which is being expressed by the one who is speaking at that moment. But, Rosenzweig argues, even when one listens quietly in such a situation, one is already engaged in responding, in formulating a reply. "In dialogue, the one who strictly listens, and not only when he strictly speaks, is also speaking, certainly not even mostly when he actually speaks, but equally as much when he raises the word onto his lips through his lively listening, through the attuned or questioning glance of his eyes at the one who is directly now speaking. It is not this listening of the eye that is meant here, but really the listening of the ears."[28] Dialogue belongs to the lingual sphere of revelation. It creates the presence and occurs in the presence; in no way

---

28 Stern, 343; Star, 328.

does it hint to that meta-lingual sphere of supreme silence, in no way does it educate us to gain the faculty of silent listening. It is much too active, much too actual.

The other kind of listening, the public listening to a speech, seems to be closer to that which Rosenzweig is aiming towards. Here the public is supposed to sit quietly and listen to the speaker. No immediate reply is expected or supposed. Nevertheless, it is also a sort of listening that does not unite the public but rather splits it into those who agree with the speaker and those who oppose.

Even the speaker before many is, as long as he is really a live speaker, only a conversant; moreover, the people listening to him, that monster of many heads, gives the public speaker his cue, also by consent and displeasure, with interruption and disturbance and its assortment of moods in which it forces him to take aside. If the public speaker wants to make himself independent of the listeners, then instead of the straightforward talking he might do, he must – at the risk of them falling asleep on him – "hold" the prepared speech learned by heart. Straightforward talk, the more straightforward it is, awakens all the more certainly two sides among the listeners, therefore just the opposite of the mutual listening of all those present. It is the essence of the "speech program" that it is "held", not spoken; at this price an assembly is supposed to be brought into unanimous accord; i.e., the speaker must necessarily turn himself into the mere lecturer of a prepared program.

A sermon is certainly a speech. A good sermon certainly contains a message which, like all non-trivial messages, bares the potency of functioning in the same schismatic way that the public speech does, dividing the congregation, and creating reactions. The authority of the preacher must also not be seen as a guarantee that the sermon will be listened to in the required way. The essential element which creates listening should lie in another dimension than the message or the personality of the speaker. The sermon gains its unique quality by being based on the "verse", namely on a sacred text, that serves as such as the foundation of the faith-community's belief.

The mutual listening that would be nothing but listening, listening where a crowd becomes "all ears", does not result from the speaker, but rather only through the drawing back of the actively speaking person behind the mere lecture, really not even behind the lecturing person, but behind the words being read aloud. The fact that the sermon must come by way of a "text" has its basis here; only the connection to the text secures for it the "devoted" listening of everyone; the straightforward words of the preacher would not at all venture to want to produce such a devotion; they would plunge like a force of separation in the listeners; but the text, which is considered to be the words of its God by the gathered community, produces for him who is reading it aloud the mutual listening of all those gathered; when he has given everything he has to say as explication of that text, he keeps that mutual listening alive during his whole sermon.

The sermon is a speech that is composed as hermeneutics of the sacred text. It brings that which the preacher wishes to express under the authority of the Holy Scripture. As such it is a component of the composition of sacred time, corresponding the liturgical moment in which it is being held. The community, gathering in the house of God in order to worship Him, can actively-silently listen to the sermon and be united through this listening, though it contains messages that could be countersealed. Through this listening to the human message that arouses from the sacred text, the community begins to learn how to create silence, how to encounter the presence of God and eternity.

It is important to note that Rosenzweig's analysis has very little to do with the actual content of modern Central European sermons, be them in liberal or in orthodox environments. He hardly expects the preacher to educate his community through the messages he delivers in his sermons, but rather in the very fact that he preaches. It is also obvious that Rosenzweig does not focus in any way on the preacher himself, only on the listening community to which the preacher serves as a no more than educational and liturgical mean. He is the creator of the situation in which the community trains itself to listen. No more than that. The active partner in the sermon is not as much the preacher but more the text.

This role of the sacred text in Rosenzweig's analysis should be carefully examined. Though most of his writings about the Bible are from a later period, one can safely say that already when writing the Star it was obvious for him that the Bible, including the Pentateuch, is a human creation, in no way a verbal Divine inspiration.[29] He must have been fully aware of the fact that this notion was taken for granted by the majority of the Central European Jews as well as many others elsewhere. These were the congregants who listened to the sermons to which he was referring in the first place. For these people, like for Rosenzweig himself, the text could contain the "word of God" only indirectly. Only as a human response to God's commandment, a human

---

29 *Joseph Turner*, The Dynamics of Religious Experience vs. the Canonical Status of Sources in Franz Rosenzweig's Understanding of Judaism, in: Franz Rosenzweigs "neues Denken" (above nr. 17), 1030–1043; *Amir*, Da'at Ma'amina (above nr. 17), 281–289.

formulation of the encounter with God,[30] could this human text be perceived as Divine.

This dialogical approach to the Bible, this perception of the Biblical text as simultaneously human and Divine, enlightens Rosenzweig's analysis of the sermon in a special light. The sermon is only the first educational step towards supreme silence. The kind of listening it creates is fully located within the sphere of language, of words, but it hints beyond that sphere. Now we learn that the text that lies behind the ability to create such a listening is by itself a liminal one. It is anchored in God's revelation but nevertheless expresses that which human beings have composed. It encounters us not directly with God, but rather with the human encounter with Him. It is a composition of words that by its nature hints beyond words, beyond language. It is no wonder that as such it can serve as an educational vehicle towards gaining the faculty of listening, of establishing contact with eternity, with eternal supreme silence.

Now we are also in a position to try to understand the groundings for Rosenzweig's ignoring of the Christian sermon. Under his interpretation Christianity is the "eternal way", while Judaism is "eternal life". Christianity carries the work of redeeming the world, while Judaism – that of anticipating redemption. The basic faith-experience of the Christian is that of "coming to God"; that of the Jew is that of "being with God".[31] This basic difference, essential to the cooperation between the two traditions, means that each tradition encounters eternity in a different way. Judaism, as an anticipation of eternity, creates a liturgical surrounding in which both redemption and eternity are being perceived as if they are mere reality. The Jew lives beyond history,[32] in a time-cycle that anticipates eternity. The Christian lives within history, within the struggle between time and eternity,

---

30 Zweistromland, 735–741.
31 *Franz Rosenzweig*, Briefe und Tagebücher, Haag 1979, 132–137. Rosenzweig reflects on the words of Jesus: "I am the way, and the truth, and the life. No one comes to the Father except through me" (John 14.6). Rosenzweig accepts the notion that no one can come to God, except through Christian revelation; but he adds: "No one comes to the father – but it is different when a person does not have to come to him any more, since he *is* already by him. And that is the case with the Jewish people (not the individual Jew)". In the Star he implements the same idea by attributing the "way" to Christianity, "life" to Judaism and "truth" to eternity towards both of them hint.
32 *Amos Funkenstein*, An Escape from History. Rosenzweig on the Destiny of Judaism, in: History and Memory 2/1990, 2, 117–135; *Yehoshua Amir*, Der Platz der Geschichte bei Franz Rosenzweig, in: Truma 1/1987, 199–211; *David M. Myers*, The Problem of History in German-Jewish Thought. Observations on Neglected Tradition. Cohen, Rosenzweig and Buber, Ramat Gan 2002.

between the two appearances of Christ. The parallelism that Rosenzweig draws between Jewish *Überwelt* and the Christian ceases in these points in which Jewish liturgical life establishes the direct encounter with eternity. This is true for the Day of Atonement; this is also true for the sermon as a step towards eternity.

If this analysis is right, it should be perceived as a clear example of the limitations from which Rosenzweig's scheme for the two religions suffers. Though one can understand within the framework of such scheme why Rosenzweig finds it difficult to deal with Christian sermon, one can hardly justify ignoring it. This difficulty is especially visible when one takes in account that, as we saw at the beginning of our discussion, the very existence and role of modern Central European Jewish sermon is a clear example of Christian influence on liberal Judaism. The fact that he finds it necessary, and possible, to ignore Christian sermon, shows how powerful and creative the schematic order in which he described the two traditions was for him. It should also serve as a proof, among many others, of how careful one must be when examining the validity and fruitfulness of Rosenzweig's scheme.

5. Rosenzweig's perception of Rabbi Nobel as a preacher

A couple of months after bringing the Star to completion[33] Rosenzweig was sent by his friend Joseph Prager, the Rabbi of Kassel'sk son, to Frankfurt am Main, were the great scholar and Talmudist Rabbi Anton (Nehemia Zvi) Nobel served as the rabbi of the moderate Orthodox congregation. The move, aimed to allow Rosenzweig to reach a new stage in his own rapid journey towards Jewish knowledge and learning, appears to be highly significant in other terms as well. It is well known that Frankfurt became the town of his own educational enterprise, *"das freie jüdische Lehrhaus"*. For our purpose it is also significant that by meeting Nobel he met for the first time in his life a preacher whom he could admire and follow. Rosenzweig makes it clear that his special relationship to Nobel is not anchored in his philosophy; it is hardly even rooted in his personality as a Talmudic teacher.[34] It was the preacher, and the prayer, to which Rosenzweig was so strongly attracted and attached.[35] Nobel was, Rosenzweig reports in a letter, "a

---

33 Rosenzweig reports that the Star was completed on February 16, 1918. Only three years later he succeeded in publishing the book.
34 See his letter to Joseph Prager, Briefe und Tagebücher (above nr. 31), 746–748.
35 It is typical to this relationship that Rosenzweig gave his son, born a few months after Nobel's sudden death, the middle name Nehamia, after his beloved teacher

Zionist, a Mystic and an Idealist (you know: in my mouth these disgraces are listed in an increasing order). [...] he speaks to the People in the way that only prophets, one might think, had the right to speak in".[36]

Living in Frankfurt and being a student and a friend of Nobel's enriched Rosenzweig's understanding of the sermon from new points of view. From then on it would not be merely an experience of a community that learns in this experience how to – actively though quietly – listen and anticipate through this experience the supreme silence of eternity. Rosenzweig will reflect on the sermon from the points of view of its content and message and, even more so, of the preacher who delivers this message.

In his eulogy to Nobel Rosenzweig wrote, referring to the first sermon he heard from him, on the first day of Passover 1918:

"I have seen for the first time in my life, so many thoughts – genuine thoughts – flow out from the podium. Each intellectual move that characterizes the Jewish *Derashah* [...]. Yes, the contradictions within the Biblical text played in many cases a role of a rhetoric 'point of departure', but in essence it was not these contradictions and tensions that he was referring to but rather the contradictions and tensions in life itself. They were metaphysic *Kashyes*[37] and, in no way metaphysic, but religious *Terutzim*.[38] In other words: human questions and divine answers.

That is, one might say, the significance of this way of thinking. The thoughts do not draw close systematic circle [...]. His flow of thought remained open, it moved in a spiral form. There were no complete, exhausting answers that would solve the question and will suck all its content. No, he led the answer to a sphere that lies far beyond that of the question; by that he left the question itself open, unsolved. He was not a man of easy, ready for use, rash solutions. Life-contradictions remained for him sharp and untouched. The puzzling questions of human freedom, of divine Being, of world's actuality remained for him puzzles; in the loneliness of his study he struggled with them again and again; they were not to be solved; only when he stood at the podium before the many at his house-of-God, he was blessed with answers and solutions. That is, in a matter of fact, the nature of these 'final' questions; we know how to answer

---

(ibid., 1189). Ernst Simon, Nobel's pupil and son in law, was asked by Rosenzweig to be the godfather of his son, as the "inheritor of his spirit and love" (ibid., 823).

36 Ibid., 726.

37 Kushiyot: questions and queries, typical to Talmudic learning and to Jewish traditional Biblical exegesis. Rosenzweig refers here to theological and ideological queries that served as the point of departure for Nobel's sermon. The twist from the pure hermeneutic query to the metaphysical one is characteristic to the modern Jewish sermon in Europe.

38 Teruzim: solutions, answers. *Teruz* is a terminus technicus in Talmudic discourse, marking the solutions offered to the *Kushiyot*.

them only when the answers are demanded, demanded by those who have the right to receive them from us."[39]

Rosenzweig describes Nobel's sermon as structured by raising questions, doubts, and problems. These are anchored in biblical and rabbinic texts and even more so "in life itself", namely in actual confrontation with theological and existential issues. The sermon aims to offer answers to these questions, to solve these difficulties. But there is an essential difference in Rosenzweig's eyes between the question and the answer. The first is strictly human. It is anchored in the human mind and belief, in sophisticated reading, and in the hermeneutical tradition. But the answers are of another dimension from that of the questions. Rosenzweig speaks of them as "Divine" answers as opposed to the "metaphysical" questions, namely questions which arise from the dialogue between human and God, between our understanding and belief, and the commandment with which God's love encounters our life.[40]

How can the preacher give "religious" answers? How can he exceed the sphere in which his reading and thinking is anchored? Rosenzweig's answer is in no way mystical. It is the demanding audience, the listening congregation that provides the preacher with the power to speak in the name of a higher truth, to provide his listeners with confidence, faith and comfort. It is the very situation of the sermon, in the house of God, at the heart of the prayer that arouses an expectation of the congregation to hear a message that will connect them with God, to be challenged by God's commandment. It is this very expectation that awards the preacher with the potency to overcome his own doubts and hesitations, everlasting questions and queries, and to provide the demanding congregation with that which they are so rightly demanding.

Rosenzweig does not give an account about the relationships between this perception of Nobel's sermons and preaching and that which he offered as a philosophy of the sermon in the Star. Nevertheless we can try to bridge that gap. In a letter to his student and successor as the Lehrhaus' head, Rudolph Hallo, he gives him practical instructions in regards of the nature of the sermon and the place of the sermon within the prayer:

---

39 Zweistromland (above nr. 19), 667–669.
40 Rosenzweig gives a reference to a "five minutes sermon" given by Nobel in an unknown occasion about the revelation to Abraham at his tent. "And God revealed himself to Abraham – and he saw there: three persons" (Briefe und Tagebücher [above nr. 31], 1005).

> "Sermon builds the bridge from the *awaudo*[41] into Talmud Torah[42] or anyway into the practical life of the community. It is, therefore, a moving out of worship, and is not only allowed but also demanded to have to a certain extent an intellectual character. It is teaching, not ritual."[43]

In the philosophic discussion offered in the Star there was no emphasis on this intellectual dimension whatsoever. Sermon was described as an opportunity to reach the unique kind of listening that only the sacred text can create. Neither the theological content nor the hermeneutic dimension were the center of gravity in this discussion. Sermon was merely part of the ritual. To a certain extent the raw model of the ritual altogether. In the letter we have seen that Rosenzweig describes things in a different way. Sermon has its place in the ritual, but it is not merely part of it; it is a bridge between the worship and the learning, the emotional and the intellectual. As such it constitutes the spiritual.

This perception of the sermon shines clear light on the significance that the exposure to Nobel's preaching had for Rosenzweig. Preaching is no longer merely an experience of the congregation, in which the preacher serves as a facilitator, but a dialogue between the two. The preacher is a teacher. He carries the authority and obligation to teach. He should build the bridge between worship and Talmud Torah, and by doing so he should build the bridge between the intellectual encounter with the texts and the religious message that the preacher wishes to bring to his audience. By doing so, by responding to the demand of the congregation to receive knowledge and guidance, he conducts a dialogue with them. This dialogue might create in one end of the congregation the ability to listen and to be united through this listening; at the other end, that of the preacher, it can stimulate the power to overcome that which stops us at every other moment of our lives and to be able to deliver a message which is anchored in God's words, in God's commandment.

---

41   Avodah – worship.
42   Talmud Torah – learning in the broadest religious meaning.
43   Briefe und Tagebücher (above nr. 31), 835.

Response

Alexander Deeg

First of all, I want to thank you, Yehoyada, for your inspiring lecture about Franz Rosenzweig, his view of religion, and his attitude towards Jewish preaching. I am very glad that you directed our attention to Franz Rosenzweig in the homiletical context, which is surely not obvious at first glance, as Rosenzweig was not a preacher. But – as you have shown impressively – there are possibilities for rich homiletical learning in Rosenzweig's thought.

In my response, I would like to stress three points and add some questions.

1. The intellectual background of Franz Rosenzweig's writings

All of Franz Rosenzweig's words and attitudes must be understood – as you have shown in your lecture – in a specific historical and intellectual background. World War I marked a considerable shift in Germany's *'Geistesgeschichte'*, in the German intellectual history. This shift can be discerned in Christian circles as well as in Jewish ones. On the Christian side theologians like Karl Barth or Eduard Thurneysen are outstanding examples of this shift away from classic liberal and enlightenment theology towards a fresh re-lecture of one's own old sources, of the sacred texts and traditional dogmatics. Theologians like Barth and Thurneysen yearned for a new thinking and a new theology – and found it theologically in the radical antithesis between God and world and aesthetically in an expressionist way of writing. The circumstances in this time of an experienced crisis produced a specific *"Theologie der Krise"*, "theology of crisis", as an answer.[1]

---

[1] Rosenzweig was very aware of these theological developments, cf. e.g. *Franz Rosenzweig*, Sprachdenken im Übersetzen, vol. 1: Jehuda Halevi. Fünfundneunzig Hymnen und Gedichte (Der Mensch und sein Werk. Gesammelte Schriften 4,1 [*Rafael N. Rosenzweig*, Ed.]), Haag/Boston (MA)/Lancaster 1983, 68–71, esp. 70.

Almost the same development can be seen in Jewish intellectual history as well – and all this had homiletical consequences, too. The Jewish reform of the 19th century produced as one of its offspring the German-Jewish sermon, which was taken over with varying emphases by the various movements which began to be differentiated in Judaism around the middle of the 19th century. The Jewish reform movement was upheld by the central paradigms of rationality and universality and also by a fundamental belief in progress. All this became questionable early in the 20th century when the irrational (the "holy"; the "subconscious/unconscious"), the particular, and the return to tradition became more and more fascinating.[2] This being the case, the modern Jewish sermon in the pedagogical form established only a few years previously in Siegmund Maybaum's "Jewish Homiletics"[3] lost much of its acceptance. Numerous young rabbis considered it a relic of past times. Consequently, looking back at the 1920's Sinai Ucko writes:

"As far as they [i.e. the younger generation of rabbis – AD] were aware, the sermon was no longer so central and one looked somewhat ironically on the homiletical rules still being taught in the rabbinic seminaries."[4]

Instead, many attempted – thus once more Sinai Ucko – "often to replace the sermon by a lecture in order thus […] to take up the old tradition of 'learning'."[5]

The return to tradition and the recent turning to the sources of Judaism, to the Talmud and Midrash, also shaped the new hermeneutics and congregational-educational conceptions which are connected with names such as Franz Rosenzweig and Martin Buber and which belong to a trend often called the "Jewish Renaissance". In his famous article *"Zeit ists"* (Hebrew: ...ל עת, English: 'It's time now!'), published in 1917, Franz Rosenzweig claimed that after 100 years of Jewish emancipation and new freedom nowadays most of the Jews were outside: outside of their own tradition, outside of Torah. What had to be done – according to Rosenzweig – was to find a new way in: into the tradition, into

---

2 Cf. *Michael Brenner*, The Renaissance of Jewish culture in Weimar Germany, New Haven (CT)/London 1996; *Steven E. Aschheim*, German Jews Beyond Bildung and Liberalism. The Radical Jewish Revival in the Weimar Republic, in: *Klaus L. Bergahn* (Ed.), The German-Jewish Dialogue Reconsidered. A Symposium in Honor of George L. Mosse (German life and civilization 20), New York et al. 1996, 125–140; 277–287 (notes).

3 Cf. *Siegmund Maybaum*, Jüdische Homiletik. Nebst einer Auswahl von Texten und Themen, Praktische Theologie 1, Berlin 1890.

4 *Sinai Ucko*, Der Rabbiner in der Kleingemeinde, in: *Schlomo F. Rülf* (Ed.), Paul Lazarus Gedenkbuch. Beiträge zur Würdigung der letzten Rabbinergeneration in Deutschland, Jerusalem 1961, 73–78; quotation: 73.

5 Ibid., 73f.

Torah. What had to be sought was a new way of teaching so that all the Jews alienated from their tradition could rediscover the richness and power of Torah and Jewish tradition.[6]

There are three interesting questions for me at this point: First: is it right to see Franz Rosenzweig as one of the many children of a large movement during the World War I-period and in the early Weimar Republic – or is he much more unique? Second: is his analysis of the hermeneutical situation of his own Jewish people correct? Did Jewish emancipation, did Jewish liberalism lead people out and away from Torah? And third: what about our situation nowadays in Germany, in Europe, in Israel, in the United States? Is it the same as it was in 1917? Are we all 'out' – and have to find new ways 'in'? And if this be the case, could we – Christians and Jews – help each other to do so?

2. Franz Rosenzweig and his homiletical hermeneutics

In Yehoyada Amir's description of Rosenzweig's homiletical approach, preaching appears as a very specific kind of "mutual listening" – and mainly "mutual listening" to the biblical texts.

In Rosenzweig's remarks about his own translation of the poems of the medieval author and poet Jehuda Halevi (1075–1141), he stressed that he wanted to show in these translations that Halevi was *not* a German writer. He wanted to make the readers feel the difference between Halevi and us. He did not want to "Germanize" Halevi's Hebrew, but to make the German sound foreign and unknown to us. He wanted to respect the difference – and this respect is according to Rosenzweig the indispensable condition for us to leap over the gap which exists between Halevi and us. And sometimes, Rosenzweig writes, there would be moments in which the wall between translation and text is broken down – magic moments for the translator and reader.[7]

In my opinion these remarks on the Halevi translation could easily be read with homiletical eyes as well. Preaching – according to Rosenzweig – would then mean *not* to bridge, but on the contrary to enlarge the gap between us and the biblical texts, to make us feel the

---

6   Cf. *Franz Rosenzweig*, Zeit ists, in: *Idem*, Zweistromland. Kleinere Schriften zu Glauben und Denken (Der Mensch und sein Werk. Gesammelte Schriften 3 [*Reinhold and Annemarie Mayer*, Eds.]), Dordrecht/Boston (MA)/Lancaster 1984, 461–481.

7   Cf. *Franz Rosenzweig*, Vorwort zu Jehuda Halevi, in: *Idem*, Sprachdenken, vol. 1 (v. supra, n. 1), 1–18.

difference, to make us listen – and thus to make the texts alluring and attractive to us.

Rosenzweig was – as Yehoyada Amir stated – attracted by the sermons of Nehemia Anton Nobel (1871–1922). These sermons were resolutely located in the context of the synagogue liturgy and drew the biblical text anew into the centre. Rosenzweig writes of a *Kohelet*-sermon by Nobel:

> "He delivered almost his entire sermon in a quiet manner, possibly for a whole hour. It was as if he were conversing with someone. But this someone was not sitting among us. Suddenly I noticed: he was not really speaking to us – in every sentence he addressed *Kohelet* directly, he did not speak *about*, he spoke *with Kohelet*. And then I saw him [i.e. Kohelet – AD] ..."[8]

If we follow Rosenzweig's description, Nobel produced a kind of dialogue with Scripture in which the listener, Rosenzweig, became a participant.

Can the implicit homiletics of Rosenzweig be characterized as a homiletics of the strange and unknown text? A text which can never be understood completely? And could we learn from this as well? Could we find a new and attractive homiletical hermeneutic in Franz Rosenzweig's traces? A homiletical hermeneutic which does not try to bridge us and the text – but instead shows us its difference and strangeness?

3. Franz Rosenzweig: The sermon in prayer context

As we have heard in Yehoyada Amir's lecture one of the main problems Franz Rosenzweig had with the Jewish sermon was that it just did not really fit in the context of Jewish prayer. Sermon always means that *one* person speaks and addresses his words to the others. The community addressing the one God and praising the one God no longer exists when one out of the community stands before the others preaching. The *bet ha-tefilla* changes its shape and becomes a specific kind of *bet-midrash*.

Actually, I think, Rosenzweig marks a fundamental problem of each sermon – as sermon can be defined as human words addressed to human beings with the purpose of edifying or interpreting or teaching in liturgical context – a context which is characterized by jointly addressing the one God in praise and lament. Especially in Protestant

---

8   *Franz Rosenzweig* in: Vorstand der Israelitischen Gemeinde Frankfurt am Main (Ed.), Nachrufe auf Rabbiner N. A. Nobel, Frankfurt/M. 1923, 44–46, here: 45f.

circles the problem of a rivalry between worship and sermon is obvious. Since the early 19th century (Schleiermacher was one of the protagonists), quite a number of Protestants have terminologically separated *Liturgy* and *Sermon,* calling liturgy everything that happens in the worship apart from the sermon.[9] The consequence in many Protestant circles is clear: liturgy somehow seems to be dispensable; the sermon of course is not!

I think Rosenzweig is right to stress this problem. And to demand a sermon which deliberately locates itself *in the context of prayer*. A sermon which does not only teach tradition or try to somehow educate the congregation in a moral sense or give its commentary on what happens in the world – but a sermon which fits in the liturgical context. Like the sermons of Nehemia Anton Nobel seem to have fitted in prayer context, because he – according to Rosenzweig's description – did not speak about Kohelet, but with him.

I ask: is the connection between sermon and liturgy or sermon and prayer still a topic in Jewish and Christian homiletical and liturgical discussions? How necessary or how dispensable is the sermon in the liturgy? And how could a sermon be shaped that really fits into its liturgical context?

---

9 Cf. *Friedrich Kalb*, Art. Liturgie I. Christliche Liturgie, in: TRE 21/1991, 358–377, here: 367.

Leo Baeck – Preacher and Teacher of Preaching

Walter Homolka

The topic of Jewish sermons in the 20th century inevitably brings us to Rabbi Leo Baeck, who was born on May 23, 1873 and died November 2, 1956. His significance as one of the greatest teachers of Judaism lifts him out of history and directly into our midst here in the present. Unfortunately, there is little opportunity to look at actual sermons of this important philosopher of 20th century Judaism in order to come to know him as a preacher and homilist.[1] Still he is a most worthy example to study Jewish preaching in the 20th century. This has as much to do with his prescient thinking as with his personality.

1. Leo Baeck's concept of a Jewish preacher

On May 4, 1913, on the occasion of Leo Baeck's inaugural lecture as a lecturer for homiletics at the *Lehranstalt für die Wissenschaft des Judentums*, Dr. Herman Veit Simon, the chairman of the board of trustees, had the following to say:

> "The Teaching Chair for Homiletics is of outstanding importance for the *Lehranstalt* and for Judaism as a whole. Whoever occupies the position is entrusted with training preachers appointed to plant the word of God in the hearts of the listeners, so that they adhere faithfully to the religion of the fathers with all their souls, with all their powers, and that they preserve them in life by changing them. Whoever occupies the office shall through religious ardour plant the seeds that will bear bloom and fruits that the appointed preacher is empowered to transmit with humble heart upon the great crowd."[2]

---

[1] Only very few sermons as scriptural interpretations are published; we have predominantly eulogies and thoughts on Jewish festivals published in Jewish periodicals or pamphlets, e.g. for soldiers in World War I, also speeches at installations and jubilees; for a full picture see Theodore Wiener, The Writings of Leo Baeck, in: Studies in Bibliography and Booklore, I, 3/1954, 108–144.

[2] „Der Lehrstuhl für Homiletik ist für die Lehranstalt und für das gesamte Judentum von hervorragender Bedeutsamkeit. Wer ihn versieht, hat Prediger heranzubilden, die berufen sind, Gottes Wort in die Herzen der Hörer zu pflanzen, damit sie mit

Baeck took a more sceptical view of the effectiveness of the sermon: "How much is said in earnestness and sincerity, how many good sermons are preached and heard – should not the world already be a perfect place if words were effective! [...] But we nevertheless must not think little of the importance of speech,"[3] he said in his farewell sermon in Oppeln in 1907.

Hans Liebeschütz remembers of Baeck:

"He always advocated the conviction that the preacher, who must preach the old lessons to his congregation in times of radical change, must in all humility be an academic, capable of reclaiming the sense of the classical source texts through independent study: only in that way is he capable of finding his own words in the pulpit and in the school room. That conviction placed Baeck firmly in the grand tradition of German Jewry as it had been formed in the first half the 19th century [...]. The two institutions from which Leo Baeck as a student had received his Jewish training, building upon the basis laid early by his father, were the 'Jewish Theological Seminar' in Breslau und the '*Lehranstalt für die Wissenschaft des Judentums*' in Berlin; both of these had their origins in that philosophical construct [...] Leo Baeck belonged in the beginning to the group of those for whom the old ideal of the learned figure in the pulpit still held sway [...]."[4]

---

der ganzen Seele, mit ganzer Kraft in Treue festhalten an der Religion der Väter und sie im Leben durch ihren Wandel bewähren. Wer ihn versieht, legt den Samen nieder, der Blüte und Frucht treiben soll durch die religiöse Begeisterung, die der berufene Prediger aus demütigem Herzen auf die große Menge zu übertragen die Macht hat." In: Zweiunddreißigster Bericht der Lehranstalt für die Wissenschaft des Judentums in Berlin 1914, 53. If not otherwise stated, the English translations of quotations from publications in German are provided by the author.

3 „Wieviel wird doch Ernst und aufrichtig gesprochen, wie viele gute Lehren werden verkündigt und gehört – müßte nicht die Welt schon vollkommen sein, wenn Worte wirken könnten! [...] Aber dennoch dürfen wir von der Bedeutung der Rede nicht gering denken." In: *Leo Baeck*, Abschiedspredigt in Oppeln am 1. Oktober 1907, in: *Idem*, Werke 6. Briefe, Reden, Aufsätze, Gütersloh 2003, 49.

4 „Er hat immer die Überzeugung vertreten, daß der Prediger, welcher seiner Gemeinde die alte Lehre in einer aufs tiefste gewandelten Zeit zu verkünden hat, in aller Bescheidenheit ein wissenschaftlicher Arbeiter sein müsse, fähig, den klassischen Quellenschriften ihren Sinn in selbständigem Studium abzugewinnen: nur so würde er imstande sein, das eigene Wort auf der Kanzel und im Schulraum zu finden. Mit dieser Überzeugung stand Baeck in der großen Tradition des deutschen Judentums, wie sie sich in der ersten Hälfte des neunzehnten Jahrhunderts gebildet hatte. [...] Die beiden Anstalten, an denen Leo Baeck als Student seine judaistische Ausbildung auf der vom Vater früh gelegten Grundlage empfing, das ‚Jüdisch-Theologische Seminar' in Breslau und die ‚Lehranstalt für die Wissenschaft des Judentums' in Berlin, hatten beide in diesem Gedankenkreis ihren Ursprung. [...] Leo Baeck gehörte von Anfang an zu der Gruppe derjenigen, für die

In 1907, "The Essence of Judaism" had already been published and had made the author widely esteemed, Leo Baeck became rabbi of Düsseldorf. Before he departed from Oppeln on October 3, 1907 he delivered his last sermon there, in which he explains how he defines the situation of the Jewish preacher:

> "If there is a danger to the community, said Baeck, then also there is a danger for the rabbi, who must not allow himself to feel he is in a position above his congregants. 'Steps lead to the pulpit, yet they are only steps of wood or stone,' he said. 'They do not lead above the community.' How easily can the rabbi 'surrender to a feeling of superiority because he is talking at a higher level and because no one opposes him [...].' Baeck asked if it were not insolent and pretentious to describe the rabbi's words 'as God's words' because, after all, the rabbi's words are 'only narrow human speech, human words.' The rabbi can be successful, but 'only where honest thinking and honest conviction strive for expression, where the spiritual way works which our wise people called the reverence before the community.' Only then can words 'have an everlasting success.'"[5]

The crutch of polished rhetoric was hence not Leo Baeck's terrain. How, we may ask, was he perceived as preacher?

2. Leo Baeck, the preacher

Baeck assumed his first post as a rabbi in 1895 in the Silesian city of Oppeln, where he remained until 1907. Unfortunately, we have little evidence of Baeck's sermons in Oppeln. Eva G. Reichmann characterizes Baeck's preaching as follows:

> "Children who had grown up in Oppeln when Leo Baeck was rabbi there recalled that they were not forced to attend services – they went willingly. They listened to Rabbi Baeck speak 'so solemn', as the children described it; as one recalled many years later, 'the world around him disappeared.'

---

das alte Ideal des Gelehrten auf der Kanzel in Kraft blieb [...]", *Hans Liebesschütz*, in: *Leo Baeck*, Aus drei Jahrtausenden, Tübingen 1958, 2–4.

5 „Stufen führen zur Kanzel hinauf, doch sie sind nur Stufen von Holz und Stein, sie führen nicht über die Gemeinde empor. Auch der, welcher von diesem Platze aus das Wort an die Gemeinde richtet, bleibt nur ein Glied der Gemeinde. [...] Kommt so zu der Gemeinde leicht von der Tatsache des Amtes die Gefahr, so nicht minder zu dem, der das Gotteswort verkündet. Wie leicht kann er der Überhebung anheimfallen, da er von einem höheren Platze aus und gleichsam in höherem Tone redet, da niemand ihm widerspricht, seiner Anklage oder seiner Verteidigung kein Urteil anderer den Anschluß gibt." In: *Leo Baeck*, Abschiedspredigt in Oppeln am 1. Oktober 1907, in: *Idem*, Werke 6. Briefe, Reden, Aufsätze, Gütersloh 2003, 49–52. The English quotations from Baeck's sermon and its paraphrase follow *Leonard Baker*, Days of Sorrow and Pain. Leo Baeck and the Berlin Jews, New York 1978, 48.

Leo Baeck avoided emotional appeals, seeking instead to offer intellectual challenges. Still, the statement suggests something of the warmth that the people came to feel for their rabbi. 'From the earliest days of my life,' said one of his young students, 'I was filled with an enthusiasm for Judaism because I saw it bound up in such a Jewish aristocrat.'"[6]

Following a move to Düsseldorf in 1907, Baeck, his wife Natalie (née Hamburg) and his daughter Ruth lived on Kasernenstraße, not at all far from the synagogue. The apartment was situated across from a theatre in which the famed Louise Dumont appeared. Baeck engaged her for speaking lessons. He was no strong orator at that point, as his Düsseldorf students had learned. And the speaking lessons did not bring about any fundamental change, felt Hermann O. Pineas: "The new rabbi, Dr. Leo Baeck, was unintelligible to us, not only what he said but how he said it. His language, his tone, the melody of his language distinguished itself in a grotesque way from the Rhenish style of speaking familiar to us, so much so that we could not refrain from laughing in the first hours. It was inconceivable to us that the community leaders could have selected such a dreadful speaker – and he must also be just as bad a preacher – as the successor of the rhetorically brilliant Dr. Hochfeld."[7] His voice would later deepen, and its gravely timbre made it interesting to listeners. Nevertheless, it is fair to say that the content of his speeches was always more enduring than his manner of presenting them.

In 1912 Leo Baeck received an invitation from Berlin to serve as a liberal congregational rabbi and a lecturer at the Hochschule. He held seminars and lectures about midrash, homiletics, history of religion, and comparative religion. His lectures were analytical, systematic and emphasised the unadorned character of his public speaking. Memories of contemporaries preserve a vivid picture of how Baeck delivered a sermon.

In Berlin Baeck's voice was "very husky, a whisper really; it had a haunting quality [...]," remembers Rabbi Herman Schaalman. "It was a very effective method of presentation, especially in Germany," said one who heard him speak often, adding, "the average German is trained to listen rather than to speak." Rudolf Simons described Baeck's preaching in the following manner: "It was something different from

---

6 *Eva G. Reichmann*, Größe und Verhängnis deutsch-jüdischer Existenz. Zeugnis einer tragischen Begegnung (Bibliotheca Judaica 2), Heidelberg 1974, 258f., 261f. The English paraphrase follows *Leonard Baker*, Days of Sorrow and Pain. Leo Baeck and the Berlin Jews, New York 1978, 36.

7 *Hermann O. Pineas*, Meine Erinnerungen an Dr. Leo Baeck. Mss. in the Leo Baeck Institute/New York, 1–3, as cited in *Leonard Baker*, Days of Sorrow and Pain. Leo Baeck and the Berlin Jews, New York 1978, 51.

what one was accustomed to by men such as Maybaum, Rosenzweig, Weisse; Baeck would not and could not compete with their theatrical talent."⁸ He refused to help his listeners through dramatics. "It was beneath his dignity to use techniques," said Joachim Prinz, a fellow rabbi in Berlin and later in New Jersey. "There was no performance," Fritz Bamberger, one of Baeck's pupils, said of him, "his rabbinical bag did not contain a well-assorted collection of Jewish tales labelled for various occasions."⁹

Listening to a sermon delivered by Leo Baeck was a challenging exercise of the mind. It demanded that one follow the development of the sermon's topic carefully, ponder its significance and stretch one's intellect to its utmost. Still, people like Henry Kellermann and Helmuth H. Galliner recalled him being on the pulpit as "the high point of the synagogue experience [...]. The structure of his sermons had a highly developed classical beauty and was exemplary. The fullness of his insight of the spirit overrode all which the liberal rabbinical tradition had to offer."¹⁰ This is even more astounding when one considers that Leo Baeck usually did not speak from a prepared manuscript. His granddaughter Marianne Dreyfus and her husband Rabbi A. Stanley Dreyfus recall that Baeck rarely, if ever, wrote out his sermons in German. He preached and taught principally without a script and did not even use cue cards on the pulpit or lectern. Instead both remember how he would memorize his words even as a lecturer at Hebrew Union College after World War II, how they would hear him walk around in his study for the purpose of concentration.¹¹ This habit helped Baeck

---

8   *Leonard Baker,* Days of Sorrow and Pain. Leo Baeck and the Berlin Jews, New York 1978, 99.
9   Ibid.
10 Ibid.
11 Interview on Baeck's preaching habits in their home in Brooklyn on April 30, 2007. When asked whether the family was aware of any sermon collections in the manuscripts of Leo Baeck both answered that they had never come across any material of this kind. Marianne Dreyfus assumed that there is little likelihood that German sermon preparations let alone whole scripts may have survived World War II in any great number since almost the complete library was lost after confiscation by the Nazis. Another reason for the absence of related manuscripts might be Baeck's manner of preparing his sermons. Marianne Dreyfus said that Baeck usually did not speak from a prepared script but used small outlines for preparations which he then memorized. On the pulpit, he spoke without any piece of paper and only from what he had memorized.
    Being asked about sermon collections of Leo Baeck at LBI archives, Dr. Frank Mecklenburg, the director of research, affirms that there are no sermons of Leo Baeck in the records of the archive. Correspondence with Dr. Frank Mecklenburg, 02–03.05.2007.

during his time in Theresienstadt when he would teach and lecture extensively right from his memory.[12]

Baeck's sermons unquestionably left behind an indelible impression on his listeners. Fritz Bamberger reports: "When Leo Baeck preached, he did not address his listeners from on high. [...] he appeared to expect an answer to his words not from the congregation, but rather from somewhere else far beyond. Baeck's sermons [...] always had a bit of a private character."[13] They were personal conversations with God.[14] A pious teacher poses questions of the Bible, a highly educated man discusses history and literature. He spoke with them, not about them. Yet, in spite of their perfect form, his sermons were largely without any definitive conclusion; they showed a human being on a quest for the truth.[15]

Leo Baeck's style is almost legendary. Albert H. Friedlander reports that he preached as he wrote: "[...] each and every word was used with the utmost caution and precision." And he continues: "Fritz Bamberger once pointed out that 'an essential of Baeck's thought-process is reflected in his tendency to hypostatise adjectives, participles, and verbs into nouns. A noun is better defined, more substantial, closer, if I may venture that far, to a Platonic idea than the fluid, moving adjective, verb or participle'."[16]

---

12 *Walter Homolka*, Leo Baeck. Jüdisches Denken – Perspektiven für heute, Freiburg 2006, 69, or Jewish Identity in Modern Times. Leo Baeck and German Protestantism, Oxford 1995, xi.

13 Fritz Bamberger berichtet weiter: "Wenn Leo Baeck predigte, wandte er sich nicht von oben herab an den Zuhörer. Er wählte sorgsam jedes Wort, er formte jeden Satz nach Gewicht und Klang, sprach etwas monoton mit einer sonderbar vibrierenden, hoch liegenden Stimme, hie und da einen Satz mit einer Bewegung seiner sensitiven Hände hervorhebend, öfter aber die Wichtigkeit eines Gedankens durch die größere Schärfe seines Blickes enthüllend; er schien die Antwort auf seine Worte nicht aus der Gemeinde, sondern von irgendwoher weit darüber hinaus zu erwarten. Baecks Predigten [...] hatten immer eine Art privaten Charakters." In: *Fritz Bamberger*, Leo Baeck. Der Mensch und die Idee, in: Eva G. Reichmann (Ed.), Worte des Gedenkens für Leo Baeck, Heidelberg 1959, 76.

14 *Eva G. Reichmann*, Größe und Verhängnis deutsch-jüdischer Existenz. Zeugnis einer tragischen Begegnung (Bibliotheca Judaica 2), Heidelberg 1974, 261.

15 „Ein frommer Gelehrter stellte Fragen an die Bibel, ein höchst gebildeter Mann besprach sich mit Geschichte und Literatur. Er sprach mit ihnen, nicht über sie. Doch trotz ihrer vollendeten Form waren seine Predigten meistens ohne endgültige Schlussfolgerung; sie zeigten einen Menschen auf der Suche nach der Wahrheit." In: *Fritz Bamberger*, Leo Baeck. Der Mensch und die Idee, in: Eva G. Reichmann (Ed.), Worte des Gedenkens für Leo Baeck, Heidelberg 1959, 76.

16 Introductory essay of Albert H. Friedlander in his translation of *Leo Baeck*, This People Israel, New York 1964, xxii.

3. Baeck, the teacher of preaching

Many of Baeck's students recount the joy and great earnestness with which he pursued his charge as a rabbi. Rabbi Bruno Italiener recalled in particular that Baeck loved sermonising and homiletics above all of his other duties:

The Homiletics class was bitter early, recalls W. Gunther Plaut,[17] at eight o'clock in the morning, and Baeck began it on time. Nathan Peter Levinson, who studied under Baeck at that time under his real name of Peter Lewinski, remembers that he once came too late and that Baeck apologised to him for having already started. He never came late again.

Formality marked the sessions, with the students wearing suits and ties and addressing Baeck as *Herr Doktor*. He – kind as he was – replied to them with *Herr Kollege*. Levinson also reported: "Every Friday morning one of the students would present a meticulously prepared sermon as part of the seminar. Baeck was in the habit of praising them highly and then presenting a new, improved form. Active Berlin rabbis regularly visited the exercises to glean ideas for the Sabbath sermons for the next morning. When it was my turn and, visibly nervous, I delivered my first practice sermon, Baeck said: 'My dear young colleague, you are very articulate. But why must you say everything that you know? I could easily take your sermon and make ten others out of it.' Given Baeck's exacting politeness, that was a crushing review that I could not so easily overcome."[18] Students were quite frightened when they had to give a practice sermon in Baeck's presence. Each student had his version of a devastating review by Leo Baeck. Heinz Warschauer remembered Baeck commenting, "Much of what you said was good and much of what you said was new. But unfortunately, what was good wasn't new and what was new, wasn't good."[19] To

---

17 *Leonard Baker*, Days of Sorrow and Pain. Leo Baeck and the Berlin Jews, New York 1978, 100.

18 „Jeden Freitagmorgen hielt einer der Studenten eine sorgfältig vorbereitete Predigt als Teil des Seminars. Baeck pflegte sie sehr zu loben und anschließend eine neue, verbesserte Form vorzutragen. Amtierende Berliner Rabbiner besuchten diese Übung regelmäßig, um noch Anregungen für die sabbatliche Predigt am nächsten Morgen zu erhalten. Als ich an der Reihe war und mit sichtlicher Nervosität meine erste Probepredigt von mir gab, meinte Baeck: 'Mein lieber junge Kollege, Sie haben eine sehr gute Aussprache. Aber warum müssen Sie alles sagen, was Sie wissen? Ich könnte aus Ihrer Predigt mit Leichtigkeit zehn andere machen.' Bei Baecks sprichwörtlicher Höflichkeit war das eine vernichtende Kritik, über die ich so bald nicht hinwegkam." In: *Nathan Peter Levinson*, Ein Ort ist, mit wem Du bist. Lebensstationen eines Rabbiners, Berlin 1996, 45ff.

19 *Heinz Warschauer*, Interview Oct. 12, 1973, quoted from *Leonard Baker*, Days of Sorrow and Pain. Leo Baeck and the Berlin Jews, New York 1978, 101.

Nelson Glueck, later President of the Hebrew Union College-Jewish Institute of Religion in America, he commented: "Your sermon is very good, except for some details. The introduction should have some connection with the text and the body of the sermon, and the language could be simpler, and the sermon would be twice as good if it were half as long; but otherwise, it is a fine sermon."[20] To his students Baeck said: "Don't forget that the preacher is in a peculiar situation: his listeners cannot pose questions to him, cannot challenge him, and he always gets in the last word."[21] He urged brevity to his class, "You may speak about anything," remembers Wolli Kaelter, a student in his class, "but for not more than twenty minutes."[22] In a less formal gathering than his class Baeck once also advised: "Only if you are leaving for Africa should you give your congregation everything you know."[23] Most important, though, was Baeck's conviction that the man is the message. A sermon is not to be delivered. It is the person who must deliver himself. The greatest message one can preach is one's life.[24]

4. The Jewish sermon as an answer to Christianity

Jewish sermon instruction in the early 20th century never tired at emphasising the Jewish origins of the modern sermon. Baeck's colleague Rabbi Dr. Max Eschelbacher (1880–1964) wrote: "It sounds like an irony of history that there was a general conception in the early decades of the 19th century that [the sermon] was utterly alien to Jewish services, that its introduction was an accommodation to the Christian culture. The only truth in this is that during the woeful times since the 15th century, the general decline was also marked by the disappearance

---

20 *Nelson Glueck*, Memorial Tribute, in: In Memoriam Leo Baeck. Gedenkfeier des Zentralrats der Juden in Deutschland und der Zentralwohlfahrtsstelle der Juden in Deutschland, Frankfurt/M. 1956 (Schriften des Zentralrats der Juden in Deutschland 1), Düsseldorf 1957, 19, quoted from *Leonard Baker*, Days of Sorrow and Pain. Leo Baeck and the Berlin Jews, New York 1978, 101.
21 „‚Vergessen Sie nicht,' sagte er zu seinen Studenten, ‚daß der Prediger in einer besonderen Lage ist, – in einer für ein menschliches Wesen kaum haltbaren Lage: seine Zuhörer können ihn nicht fragen, können ihm nicht widersprechen, er hat immer das letzte Wort.'" In: *Fritz Bamberger*, Leo Baeck. Der Mensch und die Idee, in: Eva G. Reichmann (Ed.), Worte des Gedenkens für Leo Baeck, Heidelberg 1959, 76.
22 *Wolli Kaelter*, Interview April 22, 1976, according to *Leonard Baker*, Days of sorrow and pain. Leo Baeck and the Berlin Jews, New York 1978, 100.
23 *Leonard Baker*, Days of Sorrow and Pain. Leo Baeck and the Berlin Jews, New York 1978, 101.
24 *Leo Baeck*, Werke 3. Wege im Judentum: Predigt und Wahrheit, Gütersloh 1997, 233.

of the oratory arts from the synagogue."[25] "The sermon in the narrow sense, oratory in the divine services, is a creation of Judaism [...]. Jewry first created the sermon and gave speech in the service of the house of worship a power that in other nations was only found in the court of law, the public assembly, or at the teacher's desk." (127f.) "The sermon actually achieved its summit with Moses and the prophets." (133) Eschelbacher continues, "The original Jewish sermon later experienced its greatest time in Palestine and Babylon [...]. We still know these sermons well today, because their fragments are contained in the great collections of the midrash." (134)

Leo Baeck was the one who focused on the apologetic character of the Jewish sermon in the context of other religions and overlaid this into his studies of the midrash. In 1925, over the course of his studies on the midrash, this led him to the conclusion that the oral tradition contains not just Petihot, but much rather entire sermons:[26] "It is likely that only relatively rarely did sermons come forth at that time simply from a desire to interpret or recount fables. In that time of wrestling with faith, it was largely an expression of a command to intellectual

---

25 „Es klingt wie eine Ironie der Geschichte, daß man in den ersten Jahrzehnten des 19. Jahrhunderts allenthalben der Meinung war, sie [die Predigt] sei dem jüdischen Gottesdienst überhaupt fremd, ihre Einführung sei Anpassung an den christlichen Kultus. Richtig war daran nur, daß in den traurigen Zeiten seit dem 15. Jahrhundert in dem allgemeinen Niedergang auch die Kunst der Rede aus der Synagoge geschwunden war." *Max Eschelbacher*, Die Predigt im Judentum, in: Jahrbuch für jüdische Geschichte und Literatur, 17,1/1914, 126–144, 140. "Aber die Predigt im engeren Sinne, die Rede im Gottesdienst, ist eine Schöpfung des Judentums. [...] Das Judentum erst schuf die Predigt und stellte die Macht der Rede, die bei anderen Nationen nur im Gerichtssaal, in der Volksversammlung, auf dem Katheder ihre Stätte gefunden hatte, in den Dienst des Gotteshauses." (127f.) "Die Predigt [...] hat dort [in Palästina] mit Moses und den Propheten gleich ihren Höhepunkt erstiegen" (133). "Ihre große Zeit hat die originale jüdische Predigt später in Palästina und Babylon erlebt. [...] Wir kennen diese Predigten heute noch gut, denn ihre Trümmer sind in den großen Midrasch-Sammlungen enthalten." (134)

26 *Leo Baeck*, Zwei Beispiele midraschischer Predigt, in: MGWJ 69,5/1925, 258–271. „Denn wohl nur verhältnismäßig selten ist die Predigt damals bloß aus der Lust am Deuten oder am Fabulieren hervorgegangen. In jener Zeit des Glaubensringens ist sie zumeist der Ausdruck eines Gebotes des geistigen Kampfes gewesen, welchen die alten Lehrer in Verteidigung und Angriff gegen andrängende, bedrohende Gedanken führen mussten." (261) „Von diesem Gebote der Selbstbehauptung empfing die Predigt – und die Predigt ersetzte in der Zeit der mündlichen Lehre das Buch – ihre Richtung. Man konnte hier nicht ein Judentum predigen, das von den Gedanken der Welt nichts weiß oder sie nicht beachtet." (270) „In so mancher Predigt finden wir dann auch, mehr als man es bisher wusste, das Zeugnis geistigen Kampfes mit dem Christentum." (271), or in: *Leo Baeck*, Werke 4, Aus drei Jahrtausenden – Das Evangelium als Urkunde der jüdischen Glaubensgeschichte, Gütersloh 2006, 169, 180f.

battle that the old teachers were forced to conduct in defence against and to attack concepts that crowded and threatened them." (261) Only once this is recognised does the Jewish sermon of the Talmudic age gain its religious-historical position and do the standards that it possessed become visible. "The sermon which served in place of the book in the age of oral teaching took its direction from that command to self-assertion. One could not preach a Judaism here that knew nothing of, and paid no notice to, the concepts of the world." (270) "Hence in many sermons we also find, more than one previously knew, the attestation of an intellectual struggle against Christianity."(271)

Baeck had already spoken about the relationship between Jewish and Christian sermons in his inaugural lecture at the Hochschule, entitled "Greek and Jewish Preaching," on May 4, 1913. Here, Baeck gave a history of the development of the sermon from its Greek origins to its use in contemporary Judaism. On a secondary level it was a study of how Judaism adapted the Greek concept of the sermon and transformed it into something intrinsically Jewish. On a tertiary level it was a call for rabbinical students to exert themselves to the utmost in their profession.

According to Leonard Baker, "Baeck traced the historical development of the sermon through the philosophical religions, which used it to appeal to reason. The sermon's home, he noted, was principally in the Cynico-Stoic religions, which advocated virtue and self-control."[27] Baeck himself emphasised the polymorphic nature of the Jewish sermon: "The prophets who saw divine visions and hearkened to voices from above were succeeded by the interpreters who possessed their books; the seers and their disciples were succeeded by the preachers – for the term 'sermon' ought properly to be applied not to prophetic utterance but only to this subsequent and derivative type of eloquence. The sermon, this new type of discourse, had as many forms as the different ideas of faith that it expressed."[28]

---

27 Leonard Baker, Days of Sorrow and Pain. Leo Baeck and the Berlin Jews, New York 1978, 59.

28 Leo Baeck, Greek and Jewish Preaching, in: Leo Baeck, The Pharisees and other Essays, New York 1947, 109–122, here: 110. "Auf die Suchenden, welche göttliche Gesichte schauten und Stimmen aus der Höhe vernahmen, folgen jetzt die Sprechenden, die ihr Buch besitzen, auf die Sehe und Sehergenossen folgen die Prediger – denn der Begriff der Predigt in seinem eigentlichen Sinne darf nicht auf das prophetische Wort, sondern nur auf diese nachschaffende Beredsamkeit angewandt werden. Diese Predigt ist so vielgestaltig, wie jene verschiedenen Glaubensgedanken es gewesen sind." In: Leo Baeck, Griechische und jüdische Predigt, in: Idem, Aus drei Jahrtausenden. Wissenschaftliche Untersuchungen und Abhandlungen zur Geschichte des jüdischen Glaubens, Berlin 1938, 143, or in: Leo Baeck, Werke 4, Aus

Baeck emphasises that it can be found in the Zoroastic religion, in Indian Buddhism and in China, but above all else in Greece.

Citing many of these old texts, he said there had been a widespread need for the sermon "because each of the various schools, convinced it possessed the truth, was anxious to propagate it [...]." The sermon ultimately acquired a democratic feature because of Socrates, who declared that "virtue and piety could be learned [...] were accessible to everyone and therefore could and should be preached." This democratic feature is also characteristic to modern Judaism, said Baeck: "Here, too, we have the postulate that religion can be learned: it is the Torah, the 'teaching'."[29]

Baeck said that the "Greeks' brilliance" and "elegance of style" were more of a danger than an advantage. Their search for eloquence and beauty of form, he said, "often resulted in the sacrifice of real content and conviction [...]. It has justly been said that Hellenism dies in the cult of beautiful form."[30] By contrast, Jewish sermons from the

---

drei Jahrtausenden – Das Evangelium als Urkunde der jüdischen Glaubensgeschichte, Gütersloh 2006, 152.

29 This is a paraphrase of *Leo Baeck*, Greek and Jewish Preaching, in: *Idem*, The Pharisees and Other Essays, New York 1947, 112f. "Ein Bedürfnis nach der Predigt war damals weithin vorhanden. Man besaß in den verschiedenen Schulen eine Wahrheit, an die man religiös glaubte; die Philosophie hatte hier und da fast den dogmatischen Charakter erhalten. Sie verlangte nach der Erläuterung und der Verbreitung. Bestimmend war hierfür auch der demokratische Zug, den Sokrates ihr gegeben hatte. Er hatte erklärt, daß Tugend und Frömmigkeit lernbar, also jedem Menschen zugänglich seien, daß sie daher gepredigt werden könnten und sollten. [...] Derselbe demokratische Charakter, fast möchte man sagen: diese sokratische Art, kennzeichnet das Judentum. Auch hier ist es der Grundsatz, daß die Religion lernbar ist. Sie ist Tora, die Lehre." In: *Leo Baeck*, Griechische und Jüdische Predigt, in: *Idem*, Aus drei Jahrtausenden. Wissenschaftliche Untersuchungen und Abhandlungen zur Geschichte des jüdischen Glaubens, 1938, 145f., or in: *Leo Baeck*, Werke 4, Aus drei Jahrtausenden – Das Evangelium als Urkunde der jüdischen Glaubensgeschichte, Gütersloh 2006, 154f.

30 A paraphrase of *Leo Baeck*, Greek and Jewish Preaching, in: *Idem*, The Pharisees and Other Essays, New York 1947, 113f. "Eines hatte dabei der Grieche voraus: die Technik der glänzenden Form, die Eleganz des Stils. [...] Das war ein Vorzug, aber es wurde auch die Gefahr. Die Rhetorik hat nur zu bald die Herrschaft der konventionellen Phrase mit ihrer Hohlheit und Anmaßung zuerst verstattet und endlich gefordert, und darunter sind dann Gehalt und Ernst oft verschwunden. Man hat die Rede um der Rede willen gepflegt. Mit Recht ist darauf hingewiesen worden, daß das Griechentum im Kultus der schönen Form untergegangen ist." In: *Leo Baeck*, Griechische und Jüdische Predigt, in: *Idem*, Aus drei Jahrtausenden. Wissenschaftliche Untersuchungen und Abhandlungen zur Geschichte des jüdischen Glaubens, 1938, 145f., or in: *Leo Baeck*, Werke 4, Aus drei Jahrtausenden – Das Evangelium als Urkunde der jüdischen Glaubensgeschichte, Gütersloh 2006, 155.

same period show "an almost studied indifference to artistic form."[31] Looking at the ancient Hebrew sermons "it shows that the Jews of that time did not try to evade the spiritual issues of their day." Judaism survived, while the Greek religions did not, because it is dedicated to exploration and not to intellectual and religious subjugation. This shows up especially in the existence of an oral tradition and the absence of dogma. In the absence of rigid texts they had to study ideas.[32] To the future rabbis listening to his inaugural lecture Baeck presented the concept of 'knowledge' as constant searching which one knows can never reach its end. "The history of Jewish preaching shows how we can remain faithful to what is best and most characteristic in Judaism [...]."[33]

"The preacher is entrusted with the dignity of the religion; the awareness of that fact should sharpen his conscience. He should not forget that it comes from the Holy Scripture. The office is bestowed with a soul only through the commandment, and this makes no mention of being pleasurable, but rather of instruction and elevation. This requires both a

---

31 Paraphrase of *Leo Baeck*, Greek and Jewish Preaching, in: *Idem*, The Pharisees and Other Essays, New York 1947, 114. "Im jüdischen Volk standen diesem Virtuosentum geistige und sprachliche Art entgegen, und besonders die uns überlieferten alten Predigten aus dem hebräischen Sprachgebiete oder, genauer gesagt, die Inhaltsangaben und Bruchstücke von Predigten [...] zeigen fast eine beabsichtige Gleichgültigkeit gegen die künstlerische Form." In: *Leo Baeck*, Griechische und Jüdische Predigt, in: *Idem*, Aus drei Jahrtausenden. Wissenschaftliche Untersuchungen und Abhandlungen zur Geschichte des jüdischen Glaubens, 1938, 146f., or in: *Idem*, Werke 4, Aus drei Jahrtausenden – Das Evangelium als Urkunde der jüdischen Glaubensgeschichte, Gütersloh 2006, 155.

32 Paraphrase of *Leo Baeck*, Greek and Jewish Preaching, in: *Idem*, The Pharisees and Other Essays, New York 1947, 114. "Aber dafür hatten die Juden ein anderes zu eigen, was der gesamten Predigt erst ihre Geschlossenheit gewährte. Sie besaßen die Einheit der Religion und des religiösen Grundbuches, während es bei den Griechen nur die Einheit der Schule und der Schulschriften gab. Und dazu ein Weiteres: die umfassende Bedeutung des Mündlichen gegenüber dem starren Schriftlichen, das, was das Wort Midrasch benennen will, dieses Undogmatische, dieses Recht und dieses Gebot, in der Bibel zu suchen, im Anschluß an sie auch die religiösen Gedanken zu gestalten und fortzubilden." In: *Leo Baeck*, Griechische und Jüdische Predigt, in: *Idem*, Aus drei Jahrtausenden. Wissenschaftliche Untersuchungen und Abhandlungen zur Geschichte des jüdischen Glaubens, 1938, 147, or in: *Idem*, Werke 4. Aus drei Jahrtausenden – Das Evangelium als Urkunde der jüdischen Glaubensgeschichte, Gütersloh 2006, 155f.

33 *Leo Baeck*, Greek and Jewish Preaching, in: *Idem*, The Pharisees and other essays, New York 1947, 122. "Auch die Geschichte der Jüdischen Predigt zeigt, wie man dem Eigenen und Besten des Judentums treu bleibt." *Idem*, Griechische und Jüdische Predigt, in: *Idem*, Aus drei Jahrtausenden. Wissenschaftliche Untersuchungen und Abhandlungen zur Geschichte des jüdischen Glaubens, Berlin 1938, 156, or in: *Idem*, Werke 4. Aus drei Jahrtausenden – Das Evangelium als Urkunde der jüdischen Glaubensgeschichte, Gütersloh 2006, 164.

just sensibility and a just character; only a person who is free on the inside can preach. [...] To preach means 'to learn and to teach'."³⁴

Above all else it was the debate with Adolf von Harnack (1851–1930) through which Baeck presented the legitimacy and intrinsic value of Jewish existence, so as to prevent Jews from turning their backs on their religion and crossing over to the Christian camp. In a refutation published in 1905, "The Essence of Judaism", he also developed a foundation for differentiation between Jewish and Christian sermons. He criticised in depth the sacramental character of God's word in the Church and hence the attending position of Christian preachers:

> "It is surely an acknowledgment of the old Jewish teaching if the universal priesthood of believers was proclaimed [in the Reformation] [...]. But even here, where distinct pieties for priest and people were no longer permitted to exist, a concomitance arose of authorized officials of religion, on the one hand, and of mere receivers upon the other. For wherever a religion claims to bestow miraculous gifts of grace, there will always be this inevitable division. Such a division occurred at a prominent point of doctrine. For it was due to the Reformation that the 'Word of God' was declared to be the means of salvation [...]. Thus the word is not Torah, but something sacramental. It stands beside the sacraments, and is, like them, not something which has to be fulfilled by, but something which is given to the believer. Upon its being offered and preached to the community in the right way, everything depends: the true illumination and faith, the inner experience of 'justification' and salvation. Hence it demands its officers and administrators. A special group of owners and curators of faith are thus created in the community; theologians and laymen, minors and men of age, are opposed to one another. And so the religion itself acquires a doctrinal, rationalistic character; theology sits at its centre."³⁵

---

34 Leo Baeck, Greek and Jewish Preaching, in: *Idem*, The Pharisees and other essays, New York 1947, 121f. "Die Würde der Religion ist dem Prediger anvertraut; das Bewußtsein hiervon sollte ihm das Gewissen schärfen. Er sollte nicht vergessen, daß er von der Heiligen Schrift herkommt. Das Amt erhält die Seele erst durch das Gebot, und dieses spricht nicht davon, gefallen zu sollen, sondern zu belehren und emporzuheben. Hierzu gehört allerdings wie ein gerader Verstand so ein gerader Charakter; nur ein Mensch, der innerlich frei wird, kann predigen. [...] Predigen heißt ‚lernen und lehren'." *Leo Baeck*, Griechische und Jüdische Predigt, in: *Idem*, Aus drei Jahrtausenden. Wissenschaftliche Untersuchungen und Abhandlungen zur Geschichte des jüdischen Glaubens, Berlin 1938, 156, or in: *Idem*, Werke 4. Aus drei Jahrtausenden – Das Evangelium als Urkunde der jüdischen Glaubensgeschichte, Gütersloh 2006, 163f.

35 *Leo Baeck*, The Essence of Judaism, London 1936, 45. "Zu dieser Richtung hat im Christentum die Reformation zurückführen wollen. Die alte Lehre des Judentums ist anerkannt [...]. Aber selbst hier, wo so eine gesonderte Priester- und Volksfrömmigkeit nicht mehr bestehen darf, ist es doch wieder zu einem Nebeneinander von Beauftragten und Empfängern der Religion gekommen, zu jener Scheidung, wie sie

Baeck concedes: "Judaism too did not escape a danger of this kind [...] when the codification of religious law led to the view that learning and knowledge were the main and determining things, mysticism espoused the cause of the purely religious element in piety. Thus it is due in no small measure to mysticism that Jewish piety came once more into its original rights. Life is more than doctrine or learning; that, in spite of everything, remained firmly established in Judaism."[36]

In contradiction to this he posits a decidedly different position of Judaism: the ethical character of the sermon as an admonition to each individual to break through the conventions of daily life and to reclaim strength of character.

> "Judaism created [...] certain fixed hours of reverential worship, hours in which the public conscience is allowed to speak, and the Divine will is directed towards men's souls [...]. The ethical demand is connected with public worship, and the sermon about that which we ought to be is connected with the glad certainty of that which we are. That which we should perhaps not say to one another – since we are all human beings – may, and indeed must, be pointed out to everybody by the word of God. We must be lenient, but the word of God has the right to be severe. With its greatness of feeling, with its powerful zeal for that which is right and true, with its blazing fury against baseness and maliciousness, it may rightly oppose the measured and limited feelings of every-day life which are compressed within the frame of conventionality. The hard and unyielding

---

überall schließlich eintritt, wo die Religion ihre Wundergaben besitzen will. An einem wesentlichen Punkte hat es sich so herausgebildet. Durch die Reformation wird nämlich das 'Wort Gottes' zum Mittel des Heiles erklärt [...]. Das Wort ist so nicht Thora, sondern etwas Sakramentales; es steht neben den Sakramenten, wie sie nicht etwas, was erfüllt werden soll, sondern etwas, was dem Glaubenden geschenkt wird. Davon, daß es in der richtigen Weise dargeboten, daß es der Gemeinde richtig gepredigt wird, hängt das ab, was alles bedeutet, hängt die Erleuchtung und Gläubigkeit, hängt das Erlebnis der 'Rechtfertigung' und Erlösung ab. Die richtige Theologie wird zur Bedingung des Heils. Und sie verlangt ihre Träger und Verwalter; die besondere Gruppe der Besitzenden, der Glaubenshüter wird in der Gemeinde geschaffen, Theologen und Laien, Mündige und Unmündige stehen einander gegenüber. Die Religion selbst erhält dadurch ihr Lehrhaftes wissensmäßiges Gepräge; die Theologie steht in ihrem Mittelpunkt." *Leo Baeck,* Das Wesen des Judentums, Frankfurt/M. 5[s. a.], 47f., or in: *Idem,* Werke 1. Das Wesen des Judentums, Gütersloh 2006, 80f.

36 *Leo Baeck,* The Essence of Judaism, London 1936, 46. "Auch dem Judentum ist eine ähnliche Gefahr nicht fern geblieben. [...] Als die Kodifikation des Religionsgesetzes dazu führte, daß wieder Lernen und Wissen als das Entscheidende gelten wollten, hat sie demgegenüber die Bedeutung des Religiösen vertreten. Sie hat wesentlich dazu beigetragen, daß der jüdischen Frömmigkeit ihr erstes Recht gewahrt worden ist. Hierfür hat der Inbegriff des Wortes auch maßgebend als Bekenntnis festgesetzt werden müssen [...]." *Leo Baeck,* Das Wesen des Judentums, Frankfurt/M. 5[s. a.], 48f., or in: *Leo Baeck,* Werke 1. Das Wesen des Judentums, Gütersloh 2006, 81f.

bluntness of the Hebrew Bible is needed to contradict that weak conventionality which is so easily satisfied with existing compromises, and that suave sagacity, which is only fitted to disguise a lack of character."[37]

Earlier on, in 1928, Leo Baeck had concluded in an essay called "Sermon and Truth": "Basically only a pious person can preach,"[38] thereby underlining the essentially ethical character of the Jewish sermon. So we may ask, then, what is the modern Jewish sermon?

5. The modern Jewish sermon

In 1931, Leo Baeck's colleague Georg Salzberger (1882–1975) more or less summarised Baeck's teachings in an essay entitled "The Modern Sermon":[39]

---

37   Leo Baeck, The Essence of Judaism, London 1936, 147f. "Auch die bestimmten Stunden der Ehrfurcht hat das Judentum geschaffen, Stunden, wo dem öffentlichen Gewissen Worte gegeben werden, und der göttliche Wille sich an die Seelen wendet. Auch diese Sitte, die der Verkündigung und Erklärung des Gottesgebotes, seiner geistigen Erneuung in dem Redenden wie in dem Hörenden, ist eine jener Gaben, mit denen Israel die Menschheit beschenkt hat. An die Andacht wird die sittliche Forderung geknüpft, and die frohe Gewissheit dessen, was wir sind, die Predigt von dem, was wir sein sollen. Was einer dem anderen vielleicht nicht sagen darf, – da wir ja allesamt Menschen sind – das kann und soll das Gotteswort einem jeden vorhalten. Wir sollen nachsichtig sein, das Gotteswort hat das Recht der Strenge. Den gemessenen, begrenzten Gefühlen des Alltags, die sich in den Rahmen der Rücksicht eingepreßt haben, kann es entgegentreten mit seinem großen Zug der Empfindung, mit seinen gewaltigen Eifern für das Rechte und Wahre, mit seinem lodernden Grimm gegen die Niedrigkeit und die Boshaftigkeit. Gegenüber der schwächlichen Konvention, die sich so leicht mit allem abfindet, gegenüber all der glatten Klugheit, die dazu da ist, um keinen Charakter zeigen zu müssen, ist die harte, unnachgiebige Schroffheit des Bibelwortes von nöten. Gegenüber alledem, was uns draußen richtet und beherrscht, brauchen wir die immer neue Erweckung des Bewußtseins, dass 'der Ewige unser Richter, der Ewige unser Gesetzgeber, der Ewige unser König' ist." Leo Baeck, Das Wesen des Judentums, Frankfurt/M. [5][s. a.], 159f., or in: Idem, Werke 1. Das Wesen des Judentums, Gütersloh 2006, 174.

38   "Nur ein frommer Mensch kann daher im Grunde predigen [...]", in: Leo Baeck, Predigt und Wahrheit, in: Idem, Werke 3. Wege im Judentum, Gütersloh 1997, 233.

39   Georg Salzberger, Die moderne Predigt, in: MGWJ 75,2/1931, 81–96. "Die jüdische Predigt ist ihrem Ursprung und Wesen nach eine Erklärung und Auslegung der Thora [...]." (89) "Wir meinen vielmehr, daß sie nur ein Mittel unter anderen ist, um die Gemeinde zu erziehen. Als Mittel darf sie [die Predigt] nicht überschätzt und übertrieben werden." (93) "Er ist der Lehrer seiner Gemeinde, übt also einen Beruf aus, den grundsätzlich bei gleichem Wissen und gleicher religiöser Lebensführung jeder in der Gemeinde ausüben könnte. [...] Der Rabbiner ist Lehrer. Als solcher hat er seine Gemeinde zunächst in religiösem Wissen zu unterweisen." (91) "Wenn man dem Mann nicht glaubt, daß er selbst mit allen Kräften zu leben bestrebt ist, was er lehrt, dann verfehlen auch die geistreichsten, kunst- und schwungvollsten Predigten

"The Jewish sermon is, by way of its origin and being, an explanation and interpretation of the Torah. (89) The sermon should not be underestimated as a means, yet neither should it be overestimated; it is one means among others to instruct the congregation in a religious sense (93).

The rabbi practices a profession that fundamentally could be practiced by any member of the congregation, given equal knowledge and an equally pious lifestyle. (91) The rabbi is a teacher. As such, he must first instruct his congregation in religious knowledge. (91) If one does not believe of the man that he himself is endeavouring with all his vigour those things which he is teaching, then even the most richly intellectual, artful, and spirited sermon falls short in its efficacy. (92)

On content and form: the sermon is an elucidation of the scripture. But what differentiates it from raw exegesis is its application toward the conditions and relationships of the present, so as to bring practical life into more heartfelt context with religion [...]. The sermon should be topical, but not in the sense of the timeliness of the daily press. Successful sermonising requires a realistic concept of the people for whom it is intended." (92)

Ludwig Philippson (1811–1898) had already warned of an overly unctuous tone in the pulpit. Part of the ideal is also that the Jewish preacher should preach briefly because "his listeners are even more nervous than the non-Jews".[40] The Golden Rule for a successful *derashah* was formulated by Rabbi Manuel Joel (1826–1890) in 1867: "Say the best thing, and yet, say that best thing such that not only the best understand it."[41]

---

ihre Wirkung. Aus dem Gesagten lässt sich Inhalt und Gestalt der jüdischen Predigt leicht ableiten. Sie ist im Grunde die Erklärung der Schrift. Aber was sie von der bloßen Schrifterklärung unterscheidet, ist deren Anwendung auf die Zustände und Verhältnisse der Gegenwart, um das praktische Leben in innigeren Zusammenhang mit der Religion zu bringen. [...] aber in einer Zeit wie die unsere ist die Pflicht des Predigers noch dringender geworden, auf die äußere und innere Not des heutigen Menschen, auf seine sittlichen und religiösen Fragen, Zweifel und Konflikte einzugehen. [...] Nur ist auch hier vor der Gefahr zu warnen, die in einer gewollten und gesuchten Aktualität, in der Aktualität der Tagespresse liegt" (92).

40 *Ludwig Philippson*, Die Rhetorik und jüdische Homiletik in Briefen und Abhandlungen, M. Kayserling (Ed.), Leipzig 1890, 93.
41 "Das Beste sagen und dieses Beste dennoch so sagen, daß nicht bloß die Besten es verstehen." In: *Manuel Joel*, Fest-Predigten, Breslau 1867, x.

6. Leo Baeck's homiletical legacy: Jewish existence – a sermon of truth to the world

Yet Leo Baeck was not satisfied with these parcels of advice to the judicious Jewish preacher. He went beyond the toolbox of homiletics as I have just described it.

Baeck deepened the understanding of the sermon into a theology of existence of the Jewish people.

Looking at the experiences of Jews throughout history he widens the insight that in preaching the man is the message. Baeck formulates: in its suffering for the ideal, Judaism as such became a Messianic preaching.[42] Thus, mere existence of the Jewish people became a sermon to the world.[43]

In contrast to the essential role of the Jewish community, Baeck puts little emphasis on the importance of the rabbi as a professional preacher. Far from just being listeners, each individual of the Jewish community is called to be a witness of the truth by doing God's will. In this way, preaching can become martyrdom, not testimony but suffering.[44]

In *The Essence of Judaism* he describes it as follows:

---

42   "Suffering [...] was to Judaism no mere symbol or mere poetry, but the reality of its life, the theme of its history, the experience of tragedy and of atonement. It experienced the destiny of its individuality. Its peculiar destiny became for Judaism a Messianic preaching. Jews realized how suffering for Judaism meant suffering for the ideal." In: *Leo Baeck*, The Essence of Judaism, London 1936, 257. "Das Leid hat sein Messianisches auch. Das alles ist die Wirklichkeit seines Lebens, das Thema seiner Geschichte, das Erlebnis der Tragik und der Versöhnung. Man erfuhr das Schicksal des Eigenen. Sein eigenes Schicksal wurde für das Judentum zur messianischen Predigt. Man erfuhr, wie das Leiden am Judentum ein Leiden am Ideal ist." *Leo Baeck*, Das Wesen des Judentums, Frankfurt/M. ⁵[s. a.], 278, or in: *Idem*, Werke 1. Das Wesen des Judentums, Gütersloh 2006, 272.

43   "To reproach the Jews for not having preached their religion for so long a time would be the same as to reproach a prisoner in irons for not walking out of his prison. But Jewish ideas always kept escaping and getting out. [...] It was appreciated that mere existence might be a form of promulgation, a sermon to the world." In: *Leo Baeck*, The Essence of Judaism, London 1936, 265f. "Über die Juden das Urteil zu sprechen, daß sie so lange ihre Religion nicht gepredigt hätten, das ist, dem Gefesselten es vorzuwerfen, daß er aus dem Kerker nicht hinausgehe. Aber die Gedanken zogen immer hinaus. [...] Man begriff, daß auch die Existenz eine Verkündigung sein kann, schon das Dasein eine Predigt an die Welt." (290) *Leo Baeck*, Das Wesen des Judentums, Frankfurt/M. ⁵[s. a.], 290, or in: *Idem*, Werke 1. Das Wesen des Judentums, Gütersloh 2006, 281f.

44   *Leo Baeck*, Predigt und Wahrheit, in: *Idem*, Werke 3. Wege im Judentum, Gütersloh 1997, 232ff.

"The good which is wrought by anybody is the clearest proof, the best possible witness, of God […]. It is, at the same time, the most impressive sermon about the truth of religion, more impressive than the richest richness of words can ever make that truth be heard […]. Every individual, even if the gift of speech is denied or refused him, can thus become the messenger of his faith among men, and everybody should be such a messenger."[45]

This message, however, is eternal and needs neither fashion nor ornament. In this sense, Baeck is suspicious of rhetoric and decorum,[46] he points towards the prophets who were no orators and who convinced through the congruence of man and message.[47]

Truth eventually does not need the preacher, says Baeck. It needs the Jewish community as a continuing sermon to the peoples of the world. For Leo Baeck the Jewish preacher is a servant who enables the Jewish community to dispense this allegiance to truth.[48] And this truth is essentially an ethical one, not one of faith.

Leo Baeck summed it up in his own words: "Judaism bears witness to the power of the idea as against the power of mere numbers and of outward success […]. This attitude is itself a constant preaching to the peoples of the world, to all who have ears to hear. Judaism, by its mere existence, is a never silent protest against the assumption that the multitude can be greater than right, that force may be the ruler over truth, that in the battle between spirit and the utilities, profit may have the last word."[49]

---

45   Leo Baeck, The Essence of Judaism, London 1936, 278. "Das Gute, das einer übt, ist der klarste Gottesbeweis, das deutlichste Zeugnis von Gott, das einer ablegen kann. Und das spricht auch zu aller Welt; es ist zugleich die eindringlichste Predigt von der Wahrheit der Religion, eindringlicher als der reichste Reichtum der Worte sie vernehmen zu lassen imstande ist. […] Jedermann, selbst wenn ihm das Wort verwehrt ist, kann so der Bote seines Glaubens unter den Menschen sein, und jeder soll es sein." Leo Baeck, Das Wesen des Judentums, Frankfurt/M. ⁵[s. a.], 303, or in: Idem, Werke 1. Das Wesen des Judentums, Gütersloh 2006, 293.
46   Leo Baeck, Predigt und Wahrheit, in: Idem, Werke 3. Wege im Judentum, Gütersloh 1997, 233–237.
47   Ibid., 232f.
48   Ibid., 240.
49   Leo Baeck, The Essence of Judaism, London 1936, 281. "Das Judentum bezeugt die Kraft des Gedankens gegenüber der Macht der bloßen Zahl und des äußeren Erfolges […]; auch das ist eine stete Predigt an die Völker der Welt, an alle, die zu hören vermögen. Schon durch sein Dasein ist das Judentum ein nie verstummender Widerspruch dagegen, daß die Menge mehr sein will als das Recht, daß die Gewalt Herrscherin sein will über die Wahrheit, daß in dem Kampf zwischen dem Geiste und den Nützlichkeiten der Nutzen das letzte Wort sprechen will." Leo Baeck, Das Wesen des Judentums, Frankfurt/M. ⁵[s. a.], 306, or in: Idem, Werke 1. Das Wesen des Judentums, Gütersloh 2006, 294f.

All this makes it clear that for Baeck preachers are not elevated from the community of the people of Israel. They serve Israel by administering the truth as an ethical message more than anything else. Here 'the man is the message', for only those people should preach who lead an exemplary life and practice what they preach.

Baeck is less concerned with the rhetorical aspects of the sermon and neglects the issue of ornament and decorum – yes, even trendy modernity. For him these issues are of peripheral importance.[50] Preaching is to Baeck rather a humbling act, which conveys the preacher as a teacher and at the same time as someone who still learns and who will never cease to learn.

It is this aspect that points back in a dramatic way to the midrashic origin of the Jewish sermon and to the Beth haMidrash, the House of Learning, as its source. While the current usage in public prayer and the liturgical formality of the modern synagogue may make the Jewish sermon a sister of the Christian sermon, its origin in the sphere of a circle of learning and teaching clearly identifies a dividing line. This is why Leo Baeck describes the Jewish preacher in the context of the Jewish people as a whole, with no other expertise than his personal example, his intellectual persuasiveness, and his striving for ethical refinement.

---

50 *Leo Baeck*, Predigt und Wahrheit, in: *Idem*, Werke 3. Wege im Judentum, Gütersloh 1997, 237.

Preaching the Hebrew Bible
A Christian Perspective*

Heinz-Günther Schöttler

When Christians read the Old Testament they used to understand it as "promise"¹ which has found its final and ultimate fulfilment in the Christ event. This way of interpreting the first part of the Christian Bible has been rooted in Christian tradition since antiquity. Christians believe they can justify this method of interpretation by referring Old

---

* Many thanks to my friends Claus Jungkunz (Wasserburg/Germany) and Michael A. Signer (Abrams Professor of Jewish Thought and Culture at the University of Notre Dame, Indiana/USA) for translating this text from German to English and for giving me useful hints which helped to improve this manuscript.

1 The term "promise" is in the following used as theological category which not only means facing a God-given future, but also and even more so living the present life in the face of God. The corresponding term "promise-fulfilment" cannot be found in the Old Testament and at only one place in the New Testament in Acts 13.32f. However "promise – fulfilment" exists as a theological concept in the Old Testament and has become a powerful metaphor to describe the relationship between Old and New Testament. "(32) And we preach to you the good news of the promise [*epaggelía*] made to the fathers, (33) that God has fulfilled [*Greek:* ek-plēróō] this (promise) to us, their children, in that he raised up Jesus, as it is also written in the second Psalm, 'You are my son; today I have begotten you.'" In German we have to differentiate between the term *"Verheißung"* (*Engl.:* "promise") and the term *"Weissagung"* (*Engl.:* "divination"). The latter does not represent a theological category but deals with predicting the future. At this point our irritation has to be mentioned that *Rudolf Bultmann* (1884–1976) – shortly after the Old Testament had been rejected during the time of the Nazi-Regime and the genocide of the European Jews – wrote a powerful article entitled "Weissagung und Erfüllung" (first published: 1949; printed again in *Claus Westermann* [Ed.], Probleme alttestamentlicher Hermeneutik. Aufsätze zum Verstehen des Alten Testaments, München 1960 [TB 11], 28–53). Ignoring the paradigm shift caused by the Shoah he uses a terminology which was coined by the Christocentric historic theology of Johann Christian Konrad v. Hofmann (1810–1877; cf. *Johann Christian Konrad v. Hofmann*, Weissagung und Erfüllung im alten und neuen Testamente, 2 vol., Nördlingen 1841.1844). Bultmann calls the Old Testament a *"Dokument des Scheiterns"* (*Engl.:* "document of failure") and speaks of *"Scheitern Israels an seiner Verheißung"* (*Engl:.* "Israel who has failed its promise"): "Inwiefern ist nun die alttestamentlich-jüdische Geschichte Weissagung, die in der Geschichte der neutestamentlichen Gemeinde erfüllt ist? Sie ist es in ihrem inneren Widerspruch, in ihrem Scheitern. Ein innerer

Testament passages to the second part of their Bible, the socalled "New Testament".

We can look, for example, at the Gospel of Matthew. This document holds a very significant position in the tradition of Christian interpretation. From the time of the Church Fathers up to the present it has been read and expounded with greater frequency than the other Gospels. In the Gospel of Matthew we find the following quotation formula twelve times: "Now all this took place to fulfil what was spoken by the Lord through the prophet: ..."[2] As an example, I quote from the infancy legends of Jesus in Matthew 1.20–25:

> "[20] But when he [= Joseph] had considered this, behold, an angel of the Lord appeared to him in a dream, saying, 'Joseph, son of David, do not be afraid to take Mary as your wife; for the Child who has been conceived in her is of the Holy Spirit. [21] She will bear a Son; and you shall call His name Jesus, for He will save His people from their sins.' [22] *Now all this took place to fulfil* [Greek: plēróō] *what was spoken by the Lord through the prophet:* [23] behold, the virgin [Greek: parthénos] shall be with child and shall bear a son, and they shall call his name Immanuel' – which translated means: God with us.' [24] And Joseph awoke from his sleep and did as the angel of the Lord commanded him, and took Mary as his wife, [25] but kept her a virgin until she gave birth to a Son; and he called His name Jesus."

Churchgoers hear readings like this when they are present at a Christian worship service. In the example we have just cited, Isaiah 7.14 is quoted from the Septuagint text rather than the Hebrew text.

Widerspruch durchzieht das Selbstbewußtsein wie die Hoffnung Israels und seiner Propheten. [...] Das Scheitern erweist die Unmöglichkeit, und deshalb ist das Scheitern die Verheißung. Und damit wäre es zu Ende, hätte nicht Gott in Christus einen neuen Anfang gemacht, [...] der nunmehr jederzeit offensteht für denjenigen, der dessen inne wird, daß sein Weg ins Scheitern führt ..." (ibid., 50f.). Cf. *Heinz-Günther Schöttler*, Christliche Predigt und Altes Testament. Versuch einer homiletischen Kriteriologie, Ostfildern 2001, 45f.; *Karolina de Valerio*, Altes Testament und Judentum im Frühwerk Rudolf Bultmanns (BZNW 71), Berlin/New York 1994.

2   Since "*plēróō*" has a central theological meaning which can be seen in twelve verses: 1.22f.; 2.15, 17f., 23; 4.14–16; 8.17; 12.17–21; 13.35; 21.4f.; 27.9f.; 26.54, 56 (cf. *Schöttler*, Christliche Predigt und Altes Testament, 448–455). Different in Mat. 13.14. In their case the prophecy [Greek: *hē prophēteía*] of Isaiah is being fulfilled [Greek: *ana-plēróō*], which says: "You will keep on hearing, but will not understand; you will keep on seeing, but will not perceive; (15) for the heart of this people has become dull, with their ears they scarcely hear, and they have closed their eyes, otherwise they would see with their eyes, hear with their ears, and understand with their heart and return, and I would heal them." Luz is here talking about a "unmatthäische[n] Einführungsformel. Ana-plēróō und prophēteía sind happax legomena. Warum hat sie Matthäus nicht stärker an die Einführungswendung zu den Erfüllungszitaten angepasst?" (*Ulrich Luz*, Das Evangelium nach Matthäus, vol. 2: Mt 8–17 [EKK I/2], Zürich/Braunschweig/Neukirchen-Vluyn 1990, 301 [with fn. 12]).

Matthew was quoted from the Greek text for two reasons: first, this version of the Hebrew Bible was normative to those who were called Christians at later times (compare Acts 11.26[3]). Second, the Greek word *parthénos* [= virgin], which is *ʿalmah* in Hebrew, provided a theme that was important for the infancy legends of Jesus.

In my lecture today, I would like to describe to you two quotation formulas from the New Testament. These formulas for citation have shaped the way the first part of the Christian Bible has been interpreted in the liturgy and preaching of the Christian Churches from the beginnings of Christianity until present day. Put more precisely: the Christian method of interpreting – through quotations – the Hebrew Bible, which remains Scripture for the Jewish tradition, shapes it into their Old Testament.

In order to develop this proposition, my talk will consist of three parts. First I will elaborate and explain Matthew's "quotation formula". Second, I will describe the set phrase from the New Testament which introduces Matthew's so-called Antithesis of the Law. The third and final part is an inquiry, from the Christian perspective, into the meaning of the idea that Israel, the Jewish People, is "chosen first", and how this election constitutes a special quality which is important for Christian theology and especially for Christian preaching. In this third part I shall closely follow the argument offered by Saint Paul.

1. A new understanding of the theological scheme *"promise and fulfilment"*

1.1 The traditional understanding

Matthew's quotation formula "Now all this took place to fulfil what was spoken by the Lord through the prophet: ...", which literally translated from German would be called "formula of fulfilment", has a hermeneutic purpose. It constitutes the theological scheme "promise and fulfilment", which means that the Hebrew Bible that is viewed as "Old Testament" consists of promises of fulfilment which are witnessed by the Christ Event of the "New Testament". This theological scheme of "promise and fulfilment" throughout the history of Christian

---

3 Cf. esp. *Hubert Frankemölle*, Frühjudentum und Urchristentum. Vorgeschichte – Verlauf – Auswirkungen (4. Jahrhundert v. Chr. bis 4. Jahrhundert n. Chr.), Stuttgart 2006, esp. 382–400.

biblical hermeneutics has been the common way to describe the relationship between Old and New Testament.

Especially during Advent or Christmas time Christians experience an instruction with this scheme of "promise and fulfilment". This scheme is renewed every single year and therefore has a profound deepening impact. This understanding of Scripture plays the major role in the Order of Readings for Mass and has been in use since Vatican II.[4] In the introduction to the Order of Readings for Mass ([²1981], No. 67) we can read:

> "The best instance of harmony between the Old and New Testament readings occurs when it is one that Scripture itself suggests. This is the case when the teaching and events recounted in texts of the New Testament bear a more or less explicit relationship to the teaching and events of the Old Testament. [...] [During the Advent and on Christmas] the Old Testament readings are prophecies about the Messiah and the Messianic age, especially from Isaiah."

This understanding responds to the Dogmatic Constitution on Divine Revelation *"Dei Verbum"* of Vatican II. (Art. 14–16):

> "The plan of salvation foretold [*praenuntiare*] by the sacred authors, recounted and explained by them, is found as the true word of God in the books of the Old Testament. [...] The principal purpose to which the plan of the old covenant was directed was to prepare [*praeparare*] for the coming of Christ, the redeemer of all and of the messianic kingdom, to announce this coming by prophecy [*prophetice nuntiare*] (see Luke 24.44; John 5.39; 1Peter 1.10), and to indicate its meaning through various types [*in typis significare*] (see 1Cor. 10.12). [...] God, the inspirer and author of both Testaments, wisely arranged that the New Testament be hidden [*latere*] in the Old and the Old be made manifest in the New (Augustinus). For, though Christ established the new covenant in His blood (see Luke 22.20; 1Cor. 11.25), still the books of the Old Testament [...] show forth their full meaning in the New Testament (see Mat. 5.17; Luke 24.27; Rom. 16.25–26; 2Cor. 14.16) and in turn shed light on it and explain it."

This *scheme of understanding of promise and fulfilment* notably determines how the Old Testament is understood in the liturgical praxis of the Catholic Church. If it were to be true that for Christians the promise was fulfilled in Jesus Christ the Old Testament scholar *Horst Dietrich Preuß* (1927–1993) would be correct when he said:

> "Where nowadays it is argued and proclaimed that only one word of the Old Testament is fulfilled in Christ, a conscious Christian parish is

---

4 Cf. *Schöttler*, Christliche Predigt und Altes Testament, 148–151.

compelled to query: ‚So what?!' If they are told these things, what is the use for their faith?"[5]

The members of the parish would no longer need the Old Testament because they already know everything about God from Jesus Christ or at least pretend to know everything on the basis of the New Testament. The Old Testament – as it had been practiced for centuries and perhaps still is the case today – would, therefore, only be used to tell Christians nice fairy tales that confirm what they previously had already known.

At this point let me quote *Thomas Aquinas* (1225–1274). In his "Summa theologiae" he describes the relationship between the New and the Old Testament. According to Thomas, the New Testament is a "Law of Love" and leads closer to God than the Old Testament, which is a taskmaster. However, both parts of Christian Scripture had the same purpose: to teach that the human being is subordinate to God. In *quaestio 107* Thomas says [I/II, qu. 107, art. 2 co]:

> "The New Law is compared to the Old as the perfect to the imperfect. Now everything perfect fulfils that which is lacking in the imperfect. And accordingly the New Law fulfils the Old by supplying that which was lacking in the Old Law."[6]

An example taken from Christian iconography from the Middle Ages illustrates what I have just said: In the basilica Sainte-Madelaine in Vézelay (Burgundy/France) there is a capital which was built in the second half of the 12th century. This capital is called *"mystical mill"*.[7] It does not show a biblical scene but it does have a hermeneutical goal.

---

5   *Horst Dietrich Preuß*, Das Alte Testament in christlicher Predigt, Stuttgart et al. 1984, 63.

6   *"Lex nova comparatur ad veterem sicut perfectum ad imperfectum. Omne autem perfectum adimplet id quod imperfecto deest. Et secundum hoc lex nova adimplet veterem legem, inquantum supplet illud quod veteri legi deerat."*

7   Cf. *Rudolf Voderholzer*, Geleitwort, in: *Henri de Lubac*, Typologie – Allegorie – geistiger Sinn. Studien zur Geschichte der christlichen Schriftauslegung. Aus dem

Description: Here Moses and Paul are both at work. On the left one can see Moses representing the Old Testament: he wears short clothes and simple shoes which disclose him as a slave. Moses is looking into a funnel of a mill and is filling it with grain from a sack that he is carrying on his shoulder. Paul on the right side, representing the New Testament, is wearing the long tunica of a free Roman citizen, barefoot, staring at the flour coming out of the mill with which he is filling his sack. At the centre of the scene is the mill-wheel, the spokes of which form a cross. The whole scene is following the shape of the cross: the bent position of the two persons and the folds of their clothes which are draped by the storm caused by the spirit.[8]

The theme of the capital is obvious. Only the "Christological mill" can provide adequate and proper food that nourishes the faith. Only through Christ – look at the cruciform mill wheel in the middle of the capital – can the Old Testament be processed to find its genuine meaning.

In Christian churches the approach of "promise and fulfilment" is the dominant way to describe the relationship between Old and New Testament, put more precisely, between Old Testament and the Christ event. This approach seems to be theologically inadequate by our present standards, especially "if it is used in a simplistic way for

---

Französischen übertragen und eingeleitet von Rudolf Voderholzer, Freiburg i. Br. 1999, VII–IX, here: VIII; cf. *Alois Thomas*, Art. Mühle, mystische, in: Lexikon der christlichen Ikonographie, vol. 3, Rom/Freiburg i. Br./Basel/Wien 1971, 297–299; *Michel Zink*, Moulin mystique. À propos d'un chapiteau de Vézelay: figures allégoriques dans la prédication et dans l'iconographie romanes, in: Annales. Histoire. Sciences Sociales 31/1976, 481–488; *Anne Kirsch*, Das Verhältnis von Altem und Neuen Testament im Spiegel romanischer Kirchenportale Frankreichs (SBB 56), Stuttgart 2006, 9–20.

8   The prototype of this rare setting is the so called "anagogic window" in Saint Denis Abbey near Paris (built about 1140, destroyed in 1799). Old Testament prophets carry their sacks full of wheat, which they pour into a mill that is run by Apostle Paul. Cf. *Émil Malê*, L'art religieux du XIIIe siècle en France (Paris 1898; ⁹1958), 176 fn. 2; *Louis Grodecki*, Les vitraux allegoriques de St.-Denis, in: Art de France, vol. 1, Paris 1961, 46–49 (figure 22/24). Vorderholzer assumes that the "anagogic window" was built according to a word of abbot Suger of St. Denis (about 1080–1151) written in "Liber de rebus in administratione sua gestis": "Tollis agendo molam de furfure, Paule, farinam. / Mosaicae legis intima nota facis, / Fit de tot granis verus sine furfure panis, / Perpetuusque cibus noster et angelicus." [here: Patrologia Latina 186, 1237; *German Translation*: "Den Mühlstein drehst du, o Paulus, fängst auf das Mehl aus der Kleie. / Den innersten Kern von Moses Gesetz machst du bekannt. / Aus vielen Körnern wird das wahre Brot ohne Kleie, / Speise zum ewigen Leben für Menschen und Engel."]

describing the Old Testament as promise and the New Testament as fulfilment".⁹

This approach to Christian understanding of Scripture dishonours the Jewish faith because it leaves it in the *"Pronaos* of the Temple" (the atrium of the temple), and at the same time places the Christian faith in the middle of the sanctuary.¹⁰

This careless and simplistic approach, so popular in Christian homilies, has blinded Christians to the reality that the scheme of "promise and fulfilment" exists within the Old Testament itself. This tension between promise and fulfilment is rooted in God's promise of salvation and is sustained by the continuing promise which is provided by the word of God in the Hebrew Scripture itself. Christians, on the other hand, discover the very same tension between promise and fulfilment within the New Testament without being fulfilled.

1.2 Another perspective – a biblical understanding of "promise"¹¹

I previously stated that Matthew's quotation formula "Now all this took place to fulfil *[plēróō]* what was spoken by the Lord through the prophet" functions as *hermeneutical marker* that provides essential information about how Christians interpret the Hebrew Bible. This is because the Hebrew Scripture provides the foundation for the interpretation of the Christ event. Matthew wants to warrant this Christ event for his generation. He does not intend to interpret Hebrew Scripture in a Christocentric system or to prove that the truth of the Old Testament's promise was fulfilled in Jesus, the Christ. When Matthew refers to the Prophetic word as "fulfilled" he demonstrates that the Scripture read by the Jews remains significant for his generation and that its promise will continue to be meaningful for the future.

From the hermeneutical perspective, we must distinguish between what I would call a "pro-spective" [forward looking] and a "retro-

---

9   *Christoph Dohmen/Günter Stemberger*, Hermeneutik der Jüdischen Bibel und des Alten Testaments, Stuttgart 1996, 181.
10 This point of view is found for example in the book "Heidenthum und Judenthum" written by *Johann Joseph Döllinger* (1799–1890), a main representative of the Catholic reform movement, classically named by the subtitle "Vorhalle zur Geschichte des Christentums" (Regensburg 1857). The theme of this book is coherent with the contents of evolution theory of the religious studies in the 19th century (cf. *Schöttler*, Christliche Predigt und Altes Testament, 231–235) and describes the Gentiles and Judaism – on the same level! – as *"praeparatio evangelica"*.
11 Cf. esp.: *Schöttler*, Christliche Predigt und Altes Testament, 440–485.

spective" [backward looking] reading of the Old Testament. For Christian interpretation of the Hebrew Bible, both readings are related to Christ. With this distinction in mind, I believe it is hermeneutically relevant to ask from which perspective those in the Christian Church are looking *towards* Christ as reference point. In the example from Matthew, we would argue that his approach is *prospective* as it looks forward towards Jesus as Christ.

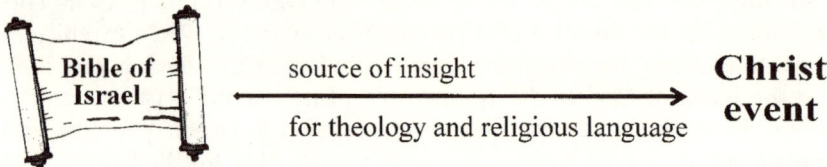

The decisive statements about Jesus in Matthew's Gospel are made within the context of theological themes and the language of the Hebrew Scriptures in their Greek translation (Septuagint). Therefore, the Hebrew Bible would remain of normative importance for Christians.

This pro-spective approach to Hebrew Scripture should be distinguished from a *retro-spective* reading of the Old Testament, which employs a contrary method.

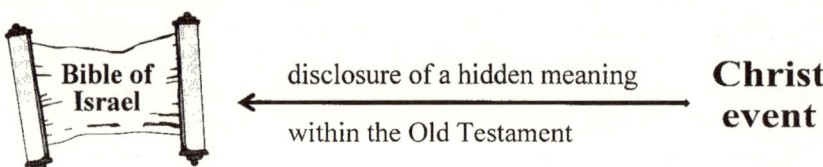

The retro-spective reading presumes that there is a Christian meaning hidden in the Hebrew Bible, and that the reader actually "discovers" this interpretation as intrinsic to the text itself. This perspective is retro-spective because it is looking from the Christ event backwards to the Old Testament. Here *the Christ event* is the *initial point*. Even if this approach is related to the Hebrew Bible, there is no need to open the book or read it carefully because this approach is convinced that it will find about Christ being proclaimed in the Old Testament. This retro-spective approach has an a priori assumption that "knows" everything at the outset.

This retrospective approach served the Christian tradition as theologians, and Church councils elaborated a more systematic approach to Christology. It has been the dominant method for Christian hermeneutic of the Hebrew Bible. However, I would argue that in our contemporary situation this method prevents us from having an unbiased point of view on the Christ event. As gentile Christians it means that we are not able to read the Hebrew Scriptures with the earlier or perhaps "original" prospective. We can no longer imagine the Christ event in the light of the Hebrew Bible like Matthew's Jewish-Christian parish because of their origins within the Jewish milieu of Roman Palestine. The retrospective reading has become so dominant over the past two thousand years that it has permanently marked our cultural memory, liturgy and piety. Thus, the great hermeneutical challenge for contemporary Christians is to find the way back to a prospective reading.

Let us return to the pro-spective reading of the Hebrew Bible. We argued that the pro-spective reading is characterised by the interpretation of the Hebrew Bible where the Christ event is the reference point about which is reported in the light of the Hebrew Bible. With the prospective reading, the Hebrew Scriptures retain their validity to Christians not because prophecy was fulfilled in Christ, but because in Christ God renews and confirms his promise and faithfulness in order to be extended for the nations. Those who believe in Jesus as the Christ, Christians, are now under the promises offered by the God of Israel. Those promises retain their validity and were not removed or made obsolete by a presumed complete fulfilment in Christ. Thus, the retrospective reading of the Hebrew Scriptures, which is identified with the theological scheme "promise and fulfilment", is not only insufficient to describe the relationship between the Old and the New Testaments, it is also an incorrect approach for the Christian understanding of the Hebrew Bible. He who is called "Jesus Christ", the "anointed one of God", *must not* be seen as *fulfilment* but as *affirmation and confirmation* of God's promise which came first to Israel and then remains valid for us Christians.

At this point it may be instructive for us to examine 2Cor. 1.18–20:

> "[18] As surely as God is faithful, our word to you has not been 'Yes and No'.[19] For the Son of God, Christ Jesus, who was preached among you by us – by me and Silvanus and Timothy – was [*Greek: egéneto*] not 'Yes and No'; but in him it is [*Greek: gégonen*] 'Yes'. [20] For as many as are the promises [*Greek: epaggelíai*] of God, in him they are 'Yes'; therefore also through him is the Amen – to the glory of God – through us."

These verses are of central theological importance as we investigate the significance of Jesus Christ in the scheme of promise and fulfilment. For Christians Jesus Christ is not the goal of promises, but he is the ultimate witness that God is faithful to humanity and that his promises cannot fail.

I want to conclude the first part of my talk with a brief linguistic hint[12] about two texts from the Hebrew Scriptures.[13] First I want to mention 1Kings 1.14. In this passage the prophet Nathan is speaking to Bathsheba the mother of King Solomon:

> "Behold, while you [= Bathsheba] are still there speaking with the king, I will come in after you and confirm your words [*Hebrew:* ומלאתי את־דבריך]."

In the term מלא את־הדברים (LXX: plēróō toùs lógous) here מלא ([ml'] Piel) does not mean "to fulfil" but has to be translated as "to affirm" or "to confirm". In a similar way we have to understand the term מלא את־דברי יהוה (LXX: plēróō tò ῥēma kyríou) in 1Kings 2.27:

> "So Solomon dismissed Abiathar from being priest to YHWH, in order to confirm the word of YHWH, which He had spoken concerning the house of Eli in Shiloh."

The Hebrew מלא ([ml'] Piel), like the Greek *plēróō* as well, could possibly lead to the misunderstanding that God's promise has become obsolete and that the promise had ended. Whenever this point has to be clarified, the Old Testament often uses קום ([qūm] Hifil) to ensure that God's promise is of remaining existence. We find this illustrated for instance in Deut. 9.5:[14]

> "It is not for your righteousness or for the uprightness of your heart that you are going to possess their land, but it is because of the wickedness of these nations that YHWH your God is driving them out before you, in order to confirm the word [ולמען הקים את־הדבר] which YHWH swore to your fathers, to Abraham, Isaac and Jacob."

In this context I want to point at an analogical use of biblical terms: When other biblical traditions use כרת ברית or נתן ברית ("to make a covenant" or "to give unto him my covenant") the priestly source utilises the term קום (Hifil) ("establish a covenant"; compare Gen. 6.18; 9.9–11, 17; 17.7–19, 21; Ex. 6.4; Lev. 26.9). This is an expression of the

---

12 Cf. *Schöttler*, Christliche Predigt und Altes Testament, 452 n. 50.
13 Cf. 1Kings 8.24 (= 2Chr. 6.15); 1Kings 8.15 (= 2Chr. 6.4); 2Chr. 36.21f. More documenting verses in *Heinz-Josef Fabry*, Art. מלא, in: Theologisches Wörterbuch zum Alten Testament, vol. 4, Stuttgart et al. 1984, 876–887, here: 880f.
14 More documenting verses: 1Sam. 3.12; 2Sam. 7.25; 1Kings 2.4; 6.12; 8.20; 12.15; Isa. 44.26; Jer. 11.5; 23.20; 28.6; 29.10; Dan. 9.12; Neh. 9.8. But in the whole LXX – only exception: Dan. 9.12 – קום is not translated with *plēróō* but with Greek *hístēmi*!

unshakeable and continuing importance, i. e. of the "affirmation of the covenant" (compare Deut. 8.19).[15]

It is important to understand the negative impact upon the person who hears the translation of the Greek verb *"plēróō"* as "to fulfil" in the readings for the Mass and school bibles. Therefore I want to advocate for translating Matthew's quotation formula as follows: "Now [all] this took place to confirm what was spoken by the Lord through the prophet (N.N.): ..." Therefore the Christian way of translating has to be revised for reasons of semantics and theology, because it used to follow a distorted point of view of the Hebrew Bible which was read as New Testament by Christians.

If Christians live their faith in the presence of the Jewish People, then and only then does "Israel" become the living evidence – which is essential and irreplaceable for the Church – that salvation has not yet come to its fulfilment. The Jewish People who continue to bear the name "Israel" become the witness within the history of the world that God's will is not yet fulfilled. By its faithful witness of "no" to the belief in Christ, the Jewish People proclaims its reservation that the eschaton has arrived in all its fulfilment.

Without this sensitive encounter with the presence of the Jewish people, the church is tempted by a "forced hope" (*"Hoffnungszwang"*)[16] to believe in a Christology of fulfilment which, in the end, leaves people hopeless. Therefore we have to construct a Christology which is located in the "gap" between promise and fulfilment, a Christology in this "lack of fulfilment", which often is painful. Christians are likely to overlook this "Christological gap" too quickly when they face the rhetorical brilliance of the "Christology of resurrection." They then ignore situations in human life where salvation remains to be realised.[17]

2. Christian identity – not at Israel's costs

An understanding, which claims that the Hebrew Scripture contradicts the New Testament and also believes that Judaism's way to salvation is blocked as "religion of law", often makes reference to that part of

---

15 Cf. *Samuel Amsler*, Art. קום, in: Theologisches Handwörterbuch zum Alten Testament, vol. 2, München/Zürich 1976, 635–641, here: 640; *Johann Gamberoni*, Art. קום, in: Theologisches Wörterbuch zum Alten Testament, vol. 6, Stuttgart/Berlin/Köln 1989, 1252–1274, here: 1263f. 1274.

16 Cf. *Heinz-Günther Schöttler*, Die Anklage Gottes als Krisenintervention. Eine erlittene Exilstheologie Israels, in: ThQ 185/2005, 158–181, here: 181.

17 About a Christology and preaching within a "painful lack of fulfilment" cf. *Schöttler*, Christliche Predigt und Altes Testament, 465–478 and 513–521.

Matthew's Sermon on the Mount which is called the "Antitheses of the Law": Mat. 5.21–48. However, neither at this point nor anywhere else in the New Testament will one find the term "antithesis". The term is taken from the ancient world. It was used as a book title by Marcion, a bishop's son and shipowner from Sinope in Asia Minor who died about A.D. 160.[18] Although it cannot be found in the original of the New Testament, the term "antithesis" was used in rubrics which were added by later translators as editorial headline. As a result today's translations and theological interpretation of Mat. 5 tend to be antithetic:

> "You have heard that the ancients were told: ... But[19] I say to you that [Greek: egò dè légo hymin hóti] ..."

It seems with the words spoken by Matthew's Jesus that the Torah of Moses became obsolete. The Jewish path to salvation by obedience to Torah was degraded as being obedient to the "law" by Christians who believed that the Jewish covenant through Torah without Christ had failed. And that is the way Christians have been accustomed to live their religion: although they retain the five books of Moses as a canonical part of their holy scriptures, the idea that Torah as "divine teaching" de facto seems to have no meaning or importance to them.

We might challenge this comfortable assumption if we look more precisely at the so called "antithesis" in Matthew's Gospel. Upon closer inspection, it becomes clear that none of them annuls even one commandment or decree of the Torah[20] – despite what average Christians believe. In these passages Matthew's Jesus does not want to show that the New Testament contradicts the Old, just the opposite is the case. The introductory verses Mat. 5.17–20 outline in an apologetic way that Jesus' interpretation of Torah must not be misunderstood as a break with the heritage of Israel. In fact this heritage is still of

---

18 The only information we have about Markion himself, his deeds, and his writings was passed on by his antagonists, especially by Justin Martyr, Irenaeus of Lyon, Tertullian, Hippolyt, and Clemens of Alexandria. From abundant literature cf. esp. *Adolf von Harnack*, Marcion. Das Evangelium vom fremden Gott. Eine Monographie zur Geschichte der Grundlegung der katholischen Kirche (1921). Neue Studien zu Marcion, Leipzig ²1924, TU 45, reprint: Darmstadt 1996; *Barbara Aland*, Art. Markion/Markioniten, in: TRE 22/1992, 89–101. – *Markion* calls his one and only writing "Antitheses". In this writing, which is lost today, he rejects the whole Old Testament and those parts of the New Testament he alleges to be Judaistic distortions. Irenaeus of Lyon sums up Markion's ideas in his writing "Adversus haereses" by clearly referring to Mat. 5.17: (Jesus) "abolished the prophets and the law, and all the works of that God who made the world, whom also he calls Cosmocrator" (Irenaeus, Adversus haereses I, 27,2).
19 The Greek particle *dé* is used as *dé*-adversativum here.
20 Cf. with detailed information *Schöttler*, Christliche Predigt und Altes Testament, 522–586.

importance for the Christian parish Matthew is writing for. The difference Matthew wants to show the Christian parish is how the approach to Torah has changed for them. They approach Torah through Jesus as mediator or, in other words, in succession of Jesus.

> Mat. 5: "[17] Do not think that I came to abolish the Law or the Prophets; I did not come to abolish but to confirm [*Greek: plēróō*]. [18] For truly I say to you, until heaven and earth pass away, not the smallest letter or stroke shall pass from the Law [*Greek: nómos*] until all is accomplished. [19] Whoever then annuls one of the least of these commandments [*Greek: entolē*], and teaches others to do the same, shall be called least in the kingdom of heaven; but whoever keeps and teaches them, he shall be called great in the kingdom of heaven. [20] For I say to you that unless your righteousness surpasses that of the scribes and Pharisees, you will not enter the kingdom of heaven."[21]

Like it has to be done with the so called *"Erfüllungsformel"*, here *"plēróō"* again has to be translated as "to confirm" or "to affirm" and not as "to fulfil" like it has been done traditionally.

We have to add that the antithetical translation of the introductory verses is only *a possible one* – although starting with Vulgate translation ("Ego *autem* dico vobis: ...") through today it has become the common one. On the other hand, according to Greek grammar, it is possible to understand the Greek particle *dé* of the introductory verses in an explicatory way (*dé explicativum*[22]), one that expands upon the meaning of the first passage. Thus, we can translate with Franz Mußner:[23]

> "You have heard that the ancients were told: ... I say to you [explaining] ... in addition [...]."

---

[21] Since the verse Mat. 5.17 is obviously contrary to his theological program, Markion finally calls it a Judaistic interpolation in his "Antitheses". Tertullian (died after 212) reports that in his writing "Adversus Marcionem": "The statement that He [Christ] came not to destroy the law and the prophets, but rather to fulfil them (Mat. 5.17) Marcion has erased as an interpolation. [...] What business, therefore, had you to erase out of the Gospel that which was quite consistent in it? [...] In vain has our man of Pontus laboured to deny this statement." (Tertullian, Adversus Marcionem IV, 7,4; IV, 9,15; V, 14,14).

[22] Cf. *Edwin Mayser*, Grammatik der griechischen Papyri aus der Ptolemäerzeit. Mit Einschluß der gleichzeitigen Ostraka und der in Ägypten verfaßten Inschriften, vol. 2/3: Satzlehre. Synthetischer Teil, Berlin/Leipzig 1934, 125ff.; *Friedrich Blass/ Albert Debrunner*, Grammatik des neutestamentlichen Griechisch, bearbeitet von Friedrich Rehkopf, Göttingen [17]1990, § 447 Nr. 1c. Ibid., however in § 447, fn. 2, the introductory formula describes the adversary use of the particle dé.

[23] Cf. *Franz Mussner*, Tractate on the Jews. The Significance of Judaism in the Christian Faith, Philadelphia (PA)/London 1984, 117f. [= *Franz Mußner*, Trakat über die Juden, München 1979, 190f.].

This kind of translation dissolves the harmful confrontation of "Torah as law" and "Gospel as grace". It follows the rabbinic halakhic way of interpreting Scripture during the period of Jesus. Therefore I want to advocate for eliminating the term "antithesis", which was added to Mat. 5.21–48 by later editors anyway. It would be far better and more authentic to follow Franz Mußner's translation, which retains the notion of Jews and Christians as faithful to the Torah. It is important for us Christians to gain a new understanding of the Jewish Torah, one which has to become a part of Christian homilies and preaching.[24]

The Christian response to the word "Torah", which was and remains polemical and negative, prevents Christians from understanding what Torah really means to Jews. This kind of reaction is motivated by a *secret fear* that the uniqueness of Jesus and Christian faith would be at risk if Christians were not in opposition to Judaism and proclaiming their Gospel is an antithesis to Torah and to the Hebrew Bible. This approach means to live separate from Judaism.

Therefore theologians and preachers sense a "threat of their faith", if Matthew's Jesus in these "Antitheses" does not annul a single commandment or decree of the Torah but to a certain extent confirms what is written in the Torah and explicates its meaning following a Jewish method of interpretation. A Christian community that defines its identity as an opposition or contrast between the Hebrew Bible and the New Testament, between "Torah and grace" or "law and Gospel", is certainly a community whose identity and integrity is severely at risk.

Christian preachers must acknowledge their "secret fear" in order to avoid homiletic traps, e. g.: when they preach about texts like Mat. 5.21–48, the so called "Antitheses of the Law", when they preach about verses containing Jesus' statements about Sabbath,[25] when the text they preach about proposes a defamatory description of the "Pharisees" in the New Testament, when they are confronted with the "seduction" of a typological exegesis that calls Jesus "the new Moses" or "the new Torah",[26] or when they are tempted to demonstrate the double

---

[24] In this context read the following from the "Catechism of the Catholic Church" (1997): "Because of sin, which it [= the Old law] cannot remove, it remains a law of bondage." [no. 1963] "The Old Law is a preparation for the Gospel." [no. 1964] "Christ is the end of the law (cf. Rom. 10.4); only he teaches and bestows the justice of God." [no. 1977] "The New Law is a law of love, a law of grace, a law of freedom" [no. 1985].

[25] Cf. esp. *Schöttler*, Christliche Predigt und Altes Testament, 604–608.

[26] Cf. *Schöttler*, Christliche Predigt und Altes Testament, 584–586.

commandment to love God and to love one's neighbour[27] represents only "Christian love", or when they preach about such verses from the New Testament, which have been understood and interpreted as antagonistic to Judaism in the Christian tradition, such as Mark 7.1–23.

Christians should not rely upon distorting descriptions in Christian sources but rather follow the fundamental principle *"lex orandi – lex credendi"*[28] ("The law of prayer constitutes what ought to be believed"). They would then be able to turn to the treasure house in the *Siddur* or Jewish prayer book and understand what Torah really means within the community of Israel as the Jewish people. Christians should read *"Ahawat-Olam-prayer"* of the Siddur, which describes God's love as revealed in Torah:[29]

> "Unending is Your love [cf. Jer. 31.3] for Your people, the House of Israel. Torah and Mitzvot, laws and precepts have You taught us. Therefore, O Lord our God, when we lie down and when we rise up, we will meditate on Your laws and rejoice in Your Torah and Mitzvot forever. Day and night we will reflect on them, for they are our life and the length of our days. Then Your love shall never depart from our hearts. Blessed is the Lord, who loves the people Israel."

---

27 For examples of homilies cf. *Schöttler*, Christliche Predigt und Altes Testament, 599–603.

28 One axiom of Christian Theology says that the prayers of the Church, especially the Liturgy, is a place where faith is practiced and therefore can be called normative as a place of Christian wisdom and of theological insight, cf. *Arno Schilson*, Art. Lex orandi – lex credendi, in: LThK 6/1997, 871f.

29 Cf. also the *"Ahawah-Rabba-prayer"*: "With abundant love have you loved us, O Lord our God; with exceedingly great pity have you pitied us. Our Father, our King, for the sake of our forefathers who trusted in You and whom You taught the decrees of life, may You be equally gracious to us and teach us. Our Father, the merciful Father, Who acts mercifully, have mercy upon us, instill in our hearts to understand and elucidate, to listen, learn, teach, safeguard, perform, and fulfil all the words of Your Torah's teaching with love. Enlighten our eyes in Your Torah, attach our hearts to Your commandments, and unify our hearts to love and fear Your Name, and may we not feel inner shame for all eternity. Because we have trusted in Your great and awesome holy Name, may we exult and rejoice in Your salvation. Bring us in peacefulness from the four corners of the earth and lead us with upright pride to our land. For You effect salvations O God; You have chosen us from among every people and tongue. And You have brought us close to You, and proclaim Your Oneness with love. Blessed are You, O Lord, Who chooses His people Israel with love."

3. "... to the Jew first" (Rom. 1.16)

The decisive factor for Christians then becomes the presuppositional knowledge where Christians encounter the Hebrew Scriptures as the Bible of the Jewish people and experience an engagement with the Jewish people. Saint Paul describes this fundamental approach in the programmatic statement at the beginning of the letter to the Romans in 1.16:

> "For I am not ashamed of the gospel, for it is the power of God for salvation to everyone who believes, to the Jew first [*Greek: prōton*] and [also] to the Greek [= *gojim*]."

This programmatic statement must be understood not merely or primarily as a temporal precedence for the history of mission, giving priority of place to the Jews before the pagans. Paul really wants to claim that the Jews have priority of election in God's plan for salvation, before the pagans, which according to Rom. 3.1–3 is of a *perduring quality*:

> "¹ Then what advantage [*Greek: tò perissón*] has the Jew? Or what is the benefit of circumcision? ² Great in every respect. First [*Greek: prōton*] of all, that they were entrusted with the words of God. ³ What then? If some did not believe, their unbelief will not nullify the faithfulness of God, will it?"

Paul emphasizes this advantage of salvation at the outset of the so-called "Israel chapters" of Rom. 9–11 when he highlights the promises among the seven gifts God gave to Israel. In these verses Paul employs the verb in the present tense, not the past.

> Rom. 9: "⁴ They are Israelites, and to them belong the adoption as sons, the glory, the covenants, the giving of the law, the worship, and the promises [*Greek: hai epaggelíai*]; ⁵ to them belong the fathers [= the patriarchs], and from them comes the Christ according to the flesh. – God who is over all shall be blessed forever. Amen."[30]

Paul says that God is faithful to his people even though it ignores the message of the Gospel. This qualitative and perduring "first" means: Israel, who was addressed first by God, has not been rejected "for the gifts and calling of God are irrevocable"[31] (Rom. 11.29). That Jesus was

---

30 On the syntax of verse 5 (doxology) cf. *Heinz-Günther Schöttler*, „Auf der Ebene ihrer je eigenen Identität verbunden" (Johannes Paul II.) – Theologische Überlegungen zu einem neuen Verhältnis von Kirche und Israel und zum christlich-jüdischen Dialog, in: *Max Peter Baumann/Tim Becker/Raphael Woebs* (Eds.), Musik und Kultur im jüdischen Leben der Gegenwart (Kulturwissenschaften 2), Berlin 2006, 33–87, here: 50 (fn. 27).

31 "Literally, 'un-repented'; God does not repent that he at one time chose Israel; the Jews remain beloved of God 'for the sake of their forefathers' [Rom. 11:29]. The election therefore endures; God does not reject Israel which he 'foreknew' (knew

not accepted by contemporary Jews led to a somewhat polemical description of the Jews in the Gospel of Matthew (e. g. Mat. 8.11f., compare also Luke 14.16–24) and permitted traditional Christian theology to proclaim that this failure to accept the Gospel meant that God had abandoned the Jews. This kind of theology was rejected as *unbiblical* by Vatican II. in the document *"Nostra Aetate* 4" where it is written:

> "that in catechetical work or in the preaching of the word of God they do not teach anything that does not conform to the truth of the Gospel and the spirit of Christ."

Following *"Nostra Aetate"* the Church must now preach that Israel has not been rejected. The Jews, "the first to hear [God's] word" (this is a quote taken from the intercessions of the ministry of the word on Good Friday), are living in an "unrevoked covenant" (Martin Buber following Rom. 11.29). Israel's history of faith, and even when it is read by Christians as Old Testament, belongs to the Jewish People as the inheritance of the first-born. The church is only able to participate. Paul puts it in Rom. 1.17f. with the image of the olive tree as follows:

> "¹⁷ But if some of the branches were broken off, and you, being a wild olive, were grafted in among them and became partaker with them [*Greek: syg-koinōnós*] of the rich root of the olive tree, ¹⁸ do not be arrogant toward the branches; but if you are arrogant, remember that it is not you who supports the root, but the root supports you."

Under the great arc of the analogy between the Hebrew Bible and the New Testament, the Church can trust that it participates in Israel's great experience of faith as a wild shoot which was grafted in.[32]

The relationship between Judaism and Christianity on a theological level and in the field of faith is a very special one that is different to all other religious relationships between Christianity and other religions. Pope John Paul II. (1920–2005) defined this special relationship in his programmatic words:

---

earlier) [Rom. 11:2], and therefore in the end even 'all Israel will be saved' [Rom. 11:26]" (*Mussner*, Tractate on the Jews, 7 [= *Mußner*, Traktat über die Juden, 21]).

32 Paul makes clear that the "Nation-Ecclesia" is only allowed to participate in the root of the olive tree "Israel" through the Greek compound *syg-koinōnós* in Rom. 11.17, which emphasizes the idea of participation. The paradigm which Paul uses here to describe the relationship between Church and Israel is the socalled "participation theory" (cf. *Bertold Klappert*, Israel und die Kirche. Erwägungen zur Israellehre Karl Barths, München 1980, esp. 32–37). Cf. Paul's methaphor "fellow heirs" (Greek: [*syg-*]*kleronómos*) of the promise in Rom. 8.17; Eph. 3.6. That, and how Christians can participate in the faith experiences of Israel about which they read in the Hebrew Bible, is seen as Old Testament by Christians cf. as a basic analysis: *Schöttler*, Christliche Predigt und Altes Testament, esp. 368–374.

"Our two religious communities are connected and closely related at the very level of their respective religious identities."[33]

Israel is not misled when it hears the word of the one and only God. The Church – in the past, today, and always – is the second one to hear the word of God which was addressed to Israel first. Christian preaching, catechesis, and religious education must never forget about this "first" of the Jews especially when they deal with texts from the Old Testament.

Israel is not an entity that belongs to the past; it is rather a contemporary community of faith. Israel, the Jewish People, lives its faith today. Christian homilies tend to ignore that Israel is alive and that Jews believe in one God who is the same for Jews and Christians. Christian preachers often speak about Israel in their homilies as something that precedes Christianity, belongs to the past, and is only of interest as a matter of history of religion. Christian proclamation must overcome its ignorance and reticence about the Jewish people for Israel's sake and for the sake of the Church itself.

Now, we have to keep in mind that we can only read the Hebrew Scriptures as Christians and that we can and must not diminish this perspective so that we preserve our own authentic identity. What is crucial for us is that we really learn to hear. This "hearing" means that we listen carefully to what Jews are telling about their faith. What I would call "listening Christian preaching" must learn how to value the present witness of Jewish faith which became Scripture in the ancient world and which remains present in the Jewish community of our own times. It can be helpful to look at the history of ecumenism where Protestants and Catholics learned to understand and respect one another, to learn from one another, to believe together, and to talk about each other.

The Protestant "grandmaster" of homiletics, Rudolf Bohren, explicitly points out in his textbook of homiletics in 1971: "Only arrogance and ignorance […] can prevent a preacher from learning from the rabbi […]: The Church cannot ignore the synagogue without losing its promises".[34] The Jews are relevant for the faith of the Church.

---

33 *Rolf Rendtorff/Hans Hermann Henrix* (Eds.), Die Kirchen und das Judentum, vol. 1, Dokumente 1945–1985, Paderborn 1988, 64.

34 *Rudolf Bohren*, Predigtlehre, München ⁶1993, 121. – Cf. the already mentioned document of the Pontifical Biblical Commission "The Jewish people and their Sacred Scriptures in the Christian Bible" (2001), no. 22: "On the practical level of exegesis, Christians can, nonetheless, learn much from Jewish exegesis practised for more than two thousand years, and, in fact, they have learned much in the course of history.[45] For their part, it is to be hoped that Jews themselves can derive profit from Christian exegetical research." Cf. also the document of the Pontifical Biblical

Unfortunately some still claim today that the Hebrew Bible is only relevant when being read through the lens of Christology.[35] However it is decisive that Christians begin to understand the truth of the Hebrew Bible as a reality which is immanent.

The Hebrew Bible has a relational value in itself for Christians. The Pontifical Biblical Commission develops this proposition in the document "The Jewish people and their Sacred Scriptures in the Christian Bible" (2001) in this way: "The Old Testament *in itself* has great value as the Word of God."[36]

A new appreciation of Israel by the Church seeks to know, to understand, and to respect Judaism as it is without looking through a Christian tradition that distorts and degrades it.

Christian preaching and catechesis of the Old Testament therefore should not refer exclusively to the Christian perspective and tradition when speaking about Judaism. Christians should also incorporate contemporary Judaism as an essential witness of faith in the one God. That is a challenge and an opportunity for us Christians to recognize the roots of our faith again in a new way and thereby learn to understand Israel as a present community of faith living in many forms, just as Christian communities do. I am more and more convinced that we understand our Christian faith more profoundly when we begin to live in the "great ecumenicism" (Karl Barth) with the Jews. We have to do this by respecting that the "Synagoga" is at eye level to the "Ecclesia"

Commission *"The Interpretation of the Bible in the Church"* (1993), I.C.2.: "Approach through Recourse to Jewish Traditions of Interpretation".

35 Compare *Peter Knauer*, Der Glaube kommt vom Hören. Ökumenische Fundamentaltheologie, Freiburg i. Br. ⁶1991, esp. 261.290; *Hans Hübner*, Das Alte Testament als Dokument der Religionsgeschichte?, in: *Bärbel Köhler* (Ed.), Religion und Wahrheit. Religionsgeschichtliche Studien. FS für Gernot Wießner, Wiesbaden 1998, 237–246. As critique of this point of view cf. esp. *Schöttler*, Christliche Predigt und Altes Testament, 99–104.

36 The *Pontifical Biblical Commission*, The Jewish people and their Sacred Scriptures in the Christian Bible (2001), no. 21. Unfortunately the context of that quote is theologically misleading because it is using old stereotypes (please notice the parts in italics): "The Old Testament in itself has great value as the Word of God. To read the Old Testament as Christians then does not mean wishing to find everywhere direct reference to Jesus and to Christian realities. True, for Christians, all the Old Testament economy is in movement towards Christ; if then the Old Testament is read in the light of Christ, one can, retrospectively, perceive something of this movement. But since it is a movement, a slow and difficult progression throughout the course of history, each event and each text is situated at a particular point along the way, at a greater or lesser distance from the end. Retrospective re-readings through Christian eyes mean perceiving both the movement towards Christ *and the distance from Christ, prefiguration and dissimilarity*. Conversely, the New Testament cannot be fully understood except in the light of the Old Testament."

and that the "Synagoga" holds a perduring qualitative "first": *"Israelitica dignitas".*[37]

---

[37] In the Church's liturgy of the Easter Vigil the reading of Ex. 14.15–15.1 is followed by the third Oration which uses the words *"Israelitica dignitas"*: "Deus, cuius antiqua miracula etiam nostris temporibus coruscare sentimus, dum, quod uni populo a persecutione Pharaonis liberando dexterae tuae potentia contulisti, id in salutem gentium per aquam regenerationis operaris, praesta, ut in Abrahae fílios et in Israeliticam dignitatem totius mundi transeat plenitudo. Per Christum Dóminum nostrum." The alternative third Oration even talks about *"Israelis privilegium"*. Unfortunately it contains a strong Christological typology overall and therefore "is getting close to a dangerous theology of substitution" (Norbert Lohfink, Die traditionellen Orationen der Ostervigil deutsch. Kritische Analyse und Neuentwurf, in: *Georg Braulik/Norbert Lohfink* [Eds.], Osternacht und Altes Testament. Studien und Vorschläge, Frankfurt/M. et al. ²2003, 139–162, here: 153 [transl.: HGS]): "Deus, qui primis temporibus impleta miracula novi testamenti luce reserasti, ut et Mare Rubrum forma sacri fontis exsisteret, et plebs a servitute liberata christiani populi sacramenta praeferret, da, ut omnes gentes, Israelis privilegium merito fídei consecutae, Spiritus tui participatione regenerentur. Per Christum Dominum nostrum."

Jewish and Christian Bible Reading Between Retro-spectivism and Pro-spectivism Response

Yehoyada Amir

The important and productive doctrine offered by Professor Schöttler is based on two major hermeneutic elements. The first has to do with the question of how the New-Testimonial word πληρόω should be translated, or to be more accurate, which understanding of the Biblical Hebrew notion of לְמַלֵּא אֶת דְּבַר הָאֵל is behind that word.[1] At stake is the crucial difference between "fulfilment" (*Erfüllung*) and "verification" (*Bestätigung*). The answer to this outlined lingual question defines two very different ways, in which the Christ event could be understood from the point of view of the New Testament and its relationship to the Hebrew Bible, or Christian-wise: the Old Testament. If one sticks to the classic Christian understanding that Jesus is the "fulfilment" of the Hebrew Biblical prophecy, then the relevancy and spiritual-religious meaning of the Hebrew Bible should be understood as exhausted by this fulfilment to an extent that may raise a serious question on whether, taking in account this exhausting fulfilment, the Hebrew Bible should be seen as relevant to the Christian altogether. Is Christianity really a "Biblical" religion in the grand sense of that term, or is it actually merely a religion of the New Testament? Does the Christian have to take seriously the reading of that exhausted book, or should she or he focus only on the message delivered in the "real", not "out-of-date" text?

As a Jew who finds the Hebrew Bible a supremely relevant and enriching spiritual and religious source, I can fully understand that Prof. Schöttler yearns for a hermeneutics that will award his life and the lives of his fellow Christians with the precious treasury of that source. As a citizen of our "global village" I share the hope that Christianity, a major factor in the design of contemporary culture and society, will adopt some powerful notions from the Hebrew Bible. Of

---

1   To the best of my reading, this phrase appears in the Hebrew Bible in three interconnected meanings: to fulfil (1Kings 2.27), to verify or strengthen (1Kings 1.14), to fulfill (1Kings 8.24; 2Chr. 36.21).

course I am also fully aware of the danger that the adoption, by Jews as well as by Christians, of quite a few very problematic Biblical notions will lead to a non-humanistic, intolerant, and conservative shape to both religions.

From the point of view of Christian-Jewish dialogue, the question would be whether we – Jews and Christians – really have substantial mutual text that would serve as the basis of the dialogue. A "fulfilment" Christian theology means that the Hebrew Bible can be perceived as Torah only to one partner, while the other sees it as an "old", out-dated, and already "fulfilled" promise. It bares nothing else but a partial, incomplete, and not entirely developed formulation of the content of the "new", and "fulfilling" covenant. Such perceptions leave a very limited space for a textual-based dialogue, for learning from each other's hermeneutics of the common text. On the other hand Christian-Jewish dialogue can flourish if Christians would adopt the perception of the Hebrew Bible as a valid, and relevant source, from which they wish to learn and which should be included in the design of contemporary Christian religiosity. Such a perception would establish a substantial groundwork to serve as a fruitful basis for the discussion of that which Jews and Christians have in common as well as that in which they differ. Christians and Jews, who read together a mutual sacred text, who struggle in parallel ways with the troubling question of what such sanctity may mean for modern/post-modern believers, and who seek to listen to the commandment and to the prophetic voice that this text awards their lives with, can quite naturally learn *with and from* each other. Encountering with a Christian perception of the Christ event as a verification of the Divine Biblical message can enrich Jewish reading of the Hebrew Bible, though for the Jew this event would be seen as an optional understanding of that potential, not as *the* verification. On the basis of such common ground Jews and Christians may learn also from those texts alien to their own corpus of sacred sources that the other religion sticks to and bases itself on: the New Testament and Christian theology on the one hand, Rabbinic and post-Rabbinic Jewish literature on the other hand.

In such a context of mutual learning one might imagine, for example, a fascinating discussion concerning the very nature of prophecy at large. In such a discussion, one might imagine, the pupil of Jewish reading of the Bible might raise the question on whether there are at the heart of prophecy really promises or forecasts of the future which might have been seen as "fulfilled", "verified", or completed. Such a reader would offer a reading of prophecy that is demanding, warning, educating, and protesting. "To prophesy" would be seen in this light not as telling that which *will* happen but rather that which *might* happen or that which should occur. In such discussion the Jewish and Christian readers would read carefully the story of Jonah, the prophet who had to learn that at the heart of his mission is the unfulfilled forecast, a warning which succeeded to the extent that it did not have to be realised. What would the Christian reader say in such a discussion? This should be left to the real, non-virtual discussion which might be constituted on the interfaith togetherness that a doctrine like that of Prof. Schöttler might potentialise.

Nevertheless, the hermeneutical question of these New Testament texts is, and must remain, a Christian issue. From a linguistic point of view both notions, that of the fulfilment and that of the verification, seem to be accurate and to correspond the same Hebrew term למלא; from a theological point of view, it is a question of religious conviction and priorities, namely a free decision that must be left to the believers of that religion alone. As a Jew I cannot and ought not offer my response. I am only allowed to offer friendship and empathy to the Christian believer who offered this hermeneutics and to appreciate his commitment to re-design and heal his faith. If there is a room for a Jewish response to this doctrine, namely for a joint sense of responsibility in regards of its religious fundaments, it lies in the second, comprehensive hermeneutic element that this doctrine is based on.

Then the lingual element was in essence only a point of departure for the principal discussion of retrospective vs. "pro-spective" reading of the scripture. The multiplicity of meanings of the Hebrew word למלא was no more than a necessary step which made it possible to develop, on the basis of legitimate and valid reading of several New Testament verses, a much farther-reaching discussion. The question of what kind of relationship the Christian reader should constitute between the two parts of the text that he or she regards as the "The Holy Scripture" is, after all, no more than an example of a comprehensive, principle question concerning the reading of holy scriptures and religious sources at large.

Prof. Schöttler offers a typology of retro-spective vs. "pro-spective" reading. The first reads the ancient text from the point of view of a younger belief, text, dogma, etc. It assumes that the old sacred text must correspond to that which is regarded as "true", "just", as "valid". In the specific case he discusses, one speaks about reading of the Hebrew Bible retrospectively from the point of view of the New Testament. The fulfilment theology is based on the notion that prophecy's meaning and potency is to be grasped only from the point of view of its full, exhausting fulfilment, namely from the Jesus event to take place hundreds of years later. The hermeneutical criteria for the accurate meaning of the old text are, hence, not its words nor our religious-intellectual comprehension, but rather a younger text that is perceived as superior in authority and Divinity. The "pro-spective" reading, on the contrary, regards the old sacred text as the hermeneutical point of departure in interpreting later texts, dogmas, beliefs, and life-situations. It is based on the notion that the text is indeed comprehensible from within, that we can and ought to learn from it.

In this light, in the case discussed by Prof. Schöttler, it is the New Testament that should be interpreted in the light of the Hebrew Bible, or Christian-wise, the second testament in light of the first one, i. e. Christ event in light of the prophetic old texts. In contradiction to that specific, strictly Christian question, as regards the general principle concerning retro-spective vs. "pro-spective" readings of sacred texts and religious sources, I feel that taking part in the discussion is not only legitimate but also required. Here I stand as a partner in an interfaith dialogue at its best. Here I share the thoughts, commitments, doubts, and deliberations of my Christian partner. Here we can learn with each other and from each other.

Retrospective reading is an essential dimension of the notions that scriptures can not be only "holy" and "divine" but also religiously relevant, and that individuals and societies can and should design their lives at the present in light of a text anchored in the past and reflecting ancient areas. Only through bridging the gap between past and present, only through renewing the antique words and awarding them a meaning that is anchored in the "here and now" of the reader, can the old text bring us God's message and commandment. Franz Rosenzweig spoke of the "ability" [*Können*] to internalize the Torah to an extent that it may actually speak from our mouth as a message of the present, as a word that stems from the reader's being and religious encounter with God.[2] He refers to the midrashic notion that interprets Ps. 1.2, speaking of the righteous: "… then God's Torah is his will, and in his Torah he dwells day and night". The midrash[3] interprets the verse not as parallelism, in which "his Torah" means "His Torah", namely the Divine one, but rather as a consequential development. The righteous yearns to be engaged in God's Torah; that portion of the Torah which he succeeds in internalising and making part of his life becomes "his Torah", the Torah of the righteous. No more does it belong only to the past, only to God's ancient revelation. Learning and interpreting it makes it also part of the present, the share of the reader, a demanding element that has its part in constituting and shaping the "here and

---

2   *Franz Rosenzweig*, Zweistromland. Kleinere Schriften, Dordrecht 1984, 687–698.
3   b. AZ 19.1.

now" of the faithful individual and community. Learning, in this sense, *must* be to a certain extent retrospective.

The retrospective reading took place in most of the classic Jewish hermeneutics from the Second Temple era onward. In the Dead Sea Scrolls it takes the form of *pesharim*, namely interpretations that attribute prophetic verses directly to contemporary reality and to its perception thereof by their authors. Rabbinic *midrash* reads Biblical texts in many cases in light of contemporary notions and conceptions, even when it is evident that the interpreter is conscious of the gap between that which he perceives as religious truth anchored in God's revelation to His people and that which the very words of the text mean. Philosophic and mystical medieval interpretation is no exception in this sense. It is only the modern era, anchored in Spinoza's harsh attack on Jewish and Christian traditions at large and hermeneutical methods in particular, that introduced the idea of "pro-spective" reading, of examining the Bible from within and freeing its interpretation from later conventions and religious interests.

Strict "pro-spective" reading robs the text of the power to take part in designing the present and the future. It is a kind of reading that may serve only religious fundamentalism on the one hand and total detachment from faith and from the Holy Scripture on the other. The first simply yearns to implement in actual present life all that is to be found in the text or at least all that it reads into the text. The latter wishes to prove that the text belongs only to the past, that it is embedded in a context which is no longer relevant, that we should free ourselves from it. It is no wonder that strictly "pro-spective" reading served in the last two centuries so many attacks on religious tradition, Jewish and Christian alike.

Pure retro-spective reading of the Bible is in no way a better way; to the contrary. The fundamentalist aims in his or her perversive way to design the present under the authority of the past, taking the Scripture strictly seriously; the opponent of religion and tradition might seek a genuine understanding of the text in order to achieve maximal effectiveness in confronting it. The pure retrospective reader does neither. Though s/he has the aspiration to design life in light of the past, s/he actually designs the past in light of the present, or at least in light of that later layer which is perceived as authoritative and formative. The pure retrospective reader does not really *read* the text but rather imposes on the text that which she or he believes to be true, that which he or she holds as Divine message, regardless of the question of what text actually says that we as if sanctify. From within, the retrospective interpretation might look convincing and solid; from an exterior point of view it cannot be viewed as but weak, non-authentic, and totally unconvincing. The Aristotelian philosopher, for example, might be fascinated by the possibility of interpreting the biblical message as being fully in line with Aristotelian notions and doctrines. A later philosopher, from a different school, will be embarrassed by such an interpretation, not only from a philosophical point of view but foremost from a hermeneutical one. In order to "save" the sacred text he would develop an alternative retrospective reading that would be in agreement with the currently leading philosophical school.

The same happens when a Jew reads the retrospective Christian interpretation. Claiming that at the essence of the Hebrew Bible is the promise exhaustingly fulfilled in the Jesus event might be viewed as convincing to some Christians and might be, for them, the solid basis of their trust in both parts of the Bible. The Jew would in no way be convinced. He would view these very verses that the retrospective Christian reading reads as talking about detailed "fulfilment" of Old Testament prophecies as no more than an artificial and superficial attempt to overtake.

Neither retro-spectivism nor "pro-spectivisim" can be seen as the right way to encounter sacred sources at large and the Holy Scripture in particular. A one-sided, pure retro-spectivism, or a one-sided, pure "pro-spectivism", leads nowhere and constitutes in no way a genuine, religious, and non-fundamental dialogue with that which we are obliged to base our lives; only a synthesis of both, only a sophisticated standpoint, which reads life from the point of view of the sacred text and which reads the text from the point of view of life, might gain the power to design our life in front of God and in line with His revealed commandment.

That is, as a matter of fact, what religious hermeneutics usually represent. It is choosing again and again when to stick to a "pro-spective" hermeneutics and to the literal meaning of the ancient text, aiming to implement it in actual life or when to develop a retrospective reading that views the Scripture from the point of view of contemporary challenges and religious convictions. This right and obligation to choose, to freely choose, between these two alternatives of reading is in the heart of the responsibility which is carried by religious interpretation of Divine message and Holy Scripture. Here is anchored the freedom of the interpreter; here is anchored his or her obligation to revive the ancient words, to bring the past and make it present, and to design the future of men and women in light of God's revelation.

That is, in essence, what we learn from Prof. Schöttler. When offering a "pro-spective" reading of the relationship between the Hebrew Bible and the New Testament he is not sticking to dogmatic, one-sided "pro-spectivism". His commitment to such a reading is not anchored in theoretical "pro-spectivism" to a further extent than it is anchored in the lingual flexibility that the Hebrew למלא offers him. The linguistic aspect, as well as the theoretical question of retro-spectivism vs. "pro-spectivism", makes it possible for him to develop his reading. But that which makes it obligatory for him, that which awards his call to reshape Christian reading of the relationship between the two testaments with a religious significance, that which makes it so urgent and acute, is not anchored in the ancient text but rather in the "here and now". The call to reshape Christian relationship to the Hebrew Bible is anchored in the conviction that contemporary Christianity, post-Holocaust, post-Hiroshima, needs to rethink its way, needs to heal itself. It is the obligation to strengthen contemporary religiosity and to constitute new bases for interfaith dialogue that motivates this courageous and powerful attempt. It is the need to award contemporary religion with prophetic, social, and moral responsibility which makes it so essential that Hebrew Biblical prophecies are not be viewed as fully fulfilled and exhausted, just because of the Christ event, and that they will still be read by Christians as demanding, as challenging, and as relevant to their lives.

This free choice about when to conduct a retrospective reading, and when to fight for the "pro-spective" one, is strictly religious. It expresses the most intimate spiritual motivations and sensitivities. This very choice that Prof. Schöttler takes gives clear voice to his direct encounter God's commandment and love, to the greatness of his soul. For me, as a Jew who listens carefully and with admiration at his brave attempt to revive humanistic, liberal, and human-loving Christianity, it makes him more than a close friend, but rather also a teacher.

"The Voice is the Voice of Jacob"
Contemporary Developments in US-American Jewish Preaching, Homiletics and Homiletical Education

Richard S. Sarason

1. Introduction and historical background

Since my topic is contemporary Jewish homiletics, I may be permitted to begin in a homiletical vein. My own teacher of *midrash* and homiletics at the Hebrew Union College, Rabbi Eugene Mihaly, of blessed memory, always spoke of the sermon as a prime instance of *torat ḥayyim*, or Living Torah – the intersection of Jewish text and tradition with the actual lived experience of each generation of Jews:

> "Torah emerges dialectically; not as a series of suspended, theoretical absolutes which may be recorded for all times, but as an ongoing dialogue within the religious consciousness of a community – a dialogue between a past and a future, the moorings and the reach. A biblical verse viewed as Torah encompasses the totality; it is timeless and ever timely; past, present, and future merge in the reality of the now. This is the uniqueness of Torah; it overcomes time."[1]

While Torah indeed overcomes time, the content and rhetorical style of sermons is grounded in very specific times and concrete social realities. The modern Jewish sermon in the vernacular is a product of the nineteenth-century entry of western Jews into the cultural, aesthetic, and religious ambience of their surrounding societies. First in the German states and later in the United States, the prevailing rhetorical and aesthetic model of modern Jewish vernacular sermons was that of the Protestant sermon aiming at edification (*Erbauung*).[2] It is not by accident that the first major work of modern Jewish scholarship in Germany, Leopold Zunz's "Die gottesdienstlichen Vorträge der Juden.

---

1   Eugene Mihaly, A Song to Creation. A Dialogue with a Text, Cincinnati (OH) 1975.
2   See *Alexander Altmann*, The New Style of Preaching in Nineteenth-Century German Jewry, in: *Idem* (Ed.), Studies in Nineteenth-Century Jewish Intellectual History, Cambridge (MA) 1964, 65–116.

Historisch entwickelt" (1832), was written as an academic defense of the modern Jewish vernacular sermon, which the Prussian authorities had viewed with suspicion as potentially revolutionary.³ Notwithstanding Zunz's learned protestations to the contrary, the Prussian authorities were basically correct: the modern Jewish sermon delivered in Hochdeutsch, modeled on contemporary Protestant sermons, and incorporating the insights of Kant, Herder, and Hegel was indeed something new, if not (to give Zunz his due) without precedent. „The voice was the voice of Jacob, yet the hands were the hands of Esau." Several decades later, that homiletical style emigrated with German Jews to America, where it came to be influenced as well by the style of English-language preaching in the major American Protestant denominations.⁴ Well into the 1960s, for example, the sermons of prominent Protestant preachers such as Harry Emerson Fosdick (1878–1969) would be held up as models for Reform Jewish sermons.⁵

The synthetic, "rule-bound" (*schulgerecht*) Protestant sermon, consisting of exordium, prayer, exposition, and blessing, drew on classical, Ciceronian oratory in its form and style. The modern Jewish

---

3   More broadly, these authorities were suspicious of any modernization of Jewish religion that would inhibit Jews from converting to Christianity. The German-language sermon was only one of a series of Jewish liturgical innovations that were prohibited by a Prussian Cabinet order on December 9, 1823. Beyond that, in the post-Napoleonic era, all social and cultural innovation was suspect. Cf. *Leopold Zunz*, Die gottesdienstlichen Vorträge der Juden. Historisch entwickelt, Frankfurt/M. ²1892, VII–XII, 463–496; *Altmann*, op. cit., and *Daniel Jeremy Silver*, The Authority of Jewish Preaching, in: CCAR Journal 17:2/1970, 34–37.

4   It is of interest that David Einhorn, a noted Jewish reformer who emigrated from Germany to the United States in 1855, steadfastly maintained German as the language of prayer and preaching in America due to his conviction that religious reform was so bound up with High German culture and philosophy that it resisted translation. See, for example, in his "Abschiedspredigt gehalten am 12. Juli 1879 im Tempel der Beth-El-Gemeinde zu New York", in: *Kaufmann Kohler* (Ed.), Dr. David Einhorn's Ausgewählte Predigten und Reden, New York 1881, 89f. In general, the relationship between modernizing Jewish worship and preaching styles in both Europe and America is nicely expressed in the old (anonymous) German-Jewish saying, *"Wie es sich christelt, so jüdelt es sich"*: "the way the Christians go, so do the Jews," as Jews have striven to adapt to the aesthetic styles and *modi operandi* of the majority culture.

5   Fosdick is twice appealed to in routine fashion as a model for Jewish preaching in the early years of the CCAR Journal: by *Robert L. Katz*, Psychology and Preaching, June, 1955, 19, and by *Julius Mark*, The Art of Preaching, January, 1960, 8 ("one of the truly great preachers of our day"); and three times during the same period in forums on homiletics at the CCAR annual meetings, as transcribed in the CCAR Yearbook: by *Julius Gordon*, CCARYB 58/1948, 249, *Robert I. Kahn*, CCARYB 62/1953, 524, and *Victor Eppstein*, CCARYB 62/1953, 540.

textual sermon, as it evolved over the period of its heyday – roughly from the last half (and particularly the last quarter) of the nineteenth century down through the first six and a half decades of the twentieth – followed the pattern of exordium, text analysis, proposition, three-part division or analysis of proposition, summary and appeal or peroration.[6] The non-textual sermon, which over time would become more frequent in Reform congregations than the textual sermon, followed the same pattern, minus the textual analysis.[7] During this period oratory in general tended to be valued in American society (partly as a spectator sport and form of entertainment).

Roughly during the century between 1850 and 1970, Jewish sermons in the United States responded to the major social and cultural upheavals in the larger world – African slavery in America,[8] the Civil War, the social and economic disparities brought about by unregulated capitalism and mass immigration, two World Wars, the Great Depression, the nuclear threat, the civil rights movement, the Vietnam war. They also, and more pervasively, responded to the social and cultural upheavals in the Jewish world: sermons helped to socialize several generations of central and eastern European immigrants into

---

6   See *Altmann*, op. cit., 65f. The first major practical Jewish treatise on homiletics was *Siegmund Maybaum*, Jüdische Homiletik nebst einer Auswahl von Texten und Themen, Berlin 1890, based on a series of lectures given in 1888–89 at the Berlin Lehranstalt für die Wissenschaft des Judenthums. In England, *Abraham Cohen* published Jewish Homiletics, with a foreword by Chief Rabbi Joseph H. Hertz, London 1937. In the United States, significant monographs on the topic have included *Israel Bettan*, Studies in Jewish Preaching, Cincinnati (OH) 1939; reprint Lanham (MD) 1987, and *Solomon B. Freehof*, Modern Jewish Preaching, New York 1941. The former volume deals more with medieval than with contemporary Jewish preaching. At Hebrew Union College-Jewish Institute of Religion, Cincinnati, *Eugene Mihaly* edited a seven-volume series of mimeographed booklets entitled "Aspects of Jewish Homiletics" between 1957 and 1961. These reproduced lectures delivered under the auspices of the Department of Midrash and Homiletics by Rabbis Robert I. Kahn (non-textual and occasional sermons), Abraham J. Feldman (What to Preach About), Ely E. Pilchik (Sources and Themes), Jacob P. Rudin (On the Nature of the Rabbi and the Nature of His Preaching), Joseph R. Narot (The Textual Sermon), Roland B. Gittelsohn (Speak to the Children of Israel), and Hyman J. Schachtel (Varieties of Preachers and Preaching). For remarks on the form of preaching, see also *Alton Meyer Winters*, Three Types of Jewish Preachers. A Suggestion for a Sermon Outline, in: CCAR Journal 10:3/1962, 42–45, 59; *Robert V. Friedenberg*, "Hear O Israel." The History of American Jewish Preaching 1654–1970, Tuscaloosa 1989, gives a good overview of historical trends in the content and rhetoric of American Jewish sermons.

7   See Freehof's complaint in 1941, in op. cit., 41f.

8   David Einhorn, for example, was an abolitionist who spoke out strongly against slavery, and had to leave his Baltimore congregation out of concern for his own safety.

the mores of middle-class American culture in both Reform and Conservative congregations as well as in some modern Orthodox ones (where the rabbi was perceived as, and took it upon himself to be, an American role model); they advocated ways to remain Jewish, to transmit Jewish identity to the next generation, and to defend Judaism and its unique values and observances within the surrounding Christian society.[9]

Before the Second World War and in the immediate postwar period, the sermon was generally agreed to be a major part of the rabbi's work (like that of his Protestant counterpart), and congregations interviewing prospective rabbis would wish to experience their sermons before making a choice. Rabbis would spend many hours a week preparing the weekly sermon (in Reform congregations, often delivered on Sunday mornings and, from the 1920s onward, more and more delivered on Friday nights, since most Jews had to work on Saturdays). Rabbis like Stephen S. Wise, Abba Hillel Silver, and Solomon B. Freehof were known nationally for their stirring oratory or learned discourses – some of which could be quite lengthy.[10] That

---

[9] In the inaugural issue of the CCAR Journal (April, 1953), Israel Bettan, then Professor of Homiletics at the Hebrew Union College-Jewish Institute of Religion in Cincinnati, published an article entitled "The Role of the Preacher", in which he remarked on the changing issues that the Jewish preacher had to address over the previous century and a half since the beginning of the emancipation of Jewry in western and central Europe: initially, "to supply the Jew with a clear understanding of his distinctive character and worth, [...] to expound the fundamental doctrines of Judaism, with special emphasis on those aspects in which they were distinguished from similar teachings of the dominant faith, [...] to vindicate the ancient faith from the menacing new ideas to which the Jew had become exposed by his freer contact with the world, [...] to reconcile if possible the old with the new [...]"(10f.); subsequently, as industrialization exacerbated social and economic differences in the United States, "there also came into the Jewish pulpit a reawakened interest in the social message of the prophets, with its passionate plea for justice and mighty protest against all forms of oppression" (11). This, of course, comported with the "social gospel" movement within mainline Protestantism in the same period. Then, beginning in the 1920s and increasingly in the 1930s and 40s, "with the revival of anti-Jewish agitation in some quarters and its intensification in others, the Jewish pulpit has been deeply immersed in the perennial problem of anti-Semitism" (11). Writing in 1953, Bettan acknowledges the uncertainties and anxieties of the postwar world, but hopes for a return to more normal, less harrowing conditions in which the preacher may be able to "concern himself more deeply with the eternal truths of religion, seeking to probe the condition of men's souls rather than merely to hold their interest." (12) To some extent (though quite idiosyncratically, as we shall note below), the current generation's interest in spirituality and Jewish tradition might be viewed as a kind of fulfillment of Bettan's hopes.

[10] During his years as the rabbi of the Free Synagogue in New York City, which he founded in 1907, Wise famously gave lengthy Sunday morning sermons at the

preaching loomed large particularly in Reform rabbinic self-understanding in this period is testified to by periodic presentations on this topic at annual conventions of the Central Conference of American Rabbis, as transcribed in the CCAR Yearbook,[11] and by the number of articles on this topic that appear in the CCAR Journal, which began publication in April, 1953.[12]

The consensus about the signal importance of preaching in the modern rabbi's job description, and of the formal sermon in the synagogue service, began to change, at first almost imperceptibly, by the early 1960s, and then more dramatically in the following decades. The shift took place from both sides of the pulpit. American Jews, benefiting from the post-war economic boom in the United States, began relocating out of the central cities to new, more prosperous suburbs, where they built new, suburban synagogues that catered to the education of their "baby-boom" children. Corporate, *gesellschaftlich* models of organization over time came to characterize these synagogues. The rabbi took on new roles as head of the religious

---

Hudson Theater and then at Carnegie Hall. Beginning in the 1930s, these sermons were recorded on aluminum discs; some of these have been transcribed and are available for research at the American Jewish Archives on the Cincinnati campus of the Hebrew Union College-Jewish Institute of Religion. Samples of this material are online at http://www.americanjewisharchives.org/aja/exhibits/wise/index.html. Freehof famously memorized his texts and preached without manuscripts or notes in order better to communicate directly with his congregation. He also forbade his assistants to preach from manuscripts or notes.

11 Gerson B. Levi, The Place of the Sermon in Jewish Worship, in: CCARYB 34/1924, 181–202; *Julius Gordon*, The Making of a Sermon, in: CCARYB 58/1948, 249–254; session on preaching, in: CCARYB 62/1953, 510–543 (papers by *Roland B. Gittelsohn, Harry Kaplan, Robert I. Kahn, Jakob K. Shankman, Paul Gorin, Victor Eppstein*); Sermonics and Sermon Techniques. A Symposium, in: CCARYB 63/1953, 492–531 (papers by *Frederic A. Doppelt, Leon I. Feuer, Nathan A. Perilman, Norbert L. Rosenthal, Samson A. Shain*, and *Samuel Teitelbaum*); Resources for Preaching, in: CCARYB 72/1962, 149–156 (papers by *Herbert C. Brichto, William G. Braude, Nathan A. Perilman*).

12 The index to the CCAR Journal, 1953–1993, lists fifty entries under the topic of homiletics. Some of these are reviews of books of collected sermons. Several items of interest have appeared since that time as well. There are no discussions of homiletics at all in the comparable journals of the Conservative Rabbinical Assembly (Conservative Judaism, which began publication in January, 1945), and the modern Orthodox Rabbinical Council of America (Tradition, which began publication in Fall, 1958). In the period in question, Conservative Judaism published a translation of a Hebrew article by *Ernst Simon* on Nehemia A. Nobel as preacher, from a volume of essays "in appreciation of the last generation of the rabbis of Germany" (Conservative Judaism 17, 1–2/1962–63, 65–69). Otherwise, only two short sermons are published, by *Jack Riemer* (in 10.3/1956, 47–51) and *Joel Orent* (in 12.3/1958, 40–43).

school, fund-raiser, and chief executive officer.[13] Many rabbis also began to develop and emphasize their roles as pastoral counselors, reflecting as well contemporary changes in the Protestant ministry. Some saw this role to be more crucial in their interaction with congregants than that of preaching.[14] In the new institutional configuration of the synagogue, they found both that they had less time to devote to preparing weekly sermons and less inclination to do so.[15] The impact of television and other entertainment media, as well as the speeding-up of communication and transportation during this period, also contributed to the shortening of attention spans and the concomitant shortening of sermons.[16]

---

13 See most recently the trenchant sociological analysis of *Jack Wertheimer*, The American Synagogue. Recent Issues and Trends, in: American Jewish Yearbook 105/2005, 3–83 (esp. 6–18), and, yet more broadly, *Jonathan D. Sarna*, American Judaism. A History, New Haven (CT) 2004, 272–293.

14 See the discussions of *Robert L. Katz*, Psychology and Preaching, in: CCARJ, June, 1955, 15–20, and The Rabbi as Preacher and/or Counselor. A Frame of Reference, in: CCARJ, June, 1958, 22–35, 46, and the cautionary remarks of *Solomon B. Freehof*, in: Israel Bettan Memorial Volume, New York 1961, 30–36.

15 As early as 1957, Jack J. Cohen muses on "the passing of the sermon?" (CCARJ, June, 1957, 20–22), remarking on the rabbi's frantic search to find weekly topics and preparation time, and the inherent problems with a frontal mode of communication that leaves listeners passive and often bored. He proposes more interactive modes of teaching as alternatives to the formal sermon. (These modes indeed would be taken up in the following decades and, as we shall see, are characteristic of the American synagogue today.) Concern over diminishing rabbinical authority across the branches of American Judaism at that time, and the perceived need to shore up the rabbinical preaching function led Rabbi Harry Essrig in 1961 to found the journal "The American Rabbi". The cover of the first issue (September, 1961) proclaims its purpose to be: "To encourage the American rabbi in his role as preacher, to enhance the art of his preaching in the American synagogue, to provide a forum for idea exchange and samples of preaching, [and] to keep open avenues of communication among leaders of the three branches of Judaism." A year earlier, then-editor of the CCAR Journal *Beryl D. Cohon* had initiated a new department in that journal that would be devoted to "text and commentary," i.e., short outlines for sermons. Cohon writes, "The deprecation of the sermon is universal in Jewry. There are even some rabbis who only put up with it as a necessary nuisance. Some have been saying – even asserting with considerable heat – that it is not even a *necessary* nuisance. We demur; hence this department" (CCARJ 8.3/1960, 36).

16 See the complaints and retrospective analysis of *Daniel Jeremy Silver*, The Core of Our Calling. Who is a Rabbi? What is a Rabbi? Why is a Rabbi? in: CCARJ 23.1/1986, 1–14, esp. 4–6. As early as 1941, Julian Morgenstern, then president of the Hebrew Union College and reflecting on his first pulpit experience some thirty-four years earlier, could write regarding sermon length: "[I]t is remarkable how impatient our congregations are and what poor listeners they have become […]. It [is] almost as if listening to a sermon [is] one of those fantastic self-tortures, exquisite and soul-satisfying for a moment, but impossible of too protracted

While social activism from the pulpit during the early phase of the civil rights movement in the first part of the 1960s may have temporarily obscured malaise about sermons, the violent social and cultural upheavals of the late '60s and early '70s in the wake of the Vietnam war and the more violent phase of the civil rights and black power movements would change the landscape entirely. Indeed, as we shall see, the contemporary situation in both the synagogue and its pulpit is a direct legacy of the 1960s.

2. The contemporary situation in the U.S. and its roots in the 1960s

2.1 Cultural styles and their formal impact on sermons

The high school and college youth of the 1960s and '70s – the "baby boomers" – would become both the rabbis and the congregants (as well as the unaffiliated) of the following decades. Their reactions against what they perceived to be the bourgeois materialist, corporate, superficial suburban synagogue culture of the postwar era – and against their parents – were the Jewish localizations of the American student counterculture of this period. That counterculture was fundamentally Romantic in its contours. It emphasized (1) individuality over social conformity; (2) spontaneity over fixed forms; (3) emotion, mysticism, and spirituality over the instrumental, scientific rationality that had given birth to the assembly line, the Holocaust, the atomic bomb, and the military-industrial complex; (4) intimate small-group interaction over impersonal rationalized corporate organization (that is, in the classic terminology of sociologist Ferdinand Tönnies, *Gemeinschaft* over *Gesellschaft*); and (5) „do-it-yourself" participation and ownership over professional expertise, authority, and performance. In a worship context – Jewish or Christian – this demographic and cultural cohort did not (and does not) wish to be prayed at, sung at, or preached at. It wants to be empowered to do for itself. It perceives the

---

endurance, through which the ordinary synagogue attendant seeks to compensate the Deity for the sins and shortcomings of his daily existence [...]. [E]ven though congregations are, in most respects, long-suffering and full of kindness, in this one respect their powers of endurance are exceedingly limited and they are anything but slow to anger and rich in mercy. An imperative need for the young rabbi is to learn that there is a time to preach, but also a time to stop preaching. And how hard is this lesson to learn!" The full cautionary anecdote bears reading, in Morgenstern's foreword to Freehof, Modern Jewish Preaching, 9–12.

role of clergy to be much more that of facilitator or enabler than that of remote, authoritarian teacher or preacher. This cohort tends to be anti-institutional in its biases; that often translates into an antipathy to organized religion and religious institutions and a privileging of personalism, personal meaning, and personal quest – even within the context of affiliation with religious institutions. Terminologically speaking, this cohort often prefers to call itself "spiritual" rather than "religious."[17] The baby-boom generation is now paying the bills in most American religious institutions – or not engaging with them at all. The counterculture of the 1960s and '70s has now, thirty to forty years later, become institutionalized, perhaps ironically given its original anti-institutional bent. Perhaps it would be more correct to say that the values and preferences of this counterculture have influenced and, in large measure, been internalized by the institutions, where they still co-exist to some extent with those of the previous generation.

The "worship wars" that have been taking place in both Christian and Jewish congregations in America over the past several decades, for example, reflect what is essentially an intergenerational conflict between two stylistic and aesthetic paradigms – "cool" formal vs. "warm" informal.[18] The differences between the two paradigms are reflected in every aspect of worship, from architecture and movement to music to the text and language of the service and how it is performed (and by whom) to the sermon or its functional equivalent.

The art of the preacher has generally been perceived by this cohort to be artifice or, worse, artificiality. The formal sermon has been regarded as fatally associated with its bourgeois origins; it is regarded as a product of the Jewish assimilation of nineteenth-century Protestant worship norms, like the organ, choral art music, and the cool, decorous worship service intoned by the clergy officiant to a mostly passive

---

17 The basic sociological literature on the impact of this cohort on contemporary religious expression in the United States is: *Wade Clark Roof*, A Generation of Seekers. The Spiritual Journeys of the Baby Boom Generation, San Francisco (CA) 1993, and *Idem*, Spiritual Marketplace. Baby Boomers and the Remaking of American Religion, Princeton (NJ) 1999; *Robert Wuthnow*, After Heaven. Spirituality in America Since the 1950s, Berkeley (CA) 1998; *Robert Bellah/Richard Madsen/ William M. Sullivan/Ann Swidler/Steven M. Tipton*, Habits of the Heart. Individualism and Commitment in American Life, Berkeley (CA) ²1996, 219–249. The basic study of Jewish religious identity in this context is *Steven M. Cohen/Arnold M. Eisen*, The Jew Within. Self, Family, and Community in America, Bloomington (IN) 2000. See also the references in note 13 above.

18 See *Thomas G. Long*, Beyond the Worship Wars. Building Vital and Faithful Worship, The Alban Institute 2001. See also *Lawrence A. Hoffman*, Re-imagining Jewish Worship, in: CCARJ, Winter, 2002, 69–87, and Common Cold and Uncommon Healing, in: CCARJ 61, 2/1994, 1–30, and *Wertheimer*, op. cit., 29ff.

congregation who are occasionally cued to respond – all of this is viewed in negative terms. Following the demise of the melting pot ideal of American society in the wake of ethnic (and particularly black) assertiveness in the late 1960s and '70s, young Jews reclaimed their ethnic roots as well, often identifying with the folk culture and piety of eastern Europe that had been cast off or attenuated in the successful attempt to Americanize. A return to tradition, or at least to some of its aesthetic, became common across the board in this cohort of American Jewry.[19] From a social-psychological perspective, we could refer to this longitudinally as "the return of the repressed."

This generation – both as rabbis and as congregants or as participants in non-congregational, small-group fellowships (*havurot*) – has preferred more participatory alternatives to the formal sermon delivered by a religious professional. Often this has meant informal group study of the weekly Torah portion where the rabbi or a knowledgeable member serves as a facilitator, either before or during the service (usually on Sabbath mornings). Or it has meant a *d'var torah* (literally, "word of Torah"), a very brief exposition of a single insight out of the weekly Torah portion, delivered in a more informal style either by the rabbi or a member of the congregation. Or it has meant sharing a Hasidic story or insight related to the Torah portion that touches on spirituality.[20]

This stylistic variety has also been fostered by the fact that there is no uniformity today in congregational expectations. Instead there is a need to appeal to different generational cohorts with different stylistic preferences, either through offering multiple service (and preaching)

---

19 Even the so-called *ba'al teshuvah* (literally, "penitent;" one who returns to the tradition after straying) movement of the 1980s and '90s, in which previously non-observant Jews embraced Orthodoxy, must be viewed in this light. See, for example, Alan T. Levenson, Reclaiming the *Ba'al Teshuva* Movement. A Liberal Critique, in: CCARJ 40,1/1993, 23–34.

20 The renewed interest in Hasidism, spurred in part by the writings of Martin Buber and Gershom Scholem and by the modeling of Zalman Schachter-Shalomi and Shlomo Carlebach, is of a piece with the cultural and aesthetic trends we have been discussing. Hasidism, as it has been presented by Scholem and others, tends to psychologize theology and to emphasize spiritual inwardness with the goal of "cleaving" to God (*devekut*) through the obliteration of the self (*bittul hayesh*). The similarity to eastern, and particularly Buddhist, meditation is obvious. Hasidism also tends to emphasize divine immanence rather than transcendence and represents a form of panentheism – also attractive to this generation. On alternatives to the formal sermon in both Reform and Conservative congregations, see also Wertheimer, op. cit., 33f., 44, and Sarah Blustain, A New Generation of Rabbis is Coming Down Off the Bimah, in: Moment 24, December, 1999, 61–65, 76–79. Wertheimer also notes changes in Orthodox homiletics, 49.

styles over different weeks of the month or by running two or more services seriatim or simultaneously on the same occasion. Examples of the former would be a Friday night monthly music service with a sermon in song, family service with a story for children, guest speaker or panel discussion after the service, brief *d'var torah*, informal sermon from notes (perhaps with the rabbi moving from behind the pulpit out into the congregation), and formal sermon from manuscript. Examples of the latter would be the conducting of early Friday evening services (before dinner) that emphasize singing and participation, with a brief (five-minute) rabbinic *d'var torah* building on the weekly Torah portion, followed by a later (after dinner) service that is more formal and includes a more formal textual or non-textual sermon. On Shabbat mornings this would include running a parallel service to the main one (which has often been perceived by congregants as "taken over" and "privatized" by the Bar or Bat Mitzvah family). The parallel service is more participatory and informal, often congregant-led, and features group Torah study instead of a formal sermon.

A survey on worship and worship styles in Reform congregations conducted by the Department of Worship of the Union for Reform Judaism in 2000 reported that:

> "While sermons delivered by rabbis are still the most frequently used form of Torah study during Erev Shabbat services, they are not the only form. A congregational service is likely to include in its place a *d'var torah*, an interactive Torah/text study, a story, teaching, or a sermon in song. During Shabbat morning services the *d'var torah* is the most common form of Torah study."[21]

As part of my research for this paper, I also conducted an unscientific, informal survey of Reform rabbis to see how often they preached formal (or informal) textual sermons and what alternative forms they used. The results are quite instructive, and comport well with the URJ statistics.[22] Out of 50 rabbis who responded to the survey, about half give sermons on Friday nights. Not all of these are textual sermons, and

---

21 The URJ survey data derives from 313 out of approximately 900 Reform congregations in North America, a participation rate of 34.8%. I am grateful to my colleague Rabbi Sue Ann Wasserman, Director of the Department of Worship, Music, and Religious Living at the Union for Reform Judaism, for supplying me with this information.

22 The survey was conducted by posting an inquiry on the electronic listserves for Reform rabbis (*ravkav*) and for alumni of the Hebrew Union College-Jewish Institute of Religion (*hucalum*). There are about 1800 Reform rabbis in the United States; 50 responded. While the survey results hardly bear statistical significance they nonetheless are anecdotally revealing and tend to correlate with other anecdotal evidence.

many are delivered from notes or an outline rather than a fully written-out text. This number goes up considerably if we include those rabbis who give Friday-night sermons once or twice a month (the other weeks generally involve multiple styles – family service with story, musical service, early evening service with no sermon, service with guest speaker, program, etc.) An additional third or so give brief, informal *divrei torah* on Friday nights. The preferred style on Saturday morning when there is no Bar Mitzvah is definitely the text discussion, followed closely by the brief *d'var torah*.

One rabbi notes, "I still think that formal preaching is important and give formal sermons with regularity, but I would observe that congregational life has evolved in such a way that I do not do that as often as I used to [...]. [What with all the other service styles that we do,] I guess I'm preaching 'formally' twice a month on average." Another remarks that "my preaching is increasingly extemporaneous. I take a mike and walk into the congregation. I find my congregation greatly prefers me to speak without notes in an informal fashion, even in our main sanctuary with 1,000 permanent seats. The times they are a-changing." A retired rabbi reports, "I am one of those who lament the demise of the well-crafted sermon and its replacement by 'informal chats.' I also find that congregants are sick and tired of hearing sermons on Friday nights about the *parashat hashavua* [the weekly Torah portion] and are appreciative of sermons that deal with a variety of other topics." Finally, one rabbi notes, "I suspect that many congregational rabbis are not confident about their sermons. In addition, most people that I have talked to leave the HUC-style [that is, the formal sermon – more on this below] behind them. This may be why your response has been so limited [...]. Besides, some rabbis just speak from notes or outlines." Such, then, is some of the anecdotal evidence from the field.[23]

---

23 A three-year in-depth (and cross-generational) survey (1994–97) of the overall worship experience of forty-seven North American Reform congregations conducted by the Central Conference of American Rabbis had this to say about sermons: "Most congregants report that the intellectual component of the worship service is important. While many speak very positively of interactive Torah study, there is concern about the decline of preaching. *As part of rabbinic training and continuing education, rabbis should learn and refine a variety of models.* [emphasis in the original; RS] It is essential for rabbis to recognize that how they present the intellectual content of the service is significant. Congregants are divided about what they need to hear and rabbis are conflicted about how they ought to present their messages. Since congregants already possess a very high degree of competence in contemporary culture, it seems clear that the congregation looks to the rabbis' [sic] Judaic expertise as an essential component of what he/she has to offer. Informality is no substitute for careful preparation." (*Rabbi Peter S. Knobel/Daniel S. Schechter*, Recommendations from Lilly Endowment Grant #930532. Lay Involvement in the

I should remark here that none of this is intrinsically "bad" or to be decried. If homiletics ultimately is the embodiment of *torat ḥayyim* – the encounter between text, tradition, and life as it is lived – then the form of the encounter should matter far less than the content and the fact of the encounter itself. The fact that the baby-boomers and their children, when interested at all in the religious and spiritual resources of Jewish tradition, wish to claim these for themselves in an active, participatory way instead of being "talked at" should be viewed as a source of positive challenge, encouragement, and opportunity.

It is also worth noting that, without exception, the rabbis surveyed still give formal sermons (though not all textual) on the High Holidays. As befits this season of solemnity and heightened Jewish self-awareness, more traditional worship forms and styles are preserved across the board – ritual, textual, musical, and homiletical.

2.2 Sermon content

If we turn now to inquire broadly about the content of contemporary sermons in the United States, the following remarks from 1988 of Rabbi Harry Essrig, the founding editor and publisher of *The American Rabbi*, a periodical featuring sermons of rabbis of all branches of Judaism, are a relevant touchstone:

> "It is my impression that the three branches of Judaism differ as to the style and content of their sermons [...]. The Reform rabbis, for instance, seem to favor a more essay-like style, in which a given thesis is examined and developed, hewing to a structure and a clearly-reasoned theme. For the most part the purpose is to instruct and to appeal to the intellect, to convince and to agitate for the position advanced in the presentation. The mind is the focus of the preacher's attention.
>
> The Conservative preachers seem to prefer the use of midrashic materials to buttress their points and depend on the various homiletical techniques available to them. Metaphor and allegory plus anecdotes and illustrative material are desiderata and not as much concern is shown for the scaffolding of the sermon. The preachers seek to engage the emotions of their audiences and to motivate them to fulfill their lives as Jews [...].
>
> The Orthodox rabbis seem to concentrate on exhorting their parishioners to maintain the traditional way of life, quote extensively from rabbinic sources, and perform their tasks in the classical sense of agitating for religious action and proper behavior in keeping with the tenets of the faith. Yet a number of very eloquent preachers have emerged in this group who

---

Development of Liturgy. Draft 24. July 25, 1997, 5; on file at the American Jewish Archives, Cincinnati).

challenge our generalization and once again underscore the fact that we should not place people in categories."[24]

Almost twenty years later, I would observe that while some aspects of this characterization remain in place, others do not. Specifically, the edges portrayed here between "Reform"- and "Conservative"-style sermons have become blurred, particularly from the Reform side. Reform sermons are much more likely today to make use of illustrative materials from Jewish tradition: midrashic, Hasidic, and otherwise. I'm inclined to think that this was also true twenty years ago, at least among younger rabbis. Briefer homiletical pieces, such as *divrei torah*, also pay less attention to scaffolding. Several observations that Essrig makes later in the article, however, remain equally true today about sermons in the context of Reform congregations. He writes:

> "Our people are interested in hearing discussions of problems affecting their personal lives and the spiritual struggles of their rabbis. There is no religious apperceptive mass within which the message can fit – there is no familiarity with our traditional sources."[25]

This comports well with some of the anecdotal evidence from the survey. Several rabbis indicated that they prefer to preach on "something happening in the lives of congregants," on "current events or issues, and self-improvement." And while many congregants are very interested in the study of traditional Jewish texts, the congregations as a whole are not familiar with much of this material. The sermon texts, sermon outlines, and *divrei torah* that rabbis shared with me indeed attempt to respond to life's ongoing challenges out of the resources of Jewish tradition. They respond to and struggle with the perennial human issues of fear, disappointment, loss, anger, conflict, forgiveness and reconciliation, choices, ultimate values as opposed to momentary gratifications, spiritual and religious grounding in the face of materialism and a coarse popular culture, and the challenges of creatively embracing Jewish identity and community in a non-Jewish society. Biblical stories and characters are often treated as paradigmatic for their "human, all too human" aspects: it is precisely as imperfect individuals who wrestle with themselves, with each other, and with God – rather than as paradigms of faith – that these characters serve as mirrors in which contemporary American Jews can see themselves reflected.[26] And that, of course, is their traditional homiletical function.

---

24 *Harry Essrig*, Impressions of Jewish Preaching Today, in: CCARJ 35:1/1988, 1–6; the passage cited is on p. 2.
25 Ibid., 4.
26 See, for example, the homiletical treatment of biblical characters in *Norman J. Cohen*, Self, Struggle, and Change. Family Conflicts in Genesis and Their Healing Insights

So, in regard to content as well, contemporary American sermons remain the latest exemplars of *torat hayyim*.

3. The current state of homiletical training in U.S. Rabbinical Seminaries

3.1 Overview

It remains for us to discuss the nature of current training in homiletics at rabbinical seminaries in the United States. Here my data is limited to the Hebrew Union College-Jewish Institute of Religion (Reform), the Jewish Theological Seminary of America (Conservative), and the Reconstructionist Rabbinical College (Reconstructionist).[27] These three schools tend to focus their homiletical training in the areas of formal sermon writing and delivery. The Reconstructionist Rabbinical College, however, also takes into account in its formal curriculum the contemporary varieties of less formal homiletical styles, and HUC-JIR and JTSA also train students in the preparation of briefer *divrei torah*. All three schools work extensively with their students on how to use traditional textual materials – midrash, medieval biblical commentaries, etc. – for homiletical purposes.

---

for Our Lives, Woodstock (VT) 1995; *Idem*, Voices From Genesis. Guiding Us through the Stages of Our Lives, Woodstock (VT) 1998; *Idem*, Hineni in Our Lives. Learning How to Respond to Others through 14 Biblical Texts and Personal Stories, Woodstock (VT) 2003; *Idem*, Moses and the Journey to Leadership. Timeless Lessons of Effective Management from the Bible and Today's Leaders, Woodstock (VT) 2007.

27 I am grateful to my colleagues at HUC-JIR, Rabbi Kenneth E. Ehrlich and Prof. Edward A. Goldman (Cincinnati), Rabbi Margaret M. Wenig (New York), and Rabbi Naamah Kelman (Jerusalem); and to Prof. Burton L. Visotzky at JTSA, and Rabbi Linda Holtzman at RRC, for sharing syllabi and other teaching materials with me, as well as their insights on homiletical instruction at their respective institutions and teaching sites. Time constraints regrettably have not allowed me to pursue information about homiletical training at the Rabbi Isaac Elchanan Theological Seminary (RIETS) at Yeshiva University (Orthodox). The question of homiletics and homiletical training in the modern Orthodox context is a fascinating topic, very much worth pursuing. *Friedenberg*, "Hear O Israel," 137, includes observations on homiletical training at RIETS from the mid-1980s, and an analysis of the sermons of Joseph Lookstein, who taught homiletics at RIETS for many years, 124–127. The same time constraints have also prevented me from seeking information about the Ziegler School of Rabbinic Studies at the University of Judaism (Conservative) or any of the "post-denominational" seminaries (the Rabbinical School of Hebrew College in Boston and the contemporary versions of the Academy for Jewish Religion in New York and Los Angeles).

3.2 Hebrew Union College-Jewish Institute of Religion (Reform)

During the first year of the rabbinical school curriculum at the Hebrew Union College-Jewish Institute of Religion, which takes place in Jerusalem, students are expected to give *divrei torah* in the College synagogue and receive training in how to use a midrashic text or a medieval Jewish commentary for this purpose. These *divrei torah* are then reviewed in a setting with faculty and students. The remaining four years of the curriculum take place stateside in either Cincinnati, New York, or Los Angeles. Students receive some limited practical training at the very beginning of the second year on preparing High Holiday sermons before their first pulpit experience in this capacity. The required homiletics course is taken in the third year, while students are serving in bi-weekly pulpits or internships.[28] The instructors, for the most part, are local area congregational rabbis who have expertise in this area.[29] Students are introduced to the preparation of both textual and non-textual sermons as well as occasional addresses, eulogies, charges, invocations, etc.

In general, the course has a reading component and a hands-on writing component. Students read many of the items listed in the footnotes to this article (e.g., selections from Cohen, Bettan, Freehof, Mihaly, Katz), as well as a variety of actual sermons[30] and, sometimes, pieces on rhetoric and sermons written by American Protestants.[31] The

---

28 In Los Angeles, the course is taken in either the second or the third year.

29 In Cincinnati, which has a more extensive resident faculty, instructors have also included regular members of the faculty and the dean of the campus, Rabbi Kenneth E. Ehrlich, who usually prepares the syllabus and supervises the course.

30 Here the Cincinnati syllabus lists the two volumes on medieval Jewish sermons by *Marc Saperstein*, Jewish Preaching 1200–1800. An Anthology, New Haven (CT) 1989, and "Your Voice Like a Ram's Horn." Themes and Texts in Traditional Jewish Preaching, Cincinnati (OH) 1996, as well as Saperstein's collection of the sermons of his father, Rabbi Harold Saperstein, Witness from the Pulpit, Lanham (MD) 2000, and *Friedenberg*, "Hear O Israel." Most of these items (and others) appear on the New York list as well.

31 The Cincinnati syllabus, for example, includes such items as *Lionel Crocker*, A Rhetorical Analysis of Harry Emerson Fosdick's Sermon, "The Power To See It Through," in: *Idem* (Ed.), Harry Emerson Fosdick's Art of Preaching. An Anthology, Springfield (IL) 1971; *Douglas Ehninger*, Toward a Taxonomy of Prescriptive Discourse, in: *Eugene White* (Ed.), Rhetoric in Transition. Studies in the Nature and Use of Rhetoric, University Park (PA) 1980; *Edmund Holt Linn*, Preaching As Counseling. The Unique Method of Harry Emerson Fosdick, Valley Forge (PA) 1966; *Wayne C. Mannebach/Joseph M. Mazza*, Speaking From the Pulpit, Valley Forge (PA) 1969; *Dale Patrick/Allan Scult*, Rhetoric and Biblical Interpretation, Sheffield 1989. Note once again the paradigmatic character of Harry Emerson Fosdick's preaching here. The New York syllabi of Rabbi Margaret M. Wenig include *Richard Lischer*,

writing component is critical, as students work in writing through the stages of text analysis, proposition outlines, sermon outlines, and actual sermon texts for both textual and non-textual sermons, as well as occasional homilies.

There are also variations on this basic formula. In recent years, Rabbi Margaret Wenig, one of the instructors in New York, has been experimenting with two different modes of teaching the course. The first is a "workshopping course" in which students prepare three complete sermons that they will deliver in their student congregations and that first will be workshopped in class. The novel element in this course is that congregant feedback is solicited for each sermon and worked through as part of the course learning. Ten congregants per student are invited to participate voluntarily and are requested to assist by: "(1) composing a prayer for your student rabbi in his/her capacity as preacher/*darshan* [parenthetically, something that Jews are far less used to doing than Christians!]; (2) explaining what you 'need' from your rabbi's sermons (i.e., what issues are you currently facing as an individual and/or what issues is your community facing collectively?); (3) recording, in writing, your responses to your student rabbi's sermons." Thus a feedback mechanism is created that can help student rabbis to improve their homiletical work in all its dimensions by actively "listening to their listeners." The instructor additionally makes presentations in class and assigns readings on the basis of the specific homiletical issues and problems that arise in the actual workshopping sessions (thus using an inductive approach to content).

The second mode utilized by Rabbi Wenig to teach this course is an intensive reading format, involving "immersion in the sermons/*derashot* of others." By the end of the semester, students will have worked carefully through, and responded in writing to, ninety sermons of all sorts, by both Jews and Christians. The theory of this course, as Rabbi Wenig explains it in her syllabus, is as follows: "A *little* practice and a *little* critique help *only a little*. More practice and more critique help much, much more. A smattering of exposure to the work of great preachers and a smattering of analysis of their artistry help a little. Exposure which becomes *immersion*, providing depth and breadth, helps much, much more."

Open Secrets, Garden City (NJ) 2001, and *Barbara K. Lundblad*, Transforming the Stone. Preaching Through Resistance to Change, Nashville (TN) 2001. Additional bibliography appears in her course reader, *Darsheini*. A Collection of Sermons, Outlines of Forms of Sermons and Thoughts about Preaching, which is updated each year.

Beyond the basic required course, HUC-JIR also offers electives (taken in the fourth or fifth year) in Cincinnati in which students each week study the weekly Torah portion together with relevant *midrashim* and medieval biblical commentaries, with an eye to using all of this material sermonically (to be demonstrated in the written final project), and a comparable elective in New York in advanced homiletics "designed to enhance skills in conceiving, shaping and writing sermons on a variety of themes: personal concerns, societal issues and challenges to Jewish life, among them." In Cincinnati, fourth-year students are required to deliver a textual sermon as part of the Shabbat morning service in the HUC synagogue and fifth-year students deliver a non-textual sermon at Monday morning services. Both sermons are prepared with the assistance of a sermon adviser from the faculty.[32] Sermon delivery is coached by a separate instructor. The sermons are videotaped and then worked through with the student by the dean, who heads the homiletics program. Comparable requirements apply as well in New York and Los Angeles.

3.3 Jewish Theological Seminary of America (Conservative)

Homiletical training at the Conservative movement's Jewish Theological Seminary of America in New York is broadly similar to that at HUC-JIR. Rabbinical students are required to take a semester course during their senior year entitled, "Senior Homiletics," that deals with sermon-writing skills and focuses on "the art of structuring and delivering sermons and *divrei torah*," paying particular attention to "accessing resources in traditional and modern sources for the preparation of rabbinic talks." The course is taught by a local area rabbi. Informal training before senior year has expanded so that students are also expected to prepare *divrei torah* for seminar classes and even, in other instances, in courses on *midrash*, Talmud, and medieval biblical commentaries.

An elective course, given periodically, that has gained a reputation for particular creativity and effectiveness in its teaching is Prof. Burton Visotzky's course, "Homiletics of Midrash" (which requires a

---

[32] Beginning in the academic year 2007/2008, the fourth-year textual sermon will be prepared for, and delivered in, the student's bi-weekly congregation so that the context is more realistic. The fifth-year sermon will be textual and delivered in the College synagogue on a Shabbat morning.

background in *midrash*, but not in homiletics).³³ This is a web-based Blackboard course that also utilizes the "workshopping" mode of instruction. Each week students study a midrashic text related to that week's Torah portion and are required to write a 750-word *d'var torah* based upon that text. These *divrei torah* are posted to the class discussion board the day before each class session, where they are shared with fellow students. The instructor responds with corrections and critique via private email to each student before the class session. Class sessions are in two parts: In the first hour, the students and the instructor "workshop" the *midrashim* they have prepared "to create [their] own, new Torah together." During the second hour, several students present their *divrei torah* to the class, allowing them "the opportunity to gently critique one another in a supportive and safe atmosphere – so that we may hone our rhetorical skills and enhance our teaching/preaching of Torah in public settings." The instructor makes available for students on-line a gathering of his own *divrei torah* ("Why," he writes, "should YOU be the only ones to stick your neck out and be vulnerable to critique?!").

The students also are required to maintain a file-folder, paper or electronic, of sermon ideas, source materials, and other resources for each of the 54 annual weekly Torah portions and for holidays, which they review individually with the instructor during the second half of the semester. The course requirements thus mimic those of congregational preaching, where a *d'var torah* must be prepared and delivered on a weekly basis, come what may, and where a file of ideas and resources for weekly sermons must be developed and maintained over time. The teaching practices of this course thus work to develop in students "a habitus or imaginative capacity for deepening their engagement with disciplinary knowledge and skills interactively with the knowledge and skills associated with clergy practices of teaching and preaching."³⁴

---

33 This course is described at some length in *Charles R. Foster/Lisa E. Dunhill/Lawrence A. Golemon/Barbara Wang Tolentino*, Educating Clergy. Teaching Practices and Pastoral Imagination, San Francisco (CA) 2006, 336–350. This volume is one of a series on preparation for the professions sponsored by The Carnegie Foundation for the Advancement of Teaching.

34 *Foster* et al., Educating Clergy, 340.

3.4 Reconstructionist Rabbinical College (Reconstructionist)

Of the three rabbinical schools chronicled here, the Reconstructionist Rabbinical College seems to be most responsive in its homiletical training to the contemporary cultural trends that we noted at the beginning of this paper. This, perhaps, is not surprising, since the school opened in 1968, during the height of the countercultural critique of American Jewish life and institutions, and has been populated since its inception by students, and now by faculty and administrators, who were formed by that counterculture and sought out Reconstructionism as "the fourth way" beyond Reform, Conservative, and Orthodox. In the basic homiletics course that students may take during any year in their course of study,[35] they learn not only how to give formal sermons, *divrei torah*, life-cycle homilies, invocations, benedictions, and occasional addresses, but also how to do storytelling, how to lead discussions, and how to give longer, educational talks and lectures "on the road." In this context, they also learn where to find materials for preaching – in books, cartoons, newspapers, and life experiences, as well as traditional texts. The weekly Torah portion will be studied with an eye to possible preaching/teaching topics, overall themes, and thematic directions. Students also spend time observing local rabbis giving sermons, *divrei torah*, and teaching *torah* to their congregations. In general, according to Rabbi Linda Holtzman, who supervises the homiletics program and teaches the basic course, the goal is for each student to find his/her own voice and, building on one's strengths, to become one's own kind of speaker rather than fitting into any particular kind of pre-existing mold. The larger message is that there is no single way to teach *torah* in the context of a worship service and that students need to practice, and become comfortable, working with a variety of approaches. Like HUC-JIR and JTS, RRC also offers elective courses in which medieval biblical commentaries and classical *midrashim* are read with an eye to their contemporary homiletical uses. The course in *darshanut* (sermonics) focuses not only on midrashic materials but also on resources in the Hasidic tradition.

---

35 This flexibility is due to the fact that each year of the rabbinic curriculum at RRC focuses on a different period of Jewish civilization (biblical, classical rabbinic, medieval, modern, contemporary); homiletical training can be shaped to fit in with any of these periods, and its typical literary materials (biblical texts; midrashic texts; medieval biblical commentaries, sermons, and ethical-pietistic texts; modern and contemporary sermonics).

3.5 Summary

Overall, there are large areas of overlap in homiletical training among the three rabbinical seminaries presented here. While students need to be familiar with a variety of styles of teaching *torah* in the context of a worship service, both the formal sermon, which is uniformly employed during the High Holy Days and more periodically throughout the year, and the informal and briefer *d'var torah* still need to be part of an American rabbi's homiletical training and professional toolbox. The crafting of oral presentations, written for the ear as opposed to the eye, and the art of speaking from outlines or notes remain important skills for the American rabbinate.[36] Beyond formal technique, rabbis still need to be schooled in the multiple ways that traditional texts can be made to speak to contemporary realities and that today's life experiences can be refracted through the prism of Jewish tradition and textuality. This is one aspect of what the Carnegie Foundation for the Advancement of Teaching calls "pastoral-rabbinic imagination" that seminaries aim to cultivate through pedagogies of interpretation, formation, contextualization, and performance.[37] It is also what my teacher Rabbi Eugene Mihaly meant by the process of *torat hayyim* – the *torah* of life that through ongoing situational reappropriation and reinterpretation is constantly becoming *our* Living Torah.

---

[36] Rabbi Margaret Wenig observed to me that most of the current generation of rabbinical students have grown up never or rarely having heard great preaching, since this is both experienced and valued far less in American Judaism than in Protestant Christianity. "That means that most students have little or no personal experience of being deeply affected by sermons (and have little faith that sermons matter to anybody). Those students don't know what great sermons (of any form) sound like. (It's difficult or impossible to learn a language if you've never heard it spoken.)" Most students have only written essays or academic papers for the eye, not artistic pieces for the ear, and "they don't have the sounds of good sermons in their heads. Can you teach a person who has never heard a violin or held a violin to play the violin on a professional level in twelve weeks (the length of one semester)? It takes years of listening to, and preparing, sermons to become a good preacher."

[37] *Foster* et al., Educating Clergy, v (Table of Contents).

Response

Martin Nicol

Dear colleague, you delivered us a fine and illuminating lecture on contemporary Jewish preaching and Jewish homiletics in the USA. I read your lecture, footnotes included, assuming that it had required a lot of research. For the last couple of weeks you often sent the respectively most current version of your lecture. This signaled to me that you were steadily working on it. Thank you so much. Let me respond to your lecture by discussing four points.

(1) First of all I have to confess that while reading your text I have become a bit proud of Protestant homiletics in Germany. In not one of the big German books on Protestant preaching and its history has the history you outlined to us ever been mentioned,[1] i.e. Jewish preaching as it emerged from 19th century. You explained to us that Jewish preaching in Germany was essentially inspired by Protestant preaching and Protestant homiletics. Afterwards, this kind of Jewish sermon emigrated to the USA where in contact with genuine American preaching, both Protestant and Jewish, it became a category of its own. As I already said, this fascinating range and impact of Protestant homiletics in Germany is not known at all in relevant German debates. I hope that as a consequence of this conference our restricted perspective will be enlarged this way.

(2) I have been happy to find in the Jewish homiletical syllabi you quoted books from the Christian homiletical context. Let me drop some names: Thomas G. Long, Barbara K. Lundblad, or Richard Lischer. I first encountered these names and a lot of others when I discovered the so-called homiletical revolution in the USA.[2] It started about 40 years ago and led among other things to the Doctor-of-Ministry-in-Preaching program with its basis in Chicago. This program was never restricted to only one denomination. Quite the contrary, several denominations worked, and still work, together. Why did I never see in this context any trace of

---

[1] In works of reference the situation is gradually changing. Cf. *Klaus Herrmann*, Art. Predigt VII. Judentum [2003], in: RGG⁴ 6, 1605–1607.

[2] Cf. *Martin Nicol*, Dramaturgical Homiletic in Germany. Preaching as Art Among the Arts, in: Homiletic 29/2004, II, 12–19.

Jewish preaching? Jewish homiletics in America seem to be close to Christian homiletics as to the way in which they shape sermons. The challenges are comparable. Both Jewish and Christian preaching look back on a long tradition in America. Why is there not a mutual exchange even beyond the level of books? I know well that there are grand and basic reasons for that lack of exchange. But let me communicate the vision I have: there will be a second homiletical revolution, but this time it will take place on both sides of the Atlantic and, most importantly, it will cover Jewish as well as Christian homileticians.

(3) You talked to us about modern challenges of Jewish preaching in the USA. The congregational expectations you outlined are not focused any longer on the well-crafted and lengthy sermon rooted in 19th century. Uniformity has given way to plurality. You presented us a lot of examples, from the *d'var torah* delivered by the rabbi, up to the congregant-led torah-study-group. And in addition to the homiletical phenomena occurring in Jewish congregations you gave us a survey of how Jewish theological schools reflect the current expectations through their homiletical education. I can say that the challenges at least in Protestant Germany seem comparable to the American Jewish ones. In my context, the sermon is increasingly going to be subsumed under the wider concept of proclamation. And proclamation is not necessarily expected in the traditional form of a sermon. Thus a variety of ways to proclaim the Christian message is emerging. This observation is ambiguous, i.e. it contains chances as well as problems.

(4) I will, at last, not talk about the chances but mark a problem. Reading the text of Professor Sarason's lecture I wondered why current homiletics does not interplay to a greater extent with current hermeneutics. It is the problem at least in German Protestantism that the expectations of both preachers and congregations are departing from an intrinsically Biblical orientation of sermons. Or, in other words, the high esteem of the Bible marking Protestantism from its origins is shifting elsewhere. Alexander Deeg and I think that we have to face this problem not by insisting on the traditional sermon and its traditional shape but by discovering anew the strange and fascinating space of the biblical text.[3] We are convinced that renewed hermeneutics lead to renewed homiletics and vice versa. In this regard, I think, both Jews and Christians should undertake some steps together.

---

3 Cf. *Martin Nicol*, Fremde Botschaft Bibel. Homiletisches Plädoyer für eine hermeneutische Schubumkehr, in: PTh 93/2004, 264–279; *Martin Nicol/Alexander Deeg*, Im Wechselschritt zur Kanzel. Praxisbuch Dramaturgische Homiletik, Göttingen 2005; *Alexander Deeg*, Skripturalität und Metaskripturalität. Über Heilige Schrift, Leselust und Kanzelrede, in: EvTh 67/2007, 5–17.

Jewish Hermeneutics and Christian Preaching
Scriptural Hermeneutics and its Homiletical Consequences

Alexander Deeg/Martin Nicol

Rudolf Bohren, Professor Emeritus of Practical Theology in Heidelberg, once wrote in his *"Predigtlehre"* (Homiletic), first published 36 years ago in 1971: "Only pride and ignorance could prevent the Protestant preacher [we are convinced that we could replace this adjective and say: "the Christian preacher" – AD/MN] from learning from the rabbi."[1] 36 years after these spirited and promising words, we want to pick up this sentence again and ask: what could homiletic learning from the rabbi mean to us?

First of all, of course, in order to answer this question and learn from 'the rabbi's preaching', we should ask *how* "the rabbi" preaches. There is obviously no simple answer to this question. We could turn to rabbinic times, to the Middle Ages, to the dramatic changes in 19th-century Germany, to the early 20th century, and to recent developments in Jewish preaching.[2] In our paper we confine ourselves to hermeneutical observations starting in rabbinic times and moving forward through the ages and thus try to get a rough overview of Jewish homiletical hermeneutics. Our main question will be whether there is something we, as Christian preachers, could learn from the ancient rabbis' ways of dealing with the sacred texts and of the subsequent hermeneutical developments.

---

1   *Rudolf Bohren*, Predigtlehre, Gütersloh ⁶1993, 121.
2   Cf. as an overview *Alexander Deeg*, Predigt und Derascha. Homiletische Textlektüre im Dialog mit dem Judentum (APTLH 48), Göttingen 2006, 63–218.

1. Scriptural hermeneutics in rabbinic times

Of course, as Professor Stemberger makes clear in his paper,[3] it is a great challenge and somehow an impossible task to find valid data about the sermon in rabbinic Judaism. Whether the rabbis preached in synagogues at all, whether the texts we find in the socalled "homiletic Midrashim"[4] are parts of real sermons – all this we do not know exactly. But we must admit that we really like the idea that at least parts of the material in the homiletic midrashim could have been real sermons or at least sermon outlines. We know that "we really like the idea" is not an academic argument at all – but we enjoy imagining that at least the P^etihot could have been synagogue sermons in rabbinic times.

According to a count made by Joseph Heinemann there are more than 2,000 p^etihot handed down in the rabbinic literature.[5] A P^etihah ends with a biblical verse, from which we can assume that this was the first verse of the Torah reading for that particular Shabbat or feast day. But it begins with a completely different biblical verse – usually from the K^etubim, the "Writings", or from the *corpus propheticum*. Between this "remote verse" with which the P^etihah begins and the verse from the reading, the *Darshan* (the interpreter, preacher) describes an arc in which he puts together separate interpretations, parables, or short stories.

Joseph Heinemann influentially represented the thesis according to which these P^etihot were the actual D^erashot in the synagogues – and not only parts or introductions to the sermons.[6]

If this was really the case, one could then picture this as something like the following: Jewish people came together to the service of worship. A fundamental constituent of the Shabbat morning service was the reading from the Torah – in *lectio continua* and in Palestine probably ensued in a

---

3   Cf. Günter Stemberger's paper "The Derashah in rabbinic times" in this volume.
4   Cf. *Günter Stemberger*, Einleitung in Talmud und Midrasch, Munich ⁸1992, 238; 284–308; *Idem*, Midrasch. Vom Umgang der Rabbinen mit der Bibel. Einführungen – Texte – Erläuterungen, Munich 1989, 143–185.
5   Cf. *Joseph Heinemann*, D^erashot baZibbur bitqufat haTalmud [Hebrew], Jerusalem 1970, 12; *Idem*, The Proem in the Aggadic Midrashim. A Form-Critical Study, in: *Idem/Dov Noy* (Eds.), Studies in Aggadah and Folk-Literature (ScrHie 22), Jerusalem 1971, 100–122, here 101. – On the whole the "homilies" in the "homiletic Midrashim" are so structured that the P^etihah (usually several P^etihot) which are introduced in more detail in what follows are succeeded by the *Injan* interpretation (interpretations on several verses of the Shabbat-*Parashah*) before a – usually shorter – eschatological section (*Hatimah*) concludes the homily (cf. *Doris Lenhard*, Die rabbinische Homilie. Ein formanalytischer Index [FJS 10], Frankfurt/M. 1998, 54–69).
6   Cf. especially the literature mentioned above in no. 5.

three-year rotation.⁷ If we assume that those attending the service had a relatively sound knowledge of the Torah, we can also surmise that the majority knew – at least roughly – what would be read on that particular Shabbat. Then the service took its course. Psalms were sung, the *Sh⁽ᵉ⁾ma Jisrael* read, the *Eighteen Benedictions* – shortened on the Shabbat – spoken. Subsequently the *Darshan* came forward and began his *D⁽ᵉ⁾rashah* – before the reading from the Torah. But he did *not* begin with the verse from the Torah with which the reading would later commence. On the contrary: he began and quoted an entirely different, far-removed biblical verse. But his listeners knew: it would be his task to come to the reading of the Torah scheduled for that Shabbat from this remote verse through the words of the *D⁽ᵉ⁾rashah*. A basic tension was provided and a way marked out for the *D⁽ᵉ⁾rashah*, a way within the textual space of the Hebrew Bible, the *Tanak*.

At first sight this prescription appears purely formal. But naturally the *P⁽ᵉ⁾tihah lemmata* were not chosen in an arbitrary fashion but in such a way that a field of tension was opened up between the *p⁽ᵉ⁾tihah lemma* and the Torah *parashah*. To give only one example of one *p⁽ᵉ⁾tihah* and the field of tension that can be found in it: A *p⁽ᵉ⁾tihah*, cited for example in Midrash Sh⁽ᵉ⁾mot Rabba, began with a *lemma* from Ps. 11: "*the LORD's throne is in heaven*" (v. 4). But it issued in Ex. 3, in the story of a God who reveals himself in the lowliness of a thorn bush in the desert. The whole *p⁽ᵉ⁾tihah* asks for the place where God can be found, asks for God's topography, and moves between the transcendence and immanence of God – and on the way from Ps. 11 to Ex. 3 joins together different interpretations and relates stories and a parable.⁸

We do not know whether the *D⁽ᵉ⁾rashot* in rabbinic times really looked like this. But at all events the *P⁽ᵉ⁾tihot* show the kind of hermeneutics which is fundamentally characteristic of the *D⁽ᵉ⁾rashah* in the rabbinic period. In short: the *D⁽ᵉ⁾rashot* led into the Torah and involved the listeners in the words of Scripture. If one were to look for a term to characterize this hermeneutic we think that *scriptural hermeneutic* would be an obvious choice. The interpreter does not speak *about* Scripture; he does not investigate *one* statement in the text but opens ways into the scripture as "Sacra Scriptura".

---

[7] Cf. *Ismar Elbogen*, Der jüdische Gottesdienst in seiner geschichtlichen Entwicklung, 2nd reprint of the 3rd improved edition, Hildesheim 1995, 155–174; *Dirk Monshouwer*, The Reading of Scripture in the Liturgy. A neglected Approach to Biblical Interpretation, in: CV 41/1999, 116–130, here: 119–128.

[8] This *p⁽ᵉ⁾tihah*, the structure of which is sketched here, is transmitted e.g. in ShemR 2.2.

The famous statement of Ben Bag Bag in m. Av 5.22⁹ sums up these scriptural hermeneutics strikingly. Ben Bag Bag says: "Turn it (the Torah) round and round, for everything is in it."

The expectation of finding "everything" in Scripture is the basis for a meticulously precise reading of the biblical text. Individual words, even letters are examined. Rabbinic interpreters ascribe the highest authority to the canonical text of the Torah. They read it convinced that every smallest particular is significant. This is justified right at the beginning of the *Midrash Tanchuma* in the exegesis of Gen. 1.1 on the grounds that even the smallest change in the consonant text of the Torah could destroy the whole world.

> Take, for example, Ps. 150.6 ("Let everything that breathes praise the LORD!"). If in the verb "praise" there were a "ḥet " (ח) in place of the letter "he" (ה), there would only be one tiny line more but the text would now read "Let everything that breathes blaspheme the LORD". The world could be destroyed by such carelessness.[10]

Frequently apposite biblical passages are drawn in such a manner that the result is an interpretation which could be described using a catchword from 20th century Literary Studies: "intertextual". In investigating the biblical words and stories and in the intertextual intertwining with other texts, the interpreters recognize that the words of Scripture do not speak of things past but are concerned with the present of the People of God.

But here it is at the same time completely clear for rabbinic interpretation that the biblical texts do not make only *one* statement which can be transmitted once and for all. On the contrary (at least in haggadic interpretation!) they are convinced that the words of the Bible do not lose any of their importance by being interpreted in many ways – but always become richer. Thus, for example, Abaje in a well-known interpretation of Ps. 62.11 ("God has spoken once, twice have I heard this …") says: "[…] a biblical passage has several meanings, but one meaning is not to be taken from different passages" (b. San 34a). In the context of the Talmud we find immediately afterwards a quotation from the school of Rabbi Ishmael: Just as the Word of God is described as a hammer which breaks a rock in pieces (Jer. 23.29), so may the manifold interpretations be understood as the many sparks produced in the process. In the medieval Midrash BemR we read that the Torah has several faces and consequently in the end has infinitely numerous

---

9　In the historical tradition we are dealing with an addition to the Mishna-tract *Avot* (Sayings of the Fathers); cf. *Günter Stemberger*, "Wende und wende sie …" (mAvot 5.22), in: BN 116/2003, 87–94.

10　Cf. *Tan* Bereshit 1.

possibilities "to confront" present-day hearers and readers (BemR *Naso* 13.15).

Rabbinic (haggadic) interpretation is characterised by its reverence for the text, the plurality of interpretation, and the intertextuality of reading. As a consequence of these characteristics, rabbinic exegesis does not take the place of the text but constantly remains *con-textualization*. Put graphically: The text is central, and around this text are grouped the varied rabbinical interpretations which only make sense together with the text. The rabbinic exegetes only achieve the new *word* of their own individual topical interpretations in the continual interplay with the scriptural *text*.

Already in the rabbinical period this con-textualization was characterised by the two terms *written* and *oral Torah*.[11] Startingpoint and constant point of reference is the *written* Torah. This is read again and again in anticipation since what Ben Bag Bag says holds true: "Turn it round and round, for everything is in it." The result of the constant turning is the continually increasing, never-ending exegesis of the written Torah which can be called the *oral Torah*. The rabbis' ability to see the most varied and even contradictory interpretations of a scriptural passage as a sign of the richness and beauty of the biblical text rather than as a problematic exegetical jungle results from their trust that the written Torah can constantly become the living Word of God. A kind of theonomically-bound reception aesthetic of the Torah is a characteristic of rabbinic biblical hermeneutics – and gives them a calm, unassuming, and frequently amusing candour. This finds expression in e.g. PesK 12.25, an interpretation of Ex. 20.2. In the introduction to the Decalogue the *whole* nation is addressed in the second person singular (!), which surprises the rabbinic exegete: "I am the LORD your (sing.) God (אלהיך)." In the *Midrash* on this we read:

> "Rabbi Levi said: The HOLY ONE, praise be to HIM, appeared to them like that statue which has a face on every side. A thousand people look at this statue and it looks at all of them. So it was with the HOLY ONE, may HE be praised: When he spoke each individual Israelite said: With me speaks the WORD. What is written here is not 'I am the LORD your (Plural) God (אלהיכם)', but 'I am the LORD, your (singular) God'." Rabbi Jossi bar Khanina said: "The WORD speaks with each individual according to his strength. Do not be surprised by this statement, for it was also so when the manna descended upon Israel: its taste differed for each individual according to his strength. [...] And just as the taste of the manna differed

---

11 Cf. *Peter Schäfer*, Das „Dogma" von der mündlichen Torah im rabbinischen Judentum, in: *Idem*, Studien zur Geschichte und Theologie des rabbinischen Judentums (AGJU 15), Leiden 1978, 153–197.

for each individual according to his strength, so each individual hears the WORD according to his strength."

The *Midrash* is a reading which combines an imaginative freedom of interpretation and academic eros in the treatment of the text with an unconditional commitment to this text, based on the expectation that God himself will make his Word again to Torah, the Word that addresses and guides.

And this is exactly what we would call *scriptural hermeneutics*. The rabbinic texts impressively show us an interpretation which, full of anticipation, meticulously searches the Torah and intertwines present-day hearers/readers in manifold ways into the words and stories of the Torah.

2. Scripturality and metascripturality in Judaism and Christianity

2.1 Metascriptural ways of Jewish hermeneutics and homiletics – and the recent fascination of Scripturality

We would suggest calling the opposite of *scriptural* hermeneutics *metascriptural* hermeneutics. *Metascriptural* hermeneutics could be characterised as a way of dealing with the text that does not lead *into the text*, its richness and variety of interpretations, but moves outward *from the text* to the interpretation derived from it. Of course this a rough confrontation, but we hope that it can prove helpful as a heuristic, as a way to orientate oneself in the large area of hermeneutical discussion.

Jewish hermeneutics are by no means *scriptural* all the times. In the history of Jewish hermeneutics there is a remarkable shift from rabbinic times to the Middle Ages and a tangible change in the way texts were interpreted.[12] Above all, the Carian criticism of the manner of rabbinic interpretation of Scripture and the influences stemming from the adoption of elementary Aristotelian philosophy resulted in many medieval D*erashot* developing philosophical or ethical statements, which they then substantiated with references from Scripture. Put bluntly, the hermeneutical direction reverses in comparison to the rabbinical period: D*erashah* no longer leads *into* the Torah and the inconsistent variety of different "sparks" which arise when the stones

---

12 This change is described, for example, by *Moshe Idel*, Preface, in: *Betty Rojtman*, Black Fire on White Fire. An essay on Jewish hermeneutics from Midrash to Kabbalah, Berkeley (CA)/Los Angeles (CA)/London 1998, ix–xii, esp. ix.

of the words and letters are carefully hewn but leads *out of* the Torah to prove a philosophical or ethical statement. Alongside this philosophical or ethical interpretation a third important direction of hermeneutics develops in the Jewish Middle Ages: the mystical interpretation. Its hermeneutics can, according to our opinion, also be described as metascriptural to the extent that mystical interpreters sought to push forward through the words of Scripture and the variety of interpretations to the real basis of the Torah hidden behind the letters, to the *unio mystica*.

We cannot go into detail concerning the Middle Ages and their hermeneutics here – this is too broad a topic for this short lecture. But we want to give another prominent example of metascriptural hermeneutics in Jewish sermons: the movement of Jewish reform – at least in its first years. Jewish reformers saw the sermon in the national language (no longer Yiddish) as an appropriate means to accomplish two urgent tasks – internally: Judaism had lost the classical plausibility structure of Jewish life as it had previously existed in Jewish communities which were relatively fenced off from their surroundings; it had to be led to an up-to-date and consequently reformed Judaism.[13] The aim was to make "Jews by fate" – as many Jewish people felt themselves to be, particularly in the cities – into "Jews by faith".[14] Outwardly, it was felt necessary to seek contact both in regard to content and form with the greater part of society which was Christian. The sermon in German appeared to be a suitable method of achieving both goals. The early sermons in that period were frequently fashioned to represent generally accepted philosophical-theological ideas or basic ethical values metascripturally from the Torah and Jewish tradition. And here again one has the typical paradigm of *metascriptural* hermeneutics. We refer to Eduard Kley as an example:

> Kley preached on the last day of the Passover Feast 5586 (1826) in the Hamburg Temple on *"Der Auszug aus Mizrajim, auch für das Alltagsleben"* ("The Exodus from Egypt – also for everyday life").[15] The title points to the basic aim and hermeneutics of the sermon: Kley wants to show how the 'old' story of the Exodus from Egypt can (still) be significant for everyday

---

13 Cf. *Michael A. Meyer*, Jüdische Identität in der Moderne, Frankfurt/M. 1992, esp. 45 n. 10; *Shulamit Volkov*, Die Erfindung einer Tradition. Zur Entstehung des modernen Judentums in Deutschland, in: *Eadem*, Das jüdische Projekt der Moderne. Zehn Essays, Munich 2001, 118–137.

14 Cf. *Ismar Schorsch*, Emancipation and the Crisis of Religious Authority: The Emergence of the Modern Rabbinate, in: *Werner E. Mosse et al.* (Eds.), Revolution and Evolution. 1848 in German Jewish History (SWALBI 39), Tübingen 1981, 205–247.

15 *Eduard Kley*, Predigten in dem neuen Israelitischen Tempel, Zweites Heft, Jahrgang 5586. Zweite Hälfte, Hamburg 1820, 65–76.

life in the present. Kley develops his sermon in three points (note the dependence on the 'pedagogical' form practiced in Christian preaching at that time!) and makes the listeners aware that the Feast of the Passover needs an everyday shape so that (1) one does not lose sight of the Feast Day, (2) one practises moderation, and (3) one remembers one's neighbours. Where this happens – thus Kley at the end of his sermon – everyday life could already become a "foretaste of bliss".[16] Three points and a conclusion – all of this based on some – relatively loose – reference to the biblical text!

This is a typically metascriptural way of hermeneutics – and its result is a thematically-oriented sermon which takes the text as a starting point and which talks about two or three points that the preacher finds important in the text.

It was striking and interesting for us to see that nowadays an impressive rediscovery of scriptural hermeneutics can be discerned, especially in the USA, but in the meantime also in other parts of the world. The pre-modern scriptural hermeneutics of the Midrash, with its emphasis on precision, intertextuality, and the plurality of readings, has again been increasingly taken into consideration and seen as a stimulating precedent for the present post-modern situation. On the theoretical level authors like Susan Handelman, David Stern, Norman Cohen, and many others[17], as well as the whole academic group of "Textual (and Scriptural) Reasoners" in the context of the "American Academy of Religion"[18], are looking for such combination of pre-modern midrashic hermeneutics in post-modern times. And there are also steps towards an altered practice in the congregations through observation of the Midrash – pursued e.g. by the "Institute for Contemporary Midrash".[19] Poems are written, films produced, plays performed, and pictures are painted to open up new levels of Torah study for present-day people.

---

16 Ibid., 76 (emphasised in the original).
17 Cf. e.g. *Susan A. Handelman*, The Slayers of Moses. The Emergence of Rabbinic Interpretation in Modern Literary Theory, Albany (NY) 1982; *Eadem*, Fragments of the Rock. Contemporary Literary Theory and the Study of Rabbinic Texts – A Response to David Stern, in: Prooftexts 5/1985, 75–95; *David Stern*, Midrash and Theory. Ancient Jewish Exegesis and Contemporary Literary Studies, Evanston (IL) 1996; *Norman Cohen*, The Way into Torah, Woodstock (VT) 2000.
18 Cf. *Peter Ochs/Nancy Levene* (Eds.), Textual Reasonings. Jewish Philosophy and Text Study at the End of the Twentieth Century, Grand Rapids (MI)/Cambridge 2002.
19 Cf. www.icmidrash.org; cf. also the periodical "Living Text" which was published by ICM between 1997 and 2000.

2.2 Are we Christians born metascripturalists?

Having collected some observations in Jewish hermeneutics and having tried to arrange the hermeneutical world by distinguishing two approaches – the scriptural and the metascriptural – let us now turn to Christian hermeneutics.

There are more than a few authors who see the Christian approach to scripture as characterised by the tendency to reduce the plurality of meanings to *the one* meaning which corresponds to the one and unique truth revealed in Jesus Christ. About ten years ago Jochen Hörisch, who teaches German literature in Mannheim, published a striking treatise on hermeneutics: *"Die Wut des Verstehens"* ("The fury of understanding").[20] He stigmatises early Christian efforts to understand the Jewish Holy Scriptures (that soon would be called by Christians "Old Testament") their way. The person he mainly aims at is Apostle Paul. According to Hörisch he is the first Christian ancestor of what, with young Schleiermacher, he calls "the fury of understanding".[21] Jesus himself still esteemed the letters of the Scriptures: "For truly I tell you, until heaven and earth pass away, not one letter, not one stroke of a letter, will pass from the law until all this is accomplished" (Mat. 5.17). In contrast Paul would soon establish an inverted way of putting letters and spirit: "Our competence is from God, who made us competent to be ministers of a new covenant, not of letter but of Spirit; for the letter kills, but the Spirit gives life" (1Cor. 3.5f.). Here we are, says Hörisch. This is the starting point of a long and dominating tradition that in complicity with Aristotelian philosophy banishes the plurality of literal meanings in favour of the one and only meaning given by the one Spirit of God. Plurality of meanings is now regarded as a defect to be overcome rather than an outstanding quality. What is said here about Christian interpretation of biblical texts may be said in general about western interpretation of any text. That "fury of understanding" can be diagnosed as a cultural pattern rather than a specifically religious or theological one.

Let us stop here. It may be enough to mark the starting point. For the following centuries we have to recognize that Hörisch's argument well captures a major stream of western interpretation of the Christian Bible. The Protestant Reformation, at least in its beginnings, may be regarded as a counterpoint to this way of unifying interpretation.

---

20 Cf. *Jochen Hörisch*, Die Wut des Verstehens. Zur Kritik der Hermeneutik, Frankfurt/M. 1988; ²1998.
21 Cf. *Friedrich Daniel Ernst Schleiermacher*, Über die Religion. Reden an die Gebildeten unter ihren Verächtern (1799) (*Günter Meckenstock*, Ed.), Berlin/New York 1999, 120.

Martin Luther fought a lifelong struggle in favour of the literal sense of the biblical texts. From Luther's times up to now others may be mentioned who tried it this way. But the Protestant mainstream of interpretation has always followed the pattern stigmatised by Jochen Hörisch. This is what we call metascripturality.[22]

2.3 Metascripturality and its homiletic consequences – or: the interrelation of homiletics and hermeneutics

It may not be astonishing that Christian preaching has been highly influenced by the metascriptural way of reading the Holy Scriptures. The way to preach the Bible and the way to read it are intrinsically tied to each other. We call it "change steps" ("*Wechselschritte*"), i.e. one cannot do the first step without doing the second one, vice-versa, and so on.[23] Homiletics and hermeneutics, indeed, are intertwined.

In modern times, the dominating western model for Christian sermons has been the three-point-sermon. The same procedure as every Sunday: the preacher starts with the biblical text, captures something in it that corresponds to ordinary dogmatic theology, and then outlines it by means of the traditional three-point-model. The biblical text turns out not to be the space to get in but the springboard to get off. Metascriptural hermeneutics have generated metascriptural homiletics and vice-versa.

This has been an admittedly rough drawing. One may no longer find the pure unadulterated model of a three-point-sermon. Real sermons ordinarily mix up metascriptural attitude with some bright spots of what may be accepted as scriptural. We quote two examples, the first one for a metascriptural attitude and the second one for a bright spot of scripturality.

The first example comes from Walter Brueggemann, Professor Emeritus of Old Testament at Columbia Theological Seminary in Decatur, Georgia. He once published an inspiring treatise on preaching: "Finally Comes the Poet. Daring Speech for Proclamation".[24] In this text he applaudably points at the poetic power of various texts in the

---

22 Cf. *Alexander Deeg*, Skripturalität und Metaskripturalität. Über Heilige Schrift, Leselust und Kanzelrede, in: EvTh 67/2007, 5–17.
23 Cf. *Martin Nicol/Alexander Deeg*, Im Wechselschritt zur Kanzel. Praxisbuch Dramaturgische Homiletik, Göttingen 2005, esp. 13–20.
24 *Walter Brueggemann*, Finally comes the Poet. Daring Speech für Proclamation, Minneapolis (MN) 1989.

Hebrew Bible and encourages Christian preachers to get inspired by biblical poetry for shaping their own sermons.

As a preacher, however, Brueggemann does not seem to be as daring as he once proposed. In the subsequent sermon[25] after about 30 seconds he reaches the sentence that has figured out to be one of the most prominent signals of metascriptural preaching:

> "All quarrels [...] are about land. It is so in rural families that endlessly quarrel about the estate. If not land then turf, power, control, security, all about scarcity. So divide it up and make sure I get mine. That's what the text is about."

"That's what the text is about." – This sentence seems to be incidental, but it is not at all. It signalizes a preacher who feels able to sum up a plurality of meanings into a short statement. He requires the authority to be the spokesman of the biblical text. Instead of preaching from within the text he takes up a position outside of it.

Our second example: the preacher is Harold Kushner, a famous American rabbi. His entire sermon[26] may not be regarded as intrinsically scriptural. Yet in the beginning he shows what rabbinic scripturality could be. In the well-known story of Adam, Eve, and the forbidden fruit he discovers a question which usually is not asked:

> "The story [...] is the story of Adam and Eve in the garden of Eden. As long as I can remember that story has bothered me. Even as a child I had this feeling that there is something fishy about this story, that doesn't come together. For one thing, it sounds like a set-up, doesn't it. Any time you have a story that begins 'Don't eat the fruit!', 'Don't open the box!', 'Don't go in the locked room!' you know what's gonna happen. You gonna do, because otherwise there is no story. The Bible would have been three pages long. If God didn't want them to eat the fruit, so don't make the fruit, I mean He is God. More than that – when they do eat the fruit [...], it bothered me, that God came down so hard on them. I remember as a child saying to myself: 'Boy if this is what God does to Adam and Eve when they did one thing wrong, what's he gonna do to me for all the things that I have done wrong?' But what bothered me about the story more than anything else, was the name of the fruit. You remember, it's not just the fruit you are not supposed to eat. How was it called? The fruit of the tree of the knowledge of good and evil. And that I could never understand. I would assume acquiring a knowledge of good and evil is a good thing. How can you be a moral person, if you don't know what's right or wrong? Why is the story told to make it seem that learning about good and evil

---

25 *Walter Brueggemann*, Videotape in the "Great Preachers" Series, Odyssey Productions, Worcester (PA).

26 *Harold Kushner*, Videotape in the "Great Preachers" Series, Odyssey Productions, Worcester (PA).

was the worst thing anybody could ever have done. But I said: 'You are a kid, you are not meant to understand this stuff. When I get older, it'll make sense.' But it never did."

The setting of the story is well-known, and well-known is the tree in the midst of the garden. It is hard to get inside a story that anybody knows so well. The rabbi, however, has the courage to ask a question he had always asked himself since he was a child: Why is this fruit called fruit of "the tree of the knowledge of good and evil"? That is what he had never been able to understand. It does not make sense that God punishes Adam and Eve for what they had done. Why is it regarded as a sin what we have always required our own children to be able to do, i.e. to identify and to discern good and evil? And so on. A well-known detail of a well-known story bothered the preacher, he didn't stop asking, but there seems to be no sense in it at all. 'Wonderful', says the homiletician. The well-known story is now open. We may pass the door, get inside the story and make discoveries, our own as well the preacher's ones.

3. Learning from the homiletic twin

3.1 Theoretical perspectives

We are convinced that in present-day homiletical and hermeneutical reality we could profit a lot, if we learned from the old, pre-modern way of Jewish midrashic scriptural hermeneutics. If we took Scripture seriously as the word given to us in order to search, search again and again – because everything is in it. If we went a way into Scripture – and not only sought ways out of it to *the* true interpretation or *the* valid message.

In our Christian tradition there are quite a lot of *scriptural* traces to be found. Martin Luther is a prominent example. In his *Kirchenpostille* of 1522 – a work which today one could perhaps most easily describe as a collection of sermon-aids or sermon-meditations – Martin Luther states that the aim of his interpretations is to carve a way to Scripture so that Scripture itself can speak. He writes:

"Therefore go right in, right in, dear Christians, and let my interpretations and those of all teachers be simply a scaffolding to the true building so that we comprehend, taste and remain at the pure, unadulterated Word of God itself; for God alone dwells there in Zion. AMEN."
("Darumb hyneyn, hyneyn, lieben Christen, und last meyn und aller lerer ausslegen nur eyn gerust seyn zum rechten baw, das wyr das blosse,

lautter gottis wort selbs fassen, schmecken unnd da bleyben; denn da wonet gott alleyn ynn Zion. AMEN.")²⁷

In learning from Jewish interpretation and preaching an exegetical and homiletic treatment of Scripture might suggest itself anew at the present time. And this could be seen as "a scaffolding to the true building" and not as beginning with the text to reach a metascriptural message which leaves the text somewhere behind.²⁸ Preaching would then be an aid for reading the text itself. It would perceive its goal as being to lead those who hear it to read the text for themselves. To do so it must keep the text alive during the whole sermon and consequently could be described as a sermon with an open Bible. The *Petihah* presented above as a possible form of a rabbinic *Derashah* which leads from a text in the words of the *Parashah* could, we believe, provide, even from a formal homiletic perspective, a stimulating potential for the shaping of a scriptural Christian sermon.

At the same time such a sermon would be anticipatory – as Jewish preaching and exegesis in dealing with the Torah was and is. In the Second Vatican Council a goal was formulated that one should prepare the "table of God's Word" more richly for the faithful and open the "treasury of the Bible" wider.²⁹ The two metaphors in the Council's declaration describe the expectation that there is in the Bible something wonderful to taste and valuable to look at. Such an expectation would make the biblical text central in the sermon and not depart from it all too quickly with metascriptural statements. It would not only show what lies on the table but would also allow the congregation to taste for themselves. It would not only talk about the treasury but would also open its doors wide. It would see its goal to be that of making the listeners expectant readers.

3.2 Practical consequences

Which practical consequences for our preaching result from this scriptural perspective? First of all, there is a problem to be pointed at: we live in a culture marked by the metascriptural pattern! In this

---

27 WA 10,1,1,728, 18–22.
28 The exegete Jürgen Ebach, taking up what he has seen in Judaism, is also of this opinion. He calls for an interpretation "which does not look for the sense of the text *behind* it but *in* it, in its words and letters" (Jürgen Ebach, Gott im Wort. Drei Studien zur biblischen Exegese und Hermeneutik, Neukirchen-Vluyn 1997, here: VII).
29 Die Konstitution des Zweiten Vatikanischen Konzils über die heilige Liturgie. Lateinisch-deutscher Text mit einem Kommentar von Joseph Lengeling (RLGD 5/6), Münster² 1965, 112 (=No. 51).

culture scriptural efforts may appear undetermined and far away from everyday experience, as somewhat clumsy and ridiculous. Academic colleagues may turn up their nose at questions without at least a tempted answer. And listeners in the pews may remain unsatisfied for they miss, towards the end of the sermon, the preacher's summary of what the sermon has been about, of what they should do next week and of what politicians all over the world have to do for peace and climate. We all are not accustomed to recover ourselves at the end of a sermon after having been thrown into the biblical text and its letters, instead of being elevated by the preacher's good ideas.

We think it might be thrilling for both Christians and Jews to rediscover the biblical text as a space to get in rather than a springboard to get off. We give only three examples of how such a scriptural approach to preaching could be arranged in our sermons.

3.2.1 Discovering and filling gaps

We already quoted Rabbi Harold Kushner asking a question which we had not been used to asking. He discovered a gap within the biblical text and marked that gap by his question. This is good rabbinic practice: discovering gaps and filling them playfully and seriously at the same time.

Take, for example, the awful story of Abraham offering his son Isaac (Gen. 22). It seems to be a story without Sarah, Isaac's mother. We only see two members of the family acting: father and son. But where is Sarah? This question leads us to a remarkable gap. Sarah must have played a role. But which one?

Arthur Strimling in his poetic re-narration of Gen. 22 sees Sarah acting, too. She observed her husband's preparations. But she did not ask anything. Quite the contrary, she stays in bed while father and son are climbing up to Mt. Moriah:

"[...]
For three days, Sarah stays in bed
Endures alone
While father and son meander to Moriah which means 'seeing'.
And Sarah sees.
[...]"

When Sarah sees what happens on Mt. Moriah, when she sees Abraham raising the knife, she starts crying:

"'Avraham!'
[...]

> Her lungs gasp for air.
> 'Avraham!'
> [...]
> Sarah's cry carries all the way to heaven,
> Passes through the throat of the angel/messenger,
> Then back down to Mt. Moriah.
>
> And Abraham freezes.
> Abraham listens to Sarah."

The story ends as it ends in the Bible (cf. Gen. 23.1f.):

> "Sarah sees, and Sarah dies."[30]

This way of locating Sarah within the well-known story is fascinating. Sarah prays, her prayer raises up all the way to heaven, it comes backwards down by the angel – and prevents Abraham from offering Isaac, her and his son.

This is not a new biblical text. This is only one way to get into the story by filling a gap. Others may fill it in a different way. Others may discover other gaps. But this time a gap was filled this way. And listeners may have been invited to get into the text through this gap as if it was a door opened by the preacher.

3.2.2 Biblical words in sermon context

The second example focuses on the difference between biblical words and the preacher's own speech. The mysterious story of Moses pleading for a glance at God's glory is well known (Ex. 33.18–23). Manfred Josuttis, Professor Emeritus of Practical Theology in Göttingen, in one of his sermons established an intriguing contrast between the demand of Moses and everyday situations in Göttingen:[31]

> "Next week the people in our city, partly in the cinema, partly on TV, will be able to see about 100 films. Crime movies, love stories, westerns, adventures in the outer space. Scenes of horror, porn pictures.
> *But 'Mose said: I beseech thee, show me your glory'.*
> Next week the 13 departments of our university will continue their research work. Deciphering a manuscript, interpreting a work of art, confirming a diagnosis, mapping the human genome, decoding atomic structures.

---

30 *Arthur Strimling*, Sarah Sees: A Shofar Story, in: Living Text. The Journal of Contemporary Midrash, No. 8/2000, 8–12.
31 *Manfred Josuttis*, Offene Geheimnisse. Predigten, Gütersloh 1999, 88–92, here: 88. Cf. *Martin Nicol/Alexander Deeg*, Im Wechselschritt zur Kanzel. Praxisbuch Dramaturgische Homiletik, Göttingen 2005, 111f.

> But *'Mose said: I beseech thee, show me your glory'*.
> Next week people will eye someone suspiciously who rang at their door. Men and women who don't know one another will watch each other full of expectation. Some will have a look at old photos. Others will draw up visions of future.
> But *'Mose said: I beseech thee, show me your glory'."*

We regard this way of establishing a contrast between the biblical text and the preacher's own speech as a good way to get into a text, for preachers as well as for listeners. Within the polarity of everyday impressions and strange biblical words people may take first steps and more into that mysterious story.

3.2.3 Telling the Story. Preaching from within – not preaching about

Don Wardlaw, Professor Emeritus of Preaching at McCormick Theological Seminary in Chicago, once gave the following advice for preachers: "You should not preach *about* a text. You should, however, preach *from within*."

Preaching from within – how is this possible? Don Wardlaw himself cultivated narrative preaching as a way to get into the biblical text. In what follows we quote the beginning of a sermon on Mat. 4.13–22, titled "Jesus comes calling by the sea".[32] The very first words leave no doubt that we already are within the biblical story.

> "We're just back from fishing in the night, as the dawn's glow stretches across the horizon. You and I pull our boat up on the beach alongside the boat of James, John, and Zebedee, their father. Peter and Andrew are close by offshore, making one more pass with the nets in the shallows as shrieking gulls dip and dive above. They're good with the nets in the shallows."

"We are back from fishing ..." – the first words establish a scene to which we (as present-day hearers) belong. There is no gap between us and the 'old' text. We can stand on the beach with the fishermen – and see, what happens. This narrative kind of sermonic shape seems to us to be an effective way of "preaching from within", but it is of course not the only one.

At any rate, a scriptural pattern should be aimed at. This pattern is for us a vision for preaching. As Christian preachers we could learn a lot from rabbinic scripturality. In our metascriptural culture it may be a task for both Christian and Jewish preachers to discover and to test ways to get into the texts. It is quite easy to get out of them but hard to

---

32 Private recording from 1994.

get in. Getting into the texts, however, fascinates. Exploring the space of a biblical text we may be able to do what Don Wardlaw once called "Preaching from within".

Through the White Fire to the Black Fire
The Bibliolog as a Path for Bible Interpretation in Judaism and Christianity[1]

Uta Pohl-Patalong

1. Christian quests for understanding and Jewish tradition

One can perceive a trend at present toward quests (*Suchbewegungen*, "search movements" [Tr.]) for deeper understanding of the nature of access to and interaction with the Bible. These movements can be seen both in homiletics and in work on Biblical texts being performed by groups. Amidst the variety of approaches, it is possible to identify tendencies that can be understood within the context of the present societal development: approaches are favoured that are hermeneutically positioned to work with different, even thoroughly contradictory, interpretations, and which to some extent possess "a competence of plurality".

An inherent part of this is a veneration of subjectivity, insofar as the subject is understood as a productive dimension of interpretation. This in turn is not restricted to learned theologians, but is instead more strongly oriented toward participation. All of this should be of little surprise in a societal landscape shaped by pluralisation, individualisation, and subjectification. At the same time, and yet not at all contradictory to the aforementioned, one can also make out tendencies toward a search for form and structure, but even more so toward a new estimation of tradition. Where tradition – classically modern – in recent decades had been largely considered something dusty and rear-facing, prescriptive and restrictive, it appears of late that the potential of tradition has been rediscovered again. Just as the "post-modernism" has been accredited with a new turning to tradition, traditions are gaining new value in daily life, and even more strongly in the sphere of religion. Yet the regard for tradition is generally linked

---

1   My heartfelt thanks here to Iris Weiss of Berlin for a critical counterreading and useful commentary from a Jewish perspective.

with a specific interaction with it, described as "plurality-ready" or "post-traditional".² To this extent, biblical texts can also gain a new appreciation and esteem after decades during which critical interaction tended to be in the theological foreground.

Interestingly – if only occasionally – these quests are now encountering Jewish ways of interacting with biblical texts and Jewish hermeneutics. Unlike in Christianity, where beyond its first centuries (during which four Gospels were set up in coexistence) it was the search for the "right," for the "true" message as distinct from the "false" one that dominated for several centuries, Judaism was always significantly more guided by an awareness that the wealth of the Torah, as the collection of human interpretations and varied exegeses, is inexhaustible. According to the Jewish understanding, exegesis is inherently brought up to date with the current era and situation. The Midrash presumes that each generation will have to interpret the Torah anew, because each generation will pose new questions or have them posed upon themselves by changed societal conditions. Various interpretations are not just tolerable for the text, but in fact serve it. Hence in the Jewish tradition it is said that each of the six hundred thousand people standing at the foot of Mount Sinai when the Torah was received (both in writing and orally) had their own opportunity to understand the Torah and that a different aspect was intended for each person. The Jewish tradition has coined the image of the "white fire" blazing between the letters of the "black fire" and opening pathways into the black fire of the text: "The Torah that the Holy One, hallowed be His name, gave unto Moses, He gave it unto him as white fire engraved with black fire. It is fire, wrapped in fire, chiselled from fire and given from fire, as it is said: 'from his right hand went a fiery law for them' (Deut. 33.2)."³

The Midrashim provide answers to questions posed by the text, but do not answer them in full or claim to provide the single definitive correct answer to the text's questions. This allows different Midrashim and different exegeses to coexist with one another. Their common basis however is a veneration of the biblical text as one to which authority is allocated and potency is entrusted. From them spring a joy in the Torah and a desire for its exegeses.

This behaviour can also be observed in modern forms of the Midrash as it has developed in recent decades, primarily in North America. The "Institute of Contemporary Midrash" brings together

---

2   Cf. *Rudolf Englert*, Vom Umgang mit Tradition im Zeichen religiöser Pluralität, in: ZPT 55/2003, 137–150.
3   y. Sheq 6.1.

many, often quite different, opportunities for continuing on the tradition of the Midrash using artistic means. This is how the inventor (or perhaps better: discoverer) of the Bibliolog, Peter Pitzele, understands the approach.⁴* Peter Pitzele is a literary scholar and pyschodramatist, yet interestingly not an academically trained theologian. Having grown up a secular Jew, through the development of the Bibliodrama he found his own new approach to the Torah. Bibliolog is – not least through psychodrama – related to what is known in Europe as "Bibliodrama," but the two differ in the methodologies, the role of the director, the orientation, and perhaps most importantly in their handling of the Biblical text in such significant ways that they must be understood as separate approaches.⁵

The fundamental element of the Bibliolog is the differentiation between the letters of the text and its empty spaces. On the one side, the Bibliolog respects the letter of the Biblical text: "The words in the Bible are canonized and immutable; the black fire cannot be modified." But "in the spirit of Midrash it searches for sub-stories and voices within that existing text; it plays with narrative inconsistencies, unanswered questions, puzzling juxtapositions. It plays with white fire."⁶ Yet it is perpetually astounding how sometimes seemingly tangential or confusing aspects prove to be key to new understanding of the text. Bibliolog sets itself the goal of bringing the white fire to a blaze, so as to achieve a living and personal access to the black fire.⁷ The Bibliolog not

---

4   He describes his approach in detail in *Peter A. Pitzele*, Scripture Windows. Toward a Practice of Bibliodrama, Los Angeles (CA) 1998. A German-language depiction of the method is provided in *Uta Pohl-Patalong*, Bibliolog. Gemeinsam die Bibel entdecken im Gottesdienst – in der Gemeinde – in der Schule, Stuttgart 2005.

*   [Translator's Note: To avoid confusion with the "Bibliodrama" as it is known in Europe, for the purposes of this essay I use the term 'Bibliolog' to refer to Pitzele's approach, so as to be clear what we are talking about. Cf. footnote 5 below.]

5   Peter Pitzele continues to refer to his approach in the USA as "Bibliodrama". In the German-speaking world, however, it quickly became clear that the word carries other connotations with it, leading Pitzele to create the neologism Bibliolog ("Bible Dialog"). He also pursues an alternative course, a more strongly self-experiential one, for which he uses the term "Bibliotherapy".

6   "The words in the Bible are canonized and immutable; the black fire cannot be modified". "But in the spirit of midrash it searches for sub-stories and voices within that existing text; it plays with narrative inconsistencies, unanswered questions, puzzling juxtapositions. It plays with white fire." (*Pitzele*, Scripture Windows, 31)

7   More extensive detail on black and white fire in *Pitzele*, Scripture Windows, 11f., 24 and 31. On the historical and hermeneutical background of the 'white fire' as Midrash, see *Tim Schramm*, Schwarzes und weißes Feuer, in: *Friedemann Green/Gisela Groß/Ralf Meister/Thorsten Schweda* (Eds.), Um der Hoffnung willen. Praktische Theologie mit Leidenschaft, Kirche in der Stadt 10, Festschrift für Wolfgang Grünberg, Hamburg 2000, 231–239, 232ff.

only accepts that understanding of biblical texts is inherently moulded by the personal, but actually uses it as the source of recognition and personal access to the text. Automatically, without the need for conscious framing and reflection, people fill the biblical roles in ways that correspond to their life experiences and worldviews.

2. Bibliolog concrete

How does a Bibliolog look in concrete terms? After a few introductory words about methodology, the director (referred to by Pitzele as the 'facilitator') opens up a scene from a biblical story. The facilitator explains the situation of a text and stirs up the imagination of the congregation or group as regards that situation. Important socio-historical information can be provided as part of the narration. At a specific point, the facilitator opens the Bible and reads a verse or a brief passage. From this verse she assigns the role of a Biblical figure to the congregation, speaks to them as if they were that figure and poses questions which are left open in the textual passage ('enrolling').

> In the story of the blessing of the firstborn (Gen. 27), I for example first asked Isaac: Isaac, you ask your son to hunt you a meal and to bring it to you in the way you like, because you are old and because you want to say a blessing over his soul before you die. Isaac, what was your motivation in stating it in that way?

All are free to express themselves (one after another) in the role of Isaac, that is, speaking in the first person, spontaneously and subjectively.[8] In doing so, the role is automatically filled by one's own life experiences and is understood in light of one's personal background, such as with:

> – I will have to move on soon, and so I want to pass on something first.
> – I want to have something good done for me by my favourite son.
> – That's quite odd, dying soon ... am I really going to die so soon?
> – Passing on my blessing, commanding my house to bring everything into order so that it can continue when I'm no longer here, I need that!

The facilitator moves about the congregation and records the – sometimes somewhat quiet and brief – statements. Using the technique of 'echoing,' she expresses the content aloud such that it can be understood by all, and honours it at the same time as comprising worthwhile subjective statements. She emphasises emotional content

---

[8] Pitzele calls this "voicing" the lynchpin of the Bibliolog: "the act of speaking in the first person singular, in the role of a biblical character or object" (*Pitzele*, Scripture Windows, 29).

that was perhaps only implied and hones statements to a point. This can potentially help the individuals gain a bit more understanding. There is also the opportunity of using 'interviewing' to clear up cases where, for example, content is only hinted at.

After several statements the facilitator guides the story further and reads the next verse or passage. The congregation is assigned a new role.

> After reading Vv. 5–10, I continued on:
> You are Rebecca. Rebecca, you tell your favourite son Jacob what he should do to receive the blessing of the firstborn. What are you really after here?
> That led to answers like:
> – Esau simply can't do it. If he assumes the job, it'll be a catastrophe! My Jacob is simply the only one who can do it!
> – And I now have to make certain that he is given the duties that he is also capable of doing.
> – And if Esau were to gain power, what would become of me?
> *(interviewing):* What are you afraid of, Rebecca?
> Than I'd go right under, wouldn't I? If Jacob has command of things here then ... *(interviewing:)* Then? (beaming) Then things would be right tidy for me!
> – I simply have to get involved here. First born or not, tradition is nice and all, but it's simply not the right thing here. Jacob is the special one, the chosen one, I simply know it! I do know my own little ones ...
> – I believe that in this case I have to take God by the arm a bit here. Sometimes he commits himself a bit and needs a little human help to see his will done ...

Thereafter Jacob and Esau can exchange words. This naturally can involve one person being queried about two different points of the story or also two people at the same spot in the text. The spots in the story where the pauses are taken, the roles that are selected, and the questions that are posed are decided upon during a thorough preparation and intensive examination of the text. In many cases the text suggests specific persons and questions. In any case it forbids certain questions, since the Bibliolog always moves within the framework of the black fire. Hence Jacob cannot be asked whether he will do what his mother said to him – since we read it thereafter in the text. He can however be questioned about his feelings and thoughts while doing it, since those questions are left open by the text. Should the participants leave the framework of the text anyway, then it is the facilitator's duty to guide things back to the text without criticising the statements – but rather by using techniques like marking them as spontaneous reaction or as a desire.

After several passages the facilitator brings things to a close, releases the congregation from the roles and guides back into the present. The various statements and hence also the various pathways to the Biblical text remain in coexistence and are not resolved into a unified message. This can seem like an unfamiliar thing in churchly settings, not least because habitual listening to mass ingrains the expectation of receiving something predetermined to carry away from the service; yet people often discover in the process that they have something thoroughly important for their lives and faith to bring out of this, something arising from their own perception and which need not be the same for all. Various fillings of the same role are expressed aloud in this way, guarding them against being posited in the absolute, since they mutually correct one another. Contradictions are not resolved but rather understood as ambivalences of the biblical roles. What is important is that all are permitted to express themselves, but that no one is obligated to do so; those who prefer to undertake their identification and debate quietly are invited to do it as they prefer as well.

3. Bibliolog and new homiletic tendencies

3.1 Bibliolog and reader-response criticism

In its implicit hermeneutic, the Bibliolog is closely related to the theoretical approach of reader-response criticism, which has grown in importance in recent years for homiletics in the German-speaking world. A brief review of reader-response criticism can hence aid with a better understanding of the hermeneutical presumptions and ramifications of the Bibliolog.[9]

The reader-reception approach[10] – developed within the framework of literary studies – levels its gaze on the happenings between the text and the recipient, and hence on the ongoing process of understanding. Instead of determining the meaning of a text in advance, one that is then communicated to others, the theory holds that the meaning of a text first emerges as part of the response process, that is, through active

---

9   More detail on Bibliolog and Homiletics, see *Uta Pohl-Patalong*, Bibliolog. Eine neue Predigtform in der homiletischen Diskussion, PTh 90/2001, 272–284, and *Eadem*, Predigt als Bibliolog. Homiletische Anstöße einer neuen Predigtform, in: *Eadem/ Frank Muchlinsky* (Eds.), Predigen im Plural. Homiletische Aspekte, Hamburg 2001, 258–268.

10 Cf. *Wolfgang Iser*, Der Akt des Lesens. Theorie ästhetischer Wirkung, München 1976; *Umberto Eco*, Lektor in Fabula. Die Mitarbeit der Interpretation in erzählenden Texten, München 1990.

contribution by the participants, who are responsible for the activity of interpretation. The texts not only foresee the role of the reader – known as the "implicit reader"[11] – they in fact require it to be understood. Hence the role of the reader can be filled culturally and individually in very different ways, depending on the preconceptions that the receiver brings into the process.[12] This approach strikes upon a problem that in homiletical terms has already been formulated by Ernst Lange, namely that there is no "sermon listener". An understanding of the sermon as "open art" by contrast supposedly "provides the listener him- or herself with the opportunity to bring his or her situation into the happenings of the sermon."[13] This makes the sermon plurivalent, with no unambiguous message that need only be relayed.

Reader-reception oriented homiletics initially drew upon arguments from communication theory to make clear that this individual reception process of the sermon is unavoidable – as "factual ambiguity". In the practical execution of sermons, this helps explain a phenomenon familiar to most preachers, namely that following the conclusion of services members of the community will offer thanks for some aspect of the sermon that the preacher is not at all certain was referenced at all. This is an expression of the multi-faceted "Auredite" of the sermon.[14] It is however also suggested that the "factual" be made into a sermon's "tactical ambiguity".[15] That means that the preacher purposefully stages a sermon's readiness and need for interpretation, indeed buttressing the need for interpretation through the very design of the sermon itself. The sermon should by this theory be so open-ended that the listeners can overlay their personal method of reading (or several variants of the same) onto the sermon.

This is precisely what Bibliolog does. It understands the Biblical texts as plurivalent and through its methodological approach opens them to the various comprehensions of the community members. Unlike the familiar settings for the sermon, the plurality of understanding

---

11   Cf. also *Iser*, Akt des Lesens, 50ff. The implied reader is not an emperical reader, but rather "embodies the totality of the preorientations that a fictional text offers its potential readers as conditions of reception" (60).
12   Cf. ibid., 65f.
13   *Gerhard Marcel Martin*, Predigt als 'offenes Kunstwerk'? Zum Dialog zwischen Homiletik und Rezeptionsästhetik, in: EvTh 44/1984, 46–58, 49.
14   The term "auredit" was coined in *Wilfried Engemann*, Semiotische Homiletik. Prämissen – Analysen – Konsequenzen, Tübingen/Basel 1993, 91, with the sense of "heard by the ears," as opposed to "manu-script" or "written with the hand".
15   "Investing in an ambiguous sermon [...] means taking seriously the recognition that the need and ability to interpret are not flaws in the message, but rather in a semiotic and theological sense the presumptions for their relevance" (ibid., 197).

can also be articulated. The individual "auredites" of a sermon, as they are known in reader-reception terminology, are continued onward by the Bibliolog into a multifaceted "oredict".[16] Through its methodology, this makes quite apparent to all – even in ambiguous sermons – that mistaking one's personal interpretation for being the only correct one is not possible. Through the articulation of the various 'oredict', an exchange and the rudiments of communication between the individual and plural approaches also becomes possible. This lends the individuals the chances to discover not only their own approach, but also the variety of others and thereby to expand, even change, their own perception. At the foundation of the Bibliolog, and frequently fascinating in its practice, is the resolution of hierarchies between those who are well versed in the biblical tradition and those who are not. The same is also true for the generations: every utterance has the same validity and contributes to an ever-richer understanding of the text. At the same time it is implicitly clear that the process of interpretation is not complete with the one Bibliolog, but rather generally cannot be brought to a conclusion at all. It makes reference beyond the group that is present and hence implicitly toward future generations. The Bibliolog is therefore also a bridge between the past, as manifested in the text, the present, and the future.

One essential presumption for the possibility of this kind of active reception process are "empty spaces" in the text, pointed out above all by Wolfgang Iser.[17] A text always says something, but never everything. Space is left open between that which is said, allowing the recipients to bear in their own experiences and fill them with elements from their own spheres of living. The empty spaces are the most important "switch-over element between text and reader" and allow for a creative relationship between one's own experiences and the external experiences of the text. It is precisely through this "dialectic of showing and silence"[18] that the communicative process between text and reader is put into motion. The empty places in the text are not simply completed with a previously existing filling, but rather they open up manifold possibilities for how they can be filled. "The author of the Biblical text has left room for the potential reader so that she can stage

---

16 Analogous with the "auredit", the "oredict" is 'spoken with the mouth.'
17 *Iser*, Akt des Lesens, 284ff. Similar argument in *Eco*, Lektor in Fabula, 63f.
18 "The thing that is kept silent forms the drive of the constitutional act, yet at the same time this stimulus for productivity is checked by that which is said, which for its part changes once that which it has pointed to is brought to occurance" (*Iser*, Akt des Lesens, 265f.). The keeping of silence in turn reminds of the quote from Yerushalmi, Shekalim 6.1: "The torah that was given to Moses is written in black fire onto white fire, sealed with fire, and cloaked in fire."

the roles intended for her as her own roles, and hence enter into the production of a new text. In cooperation with its reader, the Bible text begins to have more meaning than its author foresaw."[19]

This approach corresponds with the rabbinical talk of the "black fire" of the letters and the "white fire" of the gaps between the letters. Bibliolog lives from individuals filling in these gaps in the text for themselves and in the process expressing the content that is created. The talk in a Bibliolog is hence not just of the 'new text' of the preacher, but rather the individual comprehension of the "white fire". The subjectivity of the individual is also taken seriously through the methodology: the individual is explicitly asked for his own approaches and can articulate these as part of the happenings.[20] The encounter with the text is therefore less mediated than in the classical sermon setting. The technique of 'echoing' is used to signalise that each individual subjective utterance is esteemed and valued.

3.2 The limits of interpretation

With this comes the problem of an arbitrariness of reception, however, a problem that ranges across multiple levels: from a textual theory point of view, completely arbitrary interpretations of the text cannot be justified by the fact that they also include personal intentions and views of what is being said. From a scientific-theoretical standpoint, there is concern about a relapse into naive Bible approaches which ignore the achievements of historical-critical research. Hermeneutically, the texts would lose their character as critical counterparts that open up that which is new. Above all else, however – and this is also requested again and again during the Bibliolog – interpretations of the text shaped by personal history could so dominate the text that its own statements become completely distorted.

Umberto Eco devoted extensive consideration to this question. He referred to the 'limits of interpretation': The texts themselves restrict the arbitrary, indifferent range of interpretations by disciplining their

---

19 *Wilfried Engemann*, Der Spielraum der Predigt und der Ernst der Verkündigung, in: *Erich Garhammer/Heinz-Günther Schöttler* (Eds.), Predigt als offenes Kunstwerk. Homiletik und Rezeptionsästhetik, München 1998, 180–200, 189.

20 It is impressive – and sometimes even alarming – how many people find this aspect to be the central experience involved with getting acquainted with bibliological sermons. Heartfelt statements like "I've been attending mass for 50 years, and today was the first time that I was ever asked!" or "I was really allowed to express myself" are common both from dedicated churchgoers and from people who rarely attend services.

readers.[21] They do this primarily through "textual strategy"[22] which simulates to the readers the possibility of combining the elements of the text and organizing the repertoire of the text, and thereby moulding the processes of understanding.[23]

Eco sees the reception of a text as comprising the creation of a circle of comprehension, an interplay between text and reader: The text brings its own intentions with it, although they are not openly visible. The reader must speculate and presume an intention, something which in turn can only be done in the context of her experiences and her preconceptions – namely by filling in the blank spaces. Meaning is constituted through this experimentation. The text however begins working on its recipients at the same time as they for their part are being changed by their interaction with the text.[24] The provisional meaning is then checked against the text, since a partial text interpretation is only tenable if it is confirmed by other textual passages encountered as the reader moves forward – if it is contradicted by other portions of the text, then it must be corrected. The subjective and hence perpetually also arbitrary interpretations are hence disciplined through internal 'text coherence'.[25] Incorrect interpretations that overstep the 'limits of interpretation' can be recognised as such over the course of the reading. In this way the text remains a genuine counterpart and is not carried away by either the intentio auctoris, the intended statement of the author, or the intentio lectoris, the reader's interpretation. Through the interplay between text and interpreter, it is on the one hand the interpreter who completes the text, insofar as the text only

---

21 Cf. *Umberto Eco*, Die Grenzen der Interpretation, München 1995, 39. Similar idea also in *Iser*, Akt des Lesens, 63.
22 Cf. *Iser*, Akt des Lesens, 143ff., and *Eco*, Lektor in Fabula, 65.
23 The "idiolect" of the text, that is, the "stubbornness" based on the concrete textual strategy is to some extent the "bulwark" against the "uncontrolled nature of … the process" (*Idem*, Grenzen der Interpretation, 169).
24 "The interaction fails when the mutual projections of the partner experience no change and/or when the reader's projections are superimposed onto the text without resistance. Because the lack mobilises projective ideas, the text-reader relationship can also be changed solely through its changes. Hence the text constantly provokes a plethora of images from the reader, through which the reigning asymmetry in the totality of the situation begins to be overridden. The complexity of the text structure impedes the smooth occupancy of this situation through the reader's conceptions. Impeding means that the conceptions must be relinquished. Corrections to mobilised conceptions of this kind that are forced by the text form a referential horizon of the situation. This provides contour, allowing the reader to correct his own projections. Only in this way can he experience something that previously was not in his horizon" (*Iser*, Akt des Lesens, 263).
25 Here Eco is reaching back to Augustin, cf. *Aurelius Augustinus*, De doctrina Christiana III, in: CChrSL, XXXII, 1962, 10ff.

achieves its goal once it has been understood. Although comprehension can occur in the most varied of ways, the text remains itself during the process and provokes an understanding that is oriented toward itself – with the 'intentio operis', the intention of the text, taken seriously.

This circle of perception is made very clear through the Bibliolog: For each blank space, the participants experiment with meaning, and this process takes an effect on them as well, evoking new assumptions about meaning, although at the same time these are also methodically delimited through the textual strategy, through the fact that things always lead back to the text.[26] The text as "black fire" remains unchanged in its wording. Beyond these textual theory considerations, the subjective interpretation by the individual is also methodically relativised and corrected. Insofar as various interpretations are made aloud, it becomes clear that the personal one is one of several possible ones, and that it has its own validity alongside the other. An explicit part of the Bibliolog also involves making a critical reference to the interpretation of the last speaker. Experience also shows that – similar to what happens with Bibliodrama – texts develop a strong dynamic of their own that inhibits any subjective assimilation. Bibliologs typically include the naming of important theological insights from exegetic commentaries – albeit connected directly with their meaning for one's own belief and life. The text is fundamentally read and prized as it stands in 'black fire', and the text gets the last word, the one that envelops personal experience once again. At the same time it becomes clear that we never completely grasp and construe the text, but rather that it is always larger than our interpretations.

3.3 Staging of the Biblical texts

This insight fits with the tendency of contemporary homiletics to grasp the sermon "not as an interpretation of the text ..., but rather as a staging of a text".[27] In critiquing North American approaches to preaching, Martin Nicol more than anyone else profiled the model of "preaching as an event": "The sermon does not inform about events of

---

[26] If at a particular empty space things are expressed that are contrary to the continuation of the text, then the director uses this productively, such as through a formulation like: "Whatever your initial feelings about this were, now you have decided ... What moved you to this?" The director is – not unlike in the Bibliodrama – a lawyer for the text.

[27] *Henning Luther*, Predigt als inszenierter Text. Überlegungen zur Kunst der Predigt, in: ThPr 18/1983, 89–100, 97.

faith, but rather is itself an event in which God through His Word draws humans into his healing reality."[28]

Instead of preaching 'about' a Biblical text, this involves "preaching from within the text", or more simply and concisely, "preaching in the text". Thus a sermon should not talk about consolation, but rather should itself console. The event of the sermon is the ostensible interpretive process, as opposed to the sermon only conveying the result of an already transpired process of interpretation.[29]

The Bibliolog, it would seem to me, is related to this approach, insofar as it places the biblical text in the centre and stages its interpretation as a joint interpretation by the congregation. As a rule, a great variety of things happen for the participants during the Bibliolog. This can be taken up again in the follow-up to the Bibliolog as an explicit updating of the text, although this is not obligatory; things can also remain at the level of the individual discoveries of the subjects, what they will take for their lives from the encounter with the text. From a theological standpoint, this can be connected with the conviction that the revelation is never concluded, but rather is a constantly occurring and continuing process. The joint interpretation of the text that occurs here can lend a sense of clarity and gravitas to this permanent process of revelation. In the Jewish tradition there are two corresponding Holidays related to the Torah: Shavuot is more strongly concentrated on the giving of the Torah on Mount Sinai, while Simḥat Torah recalls the existence of the Torah and the responsible interaction with it, including in the ever progressing interpretation.

3.4 The role of the "office"

That the role of the preacher changes with a Bibliolog should be clear at this point. The Bibliolog can be understood as the methodological implementation of the "Priesthood of all Believers". In reform terms, the task of annunciation is delegated to the officer holder out of purely functional concerns. It may potentially also be that this functional determination of the annunciation duty is consistent with today's societal conditions, insofar as the person aids, structures, moderates,

---

28   *Martin Nicol*, Preaching from within. Homiletische Positionslichter aus Nordamerika, in: PTh 86/1997, 295–309, 300. Cf. also *Idem*, Einander ins Bild setzen. Dramaturgische Homiletik, Göttingen ²2005, and *Alexander Deeg/Idem*, Im Wechselschritt zur Kanzel. Praxisbuch Dramaturgische Homiletik, Göttingen 2005.
29   Cf. *Nicol*, Preaching from within, 307.

and provides space for the congregation's interpretation, instead of executing it alone.

At this point, these reflections encounter Jewish traditions and convictions which relate the religious office more strongly to teaching and judgement, and which allow for a more important role for the congregation than long was case in Christianity, at least in a de facto sense.

The Bibliolog points Christianity and the Church toward certain lines of questioning that have always been entrusted to it for reflection, not least its understanding of truth. Above all else in the end it points out to Christianity and the Church its Jewish roots and traditions of a plurality-ready interaction with the Bible which Christianity has repressed over the course of centuries.

Because of all of these factors, the astoundingly rapid approval for the Bibliolog and its dissemination in Christian spheres of the German-speaking world is a joyous event in many regards. The problem has arisen however that the Bibliolog in the Jewish realm is perceived as something Christian, which has made its reception in Jewish communities problematic. Here it would be better if the Christian side would point even more clearly toward its Jewish roots. Should it succeed in helping the Bibliolog establish a stronger foothold in the Jewish sphere, then it could offer a chance to bring Jewish and Christian interpretations into conversation with one another on the methodological basis of the Bibliolog.

Index of Biblical Texts

Gen. 1	115[9],118[20],207	Judg. 13.2–14.19	38
3.9	115[9]		
4.26	32[8]	1Sam. 3.12	164[14]
6.18	164	28.3–25	44
9.9–11	164		
9.17	164	2Sam. 7.25	164[14]
17.7–19	164		
17.21	164	1Kings 1.14	164,175[1]
18.7	13	2.4	164[14]
22.1	115[9],217	2.27	164,175[1]
23	218	6.12	164[14]
25.22	1	8.15	164
25.29–34	1	8.20	164[14]
27.1–40	1,224f.	8.24	164,175[1]
27.41–28.9	1		
33.10	1	Isa. 1.15	92[3]
33.12	3	7.14	156
33.14	3	11.2	39
		44.26	164[14]
Ex. 3	206	58.1	87
6.4	164	58.2	59
12	52[11]	61.1f.	61[54]
14.15–15.1	174[37]		
19.3	106	Jer. 11.5	164[14]
20.2	208	23.29	207
33.18–23	218	23.30	164[14]
		28.6	164[14]
		29.10	164[14]
Lev. 19.1	24	31.3	105,169
19.18	116[15]		
26.9	164	Ez. 33.30–32	58f.
		34	59
Num. 4.21–7.89	38		
		Jon. 1.8	44
Deut. 4.4	77	1.11	44
6.5	116[12]	1.12	44
6.18	24[4]	3.4b	30
8.19	165		
9.5	164	Eccles. 7.8	14
30.1	86		
30.14	80	Dan. 9.12	164[14]
33.2	222		
33.4	24[5]	Neh. 9	32
		9.8	164[14]

2Chr. 6.4	164[13]	3.11–4.4	40
6.15	164[13]	4.1	61[53]
36.21	164[13],175[1]	5.12	40,61[53]
		5.42	61[53]
2Macc. 15.9	38[17]	9.20	28[3],61[49]
		11.26	157
4Macc. 18.15	38[17]	13.5	12
Mat. 1.13	156[2]	13.5,15–41	28[3]
1.15	156[2]	13.14–44	61[49],62
1.17f.	156[2]	13.15	27
1.20–25	156	13.32f.	155[1]
1.22	156[2]	14.1–3	28[3]
4.13–23	219	14.12	33
4.14–16	156[2]	16.13f.	28[3],61[49]
5	166	17.2	61[49]
5.17	212	17.10–12,17	28[3]
5.17–21	166f.	17.18	34
5.21–48	166,168	17.32	34
8.11	171	18.4,19	28[3]
8.17	156[2]	18.24	34,34[10]
12.17–21	156[2]	18.24f.	41
13.14	156[2]	18.28	34[10]
13.35	156[2]	19.1–4	34[10]
21.4f.	156[2]	19.8	28[3],61[49]
27.9f.	156[2]	20.11	31
26.54	156[2]	21.26	61[53]
26.56	156[2]	22.1–21	33
Mark 1.21	61[49]	Rom. 1.16	170
7.1–23	169	1.17f.	171
10.17–21	42	1.18–4.25	27
		3.1–3	170
Luke 4.20f.	12	5–8	27
4.16–21	27,61f.,61[49]	8.17	171[32]
4.16–24	171	9.4f.	170
6.6	61[49]	9.10–13	1
11.32	30	9–11	27,33,170
13.10	61[49]	11.2	170[31]
22.20	158	11.17	171[32]
24.14–29	43	11.26	170[31]
24.17	158	11.29	170,171
24.44	158	12.1	34
		16,25f.	158
John 5.39	158	10.4	168[24]
6.59	61[49]		
12.20–22	33	1Cor. 1.17	31
14.6	126[31]	1.20	31
18.10	61[49]	2.1–5	33
		2.4f.	31
Acts 2.14	31	3.5f.	212
2.14–36	33	10.12	158
2.46	61[53]	11.25	158
3.1	61[53]		

2Cor. 1.18–20	163	1Thess. 5.27	27
6	33		
10.10	34	1Peter 1.10	158
14.16	158		
Eph. 3.5	171[32]	Rev. 2.9	41[19]
Col. 4.16	27		

Index of Rabbinic Texts

m. Av 5.22	207	b. San 34a	207
t. Suk 4.6	37	b. Yom 86b	81
y. Hag 2.1 (87b)	13	BemR Naso 13.15	208
y. Naz 7.2	12	Mekh Pisḥa 14	13
y. Shab 14.4 (14d)	13	Mekh Pisḥa 16	13
y. Sheq 6.1	222	PesK 12.25	208f.
b. AZ 19.1	178[3]	RutR 5.12	13
b. Ber 34b	81	ShemR 2.2	206[8]
b. BM 86b	13	Tan Bereshit 1	207

Index of Names

Aboab, Isaac	77,82,85[27]	Askani, Christoph	120[22]
Abravanel	79,80[16],85f.	Augustine	26,42,53,118[20]
Aelius Aristides	26	Averroes	76
Agobard of Lyon	50[4],75		
Alami, Solomon	87	Bach, Johann Sebastian	108
Aland, Barbara	166[18]	Baeck, Leo	110[34],136–154
Alexander (the Great)	36	Baeck, Natalie	139
Alexander (of Aphrodisias)	76	Baeck, Ruth	139
Alexander, Philip	15[17]	Baker, Leonard	138[5],139[6,7],140[8],
Altmann, Alexander	93,113[1,2],183[3],184[6]		142[17],143[22,23],145
Ambrosius	53	Bamberger, Fritz	140f.,143
Amsler, Samuel	165[15]	Barkhuizen, Jan H.	63[59]
Anatoli, Jacob	80	Barth, Karl	131,171[32],173
Anckaerts, Luc	118[18]	Bartina, Avilés	53[16]
Apollos of Alexandria	33	Basilius of Seleucia	42
Aquinas, Thomas	78,159	Bataillon, Louis	78
Arama, Isaac	75–86	Batnizky, Leora	118[18]
Aristarchus	36	Baumann, Max Peter	170[30]
Aristobulus	36	Beer, Isaac	103
Aristotle	76–78,82,180,209,212	Bellah, Robert	189[17]
Aschheim, Steven E.	132	Berger, Klaus	50[6],62[58]

Bériou, Nicole	74[3],79[15]	Dio Chrysostom	26,28
Bernardi, Jean	51[10]	Dohmen, Christoph	161[9]
Bernhard, Caspar	120[22]	Döllinger, Johann Joseph	161[10]
Bettan, Israel	184[6],185[9],187[14],196	Donaldson, James	52[11]
Billerbeck, Paul	56[29]	Doppelt, Frederic A.	186[11]
Birkenstein, Elias	92,93[5]	Dreyfus, A. Stanley	140
Blaise, Albert	26[2],32	Dreyfus, Marianne	140
Blass, Friedrich	167[22]	Dumont, Louise	139
Bloedhorn, Hanswulf	35[13],37[15],51[8], 55[26,28],62[52]	Dunhill, Lisa E.	199[33,34],201[37]
Blumenkranz, Bernard	54[20],65[66,71]	Ebach, Jürgen	216[28]
Blustain, Sarah	190[20]	Eckstein, A.	96[13]
Böhl, Felix	16	Eco, Umberto	226[10],228[17],229f.
Bohren, Rudolf	3,172,204	Egers, Sabel	96
Boyarin, Daniel	1[2]	Ehninger, Douglas	196[31]
Brändle, Rudolf	66[72],68[87,88,90]	Ehrenberg, Samuel Meyer	91f.
Braude, William G.	186[11]	Ehrlich, Ernst Ludwig	VIII
Brenner, Michael	132	Ehrlich, Kenneth E.	195[27],196[29]
Breuer, Solomon	113[4]	Einhorn, David	105,183[4],184[8]
Brichto, Herbert C.	186[11]	Eisen, Arnold M.	189[17]
Bruckstein, Almut Sh.	121[26]	Elbogen, Ismar	56[29],206[7]
Brueggemann, Walter	213f.	Eliav, Mordechai	91[1],102[21]
Buber, Martin	3,126[32],132,171,190[20]	Engemann, Wilfried	2[3],227[14],229[19]
Bucer, Martin	97	Englert, Rudolf	222[2]
Budde, Gerda	113[5]	Epictetus	26
Bulhof, Inge	4	Eppstein, Victor	183[5],186[11]
Bultmann, Rudolf	155[1]	Eschelbacher, Max	143f.
		Essrig, Harry	187[15],193f.
Caligula, Gaius	36	Euclid	36
Callimachus	36	Eunapius	42
Cameron, Averil	49[3]	Eusebius	35,57
Carlebach, Shlomo	190[20]		
Clement of Alexandria	31,42,44,52[11],64[62]	Fabry, Heinz-Josef	164[13]
Cohen, Abraham	184	Fackenheim, Emil	114[6]
Cohen, Jack J.	187	Falk, Johannes Daniel	97
Cohen, Jeremy	75[4]	Feldman, Abraham J.	184[6]
Cohen, Norman J.	194[26],196,211	Feldman, Louis	38
Cohen, Richard A.	114[6],126[32]	Feuer, Leon I.	186[11]
Cohen, Shaye J.D.	10,55[25,27],57[33]	Fine, Steven	65[65],71[1]
Cohen, Steven M.	189[17]	Fitzmyer, Joseph A.	56[30],61[51,52,53],62[55,57]
Coxe, Cleveland A.	52[11]	Flavius, Josephus	31,33,43,48,57[33]
Creizenach, Michael	104f.	Fleischer, Ezra	47
Crescas, Hasdai	78,81[19]	Fonrobert, Elisheva Charlotte	65[66],68[87]
Crocker, Lionel	196[31]	Fosdick, Harry Emerson	183,196[31]
		Foster, Charles R.	199[33,34],201[37]
Dagron, Gilbert	49[3]	Fraenkel, Yonah	23
Debrunner, Albert	167[22]	Fränkel, David	94[8]
Deeg, Alexander	72,94[9],203f.,232[28]	Frankemölle, Hubert	157[3]
Delcorno, Carlo	77[9],80[17],88[34]	Freehof, Solomon B.	184[6,7],185, 187[14,16],196
Denecke, Axel	3		
Deogratias	53	Friedenberg, Robert V.	184[6],195[27],196[30]
Déroche, Vinvent	49[3]	Friedlander, Albert H.	141

Index of Names 239

Friedrich, Johannes	VIII	Hüttenmeister, Gil	$35^{13}, 37^{15}, 51^8,$
Funkenstein, Amos	126^{32}		$55^{26,28}, 62^{52}$
Galliner, Helmuth H.	140	Ibn Esra, Moses	107
Geiger, Abraham	104	Ibn Gabirol, Solomo	107
Gerhardt, Paul	100	Ibn Musa, Hayim	76
Gersonides	79	Ibn Shem Tov, Joseph	$76^6, 80$
Gittelsohn, Roland B.	$184^6, 186^{11}$	Ibn Shem Tov, Shem Tov	81f., 84–87
Glueck, Nelson	143	Ibn Shu'eib, Joel	77
Goethe, Johann Wolfgang von	99	Idel, Moshe	209^{12}
Goldberg, Alexander	15–18	Ignatius of Antioch	31
Goldman, Edward A.	195^{27}	Iser, Wolfgang	$226^{10}, 227^{11}, 228, 230^{21,22,24}$
Golemon, Lawrence	$199^{33,34}, 201^{37}$	Italiener, Bruno	142
Gordon, Julius	$183^5, 186^{11}$		
Gorin, Paul	186^{11}	Jacobson, Israel	92, 94–96, 103
Gregory I	27	Jansen, Joost	118^{17}
Gregory Nazianzen	42	Jegher-Bucher, Verena	68^{87}
Grissom, E.A.	68^{87}	Jellinek, Adolf	106f.
Grodecki, Louis	160^8	Jelski, Julius	109^{32}
Gross, Abraham	$83, 84^{25}$	Jerome	57–60
Günsburg, Carl Siegfried	104	Joel, Manuel	151
		John Chrysostom	27, 31, 42, 44, 53, 59,
Hadrian	41^{19}		64, 66, 68f., 71
Halevi, Jehuda	$107, 131^1, 133$	Josuttis, Manfred	218
Hallo, Rudolph	129	Jungkunz, Claus	155^1
Händel, Georg Friedrich	108	Justin Martyr	$43, 52^{11}, 166^{18}$
Handelman, Susan A.	211	Justinian	$49^3, 70$
Harnack, Adolf v.	$148, 166^{16}$		
Hegel, Georg Wilhelm Friedrich	183	Kaelter, Wolli	143
Heimgartner, Martin	$66^{72}, 68^{88,90}$	Kahn, Robert I.	$183^5, 184^6, 186^{11}$
Heinemann, Joseph	$8, 9^{5,6}, 10, 56^{32}, 90^1, 205$	Kalb, Friedrich	135^9
Herder, Johann Gottfried	183	Kant, Immanuel	99, 183
Herophilus	36	Kaplan, Harry	186^{11}
Herrmann, Klaus	202^2	Karo, Isaac	82f., 85
Hertz, Joseph H.	184^6	Kasper, Walter Cardinal	VII
Herxheimer, Salomon	100f., 105	Katz, Robert L.	183^5
Herz, Henriette	103	Katz, Steven T.	$54^{23}, 187^{14}, 196$
Hill, Robert C.	53^{14}	Kedar-Kopfstein, Benjamin	57^{34}
Hirsch, Isaac	101^{20}	Kellermann, Henry	140
Hirshman, Marc	$22^1, 53^{14}, 58^{37}$	Kinzing, Wolfram	57^{34}
Hochfeld, Samson	139	Kirsch, Anne	159^7
Hoffmann, Daniel	118^{17}	Klemperer, Victor	109
Hoffmann, Lawrence A.	189^{18}	Klemperer, Wilhelm	109
Hofmann, Johann Chr.K. v.	155^1	Kley, Eduard	93, 103f., 210f.
Hofmann, Norbert	VIII	Knauer, Peter	173^{35}
Holdheim, Samuel	98f.	Knobel, Peter S.	192^{23}
Holtzman, Linda	$195^{27}, 200$	Krauss, Samuel	58f.
Homer	28	Kushner, Harold	214, 217
Horbury, William	$54^{22}, 55^{24,25}, 58^{37}, 69^{95}$		
Hörisch, Jochen	212f.	Lacerenza, Giancarlo	69^{93}
Hübner, Hans	173^{35}	Landsberger, Julius	95^{11}
Hunt, E.D.	49^1	Lange, Ernst	227

Lehmann, Matthias B. 118[21]
Lenhard, Doris 16–18,205[5]
Levenson, Alan T. 190[19]
Levi, Gerson B. 186[11]
Lévinas, Emmanuel 114[6]
Levine, Lee I. 10–12,35[12],55[25,27,28],71[1]
Levinson, Nathan Peter 142
Lewandowski, Louis 96,107f.
Lewinski, Peter 142
Libanius 42
Liebeschütz, Hans 137
Linder, Amnon 70[96]
Linn, Edmund Holt 196[31]
Lischer, Richard 196[31],202
Lohfink, Norbert 174[37]
Long, Thomas G. 189[18],202
Lookstein, Joseph 195[27]
Löwenstein, I. 97[14]
Luis, Pio de 65[67]
Lundblad, Barbara 196[31],202
Luther, Henning 231[27]
Luther, Martin 31[8],213,215
Luz, Ulrich 156[2]

MacMullen, Ramsay 53[14]
Madsen, Richard 189[17]
Maier, Joseph von 97f.
Maimonides 79,82,97,107
Malê, Émil 160[8]
Malingrey, Anne-Marie 68[87]
Mann, Jacob 20f.
Mannebach, Wayne C. 196[31]
Marcion 166f.
Mark, Julius 183[5]
Markschies, Christoph 52[11],53[14],57[34],58[36]
Martin, Gerhard Marcel 227[13]
Maybaum, Siegmund 8,19,108,132, 140,184[6]
Mayer, Wendy 53[14],68[87]
Mayser, Edwin 167[22]
Mazza, Joseph M. 196[31]
McKay, Heather A. 55[26]
Mecklenburg, Frank 140[11]
Melito of Sardis 26,41,52[11]
Mendelssohn, Moses 107
Meyer, Michael A. 94[8],113[2]
Mihaly, Eugene 182,184[6],196,201
Monshouwer, Dirk 206[7]
Morgenstern, Julian 187[16]
Morteira, Saul Levi 73
Müller, Hans Martin 52[11]
Mußner, Franz 167f.,170[31]

Nachmanides 24
Nardi, Carlo 65[68]
Narot, Joseph R. 184[6]
Neusner, Jacob 14,16[22],19[27],49
Newmann, Hillel I. 58[36]
Nicol, Martin 231f.
Nicolaus of Damascus 33
Nietzsche, Friedrich Wilhelm 108
Nobel, Nehemia Anton 127–130, 134f.,186[12]
Norden, Eduard 30

Olivar, Alexander 50[5],51[9,10],53[18]
Olmer, Heinrich VII
Orent, Joel 186[12]
Origen 27,31,44,53,57

Palmer, Gesine 118[21]
Parkes, James William 54[19]
Patrick, Dale 196[31]
Perilman, Nathan A. 186[11]
Philippson, Ludwig 151
Philo 35f.,38,41,43,45–47
Pilchik, Ely E. 184[6]
Pineas, Hermann O. 139
Pitzele, Peter 223f.
Plato 76,141
Plaut, W. Gunther 142
Plessner, Salomon 102f.
Pomerance, Aubrey 110[34]
Porton, Gary 12f.
Pradels, Wendy 66[72],68[88,90]
Prager, Joseph 127
Pratscher, Wilhelm 52[11]
Preuß, Horst Dietrich 158f.
Prinz, Joachim 140
Proclus 63f.
Ps.-Philo 26,30[6],45
Ps.-Plutarch 42f.
Ps.-Hippolytus 41
Ptolemaeus 36,76

Ravitzky, Aviezer 78
Regev, Shaul 80
Reichert, Eckhard 65[67]
Reichmann, Eva G. 138f.,141[13,14,15]
Reif, Stefan C. 55[28],56[29]
Riemer, Jack 186[12]
Ritter, Adolf Martin 68[87]
Roberts, Alexander 52[11]
Roof, Wade Clark 189[17]
Rosenfeld, Samson Wolf 96

Index of Names

Rosenthal, Karl — 110,112,186[11]
Rosenzweig, Franz — 3,113–130,131–135, 140,178
Rousseau, Philipp — 53[14]
Rouwhorst, Gerard — 1[1],52[11],55[25]
Rudin, Jacob P. — 184[6]
Rühle, Inken — 116[14]
Ruppert, Godehard — VII
Rutgers, Leonard V. — 70

Saadja Gaon — 107
Saba, Abraham — 83,84[25]
Sachot, Maurice — 50[6],51[10],56[29],57[33]
Salomon, Gotthold — 99,102
Salzberger, Georg — 150
Samely, Alexander — 18
Samuelson, Norbert M. — 117[16],122[27]
Sánchez, Manuel Ambrosio Sánchez — 80[17]
Saperstein, Harold — 196[30]
Saperstein, Marc — 196[30]
Sarason, Richard S. — 9,16
Sarna, Jonathan D. — 187[13]
Schaalman, Herman — 139
Schachtel, Hyman J. — 184[6]
Schachter-Shalomi, Zalaman — 190[20]
Schäfer, Peter — 208[11]
Schechter, Daniel S. — 192[23]
Schick, Ludwig — VII
Schilson, Arno — 169[28]
Schleiermacher, Friedrich D.E. — 93,118, 135,212
Scholem, Gershom — 190[20]
Schorsch, Ismar — 210[14]
Schrage, Wolfgang — 56[29]
Schramm, Tim — 223[7]
Schreckenberg, Heinz — 54[19],57[34],58
Schulz, Frieder — 2[3]
Schuster, Josef — VII
Schwartz, Moshe — 118[17]
Schwartz, Seth — 10,55[26,27,28],56[30]
Schwartz, Yossef — 118[21]
Scult, Allan — 196[31]
Severian of Gabala — 42
Shain, Samson A. — 186[11]
Shankman, Jakob K. — 186[11]
Sharf, Andrew — 49[3]
Shinan, Avigdor — 55[27],56[32]
Siegert, Folker — 50[6],51[7],55[24],56[31]
Signer, Michael A. — 155[1]
Silver, Daniel Jeremy — 183[3],187[16]
Silver, Hillel — 185
Simon, Ernst — 127[35]

Simon, Hermann Veit — 136,186[12]
Simon, Marcel — 54[19],68[87]
Simons, Rudolf — 139
Socrates — 146
Soloveitchik, Joseph Dov — 114[6]
Spielberg, Steven — 112
Spinoza, Baruch — 179
Stegner, William-Richard — 56[32]
Steimer, Bruno — 65[79,70]
Stemberger, Günter — VIII,55[24],56[32],57[34], 58f.,72,161[9],205,205[3,4],207[9]
Stern, David — 211
Stern, Menachem — 42[21]
Stöcker, Adolf — 96
Stowers, Stanley K. — 33
Strack, Hermann L. — 56[29]
Strimling, Arthur — 217f.
Sullivan, William M. — 189[17]
Sulzer, Salomon — 96
Swidler, Ann — 189[17]

Teitelbaum, Samuel — 186[11]
Tertullian — 43,166[18],167[21]
Themistius — 76
Theocritus — 36
Theophilus of Antioch — 31
Thomas, Alois — 159[7],160[8]
Thümmel, Hans G. — 52[12]
Thurneysen, Eduard — 131
Thyen, Hartwig — 56[31]
Tipton, Steven M. — 189[17]
Tönnies, Ferdinand — 188
Treitschke, Heinrich von — 95
Turner, Joseph — 115[10],116[11],125[26]

Ucko, Sinai — 132

Valentinus — 31,52[11]
Valerio, Karolina de — 156[1]
Varnhagen, Rahel — 103
Veltri, Giuseppe — 70[96]
Visotzky, Burton — 19,195[27],198
Voderholzer, Rudolf — 159[7]
Volkmann, Evelina — 2[3]
Volkov, Shulamit — 210[13]

Wang Tolentino, Barbara — 199[33,34],201[37]
Wardlaw, Don — 219f.
Warschauer, Heinz — 142
Wasserman, Sue Ann — 191[21]
Weiss, Iris — 221[1]
Weisse, Samson — 140

Wenig, Margaret M. $195^{27},196^{31},197,201^{36}$
Werden, Johannes von 85^{28}
Wertheimer, Jack $187^{13},189^{18},190^{20}$
Wick, Peter $55^{28},61^{50}$
Wiener, Theodore 136^{1}
Wilken, Robert Louis $66^{75},68^{87},69^{92,93,95},70^{96}$
Winters, Alton Meyer $184^{6},210^{13}$
Wise, Stephen S. 185

Wuthnow, Robert 189^{17}

Xenophon 31

Zink, Michel 159^{7}
Zink, W.S. $97^{14},159^{7}$
Zunz, Leopold 7–9,56,91–93, 95,109,113^{1},114,182f.

Index of Subjects

Aesthetic(s)/aesthetical 71,86,90,108,114, 118–121,131,182,183^{4},189f.,208
Aggadah/aggadic ⇨ see Haggadah/haggadic
Alexandria 34–37,47
Aramaic 8,33,46,72
Authority 83,114,124f.,130,178f., 187^{15},188,207,214,222

Baby-boomers 188f.,193
Bar Mitzvah 92f.,102f.,108f.,192
Bat Mitzvah 106,191
Bibliodrama 223
Buddhism 146,190^{20}

Catechism 95
Catholic 101,109,158,172
Christian-Jewish Dialogue
⇨ see Jewish-Christian Dialogue
Church Fathers 31,42,58,156
Civil Rights Movement 184,188
Clergy 189f.,199
Communication theory 227
Community/Gemeinschaft 12,28,51,92, 97,100f.,119,117,128–130,134,154, 168f.,188,194
Conservative 104,185,193–195,200

Derashah 7–21,25,29,72,122,128,197, 205f.,209,216
Diaspora 9,25,34f.,45,47,55,72
Dogma/Dogmatics 2,54,131,146^{29},147, 158,177f.,213

Ecclesia 171^{32},173
Ecumenism 172

Edification 20,92,182
Enlightenment 92,94f.,97–100,103,131
Eretz Israel 22,55
Eternity 80,118–121,125–127
Ethic(s)/ethical 40,76,87,149f.,153f.,209f.
Exegesis/exegetical/exegete 2,13,18f., 42–44,52,52^{11},54,57,62,81,86, 128^{37},168,208,216,222,231
Expulsion (Spain) 76,79,82

French Revolution 94

Germany 113,131,133,139,182, 183^{4},202f.,205
Gnosticism 31
Gospel 29,156,162,166–168,170f.
Greek 19,61f.,146

Haftarah 15,20,28,36,60,61^{54},86
Haggadah/haggadic 7f.,23,82,207f.
Hagiographa 14,21,25,74
Halakhah 23f.
Ḥatimah 15–21
Hellenism 146
Heresy/heretical 10,59,79,83,85^{27}
Hermeneutic(s)/hermeneutical 38,44f., 76,125,128^{37},133f.,157–165, 175–181,204–220,226

Implicit reader 227
Intertextual 72,90^{1},207f.,211
Islam 118,118^{21}

Jewish-Christian Dialogue VIIf.,1f., 176–181
Jewish Renaissance 132

Index of Subjects

Liberal 107,113f.,125,127,133,140
Liturgy/liturgical 4,7f.,10f.,15,19,30, 45,121f.,134f.,169[28]

Midrash/midrashic 7–9,12f.,15f.,18–20, 56,90[1],114[6],139,144,154,178f., 193,205,209,211,215,222f.
Music 94,96,107f.,114,117,121, 189,191–193
Mysticism/mystic 128,149,159,179, 188,210

Nosé 74f.
Nostra aetate 5,171

Orthodox 93,96,101,109,113,125, 185,190[19],193,200

Panegyric 26,30f.,37,40–42,46,50
Passover 67,78,110,122,128,210f.
Pericope 16,27,41,44
Petiḥah 14–21,56,74,90[1],144,205f.,216
Pietism 98
Piyyutim 14[16],47,56
Prophets 25,60,62,76,81,86[30],128, 144f.,153,160[8],166[18],185[9]
Protestantism/protestant 3,93–101,114, 122,134f.,172,182f.,189,202f.

Rabbinical Assemblies 96,98
Reform Jews 101,183,191
Reform movement 7,92,95f.,98,107f.,132
Repentance 39,73,79–88
Rhetoric/rhetorical 3,8,15f.,20f.,25–44,72, 89f.,128,138f.,153f.,183,196,199

Scholastic/Scholasticism 74f.,78f.,81[19], 83,86[30],89

Second Temple 46,56[28],179
Sephardic 75,79
Septuagint 25,36,38,70,156,162,164
Sermon on the Mount 30,166
Shabbat 12–14,35,38,54,60,67,78f., 113f.,120,122,206
Shema Yisrael 106
Shoa 110,112,155[1]
Siddur 97,169
Sitz im Leben 15,26,35,37,40,46, 50f.,70[98],114
Sunday 52[11],91,120,122,185,185[10],213
Synagogues 9–14,22,28f.,33–36,45, 50,55f.,61–70,87,94–98,104, 106–108,173f.,186–188

Talmud 92,105–107,132,198
Targum 15,47,56f.
Theatre 29,32,42,59,65,139,185[10]
Torah 14f.,21,25,47,60,76,79f.,92,106, 120,133,146,151,166–168,178, 182,205–210,222f.,232

USA 211,223[5]

Vatican II 5,158,171,216

Woman/Women 67,81,87,103–108
World War 131,133,140,184f.
Worship 26,34–36,107,114,125, 130,135,149,183[4],189, 191–193,200f.

Yelamdenu 16[20],17f.,89
Yom Kippur 38f.,47,86,122

List of Contributors

Amir, Yehoyada, Prof. Dr.

Associate Professor for Jewish Thought and the Director of *The Israel Rabbinic Program*, Hebrew Union College, Jerusalem, Israel. Author of: *"Da'at Ma'amina – Iyyunim be'Mishnato shel Franz Rosenzweig"* (Cognition out of Faith – The Philosophy of Franz Rosenzweig), published 2004 in Tel Aviv and the editor of various books in Modern Jewish Philosophy.

Deeg, Alexander, Dr.

Assistant at the Chair of Practical Theology, Friedrich-Alexander-University Erlangen-Nürnberg, Germany, protestant pastor and vice-president of BCJ.Bayern (Begegnung von Christen und Juden; www.bcj.de). Author of "Predigt und Derascha. Homiletische Textlektüre im Dialog mit dem Judentum", published in Göttingen 2006.

Herrmann, Klaus, Dr.

Senior Lecturer for Judaic Studies, Berlin, Germany. Primary areas of interest are the study of the Hekhalot-Literature and German Judaism in the 19th century.

Homolka, Walter, Rabbi Prof. Dr.

Rector of the Abraham Geiger College at Potsdam University (Germany) and Adjunct Full Professor in the Department of Philosophy, there. Chairman of the Leo Baeck Foundation and Member of the Executive Board of the World Union for Progressive Judaism. Author of (among others) "Leo Baeck. Jüdisches Denken. Perspektiven für heute," Freiburg 2006, and "Jewish Identity in Modern Times. Leo Baeck and German Protestantism," Oxford 1995.

Kosman, Admiel, Prof. Dr.

Professor of Rabbinics and Academic Director of the Abraham Geiger-College at Potsdam University, Potsdam/Berlin, Germany. Several publications on Midrash and Midrashic Hermeneutics.

Nicol, Martin, Prof. Dr.

Professor of Practical Theology, Friedrich-Alexander-University Erlangen-Nürnberg, Germany, homiletical education for pastors (www.atelier-sprache.de). Books on homiletics: "Einander ins Bild setzen. Dramaturgische Homiletik", Göttingen ²2005; M.N./Alexander Deeg, "Im Wechselschritt zur Kanzel. Praxisbuch Dramaturgische Homiletik", Göttingen 2005.

Pohl-Patalong, Uta, Prof. Dr.

Professor of Practical Theology at Christian-Albrechts-University Kiel, Germany, offers courses in "Bibliolog" (see: "Bibliolog. Gemeinsam die Bibel entdecken – im Gottesdienst – in der Gemeinde – in der Schule", Stuttgart ²2007).

Saperstein, Marc, Prof. Dr.

Principal of the Leo Baeck College, London, United Kingdom, author of "Jewish Preaching 1200–1800" (1989), "'Your Voice Like a Ram's Horn'. Themes and Texts in Traditional Jewish Preaching" (1996), "Exile in Amsterdam: Saul Levi Morteira's Sermons to a Congregation of 'New Jews'" (2005), "Jewish Preaching in Times of War, 1800–2001" (2007).

Sarason, Richard S., Prof. Dr.

Professor of Rabbinic Literature and Thought, Hebrew Union College-Jewish Institute of Religion, Cincinnati, Ohio, USA. Associate Editor of the Hebrew Union College Annual. Author of (among others) "A History of the Mishnaic Law of Agriculture. A Study of Tractate Demai", Leiden 1979, ²2005; "The Talmud of the Land of Israel. A Preliminary Translation and Explanation. Demai", Chicago 1993; "Midrash in Liturgy", in: Jacob Neusner/Alan J. Avery-Peck (Eds.), Encyclopaedia of Midrash: Biblical Interpretation in Formative Judaism, Leiden 2005.

Schöttler, Heinz-Günther, Prof. Dr.

Professor of Pastoral Theology and Kerygmatics, Regensburg and Bamberg, Germany, member of the "Gesprächskreis Christen und Juden" at the "Zentralkomitee der deutschen Katholiken", and "Ephraim-Veitel-Lecturer" for homiletics at Abraham Geiger College (Potsdam). Author of (among others) "Christliche Predigt und Altes Testament. Versuch einer homiletischen Kriteriologie", Ostfildern 2001; "Der Leser begreife!" Vom Umgang mit der Fiktionalität biblischer Texte, Münster 2006.

Siegert, Folker, Prof. Dr.

Professor of New Testament and Jewish Studies, Director of the Institutum Judaicum Delitzschianum, Münster University, Germany. Further Publications: „Argumentation bei Paulus, gezeigt an Röm 9–11", Tübingen 1980; „Zwischen Hebräischer Bibel und Altem Testament. Eine Einführung in die Septuaginta", 2 vol., Münster 2001–2002; „Das Evangelium des Johannes in seiner ursprünglichen Gestalt. Wiederherstellung und Kommentar", Göttingen 2007.

Stemberger, Günter, Prof. Dr.

Professor in the Department of Judaic Studies, University of Vienna, Austria. Areas of research: Rabbinic literature, history of the Jews in the Talmudic period, history of Jews and Christians in Palestine before the advent of Islam. Main publications: "Introduction to the Talmud and Midrash", Edinburgh ²1996; "Jews and Christians in the Holy Land. Palestine in the Fourth Century", Edinburgh 2000.

Stockhausen, Annette von, Dr.

Assistant at the Chair of Early Christianity, Friedrich-Alexander-University Erlangen-Nürnberg, Germany; primary areas of interest are 4th-century Christianity and the literature of the Church Fathers.